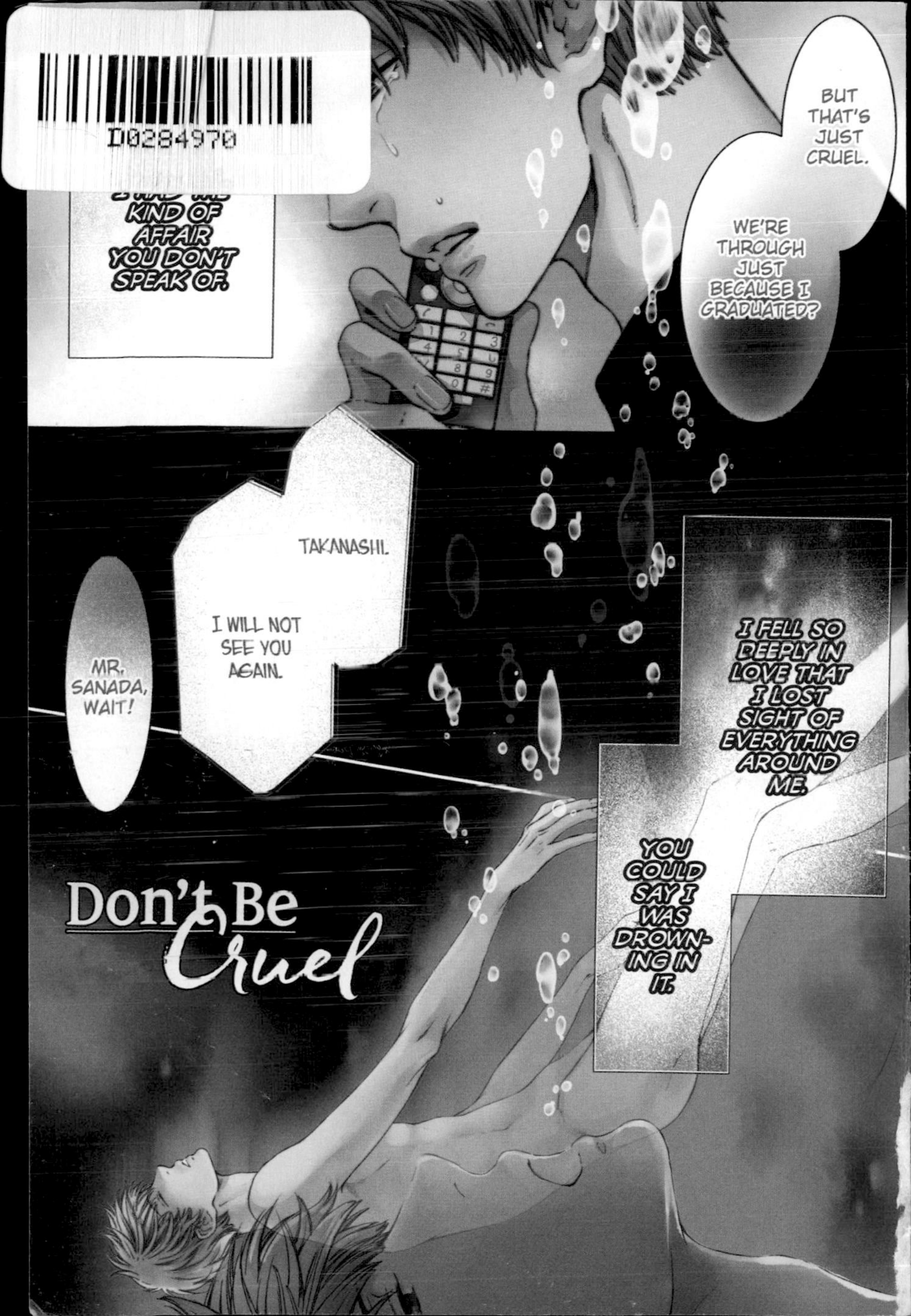
BUT THAT'S JUST CRUEL.
WE'RE THROUGH JUST BECAUSE I GRADUATED?
KIND OF AFFAIR YOU DON'T SPEAK OF.
I FELL SO DEEPLY IN LOVE THAT I LOST SIGHT OF EVERYTHING AROUND ME.
YOU COULD SAY I WAS DROWN-ING IN IT.
TAKANASHI.
I WILL NOT SEE YOU AGAIN.
MR. SANADA, WAIT!
Don't Be Cruel

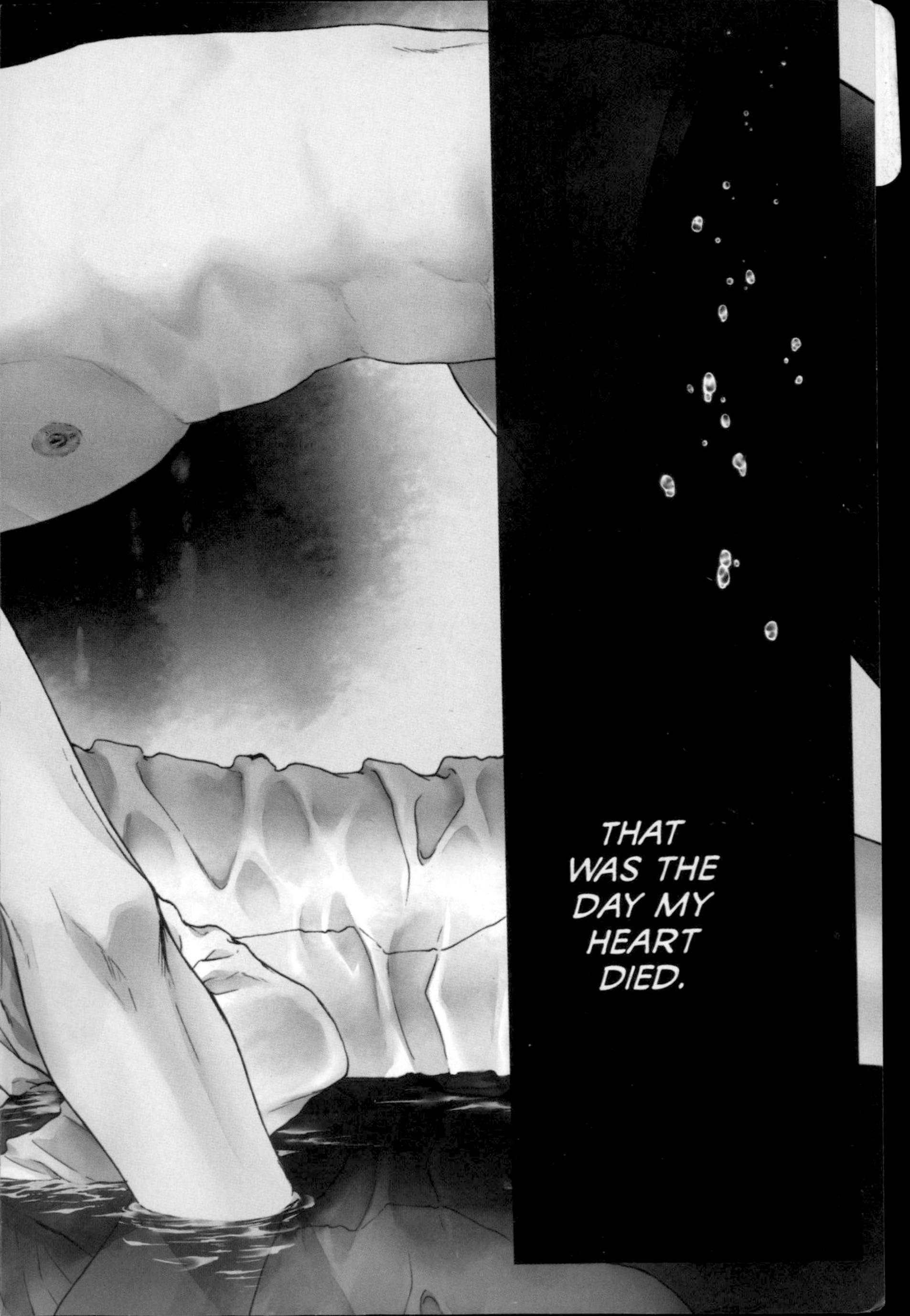
THAT WAS THE DAY MY HEART DIED.

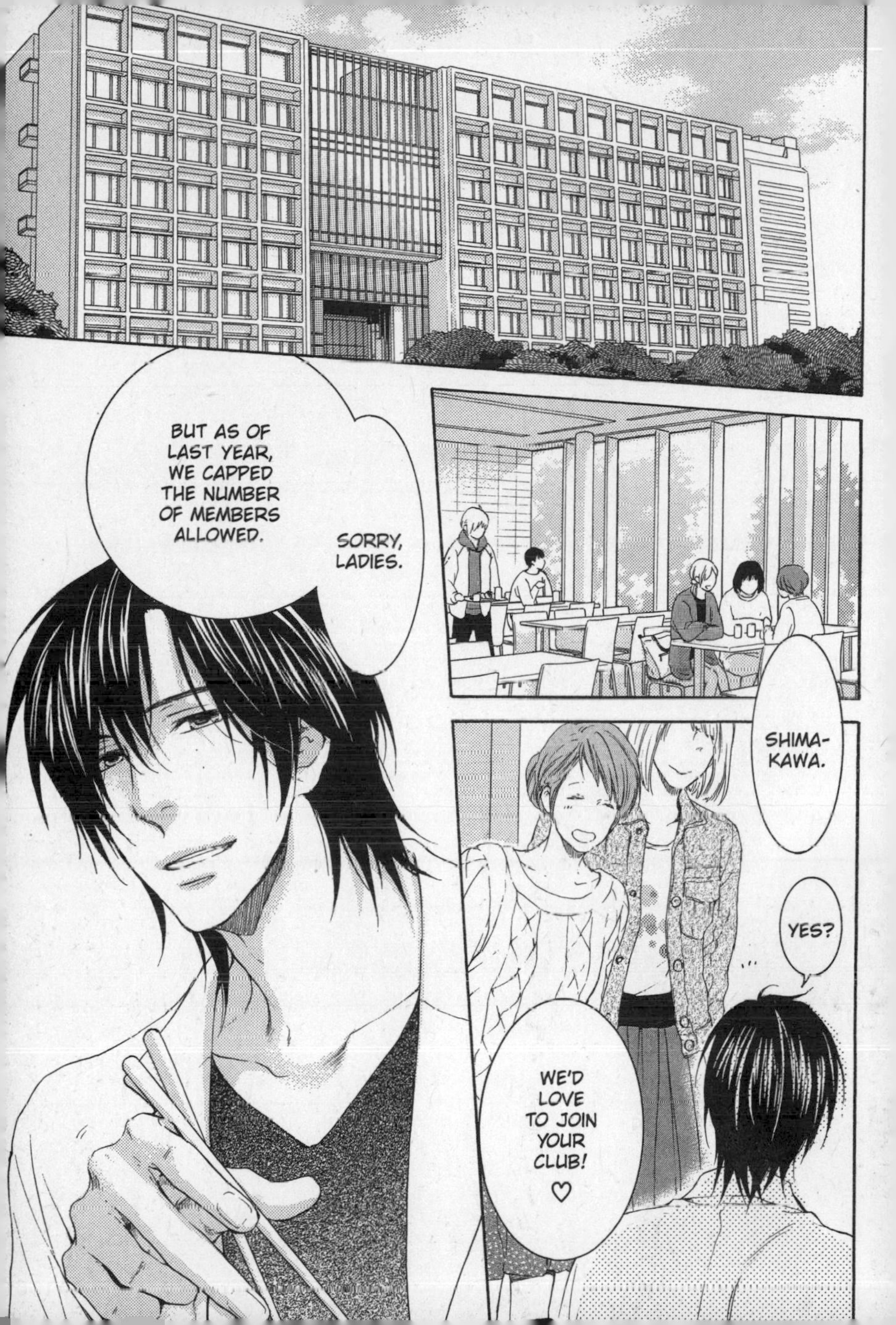
SHIMA-KAWA.
YES?
WE'D LOVE TO JOIN YOUR CLUB! ♡
BUT AS OF LAST YEAR, WE CAPPED THE NUMBER OF MEMBERS ALLOWED.
SORRY, LADIES.

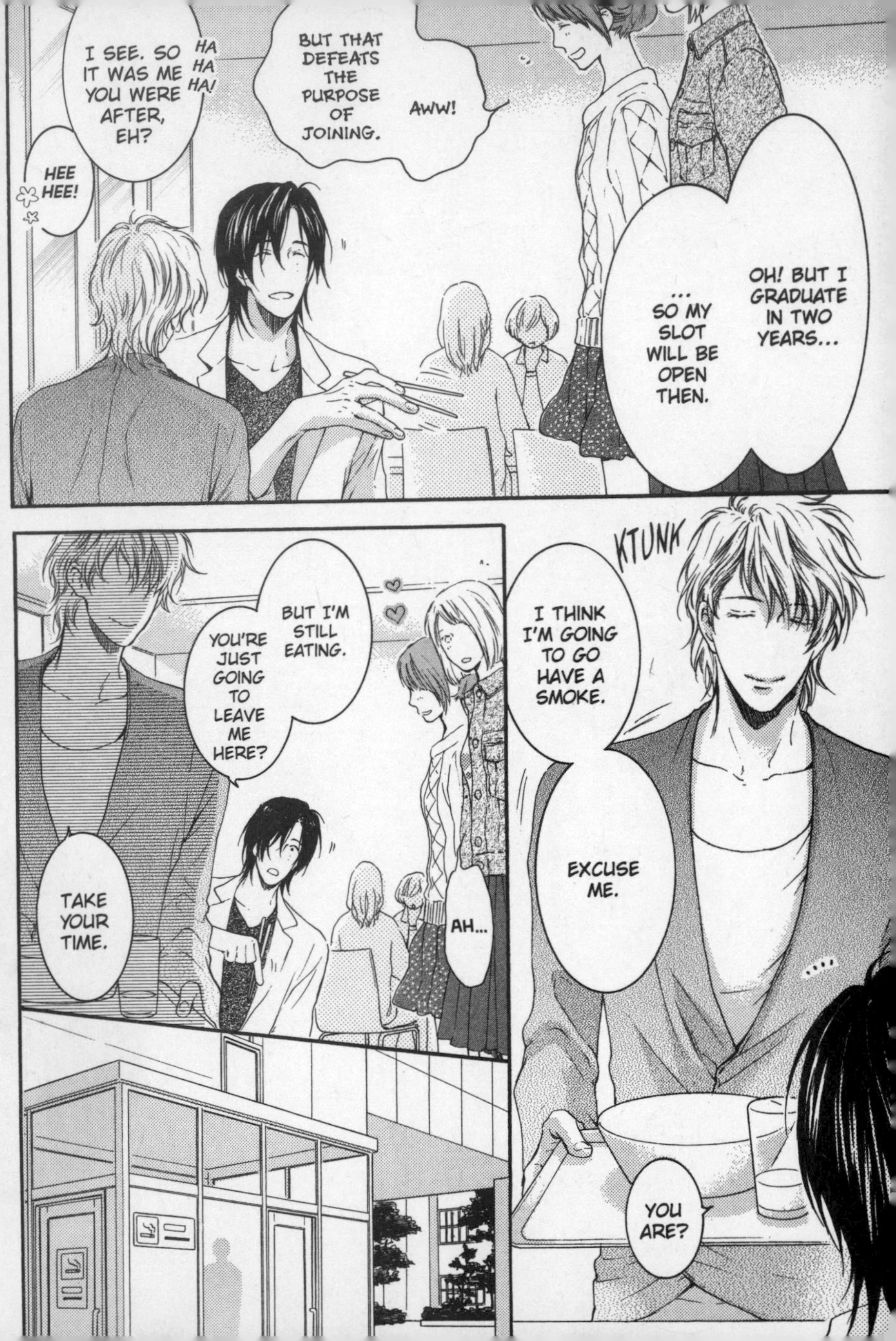
OH! BUT I GRADUATE IN TWO YEARS...
... SO MY SLOT WILL BE OPEN THEN.
BUT THAT DEFEATS THE PURPOSE OF JOINING.
AWW!
I SEE. SO IT WAS ME YOU WERE AFTER, EH?
HA HA HA!
HEE HEE!
KTUNK
I THINK I'M GOING TO GO HAVE A SMOKE.
EXCUSE ME.
...
YOU ARE?
BUT I'M STILL EATING.
YOU'RE JUST GOING TO LEAVE ME HERE?
AH...
TAKE YOUR TIME.

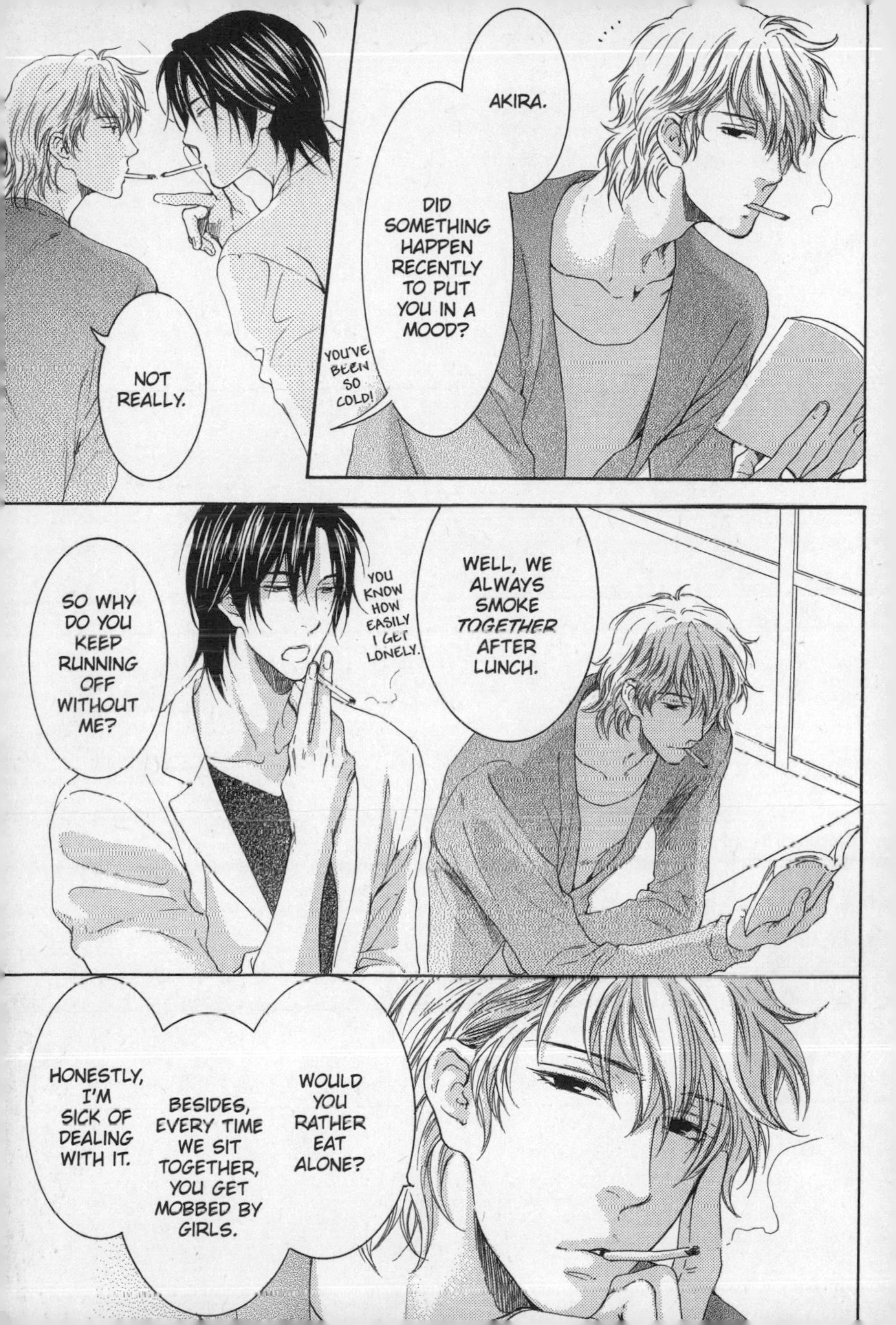
....
AKIRA.
DID SOMETHING HAPPEN RECENTLY TO PUT YOU IN A MOOD?
YOU'VE BEEN SO COLD!
NOT REALLY.
WELL, WE ALWAYS SMOKE *TOGETHER* AFTER LUNCH.
YOU KNOW HOW EASILY I GET LONELY.
SO WHY DO YOU KEEP RUNNING OFF WITHOUT ME?
WOULD YOU RATHER EAT ALONE?
BESIDES, EVERY TIME WE SIT TOGETHER, YOU GET MOBBED BY GIRLS.
HONESTLY, I'M SICK OF DEALING WITH IT.

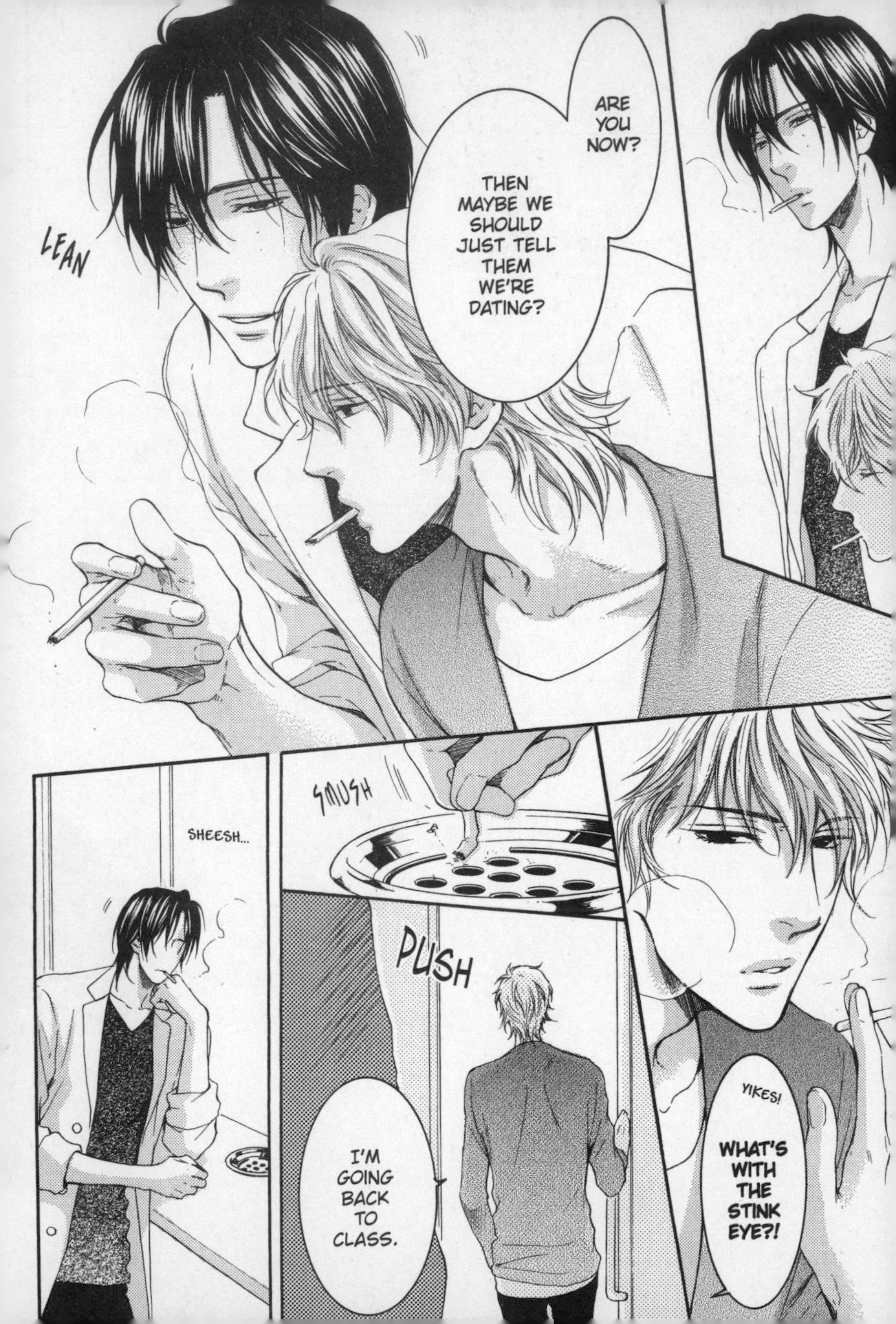
ARE YOU NOW?
THEN MAYBE WE SHOULD JUST TELL THEM WE'RE DATING?
LEAN
YIKES!
WHAT'S WITH THE STINK EYE?!
SMUSH
PUSH
I'M GOING BACK TO CLASS.
SHEESH...

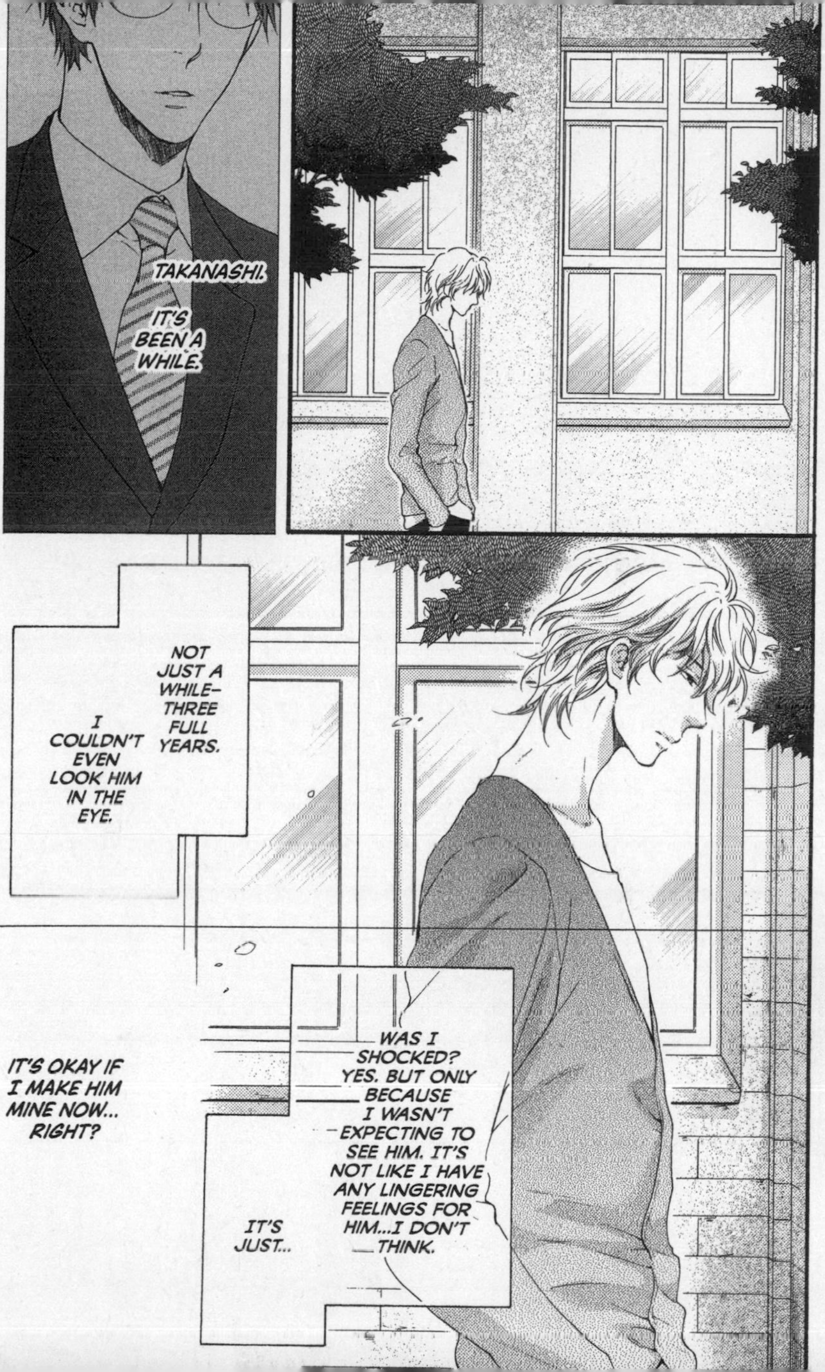
TAKANASHI.
IT'S BEEN A WHILE.
NOT JUST A WHILE— THREE FULL YEARS.
I COULDN'T EVEN LOOK HIM IN THE EYE.
WAS I SHOCKED? YES. BUT ONLY BECAUSE I WASN'T EXPECTING TO SEE HIM. IT'S NOT LIKE I HAVE ANY LINGERING FEELINGS FOR HIM...I DON'T THINK.
IT'S JUST...
IT'S OKAY IF I MAKE HIM MINE NOW... RIGHT?

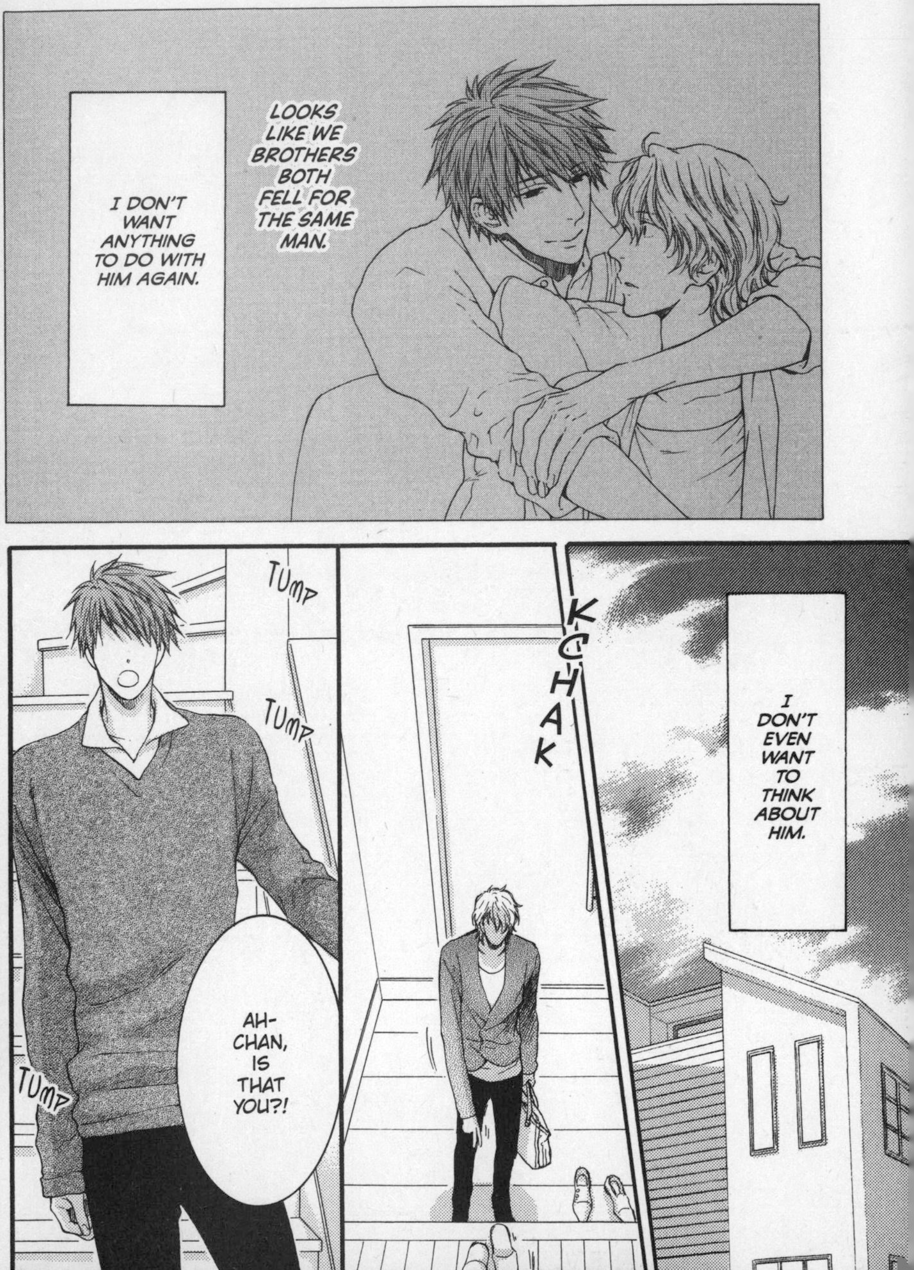
LOOKS LIKE WE BROTHERS BOTH FELL FOR THE SAME MAN.
I DON'T WANT ANYTHING TO DO WITH HIM AGAIN.
I DON'T EVEN WANT TO THINK ABOUT HIM.
KCHAK
TUMP
TUMP
TUMP
AH-CHAN, IS THAT YOU?!

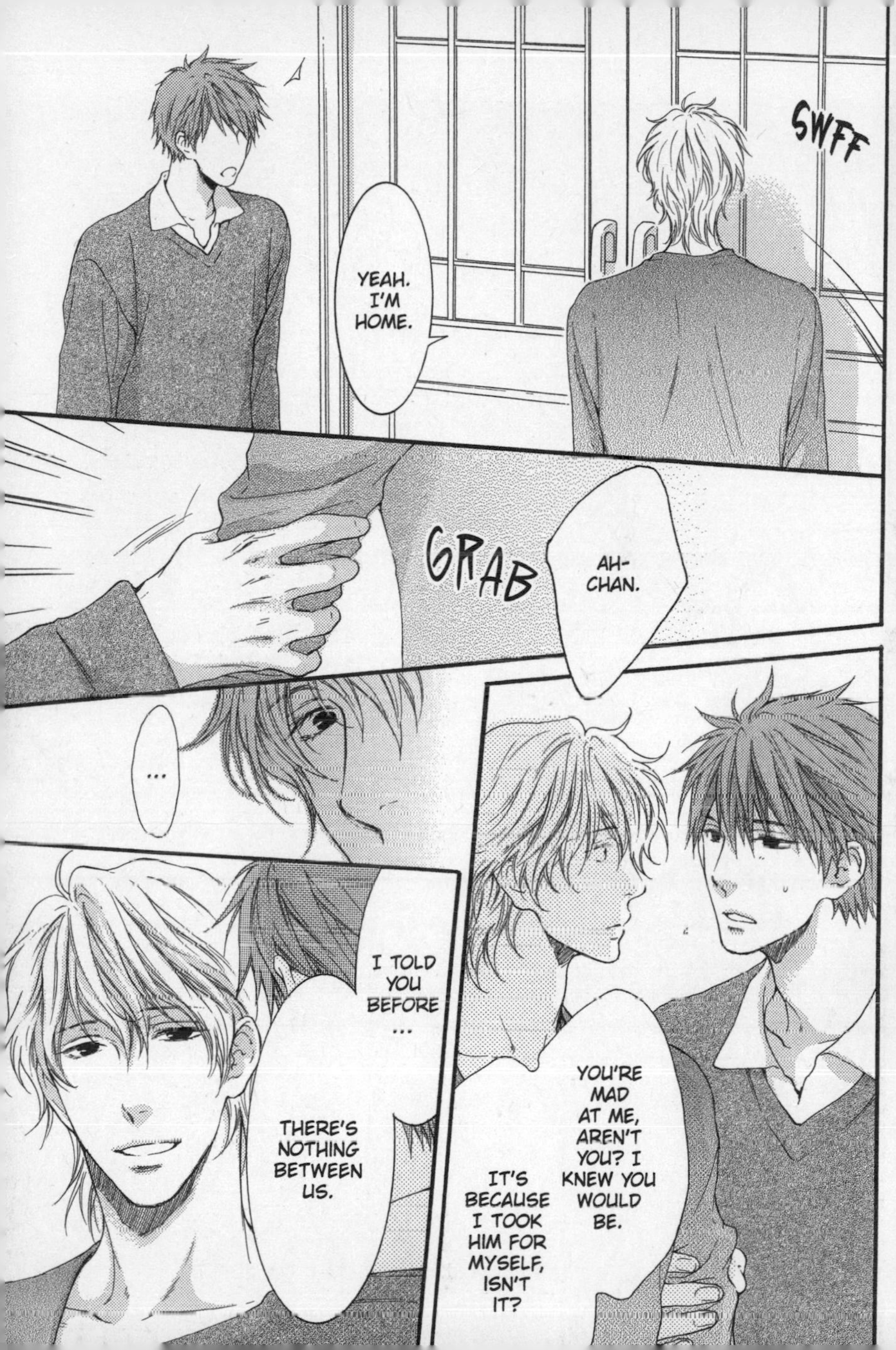
SWFF
YEAH. I'M HOME.
AH-CHAN.
GRAB
YOU'RE MAD AT ME, AREN'T YOU? I KNEW YOU WOULD BE.
IT'S BECAUSE I TOOK HIM FOR MYSELF, ISN'T IT?
...
I TOLD YOU BEFORE...
THERE'S NOTHING BETWEEN US.

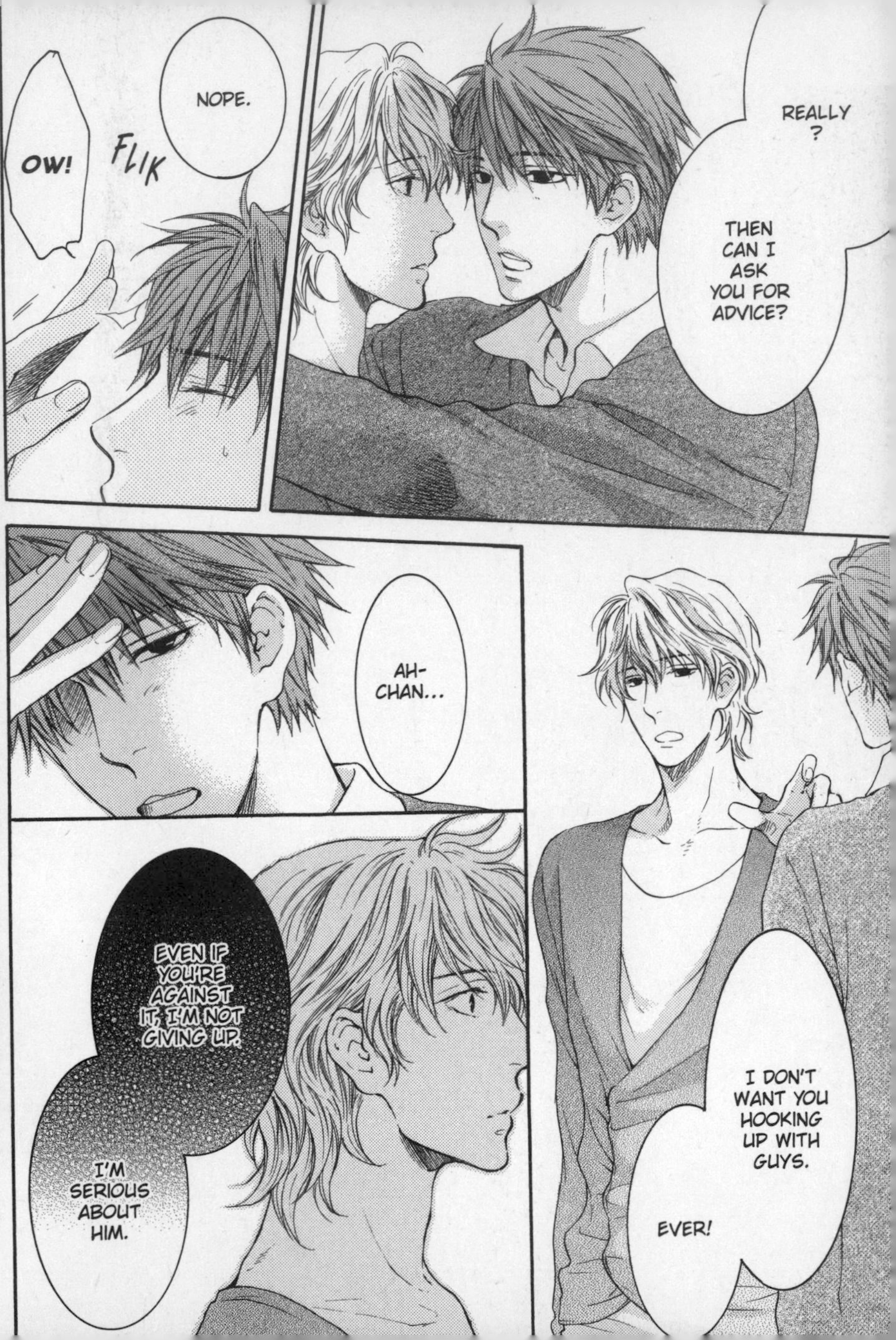
REALLY?
THEN CAN I ASK YOU FOR ADVICE?
NOPE.
FLIK
OW!
I DON'T WANT YOU HOOKING UP WITH GUYS.
EVER!
AH-CHAN...
EVEN IF YOU'RE AGAINST IT, I'M NOT GIVING UP.
I'M SERIOUS ABOUT HIM.

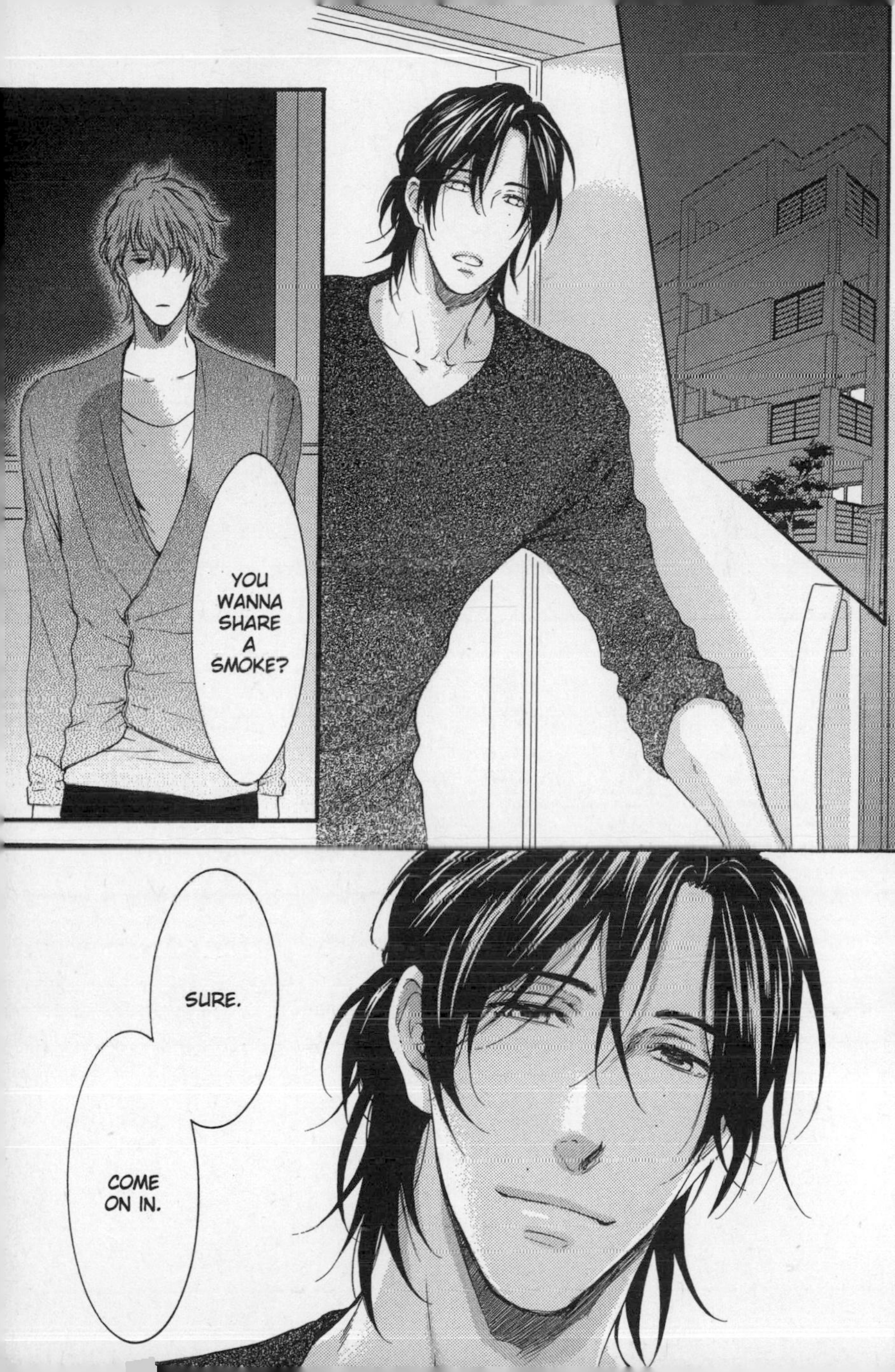
YOU WANNA SHARE A SMOKE?
SURE.
COME ON IN.

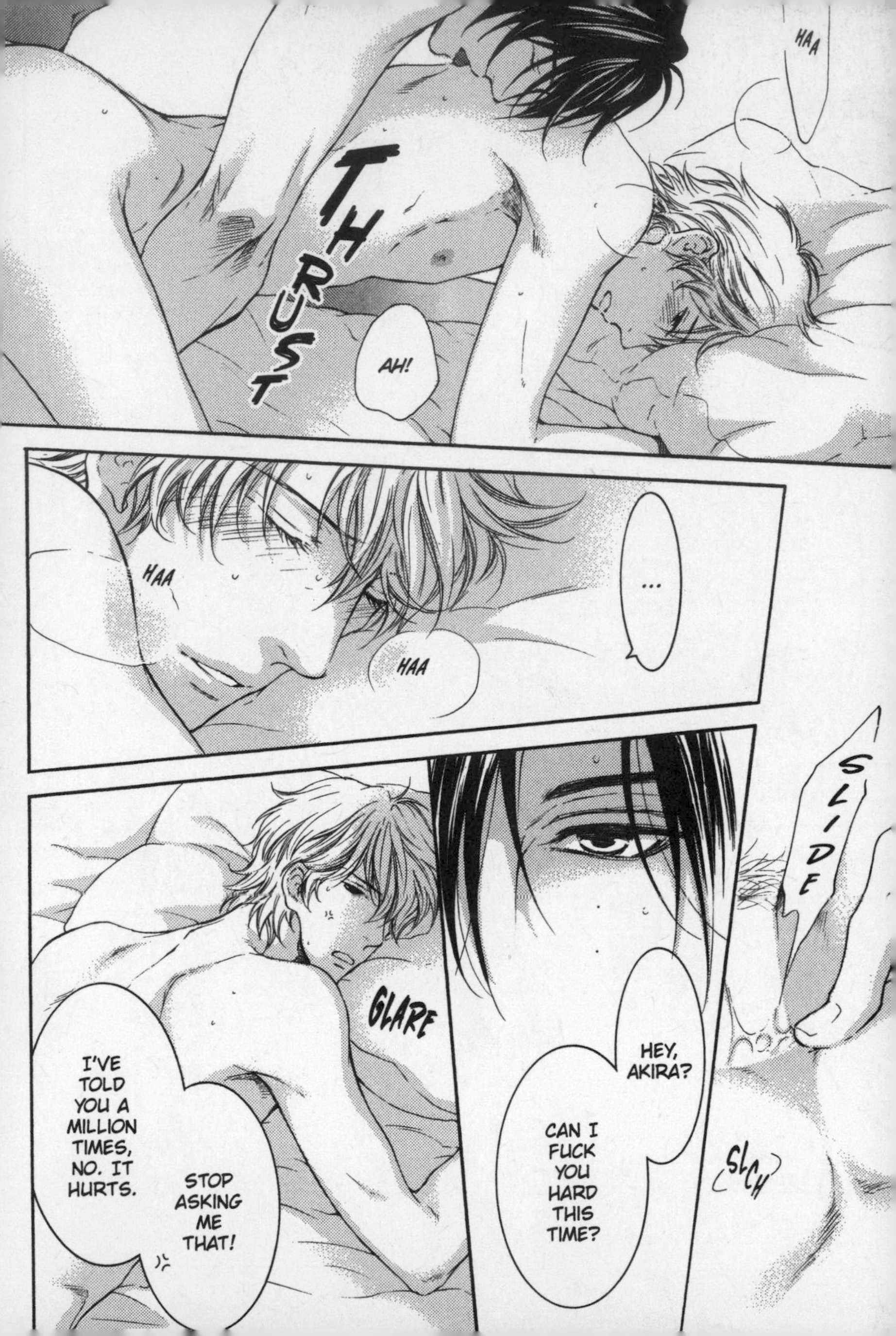
HAA
THRUST
AH!
...
HAA
HAA
SLIDE
HEY, AKIRA?
CAN I FUCK YOU HARD THIS TIME?
SLCH
GLARE
I'VE TOLD YOU A MILLION TIMES, NO. IT HURTS.
STOP ASKING ME THAT!

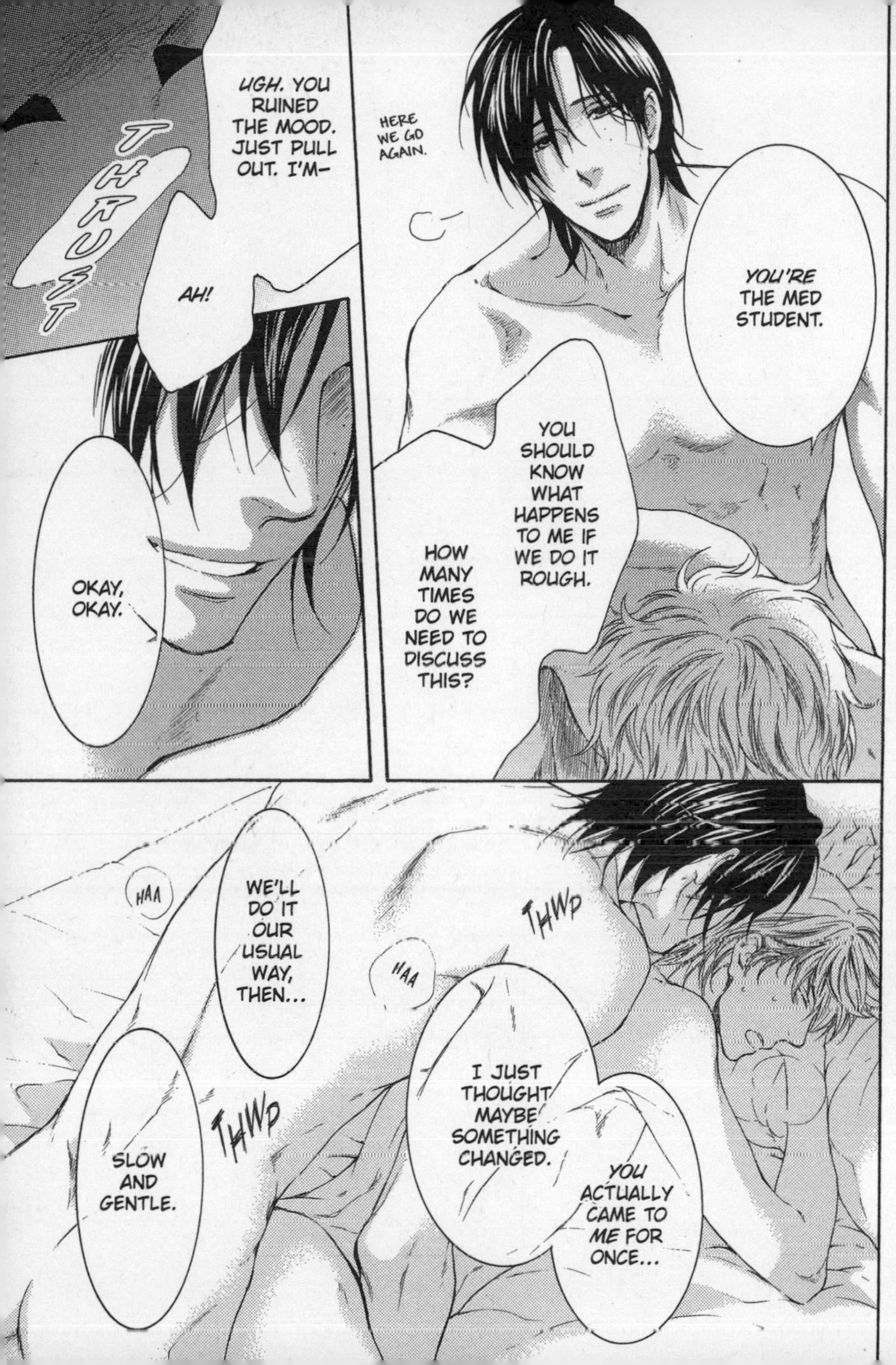
YOU'RE THE MED STUDENT.
YOU SHOULD KNOW WHAT HAPPENS TO ME IF WE DO IT ROUGH.
HOW MANY TIMES DO WE NEED TO DISCUSS THIS?
HERE WE GO AGAIN.
UGH. YOU RUINED THE MOOD. JUST PULL OUT. I'M-
THRUST
AH!
OKAY, OKAY.
YOU ACTUALLY CAME TO ME FOR ONCE...
I JUST THOUGHT MAYBE SOMETHING CHANGED.
HAA
THWP
WE'LL DO IT OUR USUAL WAY, THEN...
HAA
THWP
SLOW AND GENTLE.

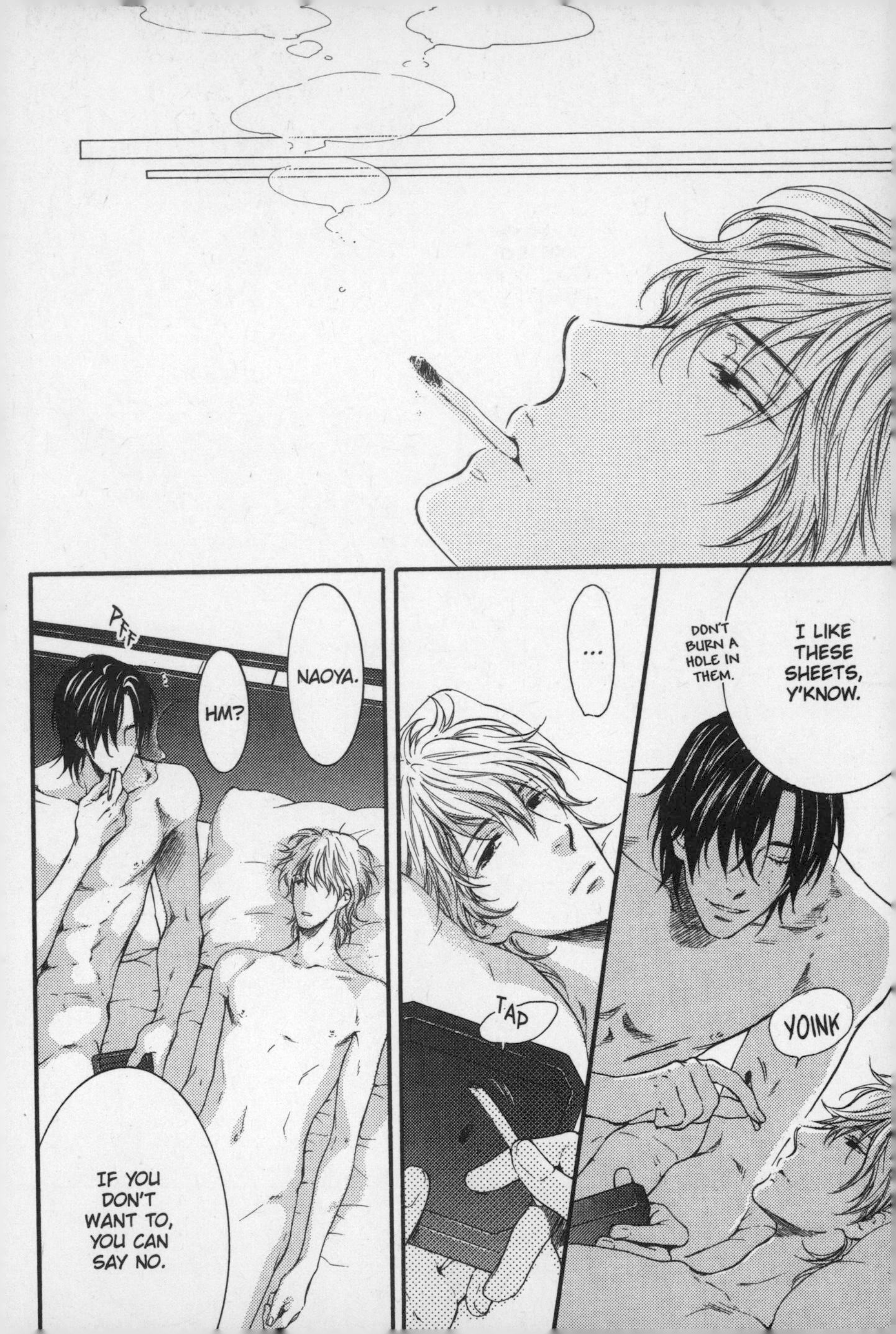
I LIKE THESE SHEETS, Y'KNOW.
DON'T BURN A HOLE IN THEM.
YOINK
...
TAP
NAOYA.
HM?
PFF
IF YOU DON'T WANT TO, YOU CAN SAY NO.

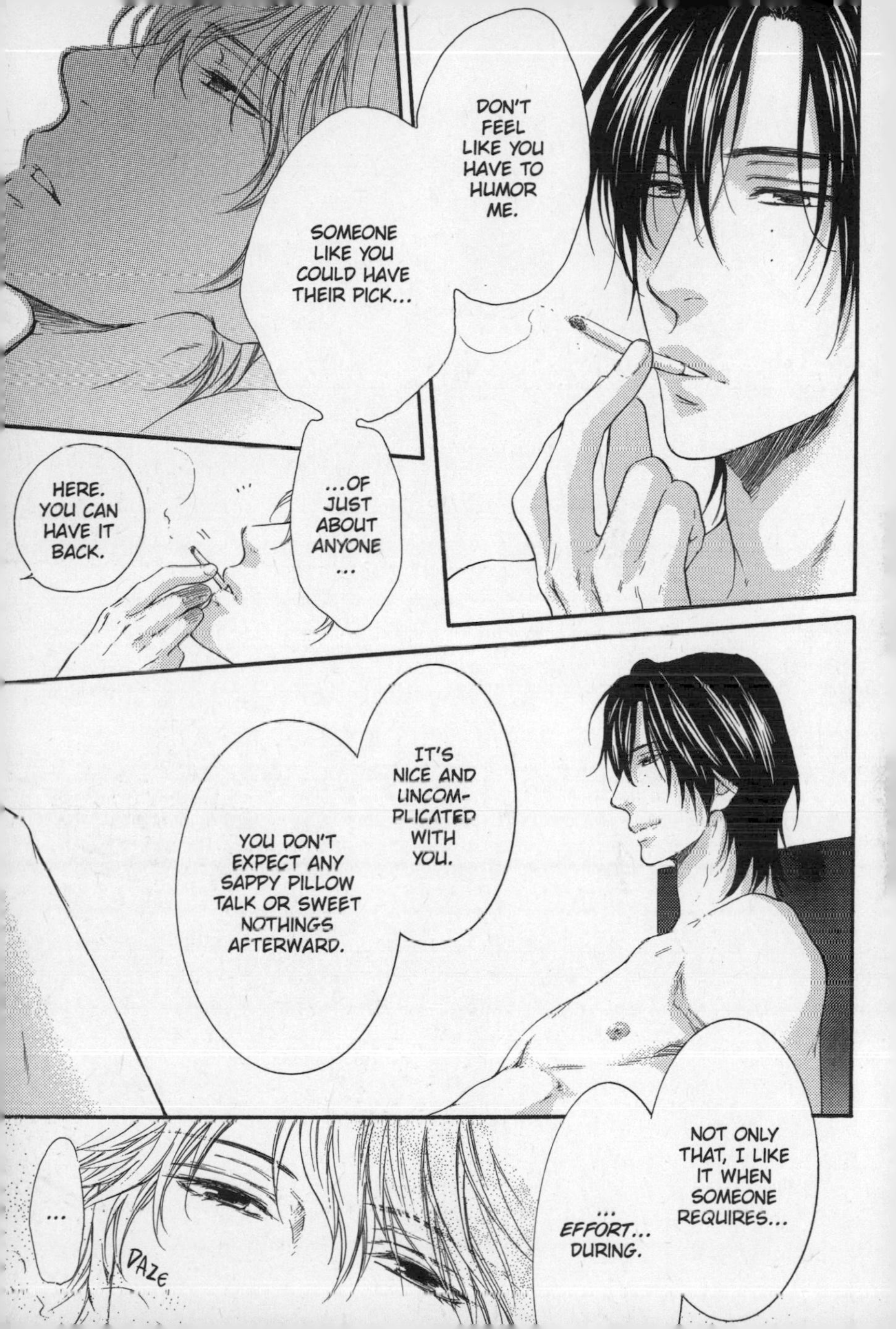
DON'T FEEL LIKE YOU HAVE TO HUMOR ME.
SOMEONE LIKE YOU COULD HAVE THEIR PICK...
...OF JUST ABOUT ANYONE ...
...
HERE. YOU CAN HAVE IT BACK.
IT'S NICE AND UNCOM-PLICATED WITH YOU.
YOU DON'T EXPECT ANY SAPPY PILLOW TALK OR SWEET NOTHINGS AFTERWARD.
NOT ONLY THAT, I LIKE IT WHEN SOMEONE REQUIRES...
... EFFORT... DURING.
...
DAZE

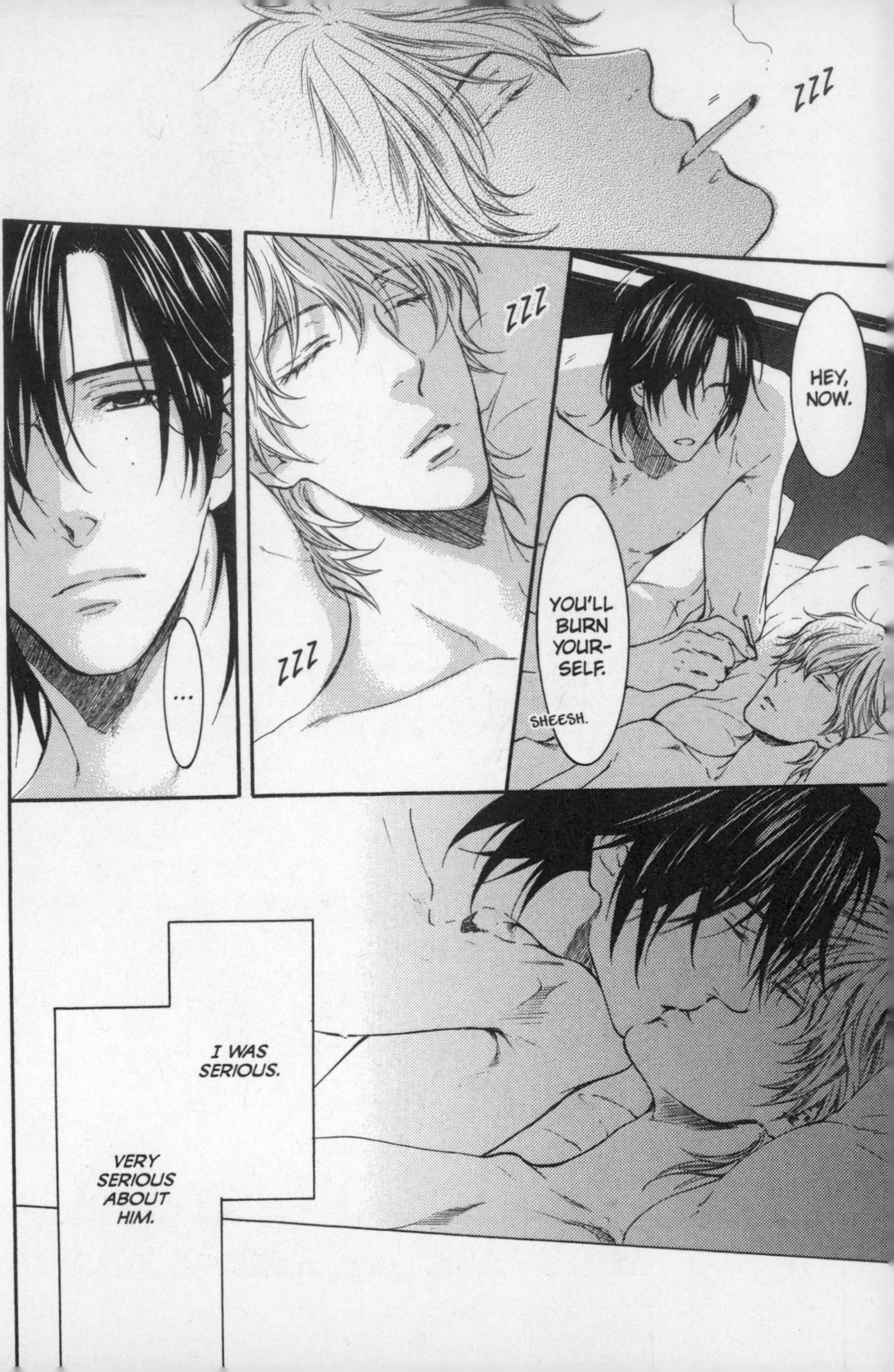
ZZZ
HEY, NOW.
YOU'LL BURN YOURSELF.
SHEESH.
ZZZ
ZZZ
...
I WAS SERIOUS.
VERY SERIOUS ABOUT HIM.

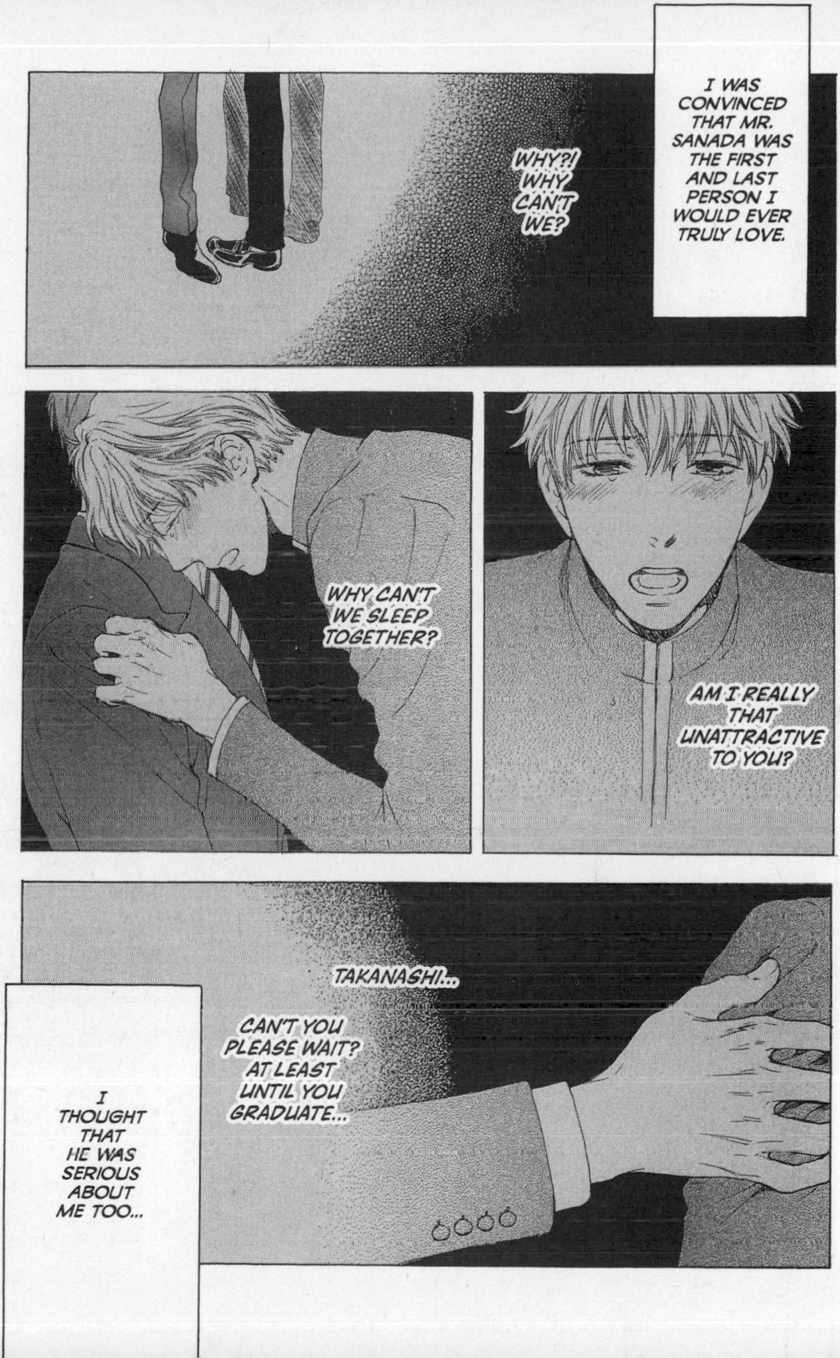
I WAS CONVINCED THAT MR. SANADA WAS THE FIRST AND LAST PERSON I WOULD EVER TRULY LOVE.
WHY?! WHY CAN'T WE?
AM I REALLY THAT UNATTRACTIVE TO YOU?
WHY CAN'T WE SLEEP TOGETHER?
TAKANASHI...
CAN'T YOU PLEASE WAIT? AT LEAST UNTIL YOU GRADUATE...
I THOUGHT THAT HE WAS SERIOUS ABOUT ME TOO...

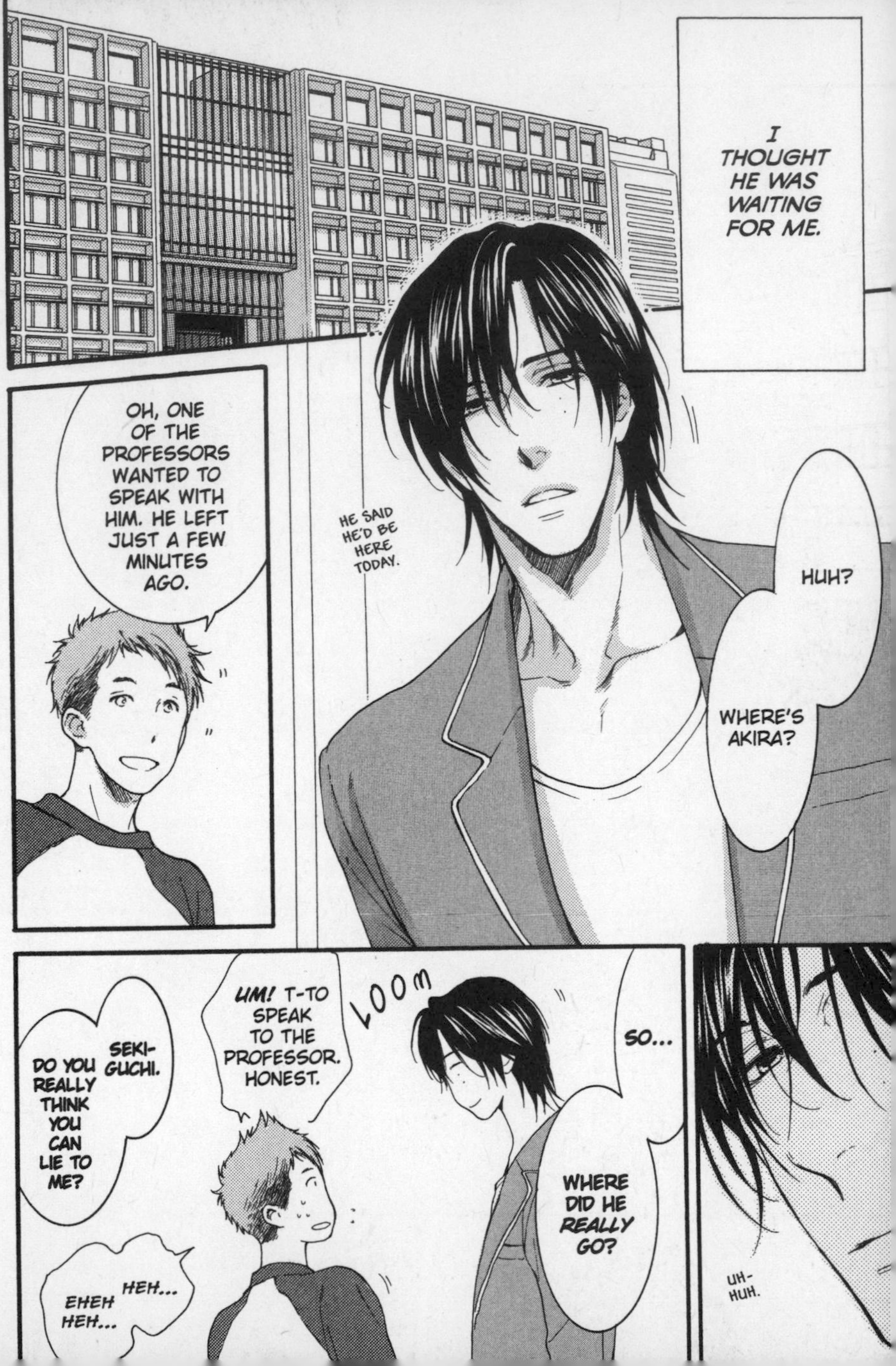
I THOUGHT HE WAS WAITING FOR ME.
HUH?
WHERE'S AKIRA?
HE SAID HE'D BE HERE TODAY.
OH, ONE OF THE PROFESSORS WANTED TO SPEAK WITH HIM. HE LEFT JUST A FEW MINUTES AGO.
UH-HUH.
SO...
WHERE DID HE REALLY GO?
UM! T-TO SPEAK TO THE PROFESSOR. HONEST.
LOOM
SEKI-GUCHI.
DO YOU REALLY THINK YOU CAN LIE TO ME?
HEH... EHEH HEH...

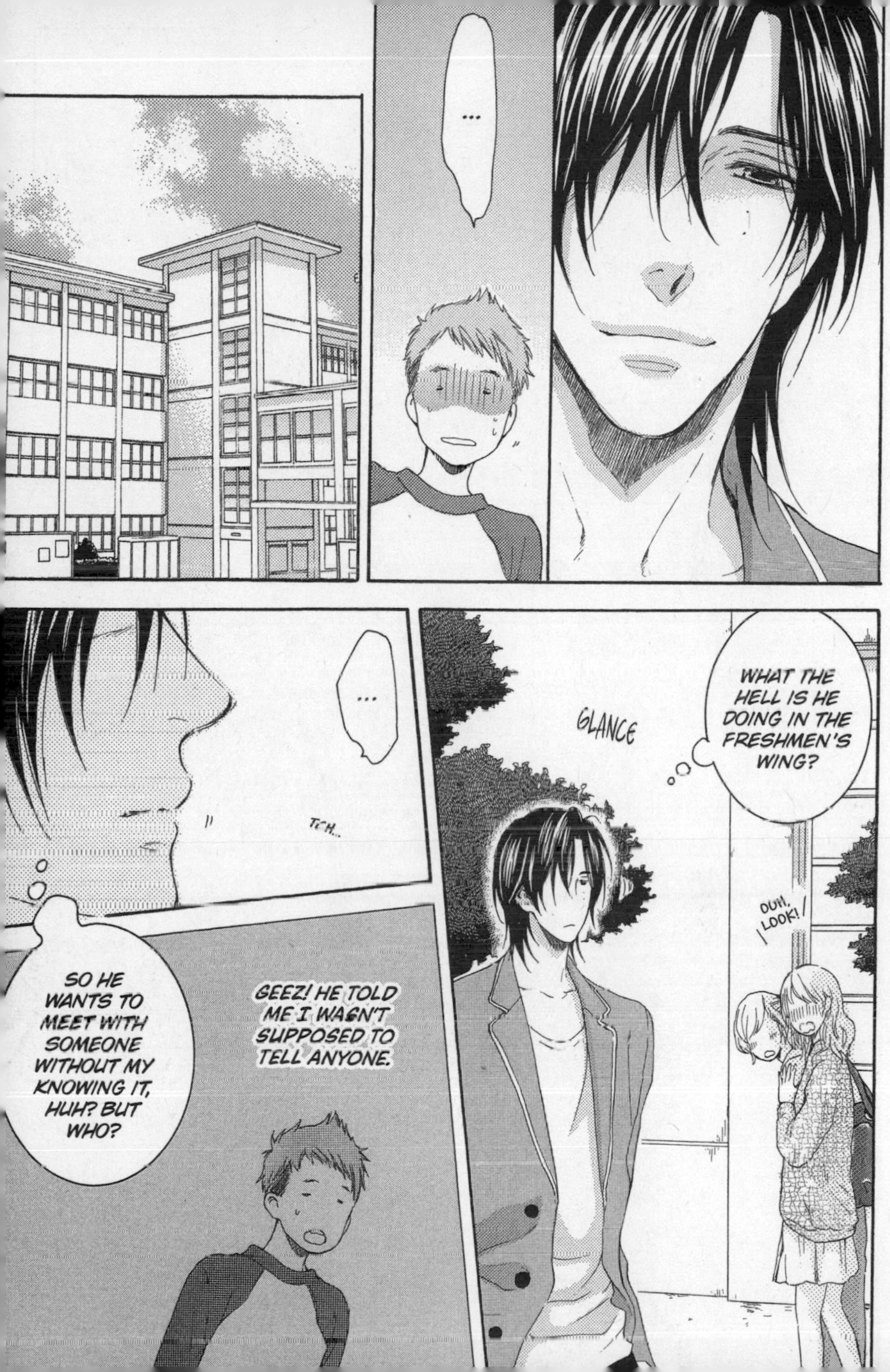
...
WHAT THE HELL IS HE DOING IN THE FRESHMEN'S WING?
GLANCE
OUH, LOOK!
...
TCH...
SO HE WANTS TO MEET WITH SOMEONE WITHOUT MY KNOWING IT, HUH? BUT WHO?
GEEZ! HE TOLD ME I WASN'T SUPPOSED TO TELL ANYONE.

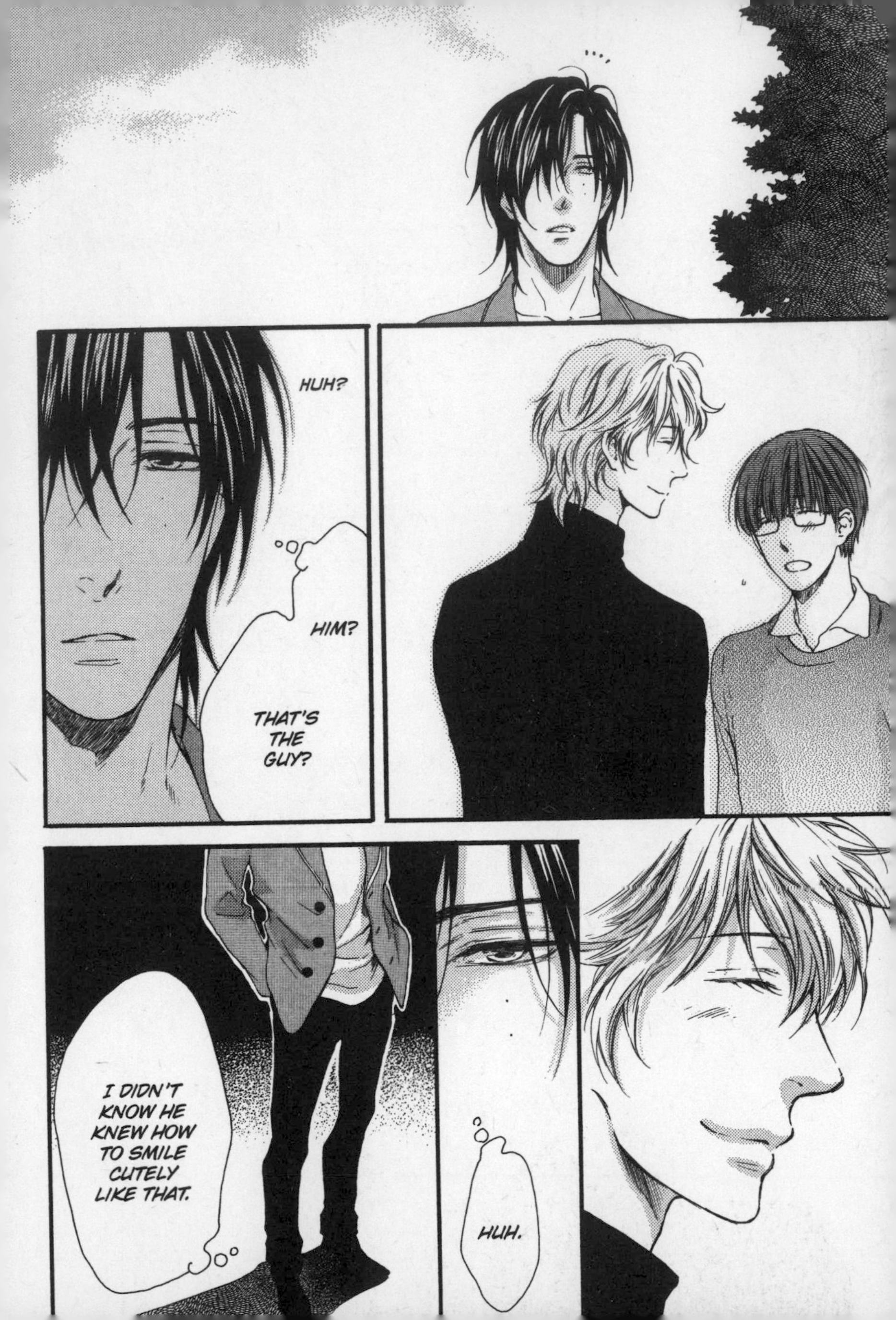
HUH?
HIM?
THAT'S THE GUY?
HUH.
I DIDN'T KNOW HE KNEW HOW TO SMILE CUTELY LIKE THAT.

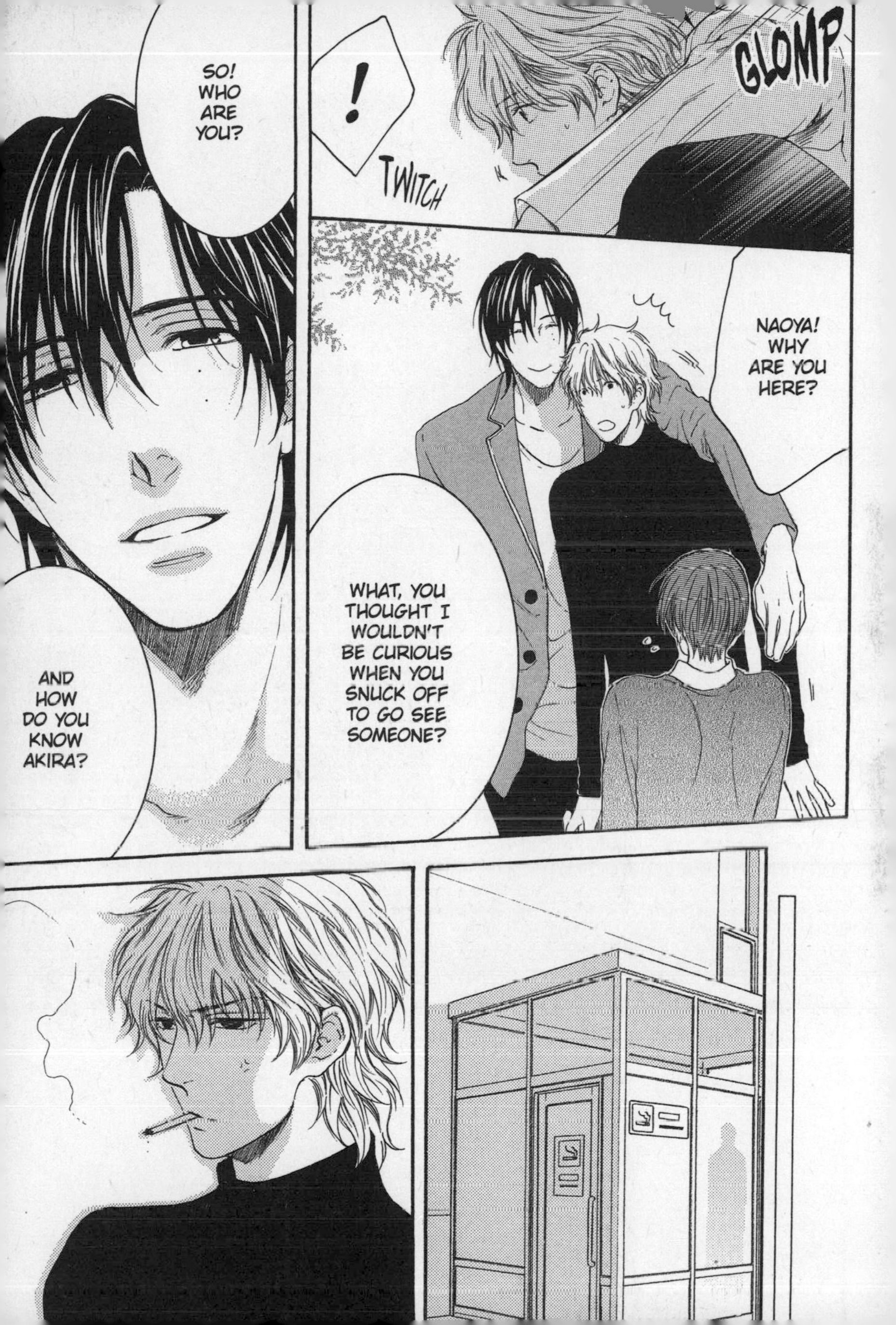
GLOMP
!
TWITCH
NAOYA! WHY ARE YOU HERE?
WHAT, YOU THOUGHT I WOULDN'T BE CURIOUS WHEN YOU SNUCK OFF TO GO SEE SOMEONE?
SO! WHO ARE YOU?
AND HOW DO YOU KNOW AKIRA?

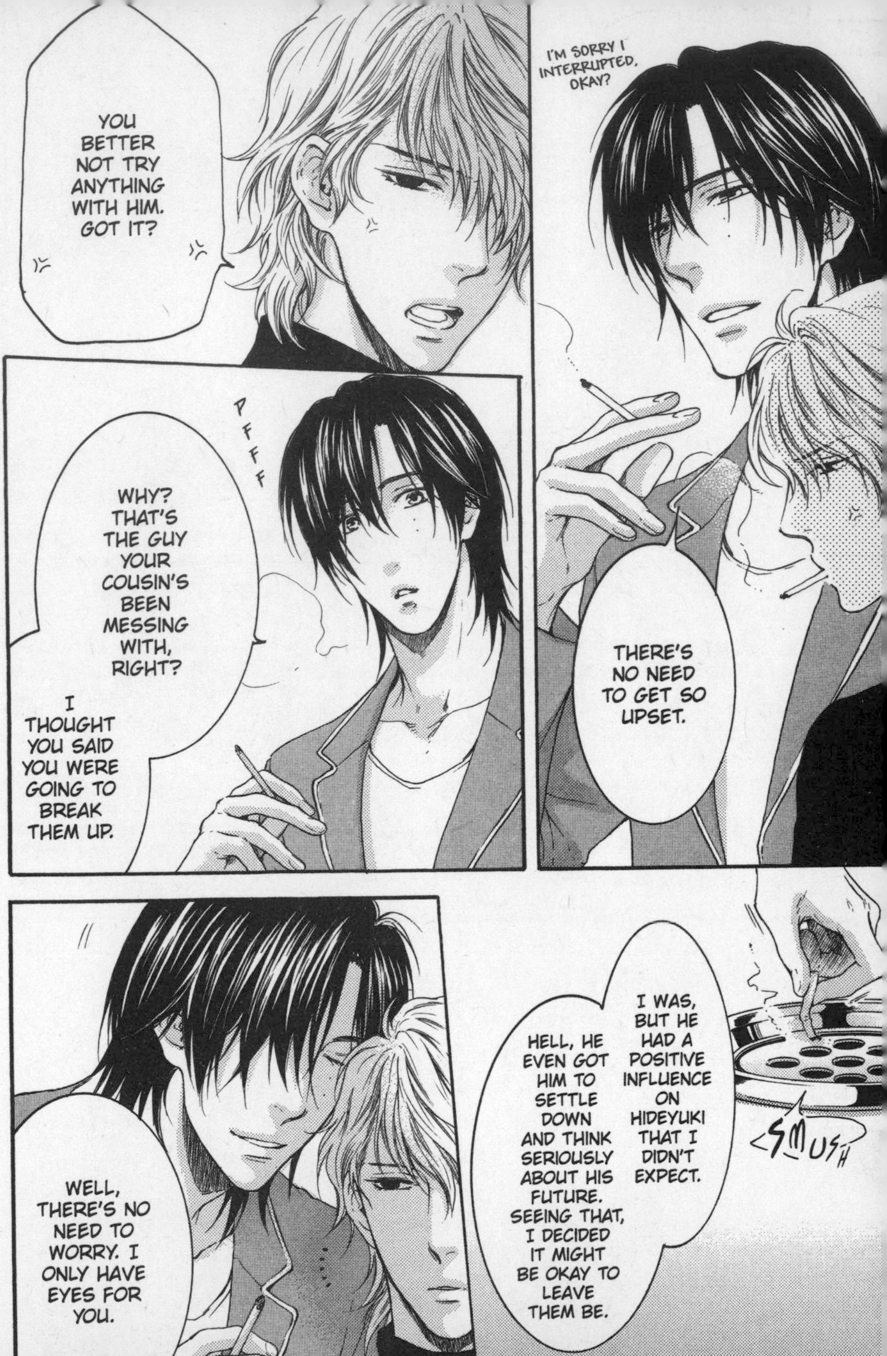
I'M SORRY I INTERRUPTED, OKAY?
THERE'S NO NEED TO GET SO UPSET.
YOU BETTER NOT TRY ANYTHING WITH HIM. GOT IT?
PFFF
WHY? THAT'S THE GUY YOUR COUSIN'S BEEN MESSING WITH, RIGHT?
I THOUGHT YOU SAID YOU WERE GOING TO BREAK THEM UP.
SMUSH
I WAS, BUT HE HAD A POSITIVE INFLUENCE ON HIDEYUKI THAT I DIDN'T EXPECT.
HELL, HE EVEN GOT HIM TO SETTLE DOWN AND THINK SERIOUSLY ABOUT HIS FUTURE. SEEING THAT, I DECIDED IT MIGHT BE OKAY TO LEAVE THEM BE.
WELL, THERE'S NO NEED TO WORRY. I ONLY HAVE EYES FOR YOU.

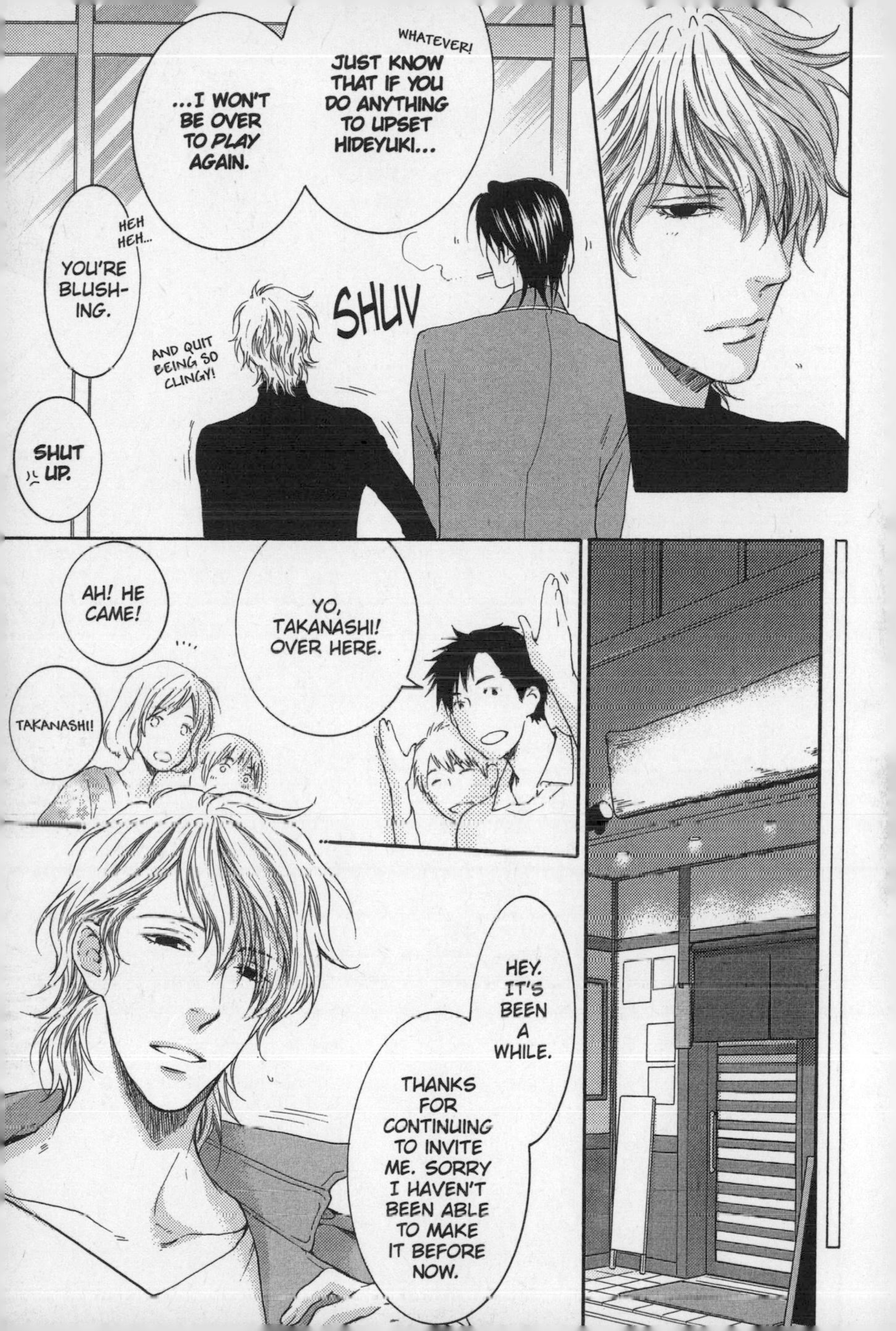
WHATEVER!
JUST KNOW THAT IF YOU DO ANYTHING TO UPSET HIDEYUKI...
...I WON'T BE OVER TO PLAY AGAIN.
SHUV
HEH HEH...
YOU'RE BLUSH-ING.
AND QUIT BEING SO CLINGY!
SHUT UP.
YO, TAKANASHI! OVER HERE.
AH! HE CAME!
...
TAKANASHI!
HEY. IT'S BEEN A WHILE.
THANKS FOR CONTINUING TO INVITE ME. SORRY I HAVEN'T BEEN ABLE TO MAKE IT BEFORE NOW.

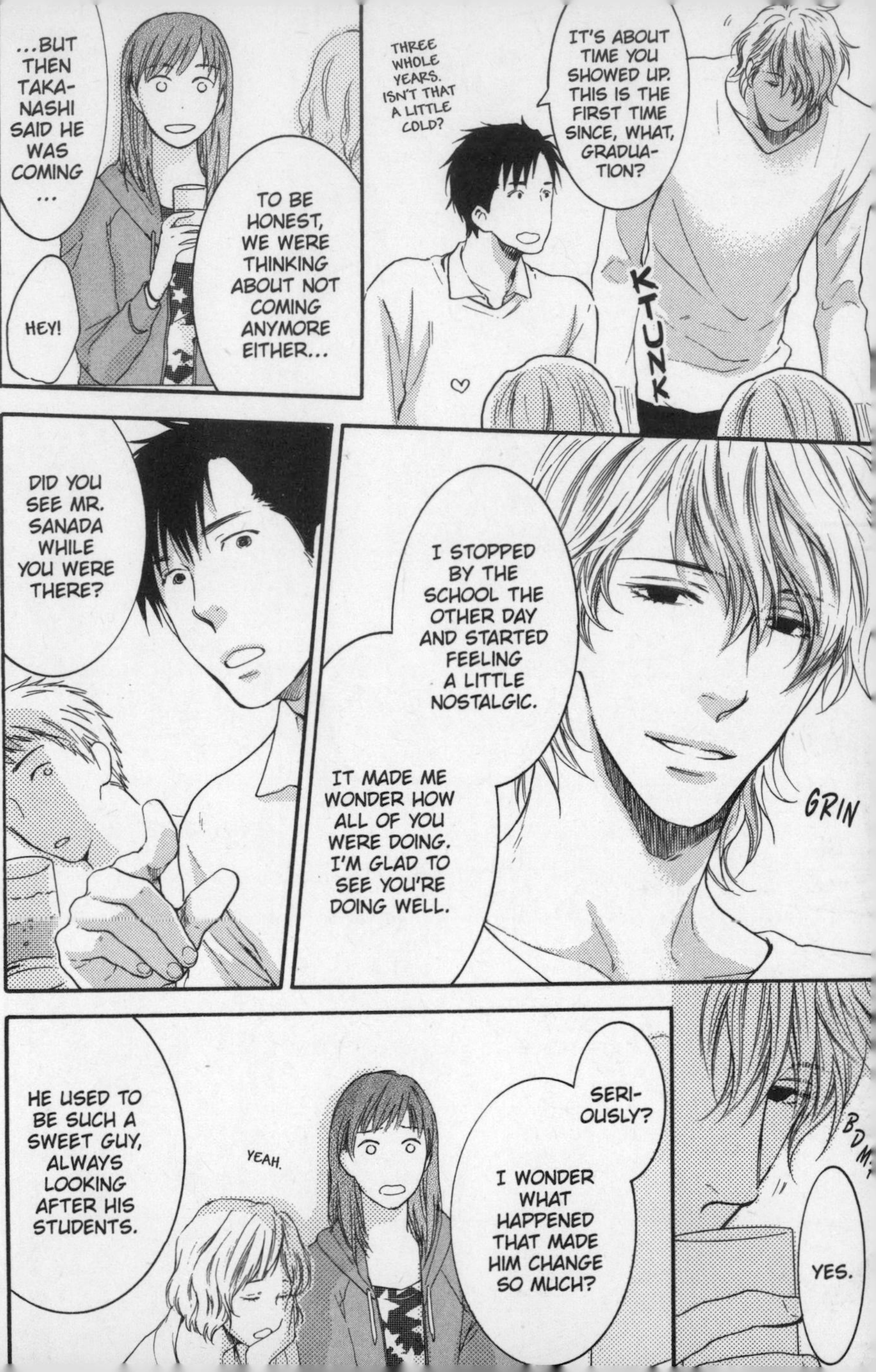
IT'S ABOUT TIME YOU SHOWED UP. THIS IS THE FIRST TIME SINCE, WHAT, GRADUATION?
THREE WHOLE YEARS. ISN'T THAT A LITTLE COLD?
KTUNK
...BUT THEN TAKANASHI SAID HE WAS COMING...
TO BE HONEST, WE WERE THINKING ABOUT NOT COMING ANYMORE EITHER...
HEY!
I STOPPED BY THE SCHOOL THE OTHER DAY AND STARTED FEELING A LITTLE NOSTALGIC.
IT MADE ME WONDER HOW ALL OF YOU WERE DOING. I'M GLAD TO SEE YOU'RE DOING WELL.
GRIN
DID YOU SEE MR. SANADA WHILE YOU WERE THERE?
BDM
YES.
SERIOUSLY?
HE USED TO BE SUCH A SWEET GUY, ALWAYS LOOKING AFTER HIS STUDENTS.
YEAH.
I WONDER WHAT HAPPENED THAT MADE HIM CHANGE SO MUCH?

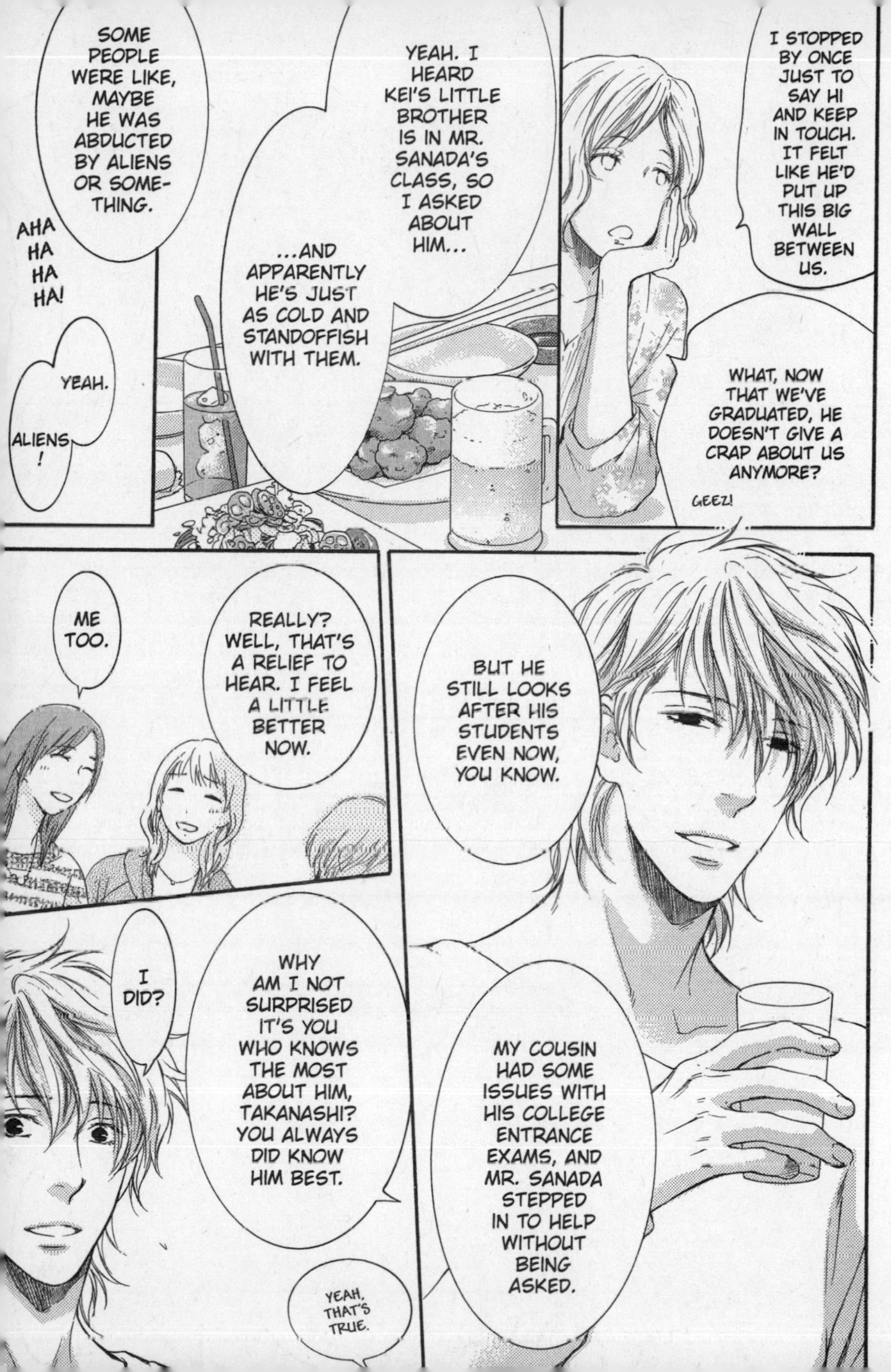
I STOPPED BY ONCE JUST TO SAY HI AND KEEP IN TOUCH. IT FELT LIKE HE'D PUT UP THIS BIG WALL BETWEEN US.
WHAT, NOW THAT WE'VE GRADUATED, HE DOESN'T GIVE A CRAP ABOUT US ANYMORE?
GEEZ!
YEAH. I HEARD KEI'S LITTLE BROTHER IS IN MR. SANADA'S CLASS, SO I ASKED ABOUT HIM...
...AND APPARENTLY HE'S JUST AS COLD AND STANDOFFISH WITH THEM.
SOME PEOPLE WERE LIKE, MAYBE HE WAS ABDUCTED BY ALIENS OR SOME-THING.
AHA HA HA HA!
YEAH.
ALIENS!
BUT HE STILL LOOKS AFTER HIS STUDENTS EVEN NOW, YOU KNOW.
MY COUSIN HAD SOME ISSUES WITH HIS COLLEGE ENTRANCE EXAMS, AND MR. SANADA STEPPED IN TO HELP WITHOUT BEING ASKED.
REALLY? WELL, THAT'S A RELIEF TO HEAR. I FEEL A LITTLE BETTER NOW.
ME TOO.
WHY AM I NOT SURPRISED IT'S YOU WHO KNOWS THE MOST ABOUT HIM, TAKANASHI? YOU ALWAYS DID KNOW HIM BEST.
I DID?
YEAH, THAT'S TRUE.

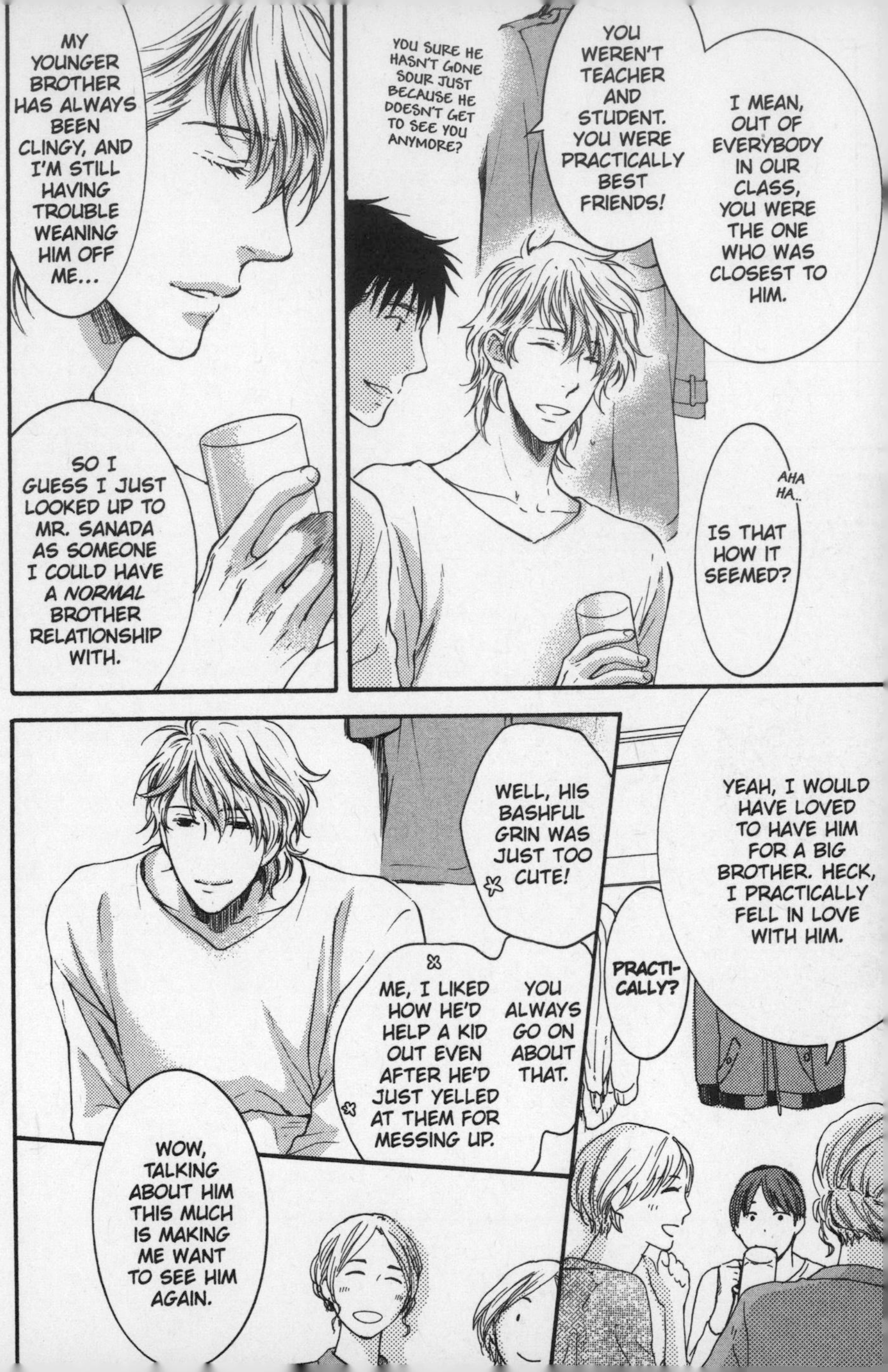
YOU WEREN'T TEACHER AND STUDENT. YOU WERE PRACTICALLY BEST FRIENDS!
I MEAN, OUT OF EVERYBODY IN OUR CLASS, YOU WERE THE ONE WHO WAS CLOSEST TO HIM.
YOU SURE HE HASN'T GONE SOUR JUST BECAUSE HE DOESN'T GET TO SEE YOU ANYMORE?
AHA HA..
IS THAT HOW IT SEEMED?
MY YOUNGER BROTHER HAS ALWAYS BEEN CLINGY, AND I'M STILL HAVING TROUBLE WEANING HIM OFF ME...
SO I GUESS I JUST LOOKED UP TO MR. SANADA AS SOMEONE I COULD HAVE A *NORMAL* BROTHER RELATIONSHIP WITH.
YEAH, I WOULD HAVE LOVED TO HAVE HIM FOR A BIG BROTHER. HECK, I PRACTICALLY FELL IN LOVE WITH HIM.
PRACTI-CALLY?
WELL, HIS BASHFUL GRIN WAS JUST TOO CUTE!
ME, I LIKED HOW HE'D HELP A KID OUT EVEN AFTER HE'D JUST YELLED AT THEM FOR MESSING UP.
YOU ALWAYS GO ON ABOUT THAT.
WOW, TALKING ABOUT HIM THIS MUCH IS MAKING ME WANT TO SEE HIM AGAIN.

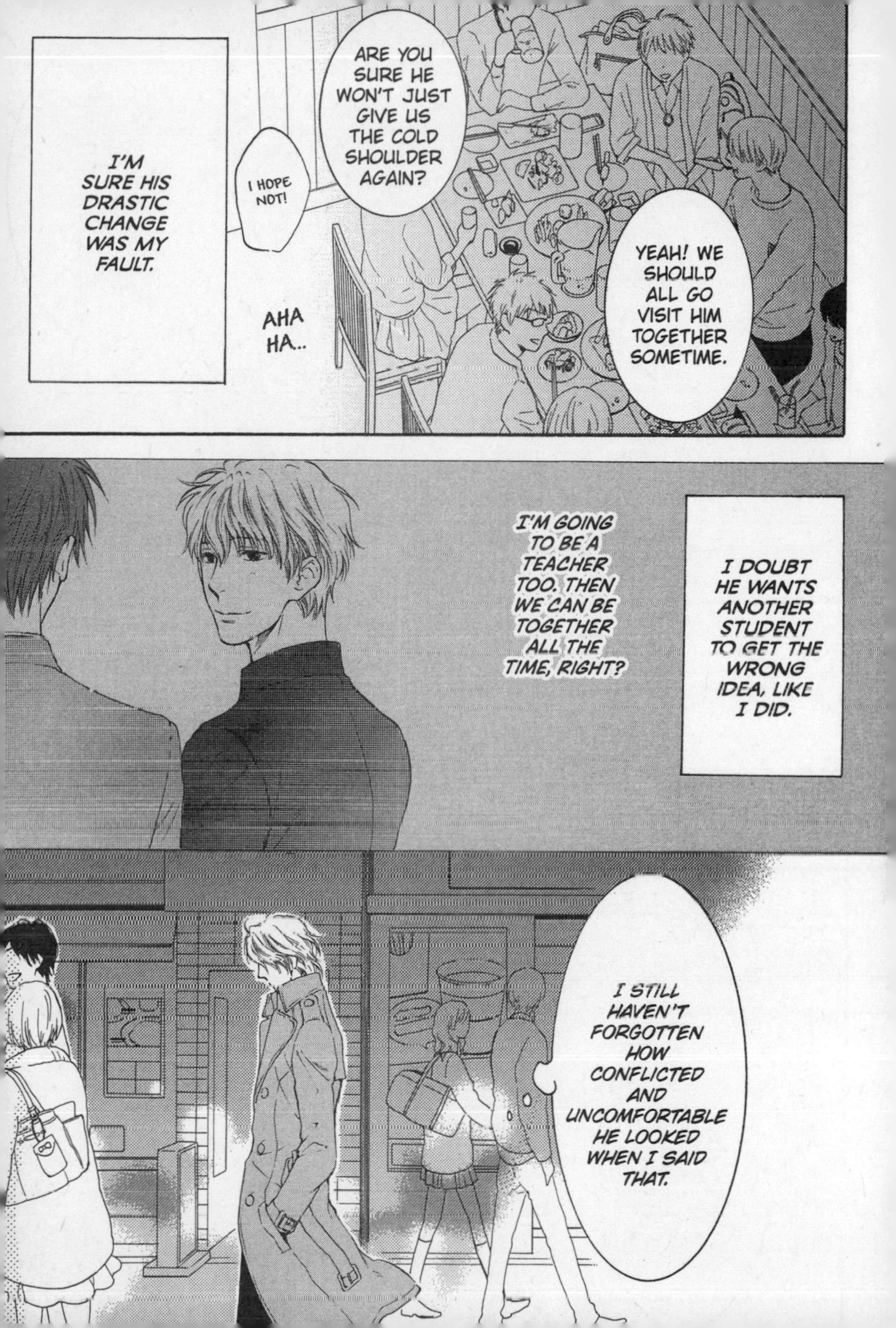
ARE YOU SURE HE WON'T JUST GIVE US THE COLD SHOULDER AGAIN?
I HOPE NOT!
YEAH! WE SHOULD ALL GO VISIT HIM TOGETHER SOMETIME.
AHA HA...
I'M SURE HIS DRASTIC CHANGE WAS MY FAULT.
I'M GOING TO BE A TEACHER TOO. THEN WE CAN BE TOGETHER ALL THE TIME, RIGHT?
I DOUBT HE WANTS ANOTHER STUDENT TO GET THE WRONG IDEA, LIKE I DID.
I STILL HAVEN'T FORGOTTEN HOW CONFLICTED AND UNCOMFORTABLE HE LOOKED WHEN I SAID THAT.

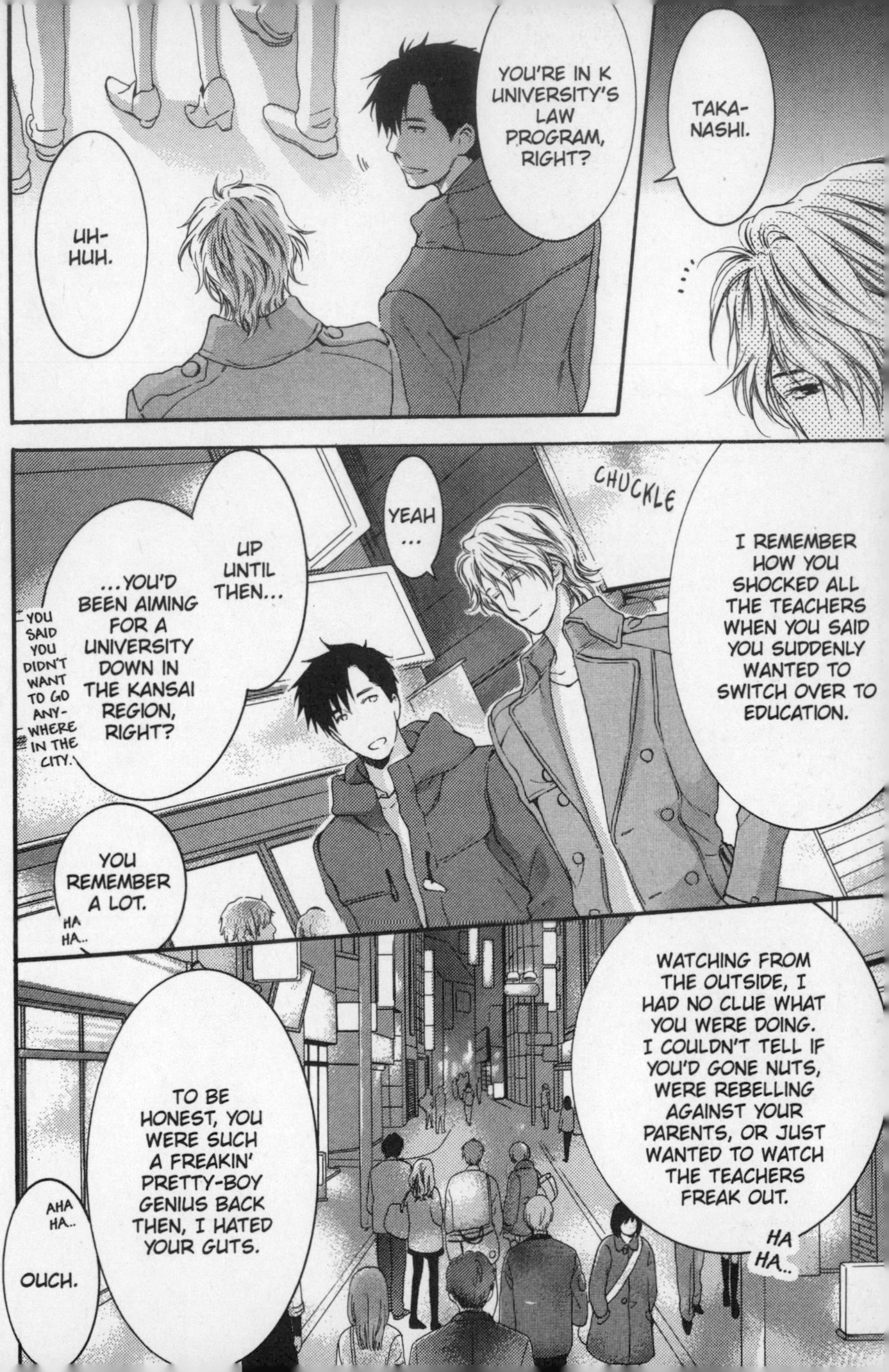
TAKA-NASHI.
...
YOU'RE IN K UNIVERSITY'S LAW PROGRAM, RIGHT?
UH-HUH.
CHUCKLE
I REMEMBER HOW YOU SHOCKED ALL THE TEACHERS WHEN YOU SAID YOU SUDDENLY WANTED TO SWITCH OVER TO EDUCATION.
YEAH ...
UP UNTIL THEN...
...YOU'D BEEN AIMING FOR A UNIVERSITY DOWN IN THE KANSAI REGION, RIGHT?
YOU SAID YOU DIDN'T WANT TO GO ANY-WHERE IN THE CITY.
YOU REMEMBER A LOT.
HA HA..
WATCHING FROM THE OUTSIDE, I HAD NO CLUE WHAT YOU WERE DOING. I COULDN'T TELL IF YOU'D GONE NUTS, WERE REBELLING AGAINST YOUR PARENTS, OR JUST WANTED TO WATCH THE TEACHERS FREAK OUT.
HA HA..
TO BE HONEST, YOU WERE SUCH A FREAKIN' PRETTY-BOY GENIUS BACK THEN, I HATED YOUR GUTS.
AHA HA..
OUCH.

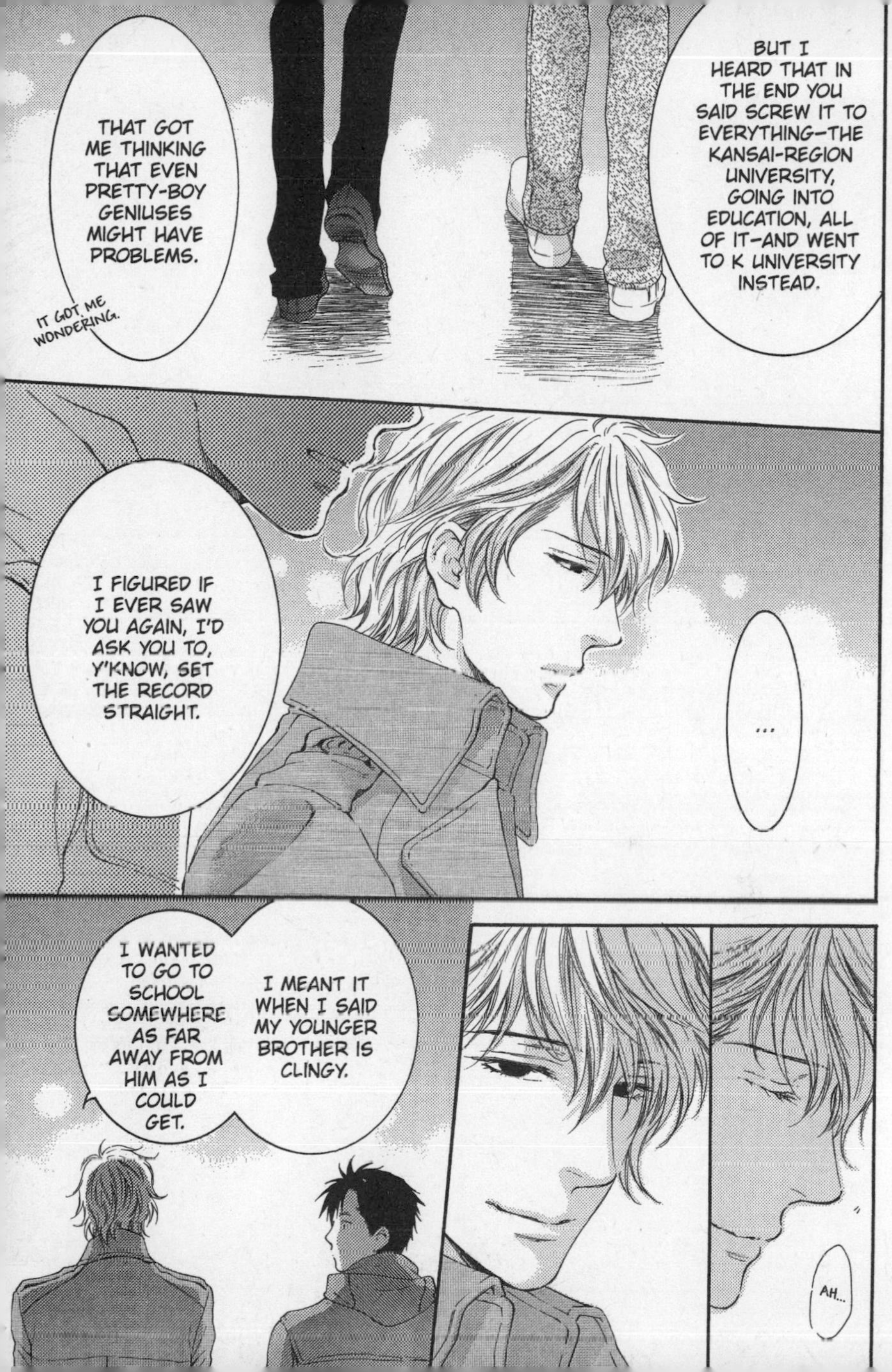
BUT I HEARD THAT IN THE END YOU SAID SCREW IT TO EVERYTHING—THE KANSAI-REGION UNIVERSITY, GOING INTO EDUCATION, ALL OF IT—AND WENT TO K UNIVERSITY INSTEAD.
THAT GOT ME THINKING THAT EVEN PRETTY-BOY GENIUSES MIGHT HAVE PROBLEMS.
IT GOT ME WONDERING.
...
I FIGURED IF I EVER SAW YOU AGAIN, I'D ASK YOU TO, Y'KNOW, SET THE RECORD STRAIGHT.
AH...
I MEANT IT WHEN I SAID MY YOUNGER BROTHER IS CLINGY.
I WANTED TO GO TO SCHOOL SOMEWHERE AS FAR AWAY FROM HIM AS I COULD GET.

WHAT?! NO WAY!

GOD, I'M SORRY! I SHOULDN'T HAVE ASKED!

BUT THEY TURNED ME DOWN.

BUT THEN I MET SOMEONE.

SOMEONE WHO I THOUGHT COULD BE THE ONE...

BTAM

WELCOME HOME. WERE YOU OUT DRINKING?

A LITTLE.

BTAM

BUT I WANT TO.

THEN DON'T CLING TO ME.

A LITTLE, HUH? YOU REEK OF BOOZE.

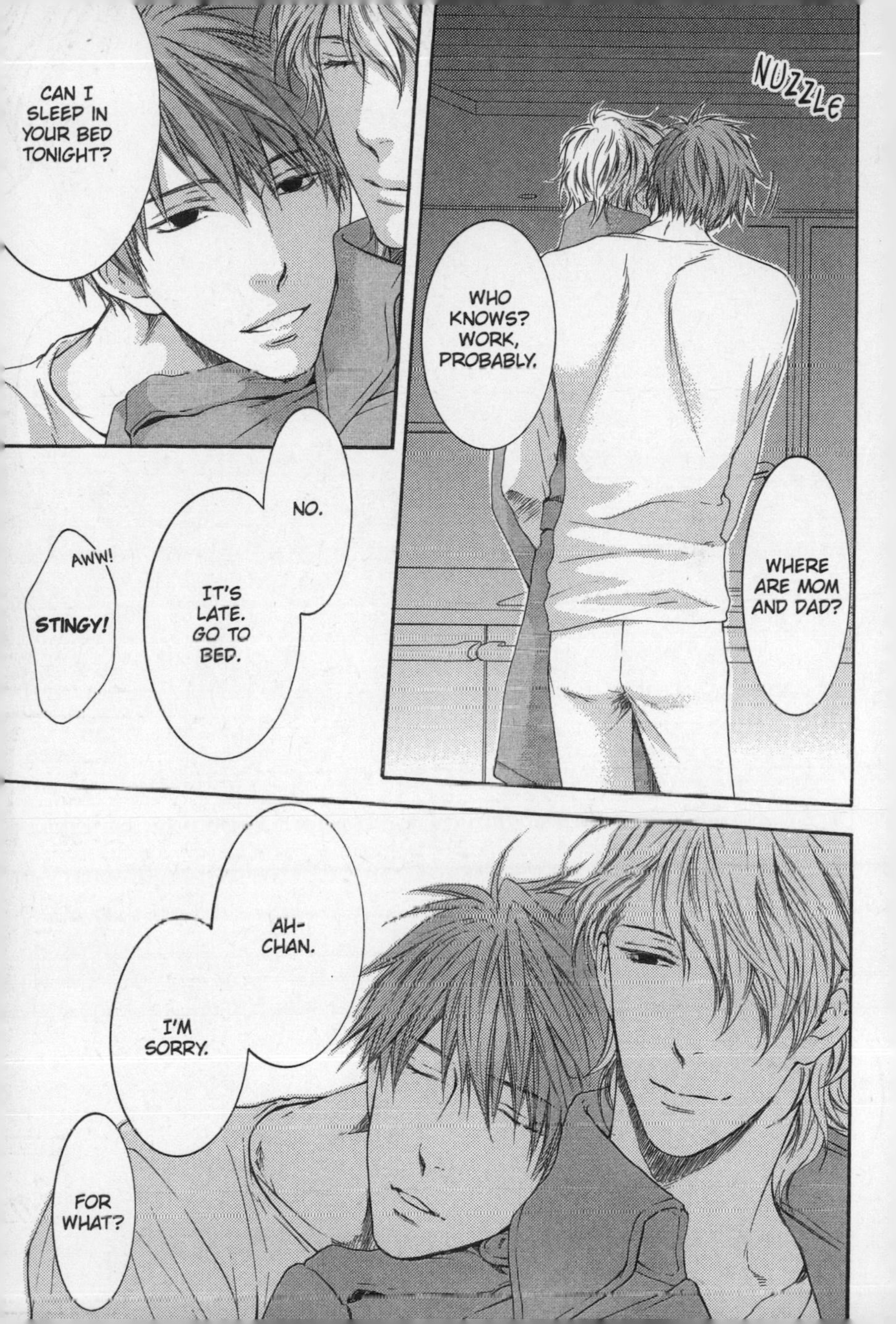
NUZZLE
WHERE ARE MOM AND DAD?
WHO KNOWS? WORK, PROBABLY.
CAN I SLEEP IN YOUR BED TONIGHT?
NO.
IT'S LATE. GO TO BED.
AWW!
STINGY!
AH-CHAN.
I'M SORRY.
FOR WHAT?

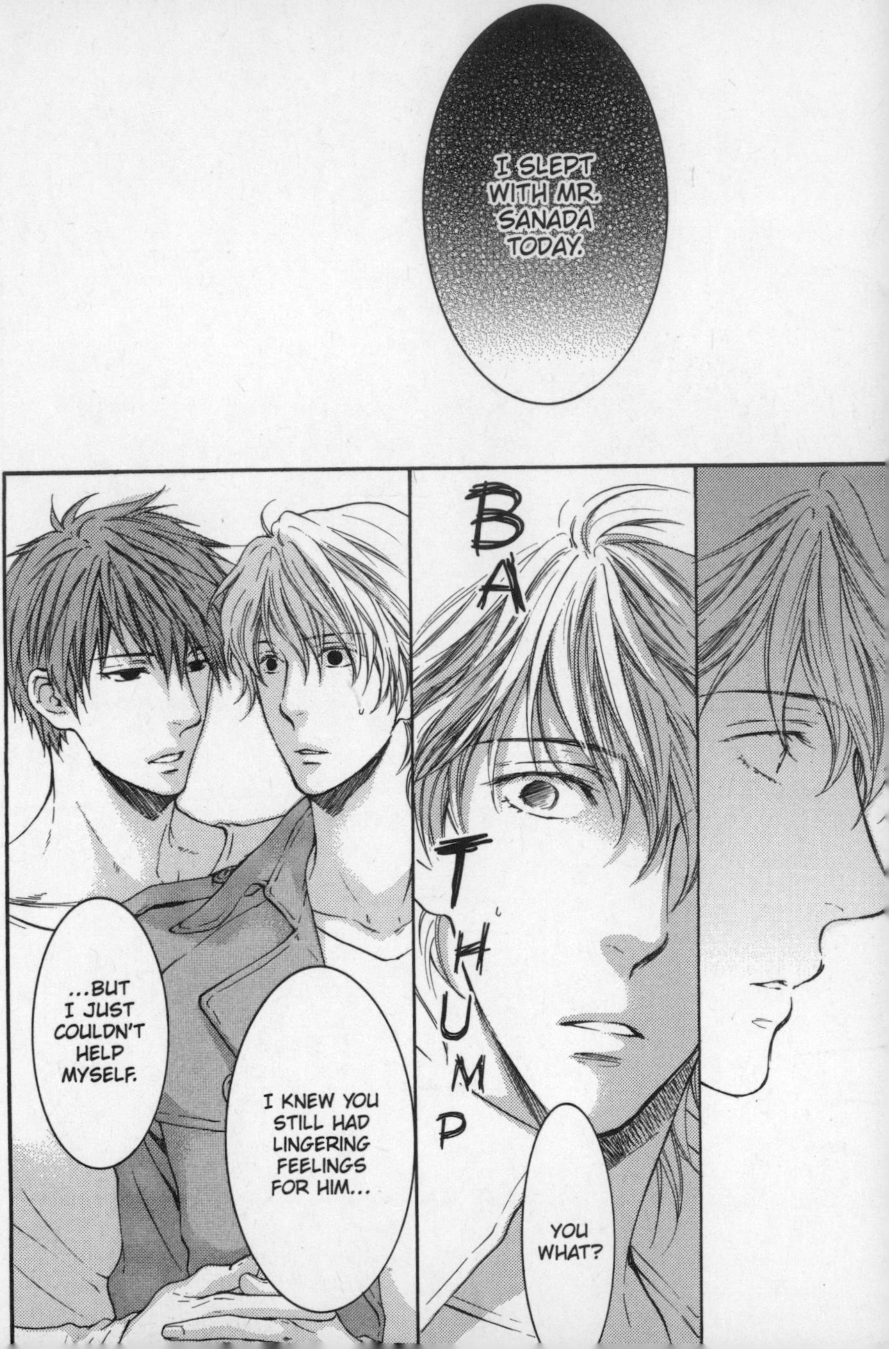
I SLEPT WITH MR. SANADA TODAY.
BA THUMP
YOU WHAT?
I KNEW YOU STILL HAD LINGERING FEELINGS FOR HIM...
...BUT I JUST COULDN'T HELP MYSELF.

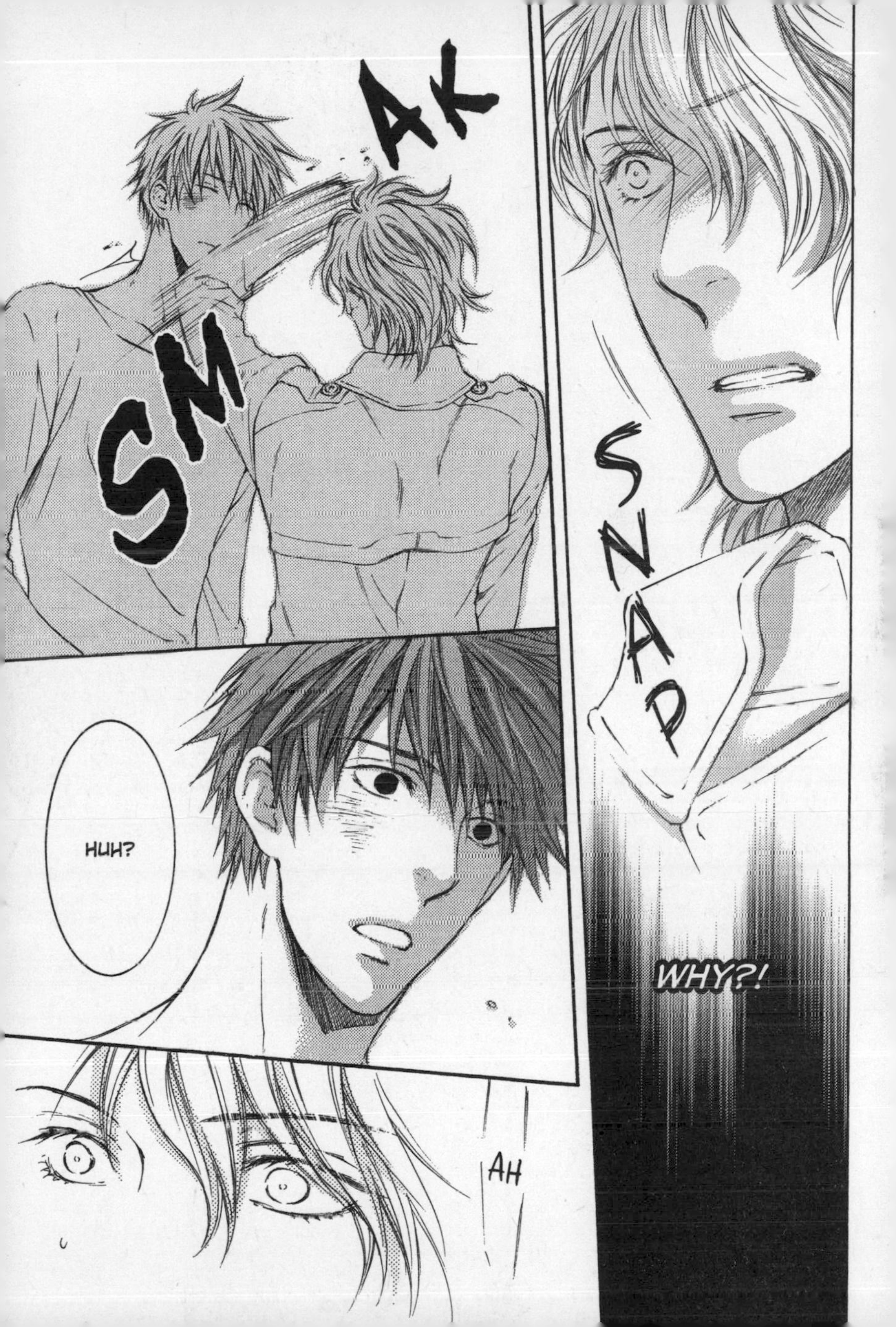
SNAP
WHY?!
SM AK
HUH?
AH

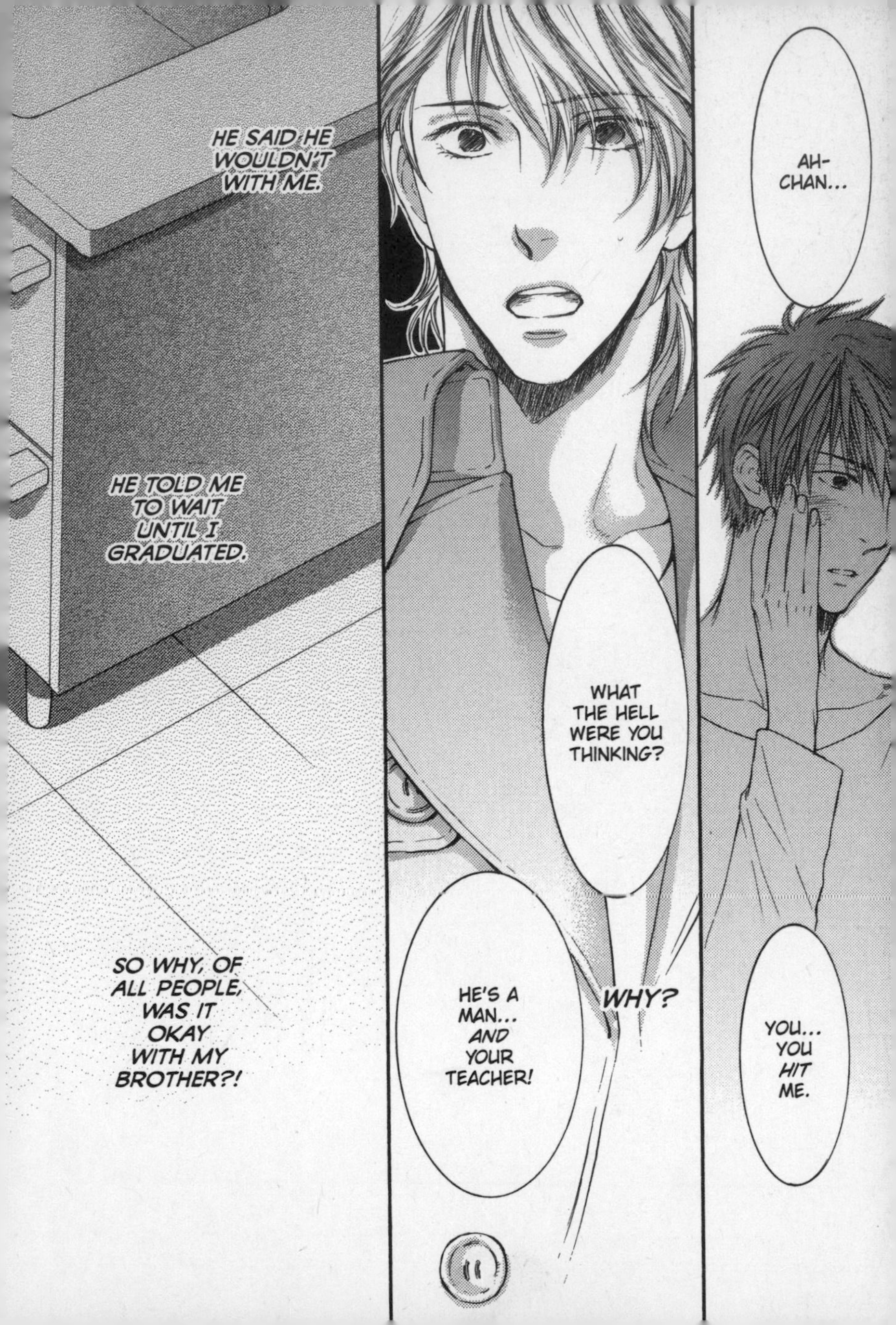
AH-CHAN...
YOU... YOU HIT ME.
WHAT THE HELL WERE YOU THINKING?
WHY?
HE'S A MAN... AND YOUR TEACHER!
HE SAID HE WOULDN'T WITH ME.
HE TOLD ME TO WAIT UNTIL I GRADUATED.
SO WHY, OF ALL PEOPLE, WAS IT OKAY WITH MY BROTHER?!

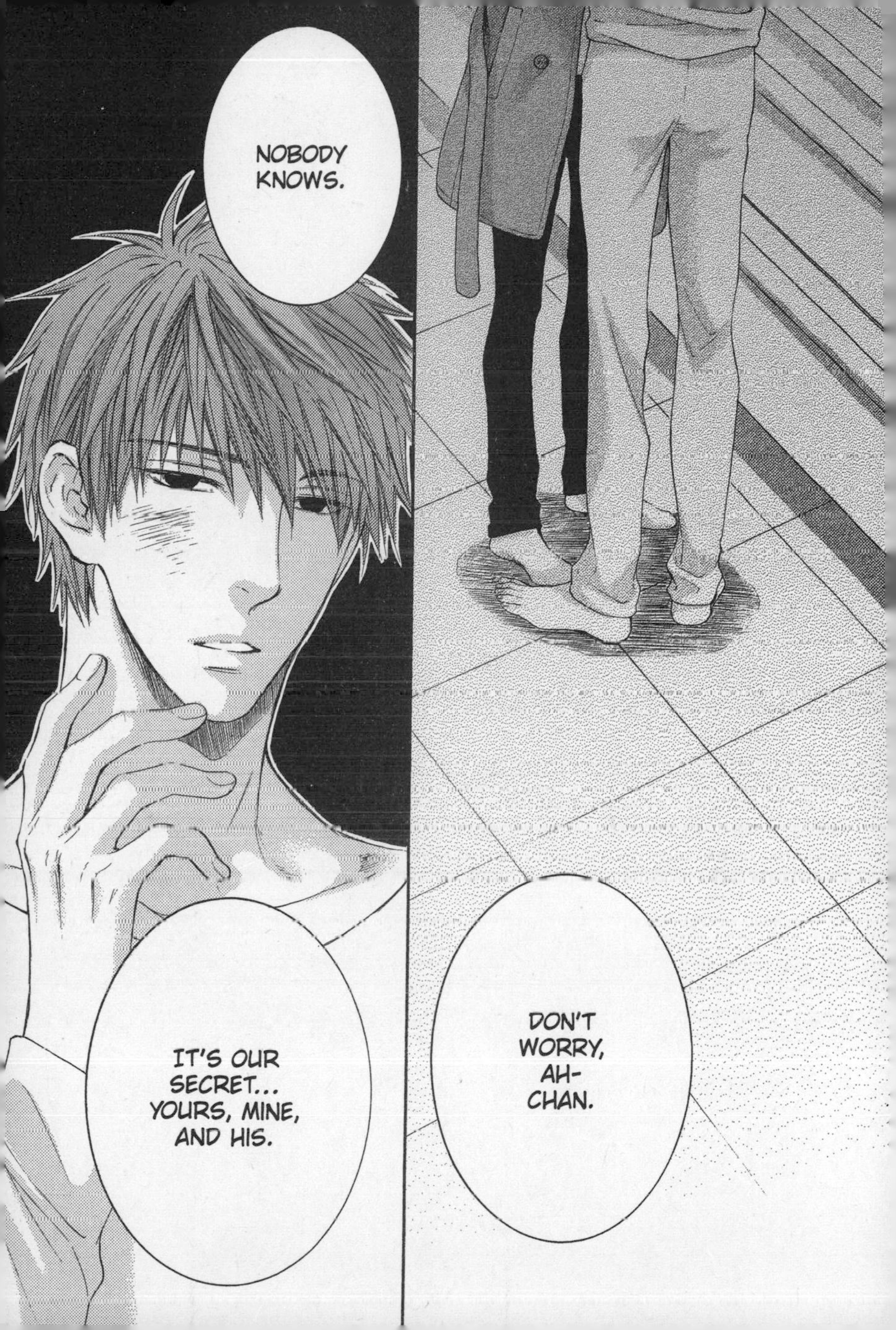
DON'T WORRY, AH-CHAN.
NOBODY KNOWS.
IT'S OUR SECRET... YOURS, MINE, AND HIS.

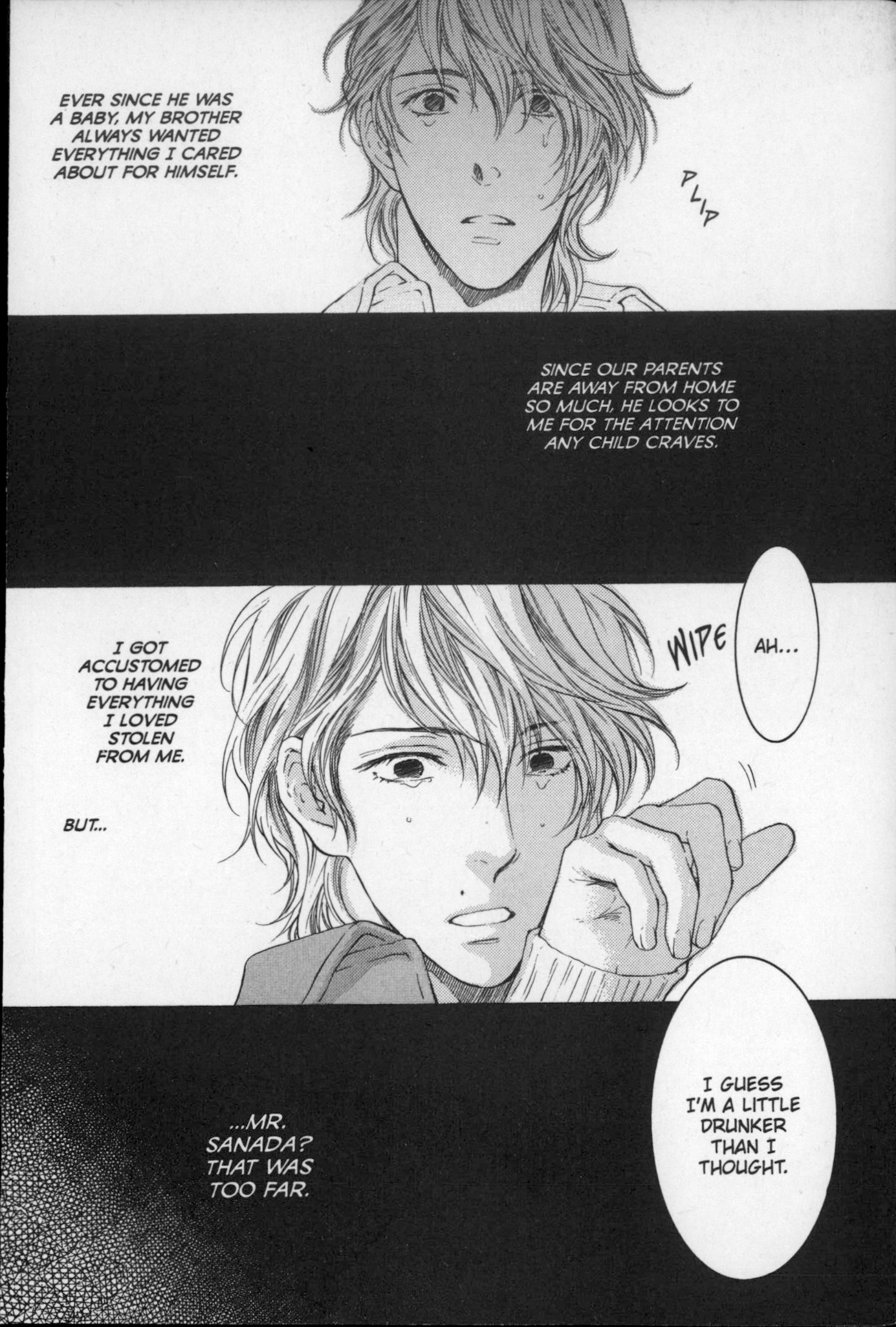
EVER SINCE HE WAS A BABY, MY BROTHER ALWAYS WANTED EVERYTHING I CARED ABOUT FOR HIMSELF.
PLIP
SINCE OUR PARENTS ARE AWAY FROM HOME SO MUCH, HE LOOKS TO ME FOR THE ATTENTION ANY CHILD CRAVES.
AH...
WIPE
I GOT ACCUSTOMED TO HAVING EVERYTHING I LOVED STOLEN FROM ME.
BUT...
I GUESS I'M A LITTLE DRUNKER THAN I THOUGHT.
...MR. SANADA? THAT WAS TOO FAR.

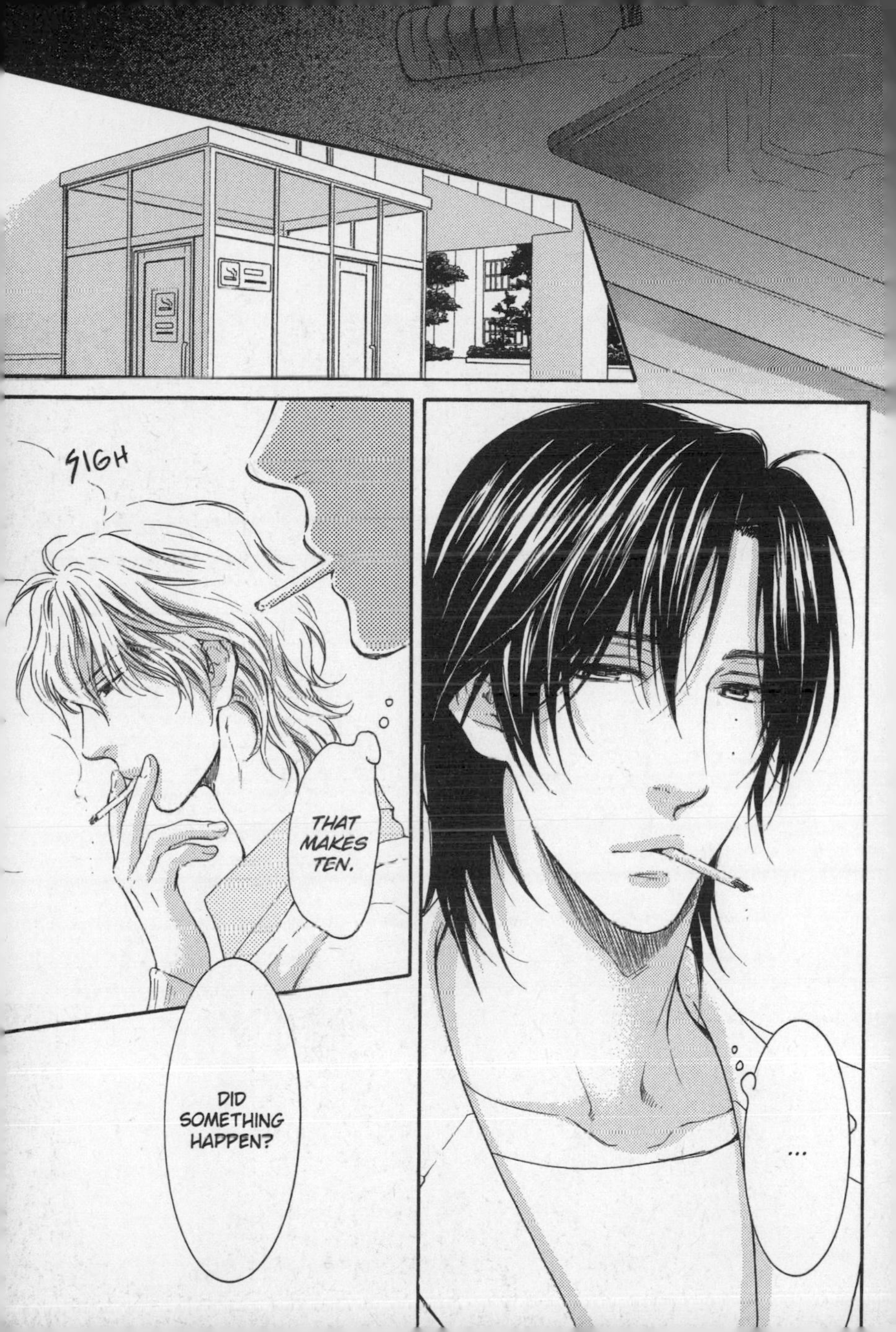
...
SIGH
THAT MAKES TEN.
DID SOMETHING HAPPEN?

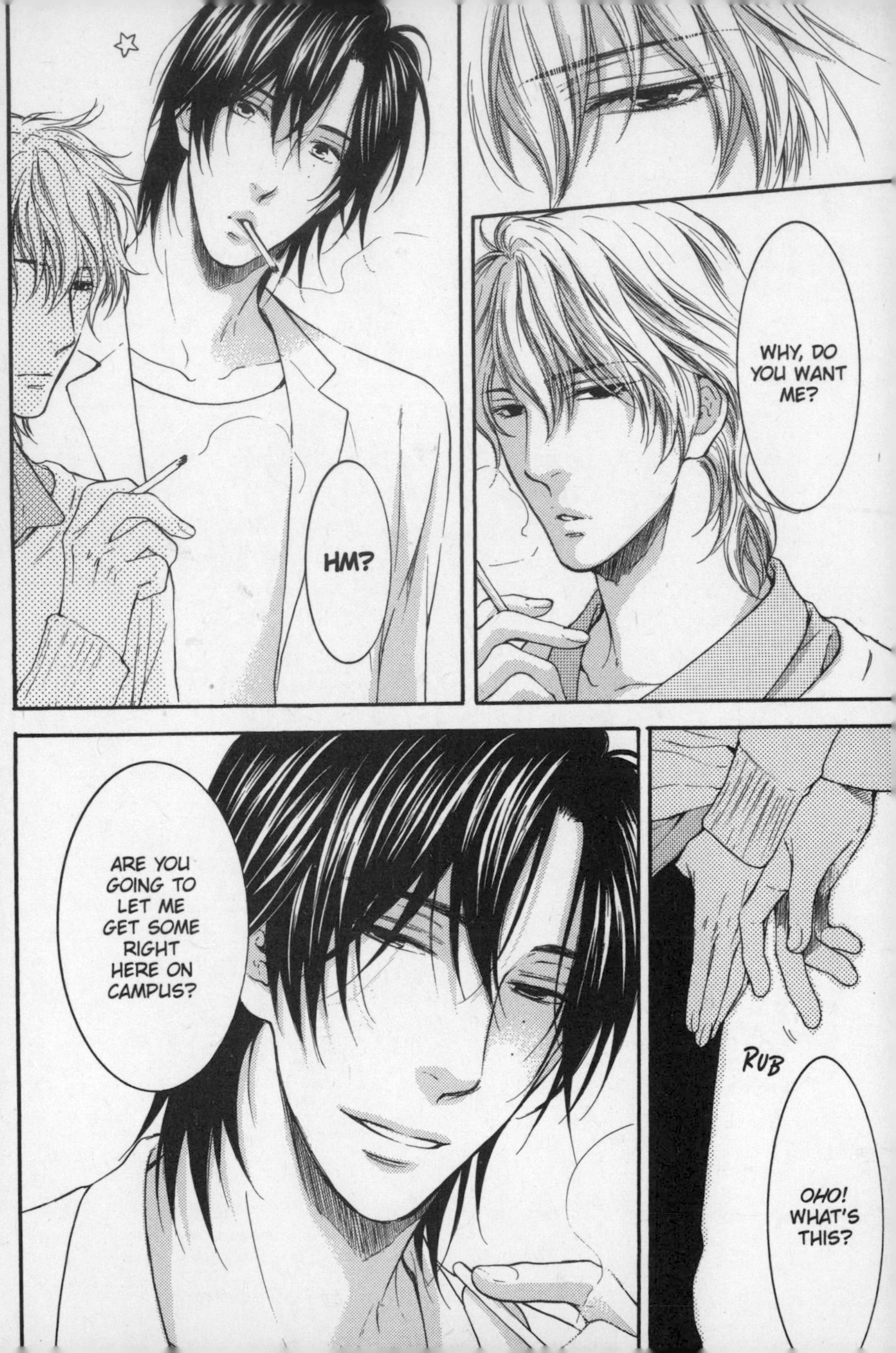
WHY, DO YOU WANT ME?
HM?
RUB
OHO! WHAT'S THIS?
ARE YOU GOING TO LET ME GET SOME RIGHT HERE ON CAMPUS?

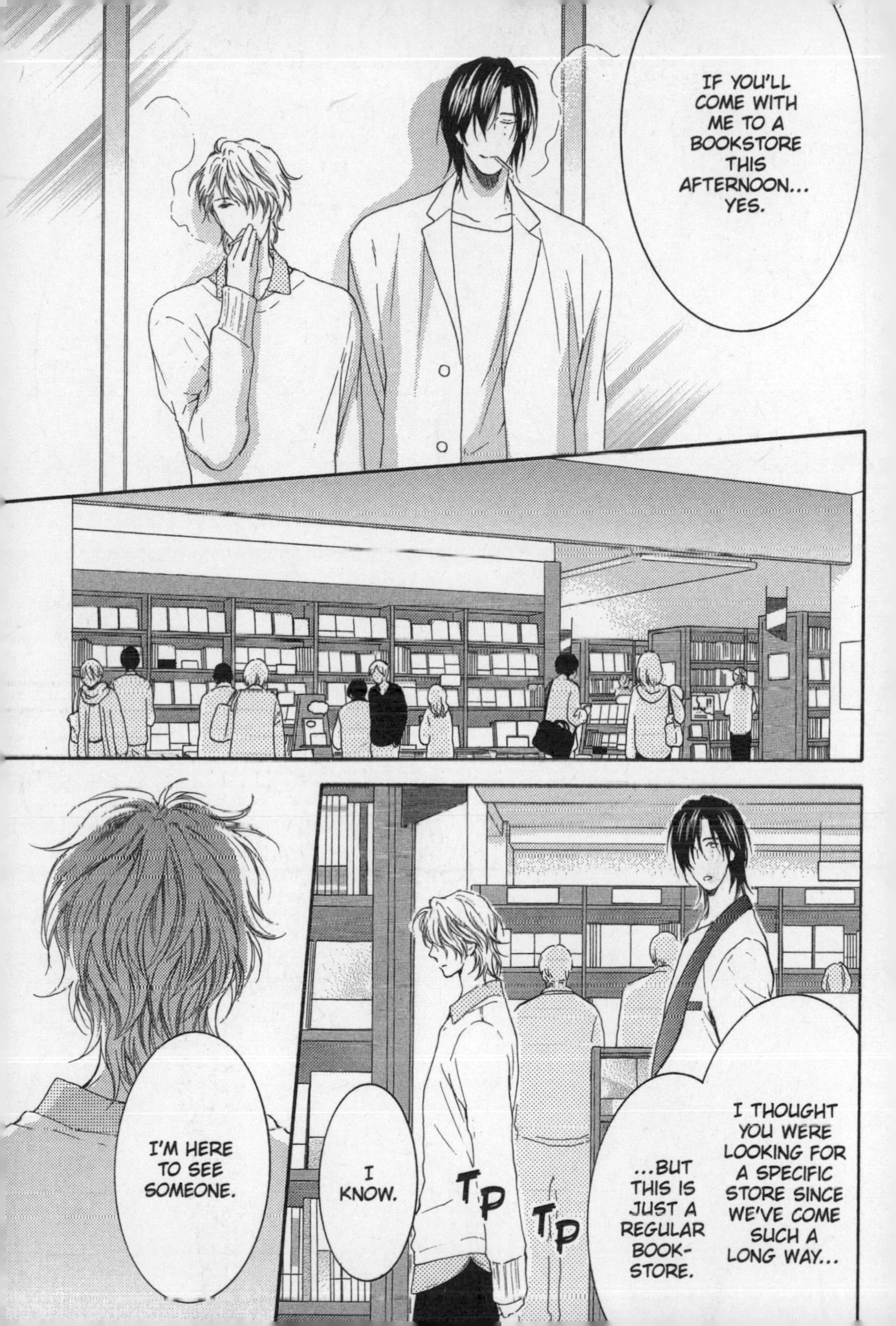
IF YOU'LL COME WITH ME TO A BOOKSTORE THIS AFTERNOON... YES.
I THOUGHT YOU WERE LOOKING FOR A SPECIFIC STORE SINCE WE'VE COME SUCH A LONG WAY...
...BUT THIS IS JUST A REGULAR BOOK-STORE.
TP TP
I KNOW.
I'M HERE TO SEE SOMEONE.

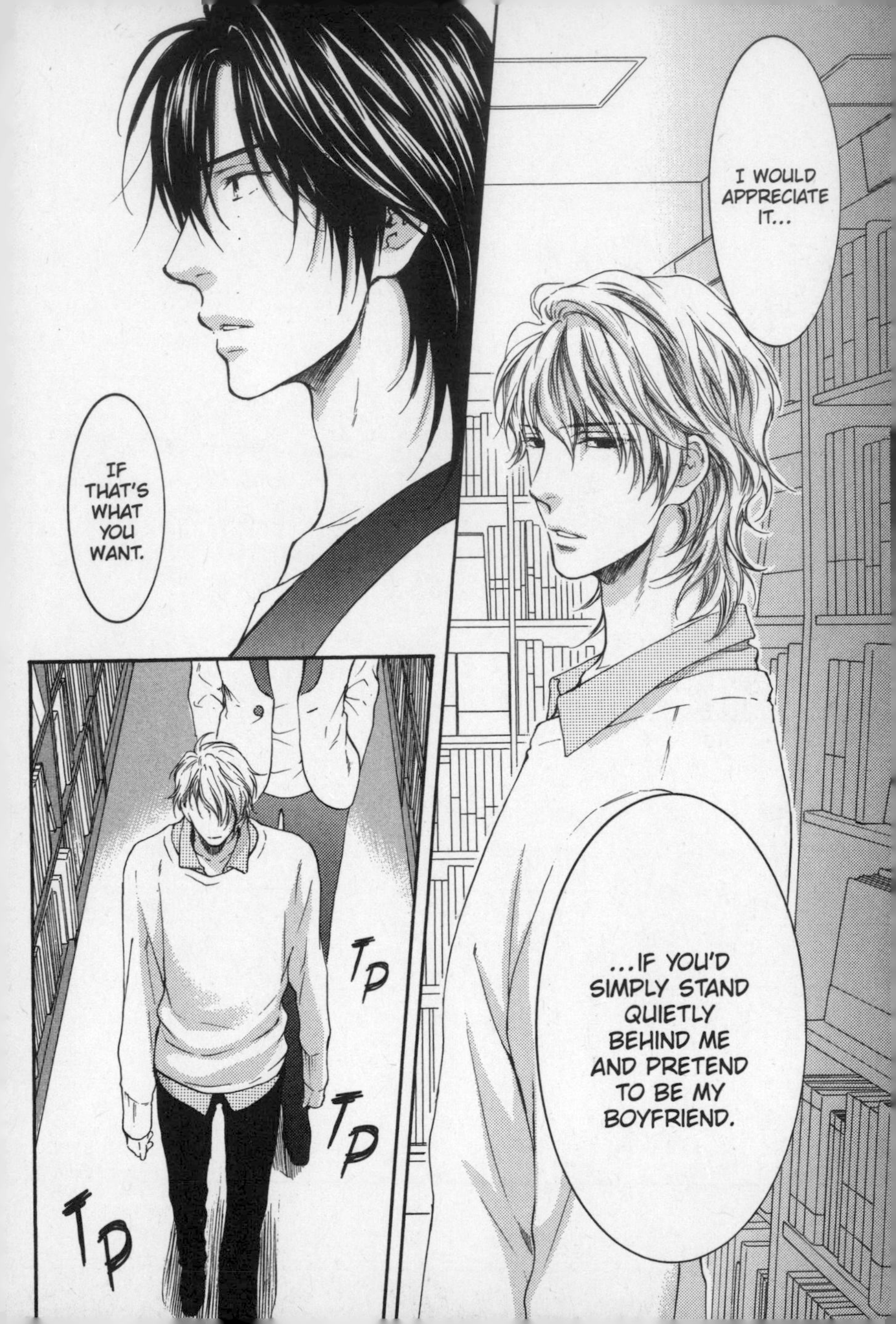
I WOULD APPRECIATE IT...
...IF YOU'D SIMPLY STAND QUIETLY BEHIND ME AND PRETEND TO BE MY BOYFRIEND.
IF THAT'S WHAT YOU WANT.
TP
TP
TP

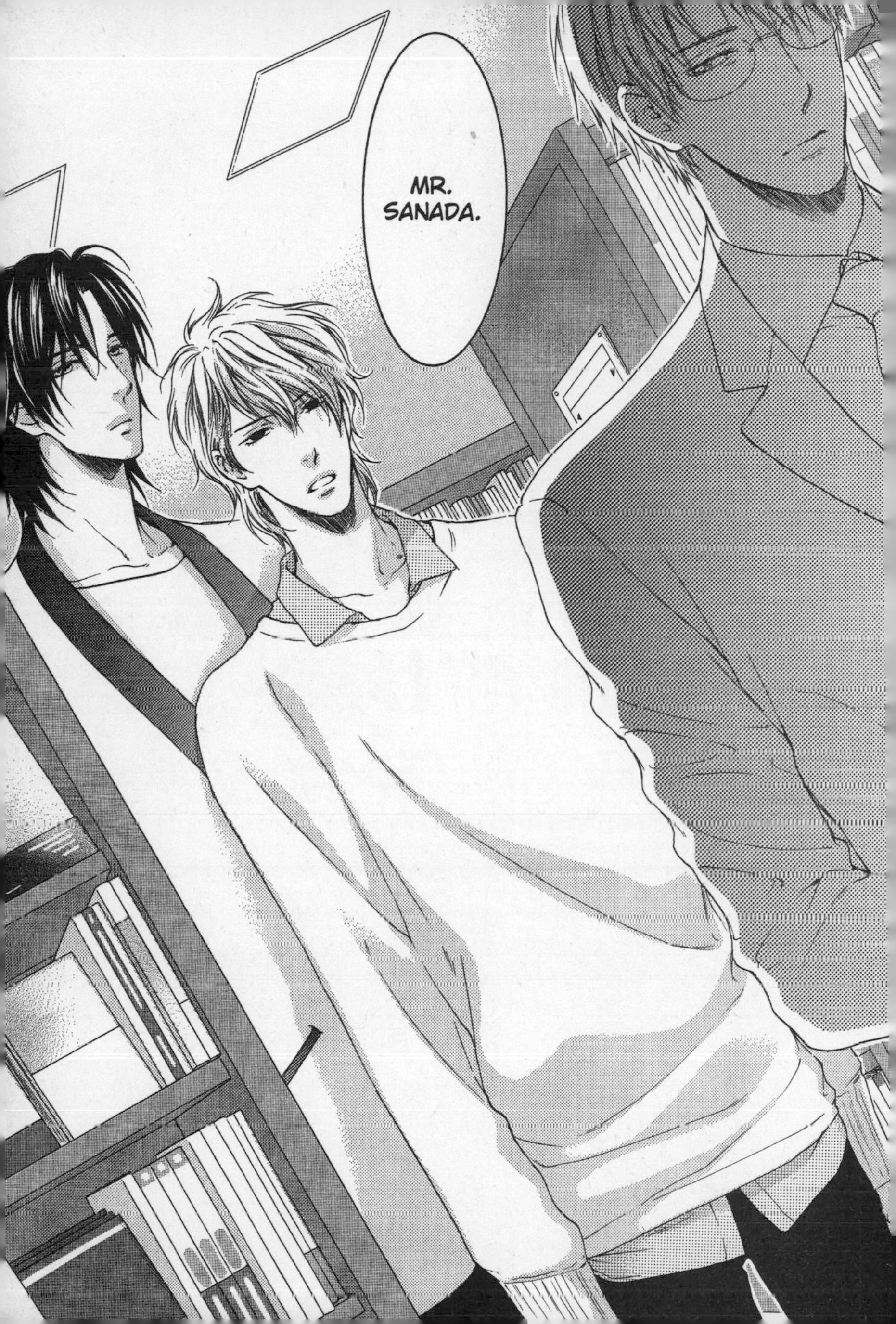
MR. SANADA.

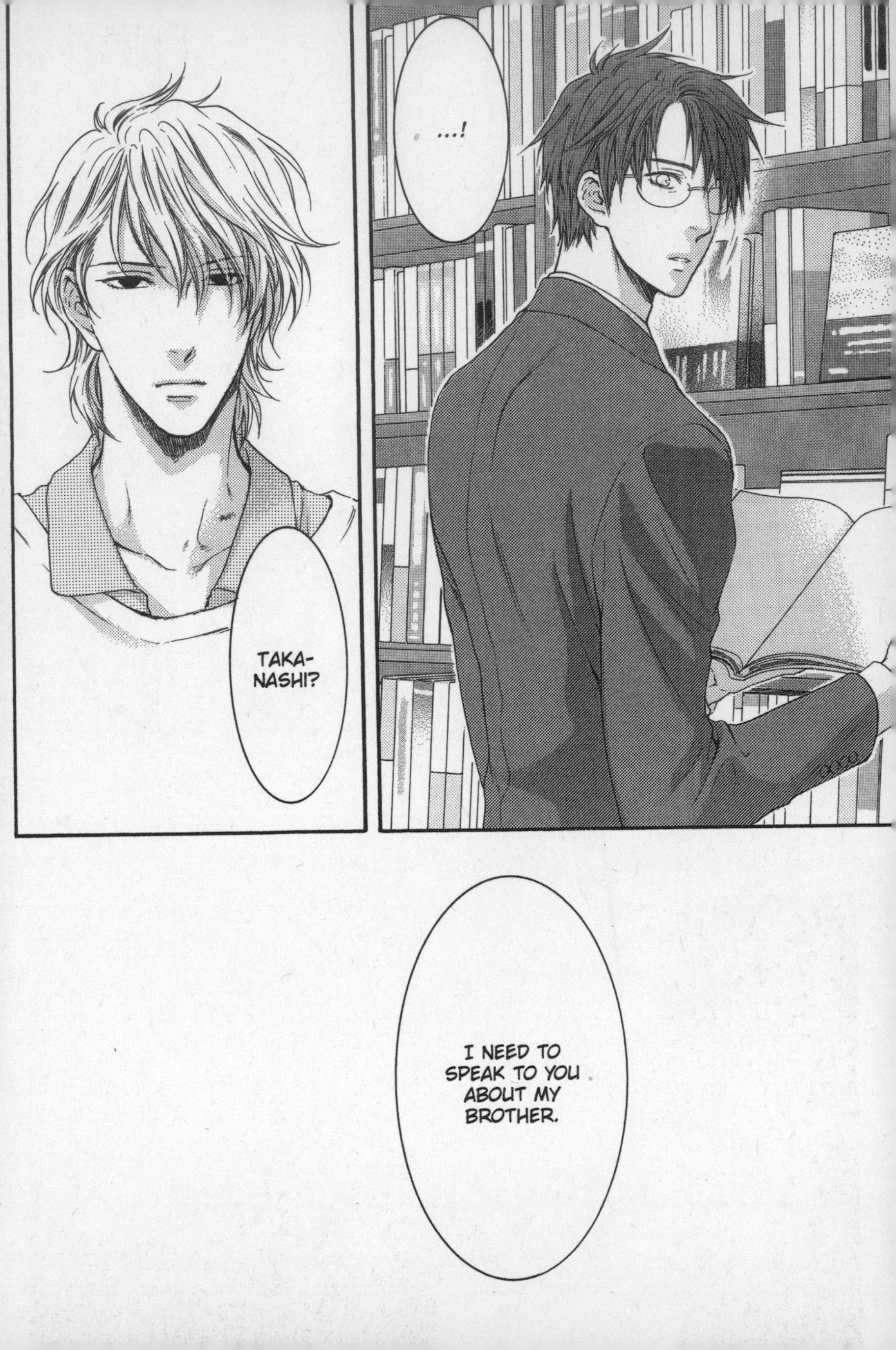
...!
TAKA-NASHI?
I NEED TO SPEAK TO YOU ABOUT MY BROTHER.

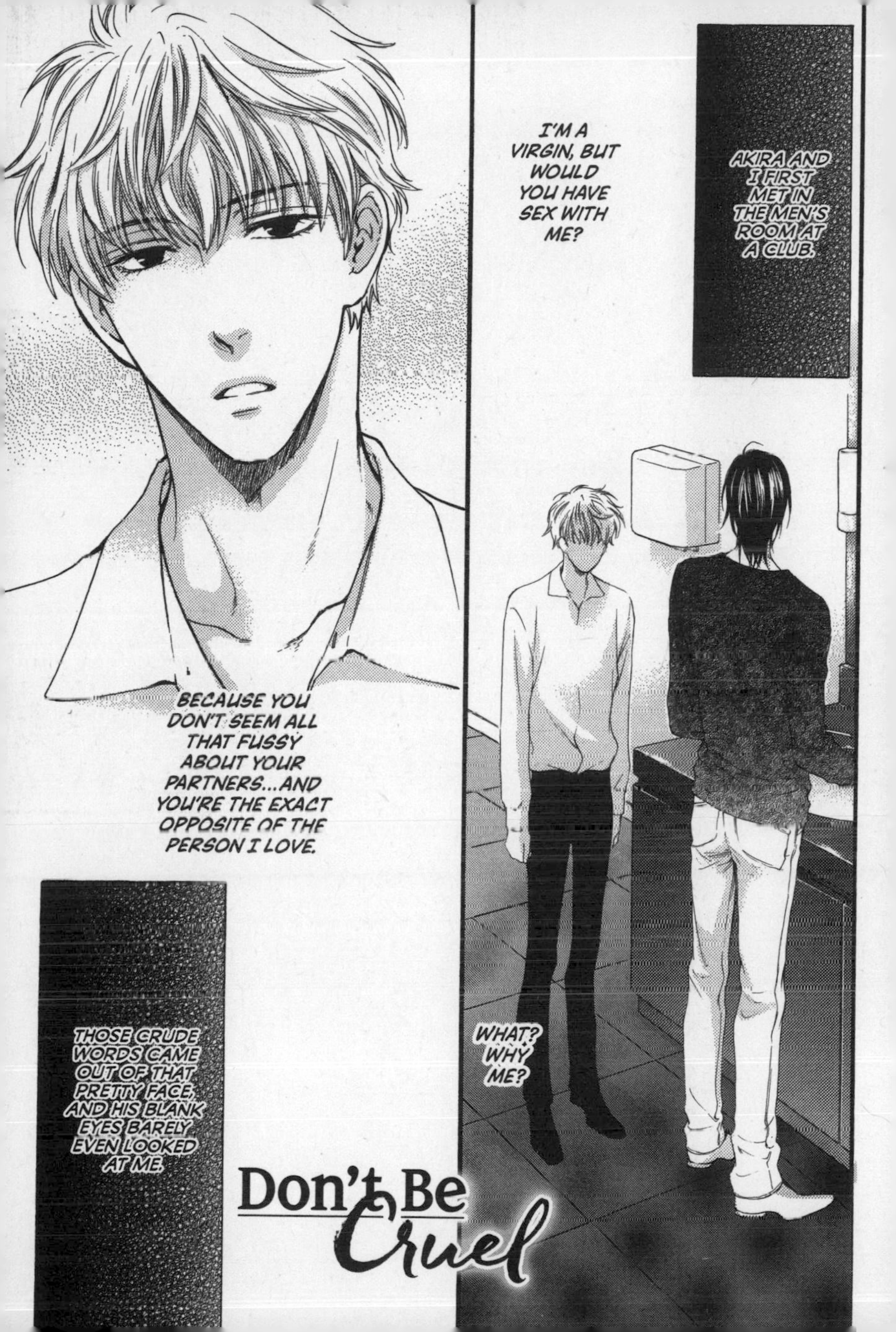
AKIRA AND I FIRST MET IN THE MEN'S ROOM AT A CLUB.
I'M A VIRGIN, BUT WOULD YOU HAVE SEX WITH ME?
WHAT? WHY ME?
BECAUSE YOU DON'T SEEM ALL THAT FUSSY ABOUT YOUR PARTNERS...AND YOU'RE THE EXACT OPPOSITE OF THE PERSON I LOVE.
THOSE CRUDE WORDS CAME OUT OF THAT PRETTY FACE, AND HIS BLANK EYES BARELY EVEN LOOKED AT ME.
Don't Be Cruel

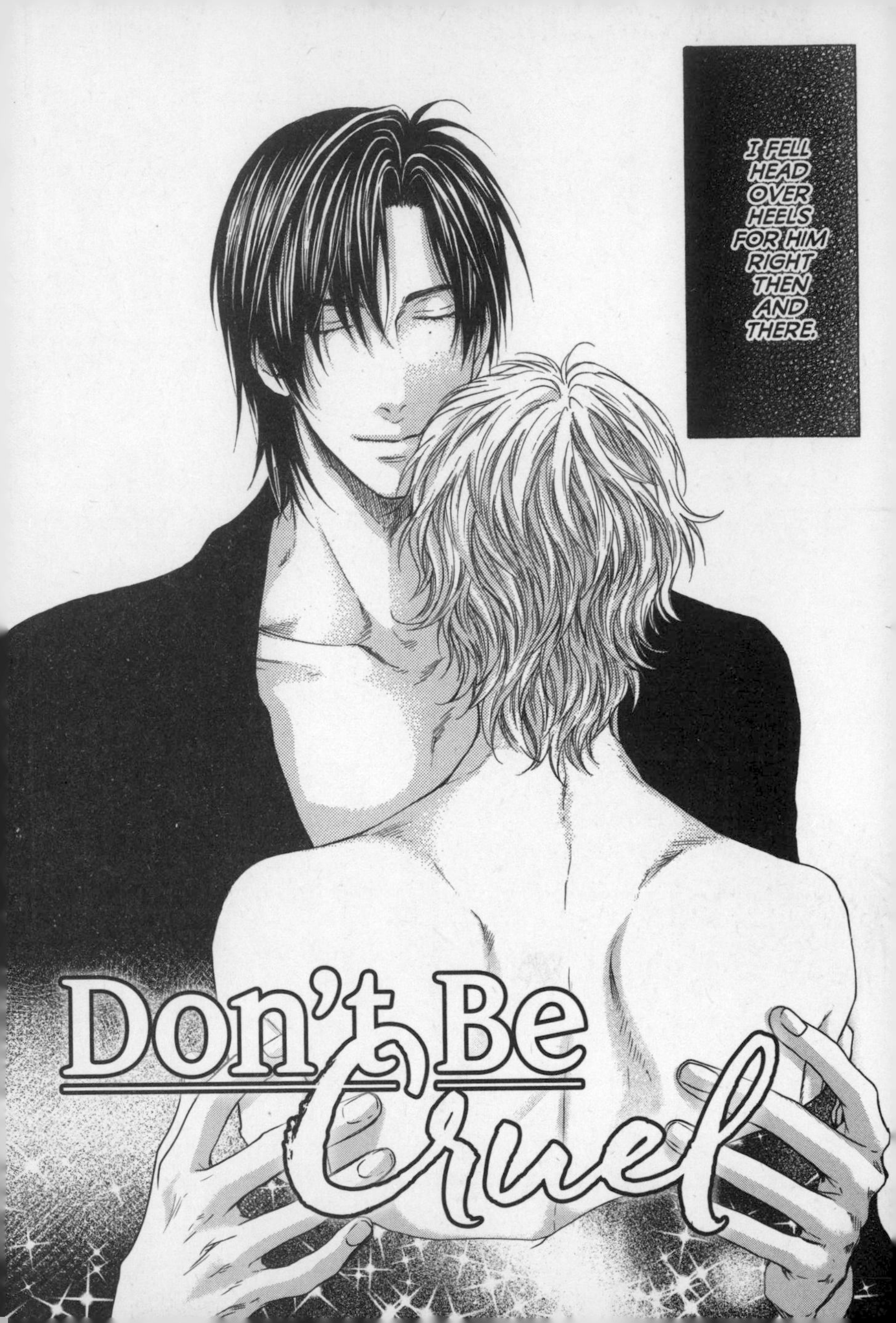
I FELL HEAD OVER HEELS FOR HIM RIGHT THEN AND THERE.
Don't Be Cruel

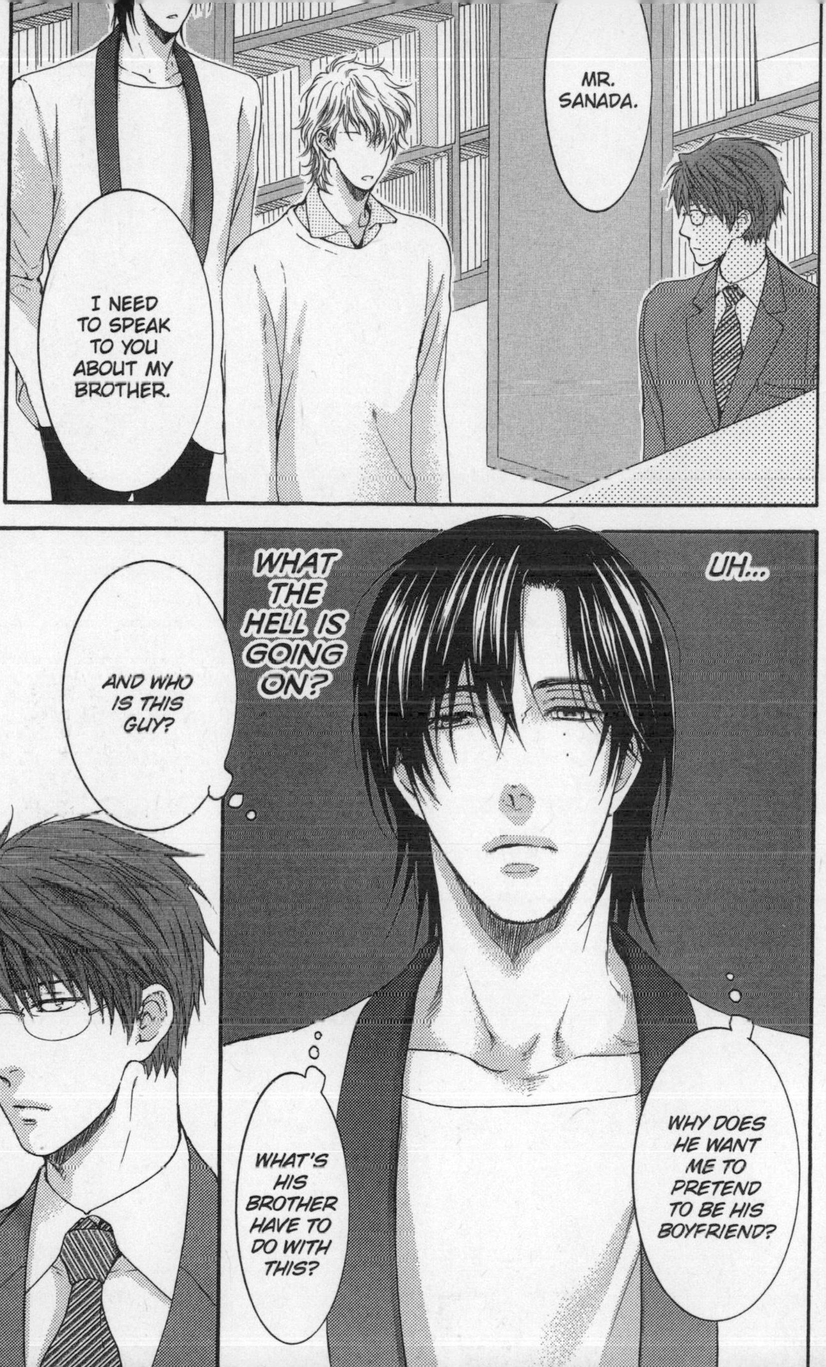
MR. SANADA.
I NEED TO SPEAK TO YOU ABOUT MY BROTHER.
UH...
WHAT THE HELL IS GOING ON?
WHY DOES HE WANT ME TO PRETEND TO BE HIS BOYFRIEND?
WHAT'S HIS BROTHER HAVE TO DO WITH THIS?
AND WHO IS THIS GUY?

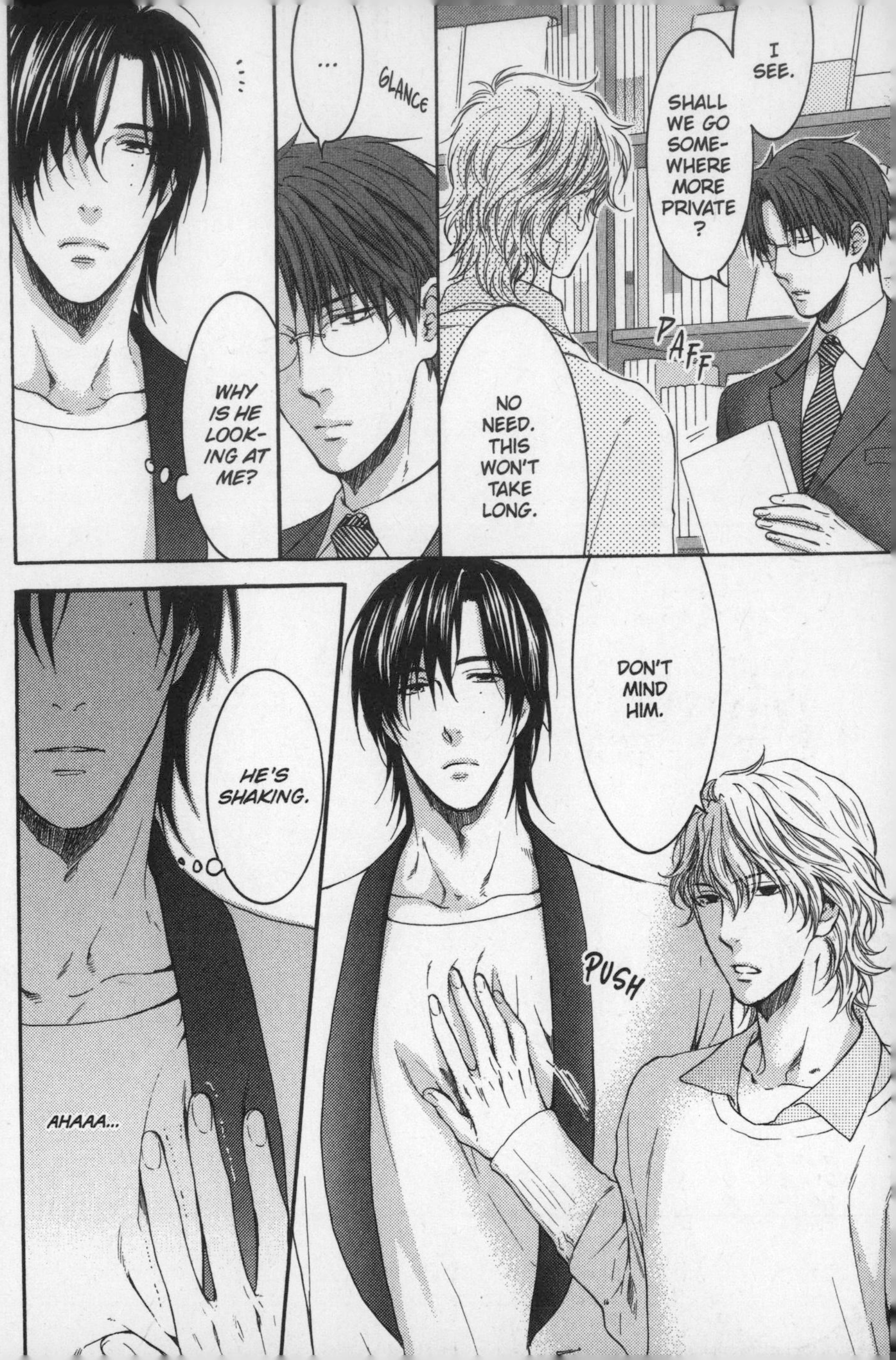
I SEE.
SHALL WE GO SOME-WHERE MORE PRIVATE?
PAFF
NO NEED. THIS WON'T TAKE LONG.
...
GLANCE
…
WHY IS HE LOOKING AT ME?
DON'T MIND HIM.
PUSH
HE'S SHAKING.
AHAAA...

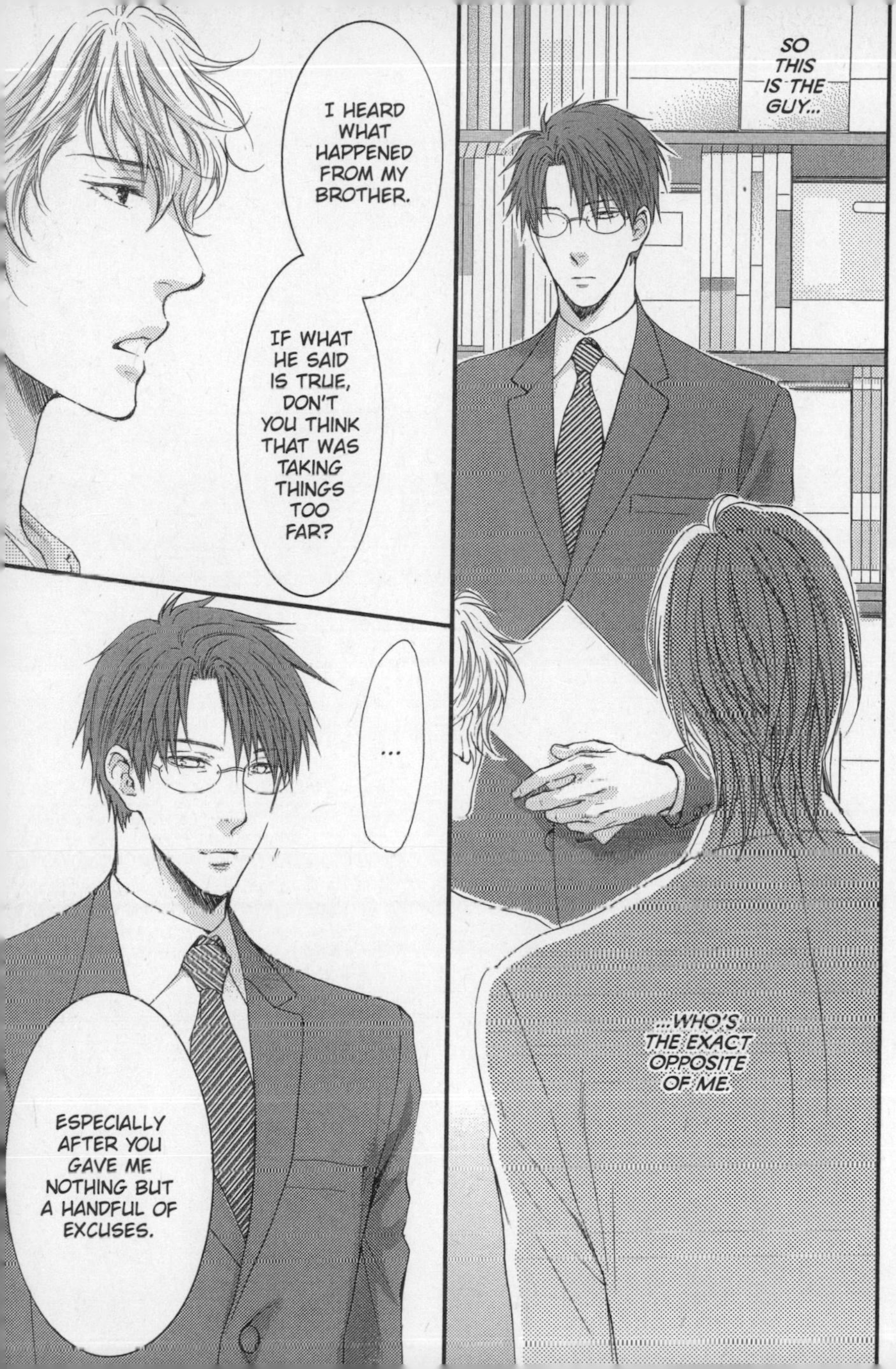
SO THIS IS THE GUY...
...WHO'S THE EXACT OPPOSITE OF ME.
I HEARD WHAT HAPPENED FROM MY BROTHER.
IF WHAT HE SAID IS TRUE, DON'T YOU THINK THAT WAS TAKING THINGS TOO FAR?
...
ESPECIALLY AFTER YOU GAVE ME NOTHING BUT A HANDFUL OF EXCUSES.

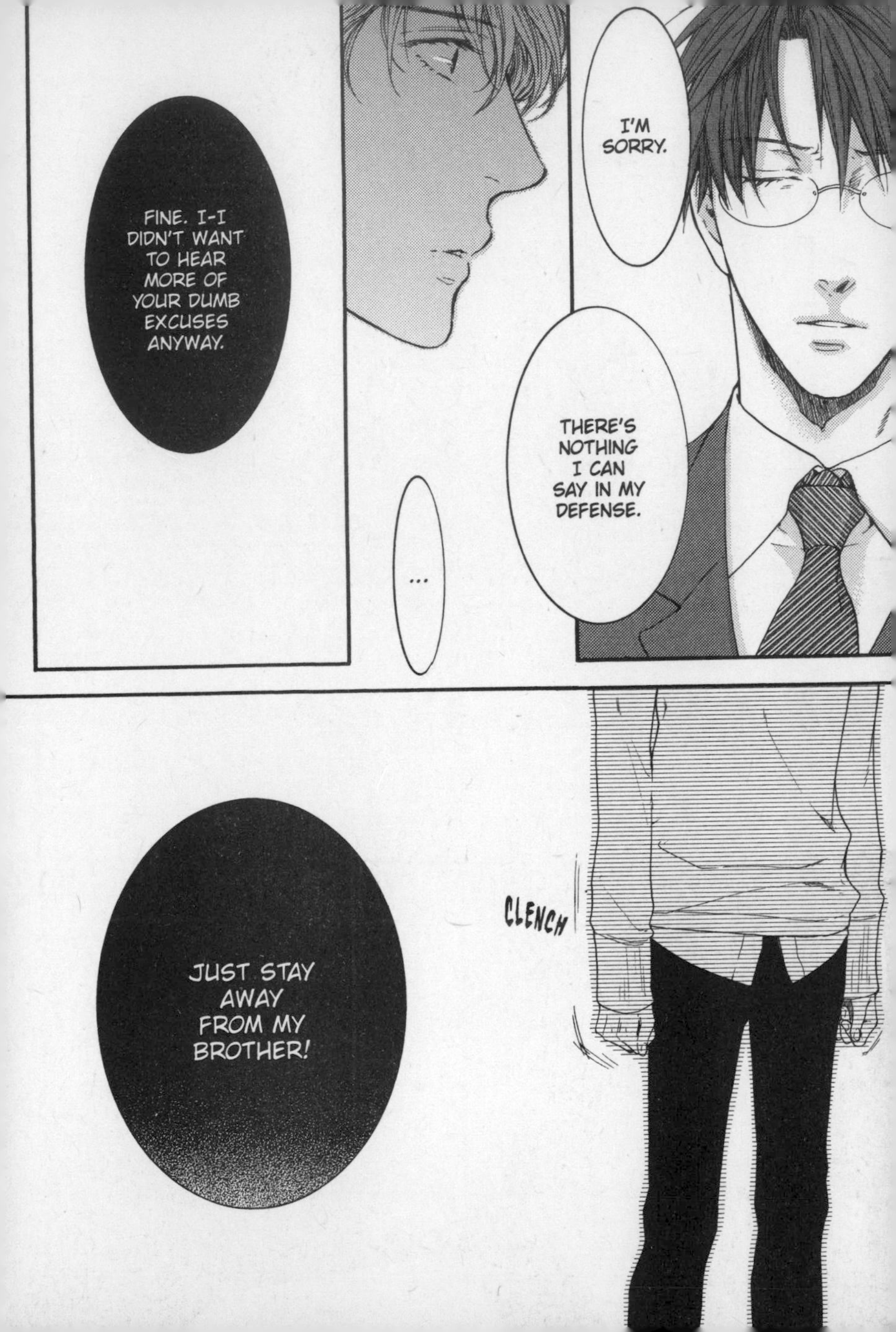
I'M SORRY.
THERE'S NOTHING I CAN SAY IN MY DEFENSE.
...
FINE. I-I DIDN'T WANT TO HEAR MORE OF YOUR DUMB EXCUSES ANYWAY.
CLENCH
JUST STAY AWAY FROM MY BROTHER!

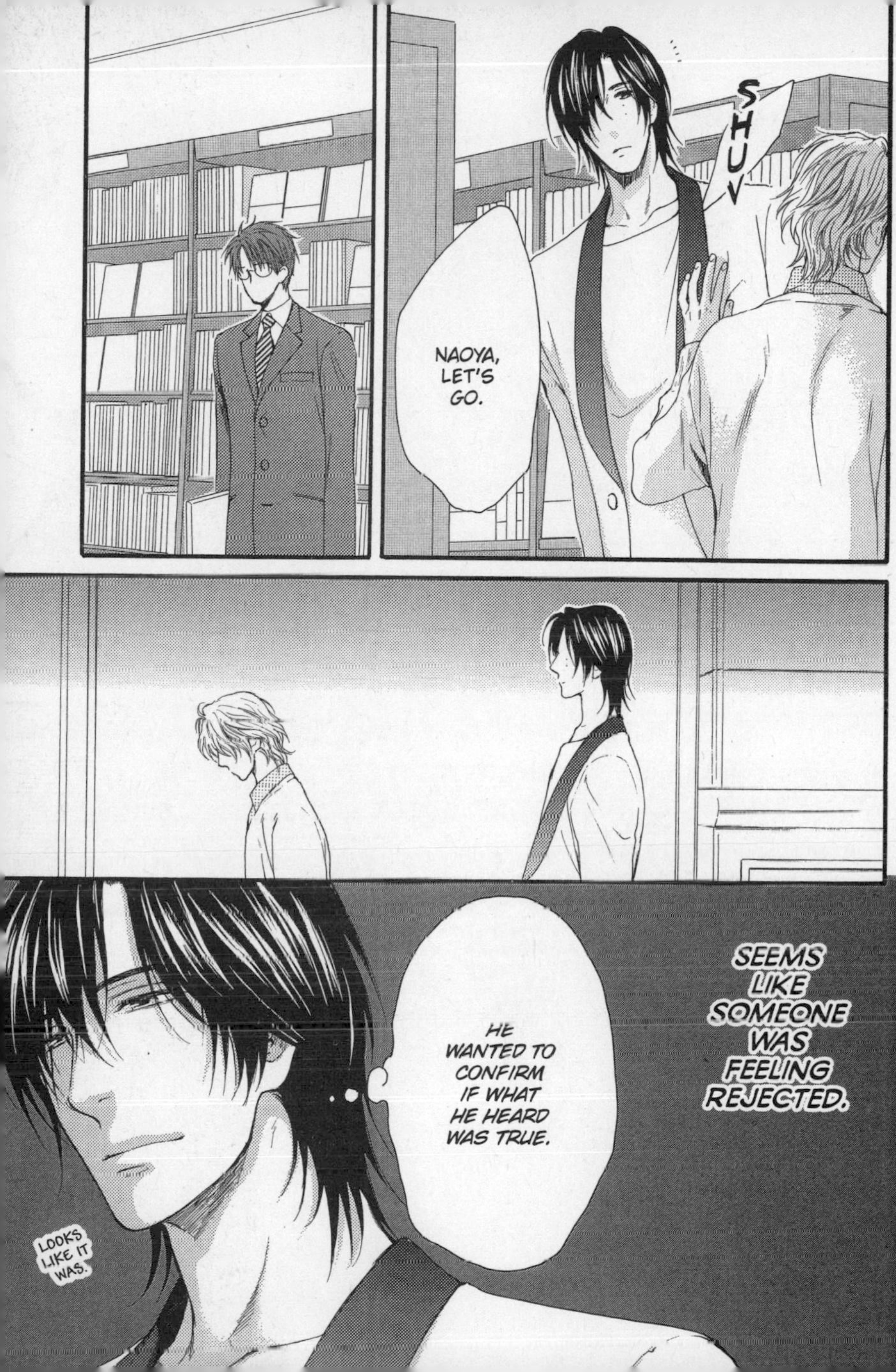
SHUV
NAOYA, LET'S GO.
SEEMS LIKE SOMEONE WAS FEELING REJECTED.
HE WANTED TO CONFIRM IF WHAT HE HEARD WAS TRUE.
LOOKS LIKE IT WAS.

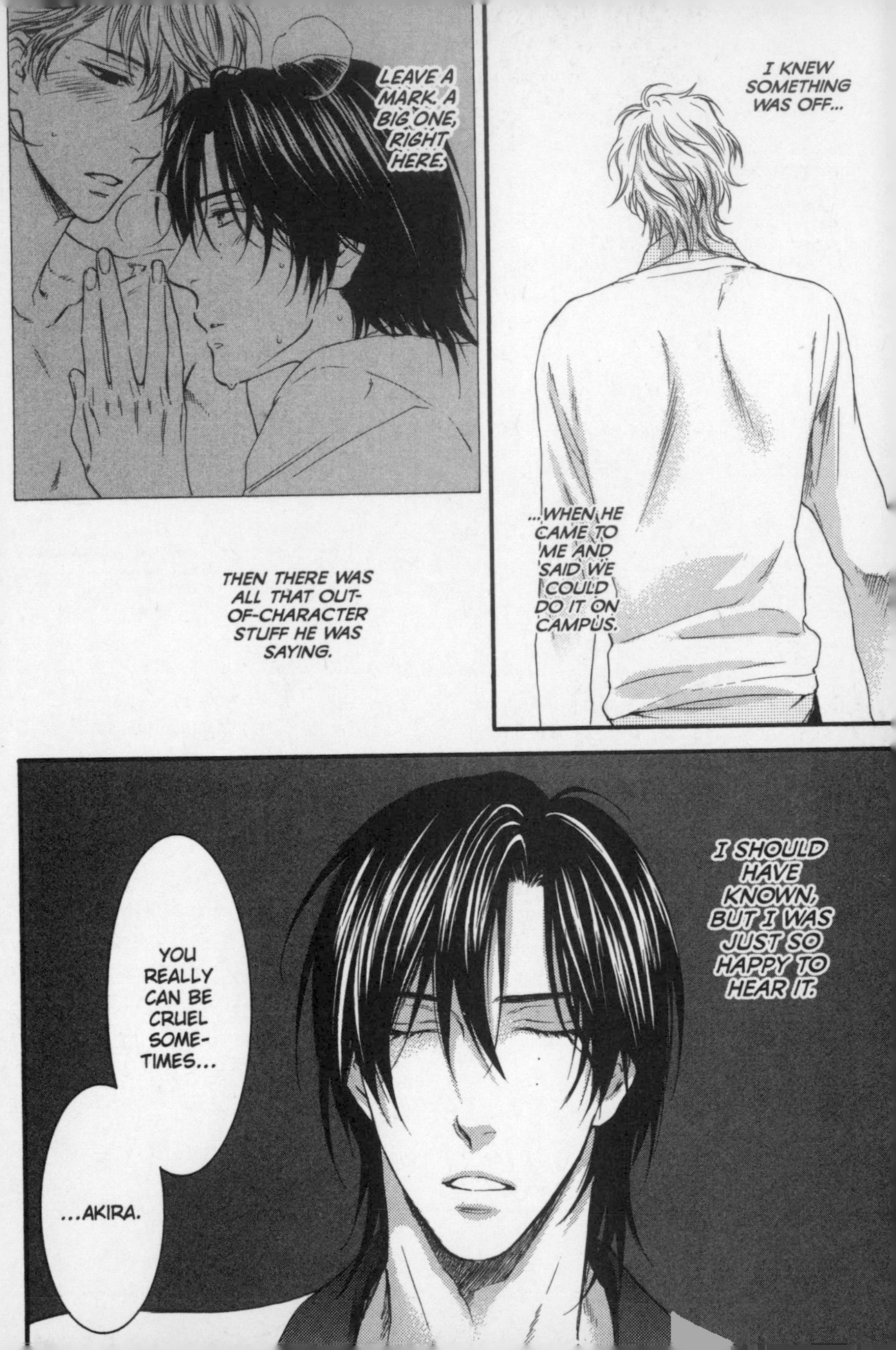
I KNEW SOMETHING WAS OFF...
...WHEN HE CAME TO ME AND SAID WE COULD DO IT ON CAMPUS.
LEAVE A MARK. A BIG ONE, RIGHT HERE.
THEN THERE WAS ALL THAT OUT-OF-CHARACTER STUFF HE WAS SAYING.
I SHOULD HAVE KNOWN, BUT I WAS JUST SO HAPPY TO HEAR IT.
YOU REALLY CAN BE CRUEL SOME-TIMES...
...AKIRA.

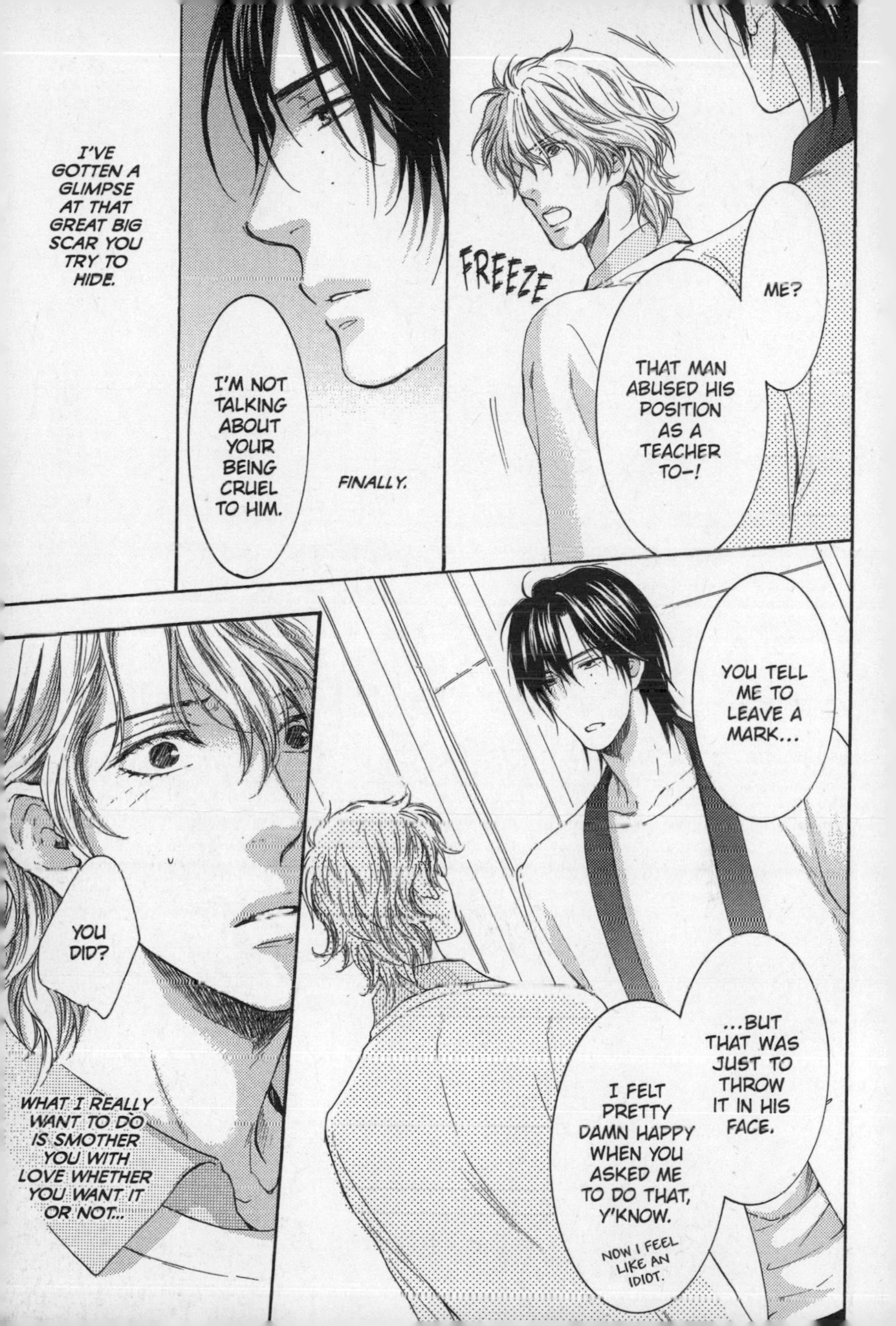
ME?
THAT MAN ABUSED HIS POSITION AS A TEACHER TO-!
FREEZE
I'M NOT TALKING ABOUT YOUR BEING CRUEL TO HIM.
FINALLY.
I'VE GOTTEN A GLIMPSE AT THAT GREAT BIG SCAR YOU TRY TO HIDE.
YOU TELL ME TO LEAVE A MARK...
...BUT THAT WAS JUST TO THROW IT IN HIS FACE.
I FELT PRETTY DAMN HAPPY WHEN YOU ASKED ME TO DO THAT, Y'KNOW.
NOW I FEEL LIKE AN IDIOT.
YOU DID?
WHAT I REALLY WANT TO DO IS SMOTHER YOU WITH LOVE WHETHER YOU WANT IT OR NOT...

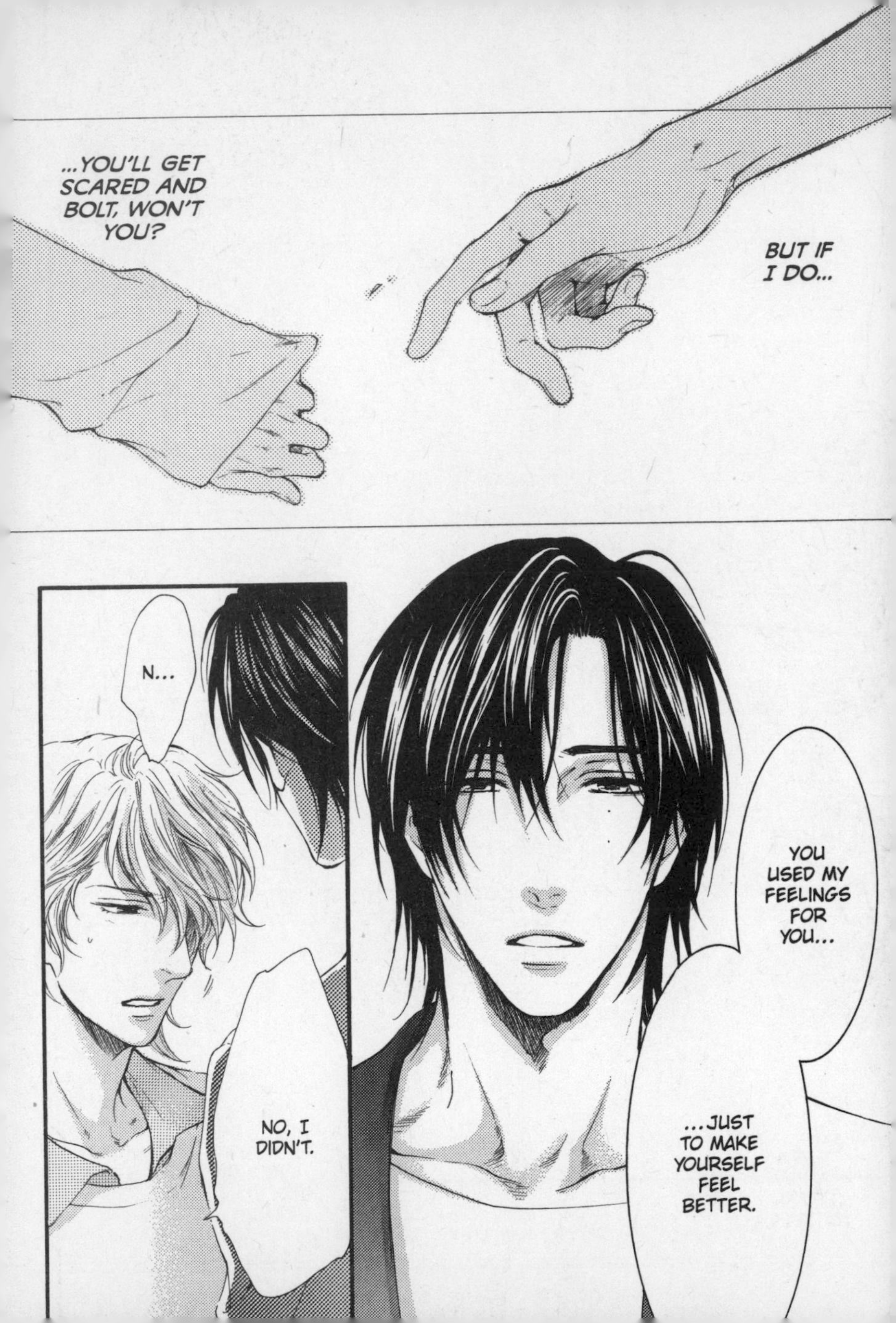
BUT IF I DO...
...YOU'LL GET SCARED AND BOLT, WON'T YOU?
YOU USED MY FEELINGS FOR YOU...
...JUST TO MAKE YOURSELF FEEL BETTER.
N...
NO, I DIDN'T.

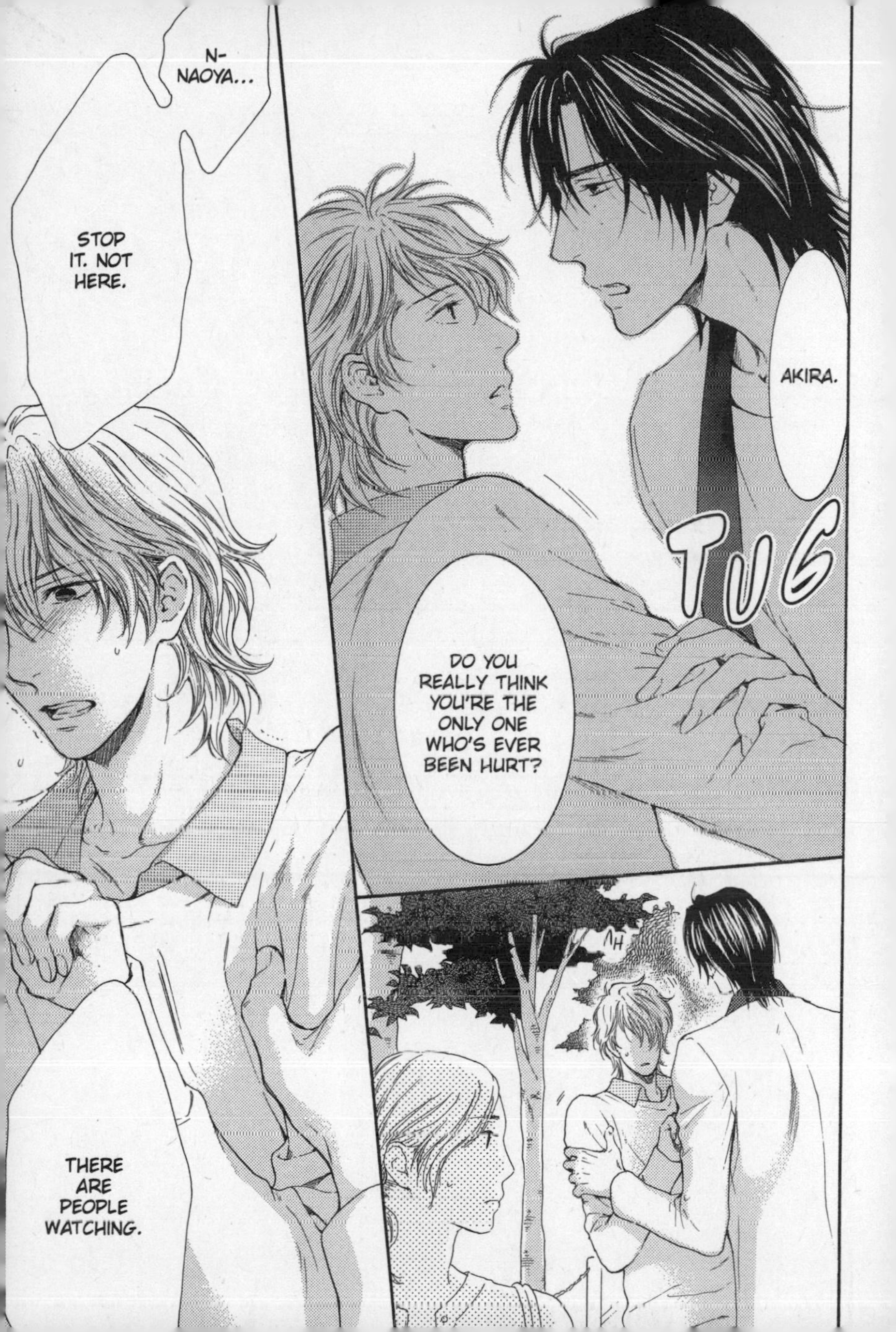
AKIRA.
TUG
DO YOU REALLY THINK YOU'RE THE ONLY ONE WHO'S EVER BEEN HURT?
AH
N- NAOYA...
STOP IT. NOT HERE.
THERE ARE PEOPLE WATCHING.

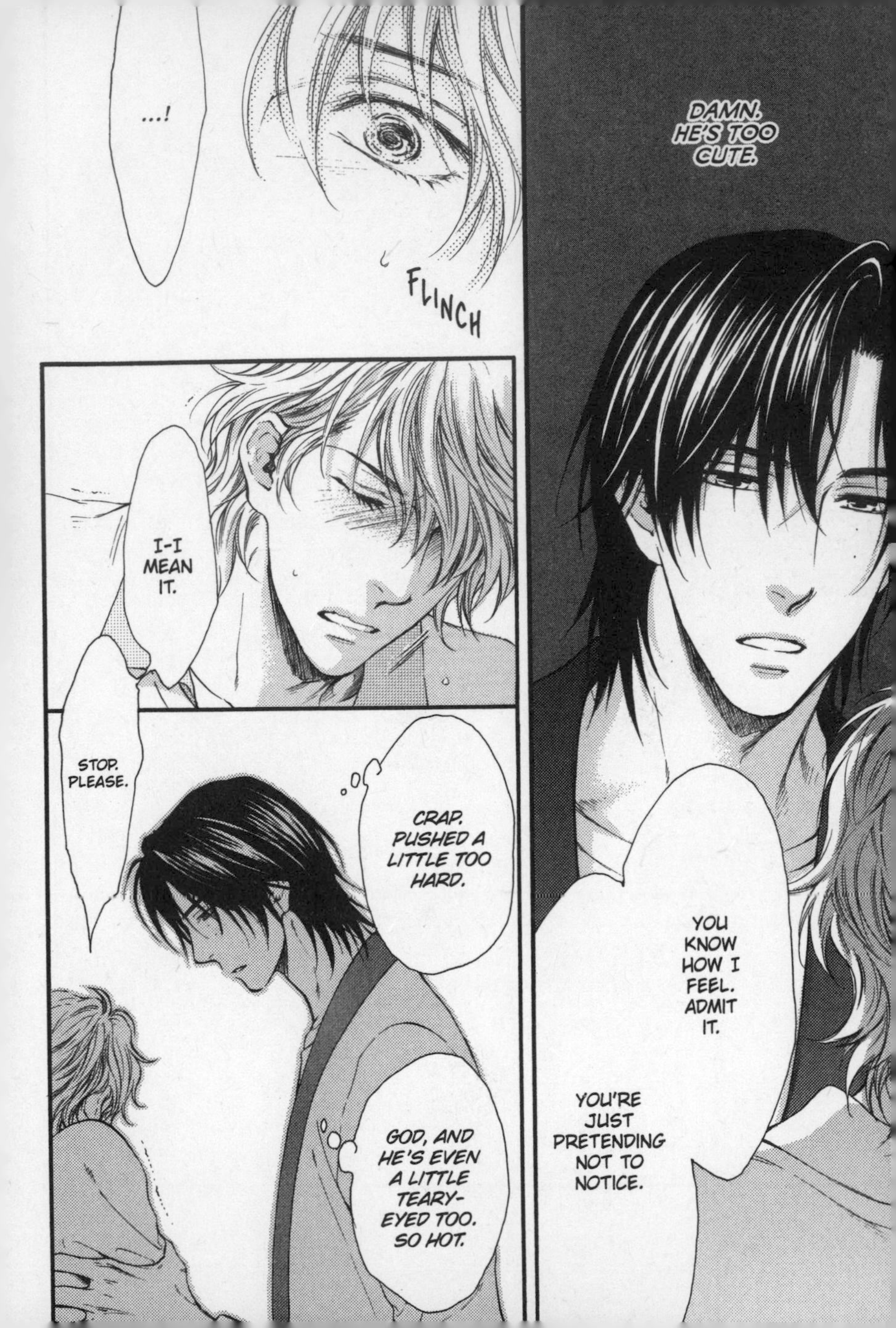
DAMN. HE'S TOO CUTE.
YOU KNOW HOW I FEEL. ADMIT IT.
YOU'RE JUST PRETENDING NOT TO NOTICE.
...!
FLINCH
I-I MEAN IT.
STOP. PLEASE.
CRAP. PUSHED A LITTLE TOO HARD.
GOD, AND HE'S EVEN A LITTLE TEARY-EYED TOO. SO HOT.

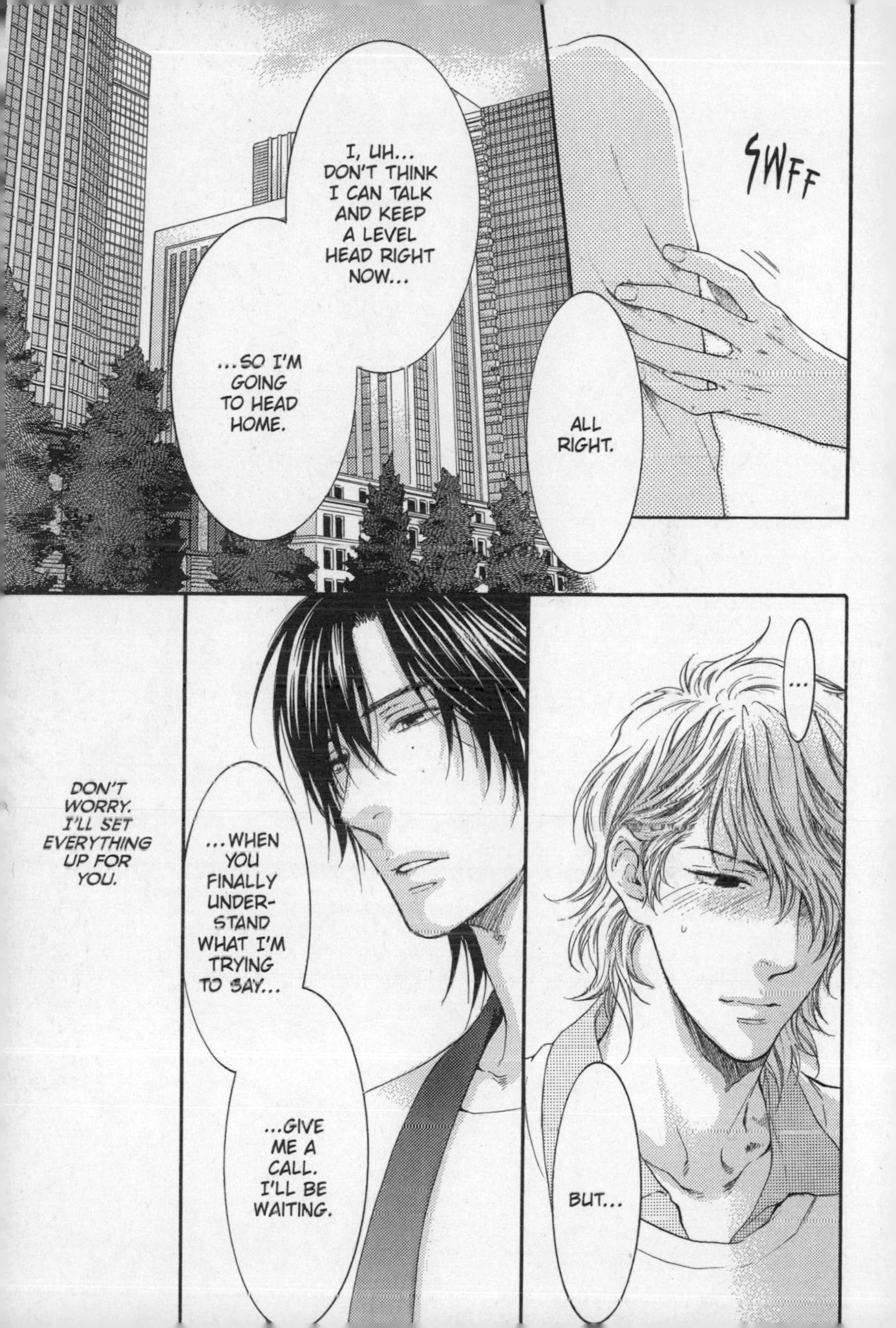
I, UH... DON'T THINK I CAN TALK AND KEEP A LEVEL HEAD RIGHT NOW...
...SO I'M GOING TO HEAD HOME.
SWFF
ALL RIGHT.
...
BUT...
...WHEN YOU FINALLY UNDER-STAND WHAT I'M TRYING TO SAY...
...GIVE ME A CALL. I'LL BE WAITING.
DON'T WORRY. I'LL SET EVERYTHING UP FOR YOU.

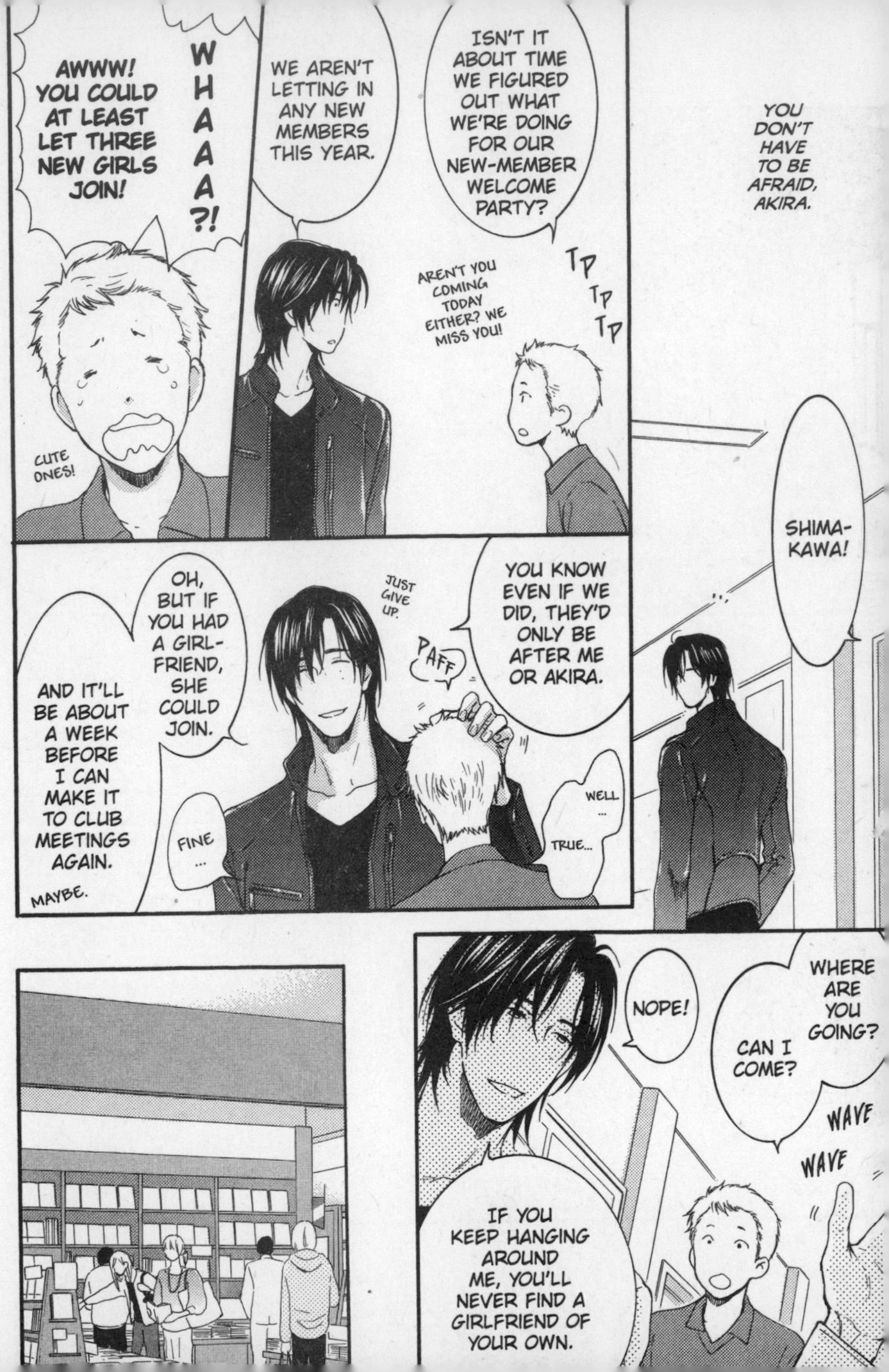
YOU DON'T HAVE TO BE AFRAID, AKIRA.
SHIMAKAWA!
ISN'T IT ABOUT TIME WE FIGURED OUT WHAT WE'RE DOING FOR OUR NEW-MEMBER WELCOME PARTY?
TP TP TP
AREN'T YOU COMING TODAY EITHER? WE MISS YOU!
WE AREN'T LETTING IN ANY NEW MEMBERS THIS YEAR.
WHAAAA?!
AWWW! YOU COULD AT LEAST LET THREE NEW GIRLS JOIN!
CUTE ONES!
YOU KNOW EVEN IF WE DID, THEY'D ONLY BE AFTER ME OR AKIRA.
JUST GIVE UP.
PAFF
WELL... TRUE...
OH, BUT IF YOU HAD A GIRL-FRIEND, SHE COULD JOIN.
FINE...
AND IT'LL BE ABOUT A WEEK BEFORE I CAN MAKE IT TO CLUB MEETINGS AGAIN.
MAYBE.
WHERE ARE YOU GOING? CAN I COME?
NOPE!
WAVE
WAVE
IF YOU KEEP HANGING AROUND ME, YOU'LL NEVER FIND A GIRLFRIEND OF YOUR OWN.

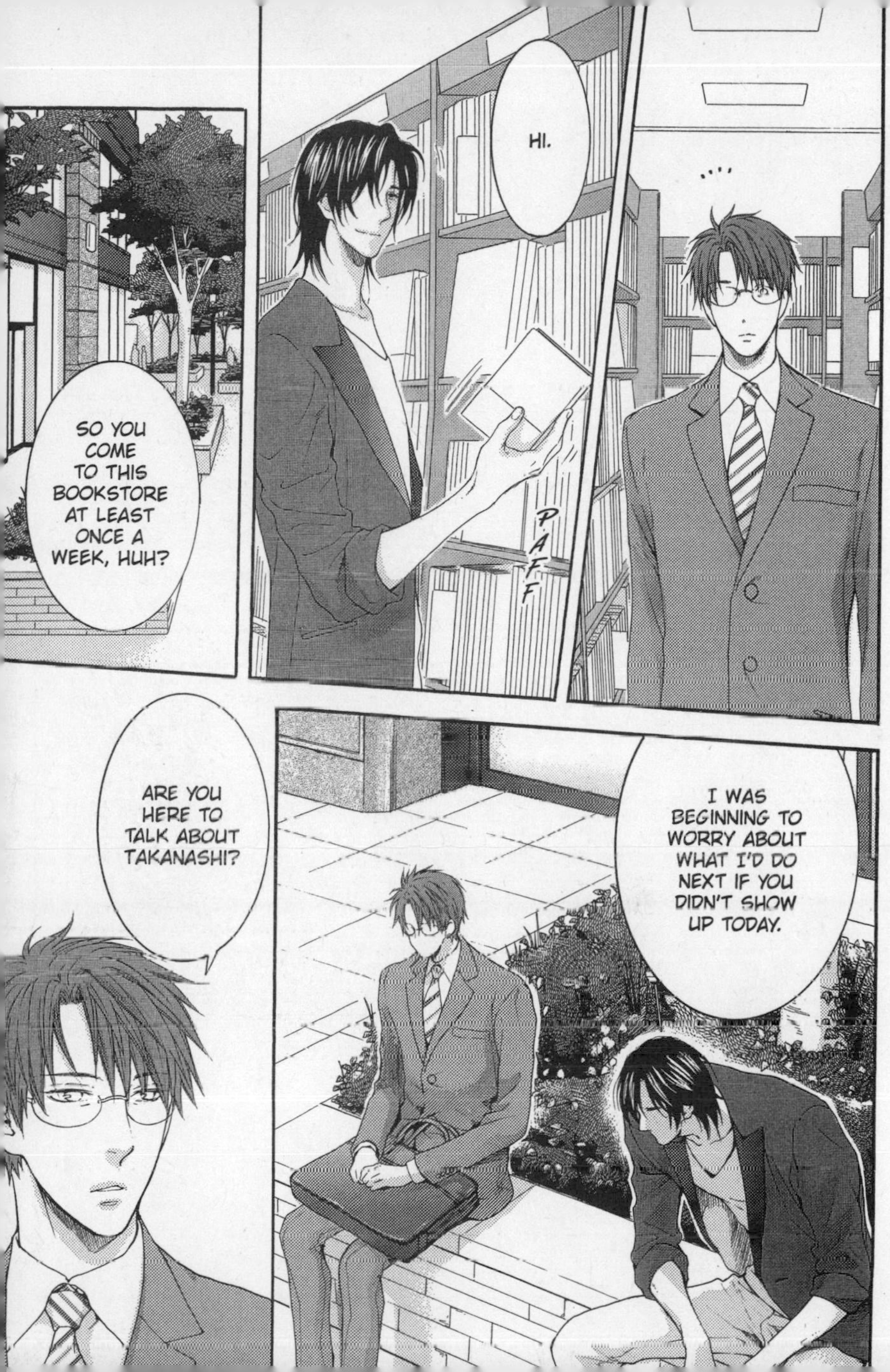
...
HI.
PAFF
SO YOU COME TO THIS BOOKSTORE AT LEAST ONCE A WEEK, HUH?
I WAS BEGINNING TO WORRY ABOUT WHAT I'D DO NEXT IF YOU DIDN'T SHOW UP TODAY.
ARE YOU HERE TO TALK ABOUT TAKANASHI?

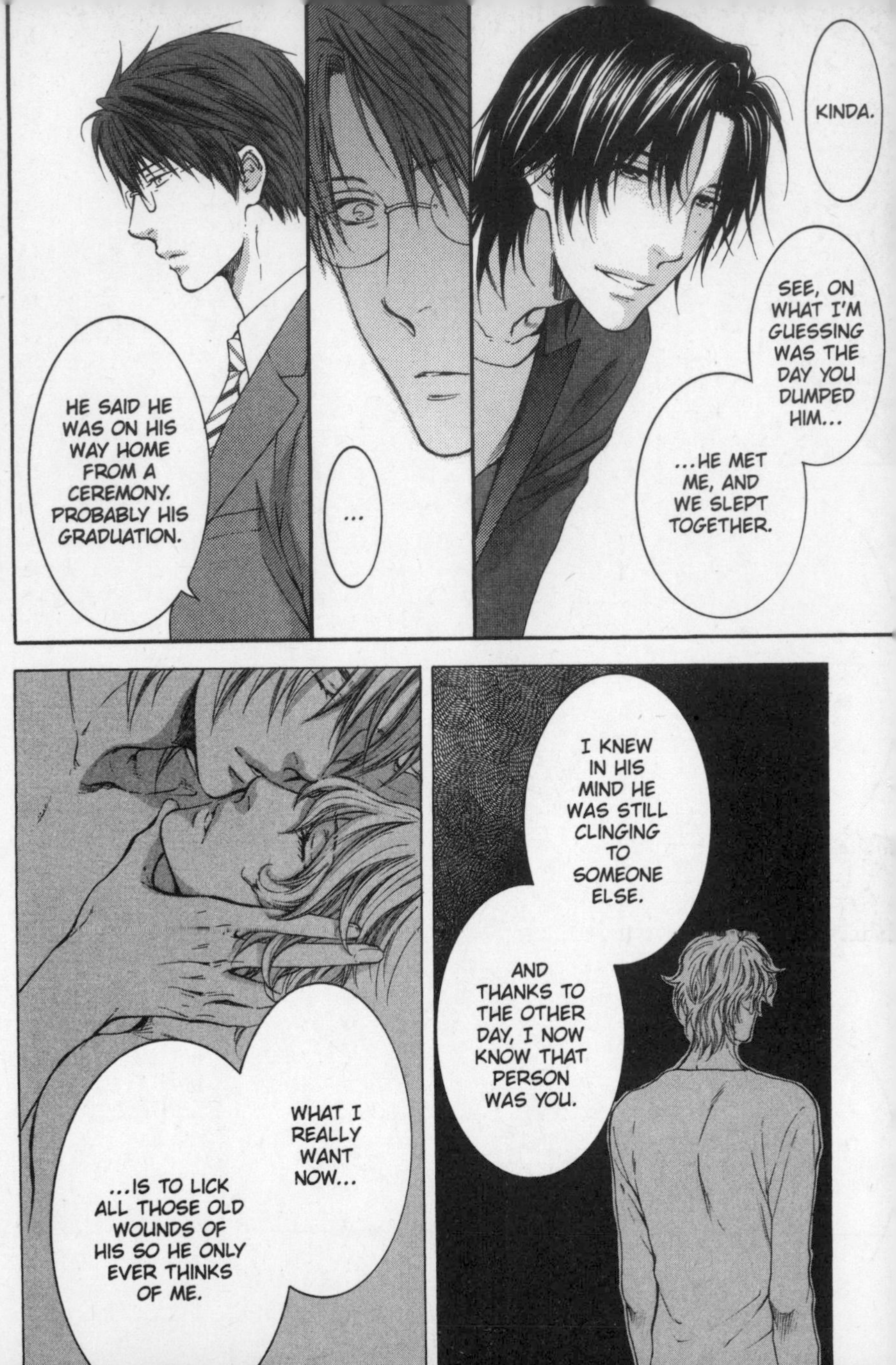
KINDA.
SEE, ON WHAT I'M GUESSING WAS THE DAY YOU DUMPED HIM...
...HE MET ME, AND WE SLEPT TOGETHER.
...
HE SAID HE WAS ON HIS WAY HOME FROM A CEREMONY. PROBABLY HIS GRADUATION.
I KNEW IN HIS MIND HE WAS STILL CLINGING TO SOMEONE ELSE.
AND THANKS TO THE OTHER DAY, I NOW KNOW THAT PERSON WAS YOU.
WHAT I REALLY WANT NOW...
...IS TO LICK ALL THOSE OLD WOUNDS OF HIS SO HE ONLY EVER THINKS OF ME.

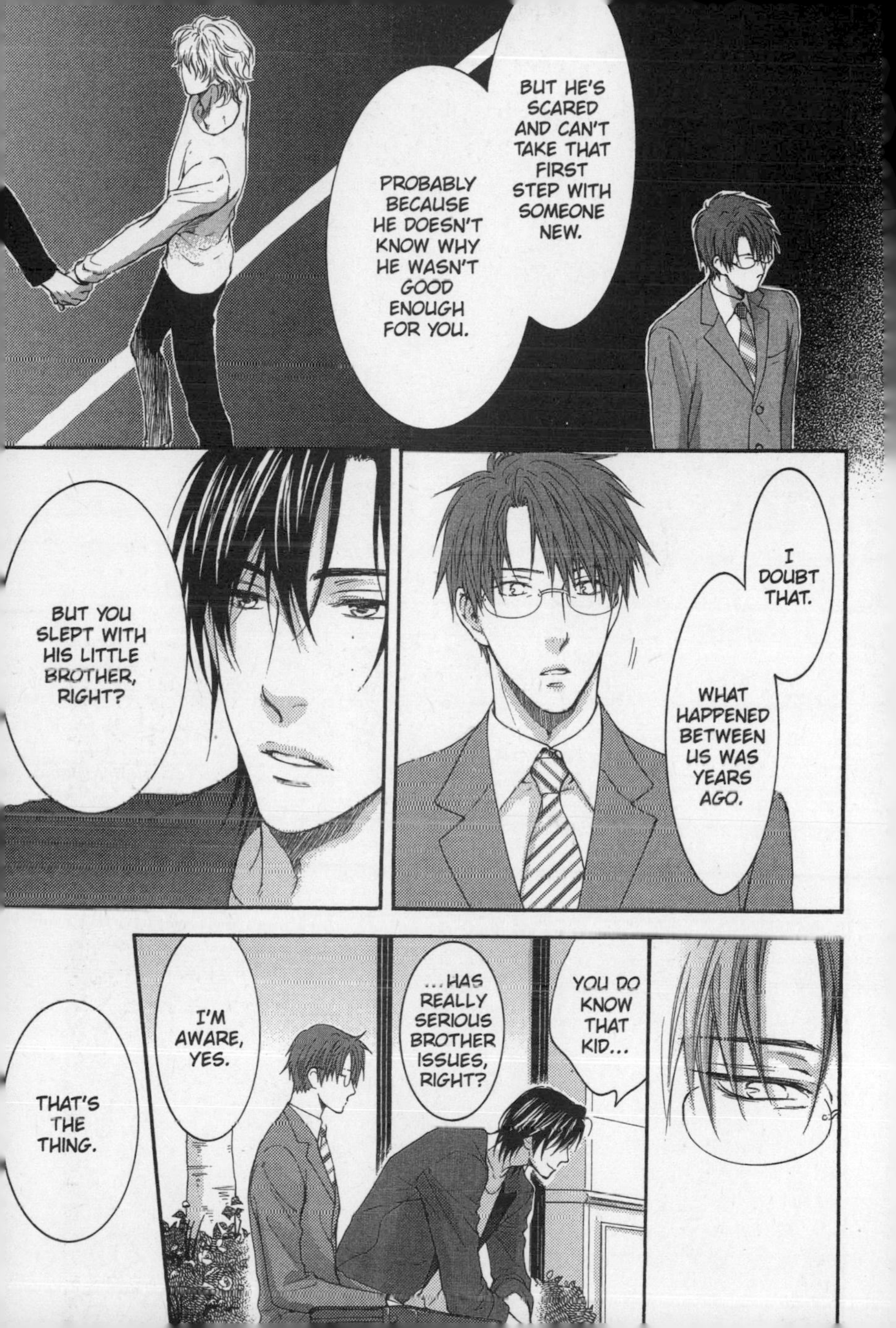
BUT HE'S SCARED AND CAN'T TAKE THAT FIRST STEP WITH SOMEONE NEW.
PROBABLY BECAUSE HE DOESN'T KNOW WHY HE WASN'T GOOD ENOUGH FOR YOU.
I DOUBT THAT.
WHAT HAPPENED BETWEEN US WAS YEARS AGO.
BUT YOU SLEPT WITH HIS LITTLE BROTHER, RIGHT?
YOU DO KNOW THAT KID...
...HAS REALLY SERIOUS BROTHER ISSUES, RIGHT?
I'M AWARE, YES.
THAT'S THE THING.

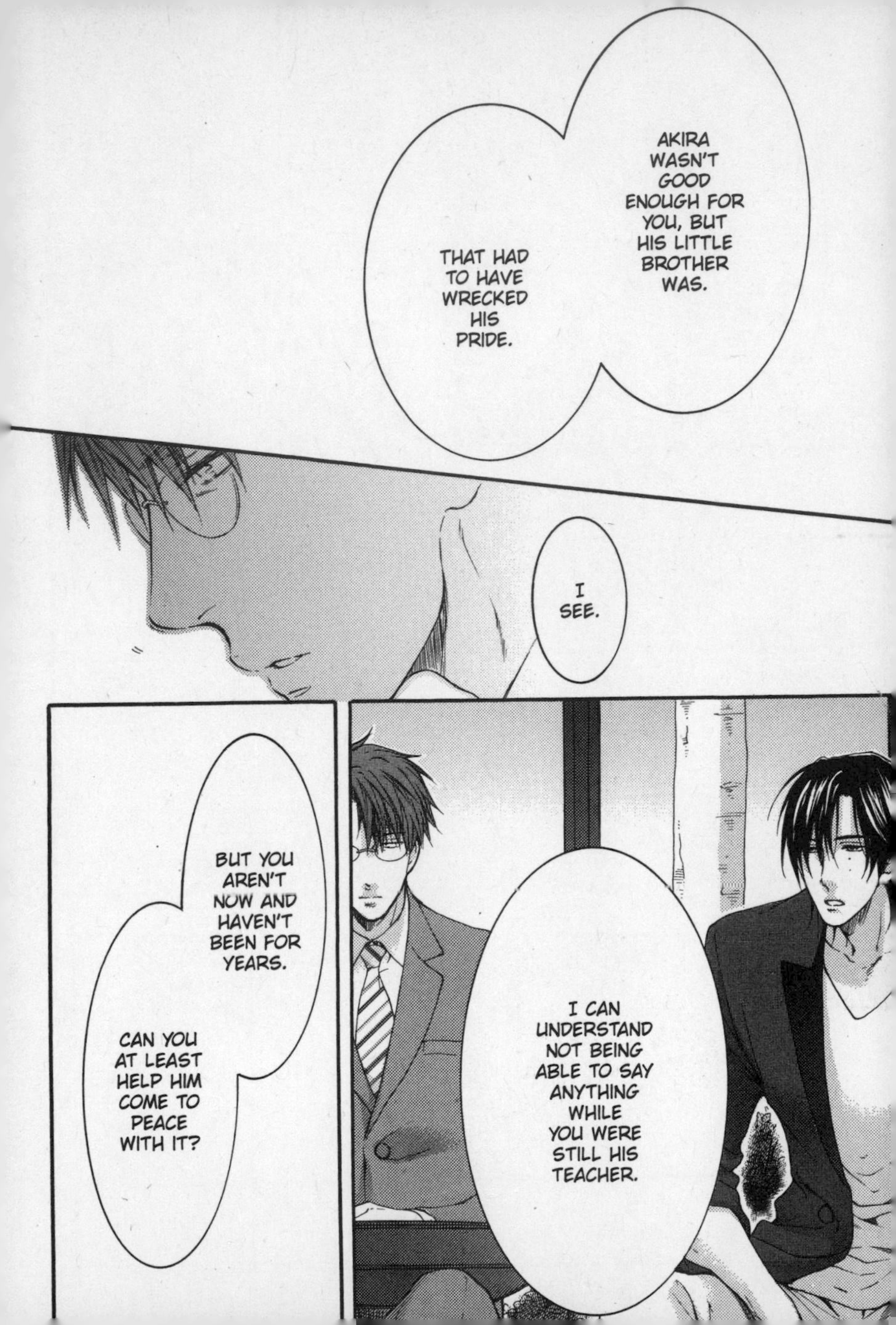
AKIRA WASN'T GOOD ENOUGH FOR YOU, BUT HIS LITTLE BROTHER WAS.
THAT HAD TO HAVE WRECKED HIS PRIDE.
I SEE.
I CAN UNDERSTAND NOT BEING ABLE TO SAY ANYTHING WHILE YOU WERE STILL HIS TEACHER.
BUT YOU AREN'T NOW AND HAVEN'T BEEN FOR YEARS.
CAN YOU AT LEAST HELP HIM COME TO PEACE WITH IT?

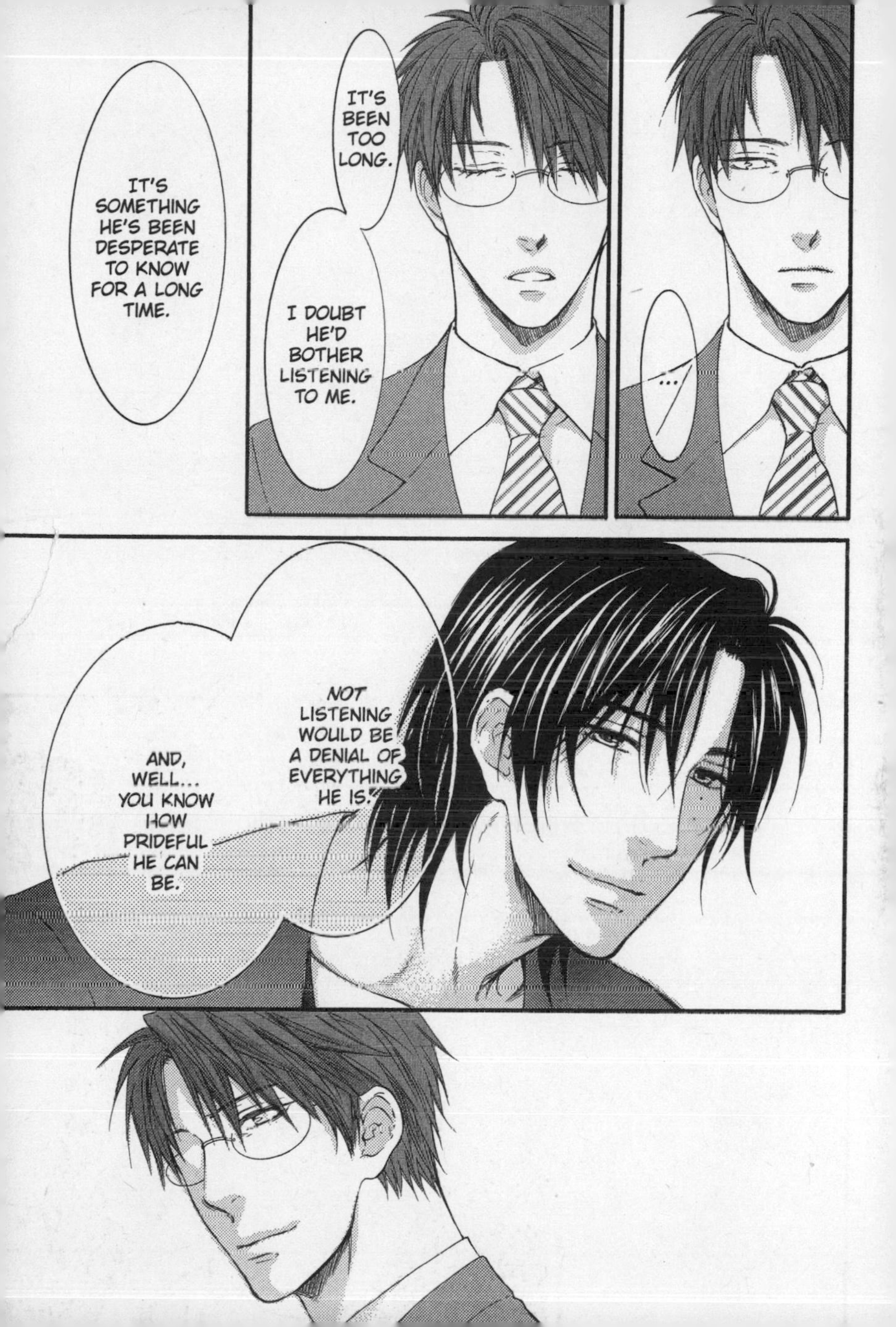
...
IT'S BEEN TOO LONG.
I DOUBT HE'D BOTHER LISTENING TO ME.
IT'S SOMETHING HE'S BEEN DESPERATE TO KNOW FOR A LONG TIME.
NOT LISTENING WOULD BE A DENIAL OF EVERYTHING HE IS.
AND, WELL... YOU KNOW HOW PRIDEFUL HE CAN BE.

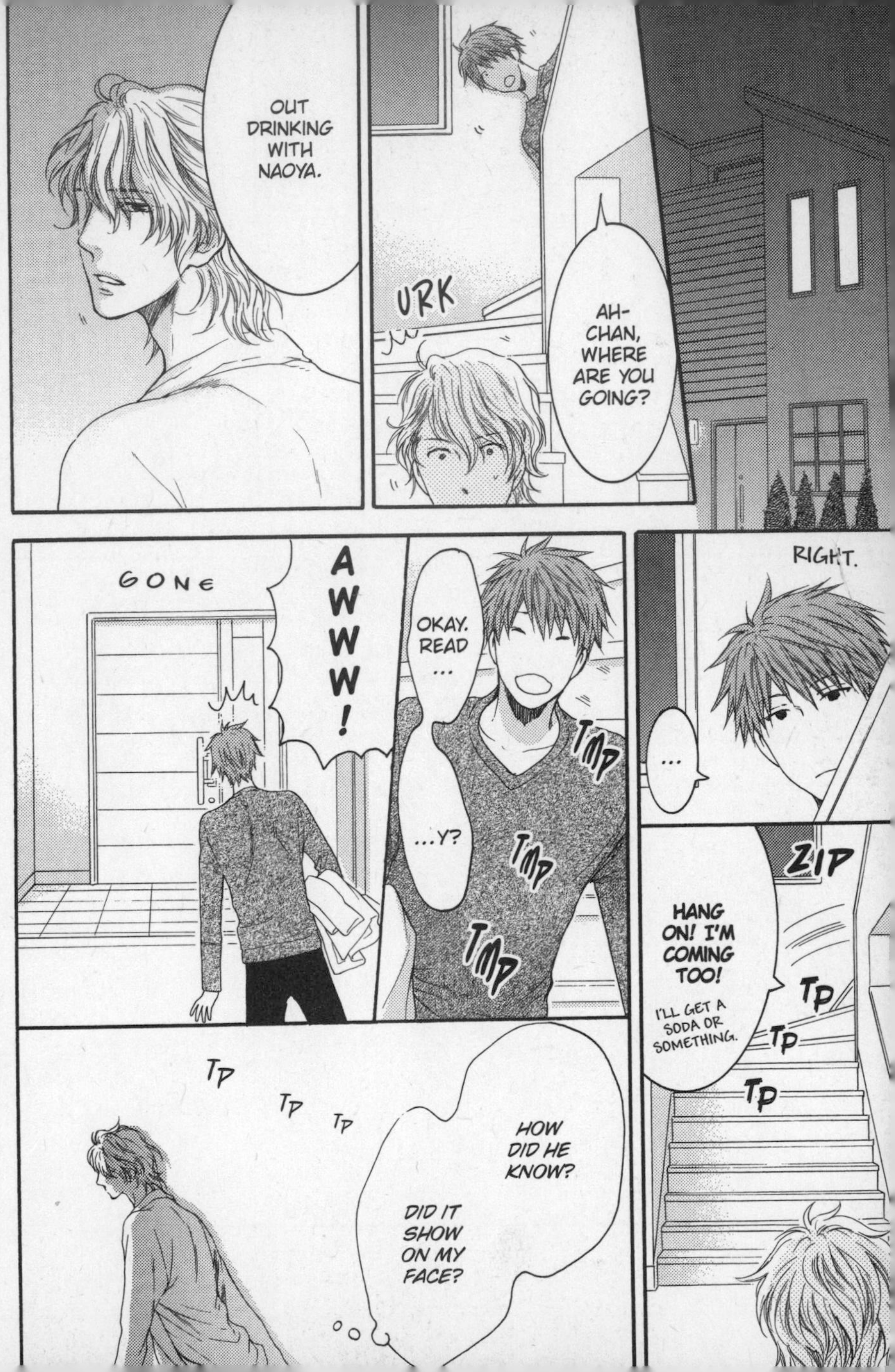
URK
AH-CHAN, WHERE ARE YOU GOING?
OUT DRINKING WITH NAOYA.
RIGHT.
...
OKAY. READ ...
...Y?
TMP
TMP
TMP
AWWW!
GONE
ZIP
HANG ON! I'M COMING TOO!
I'LL GET A SODA OR SOMETHING.
TP
TP
TP
TP
TP
TP
HOW DID HE KNOW?
DID IT SHOW ON MY FACE?

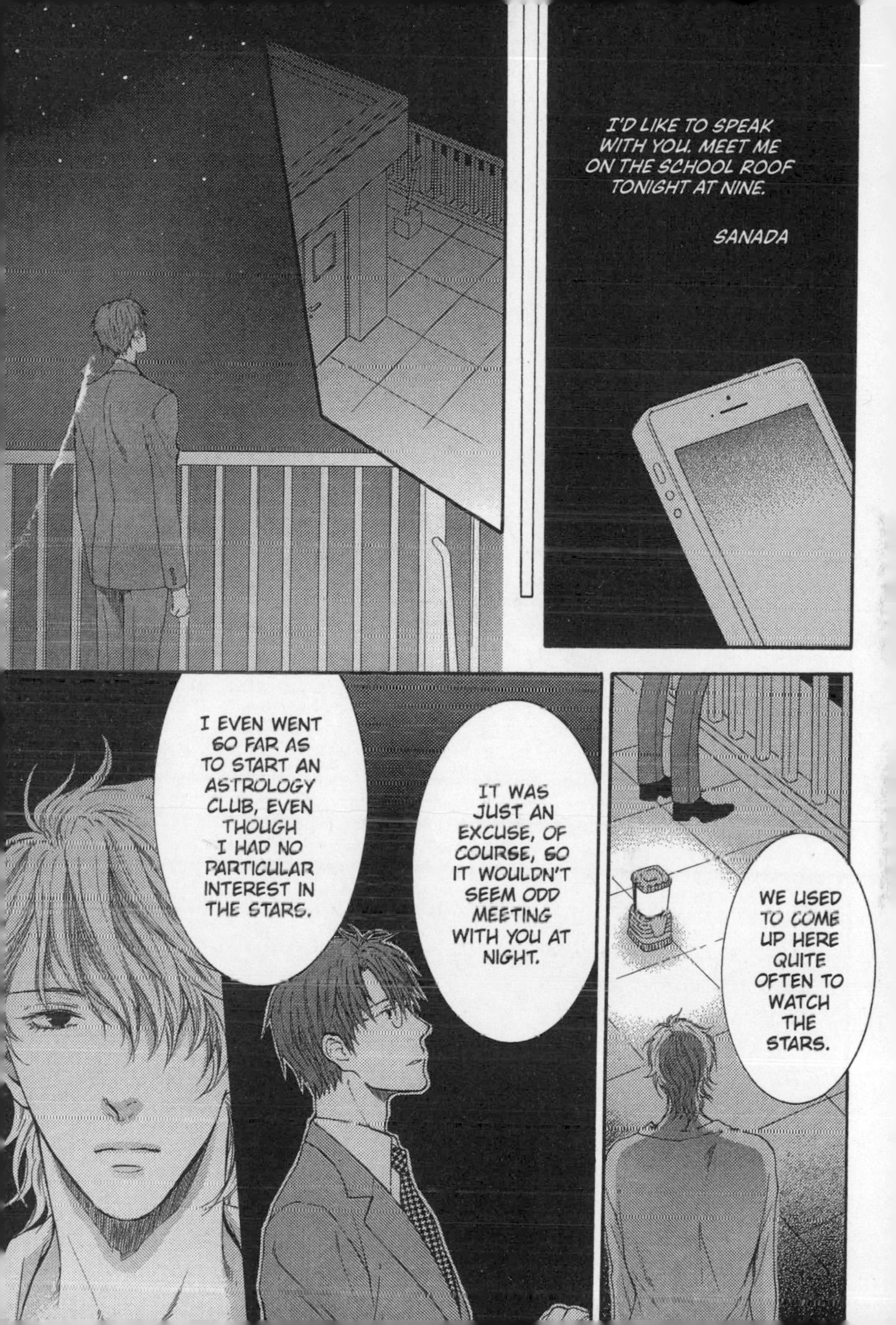

I'D LIKE TO SPEAK WITH YOU. MEET ME ON THE SCHOOL ROOF TONIGHT AT NINE.
SANADA
WE USED TO COME UP HERE QUITE OFTEN TO WATCH THE STARS.
I EVEN WENT SO FAR AS TO START AN ASTROLOGY CLUB, EVEN THOUGH I HAD NO PARTICULAR INTEREST IN THE STARS.
IT WAS JUST AN EXCUSE, OF COURSE, SO IT WOULDN'T SEEM ODD MEETING WITH YOU AT NIGHT.

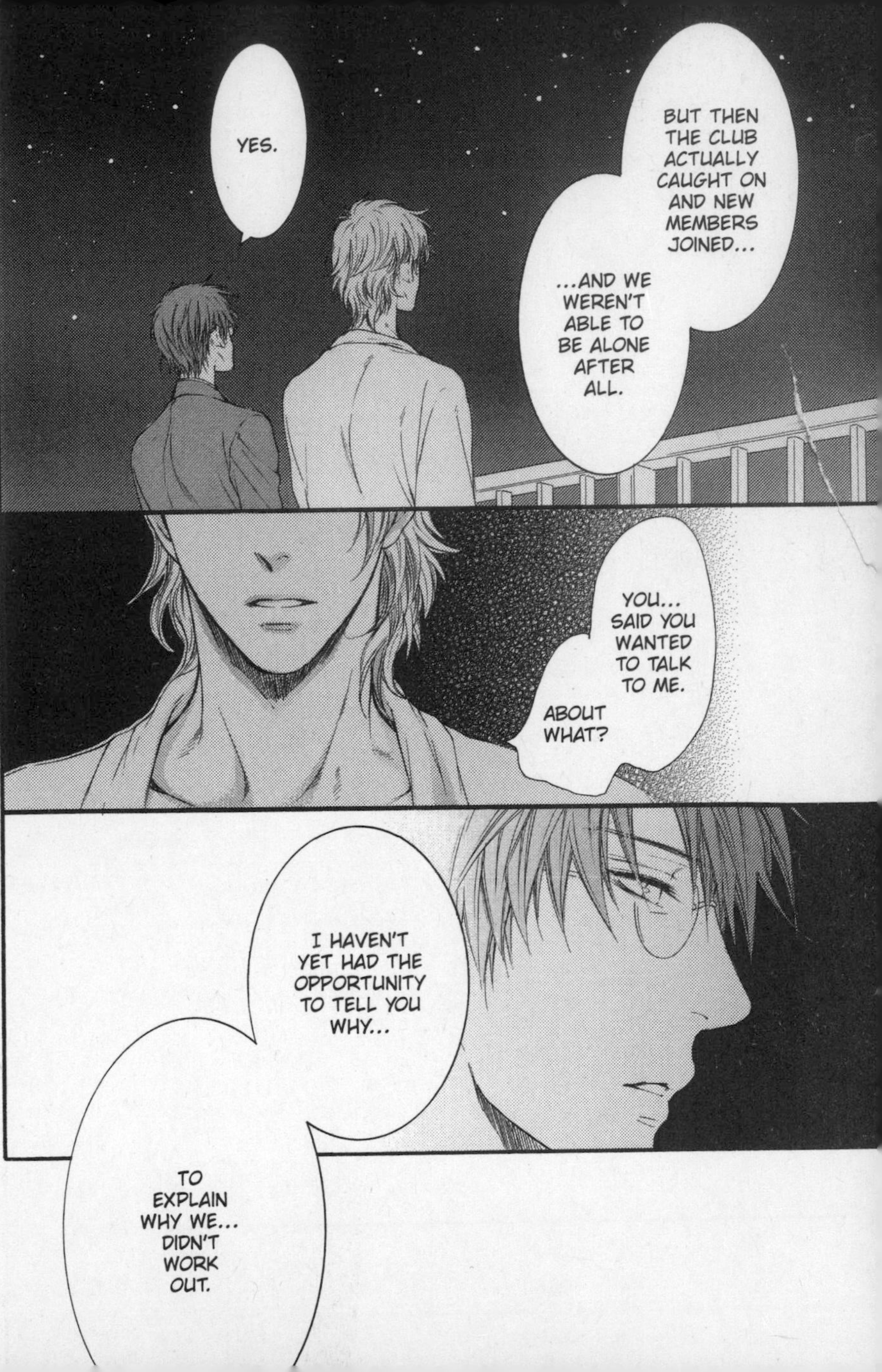
BUT THEN THE CLUB ACTUALLY CAUGHT ON AND NEW MEMBERS JOINED...
...AND WE WEREN'T ABLE TO BE ALONE AFTER ALL.
YES.
YOU... SAID YOU WANTED TO TALK TO ME.
ABOUT WHAT?
I HAVEN'T YET HAD THE OPPORTUNITY TO TELL YOU WHY...
TO EXPLAIN WHY WE... DIDN'T WORK OUT.

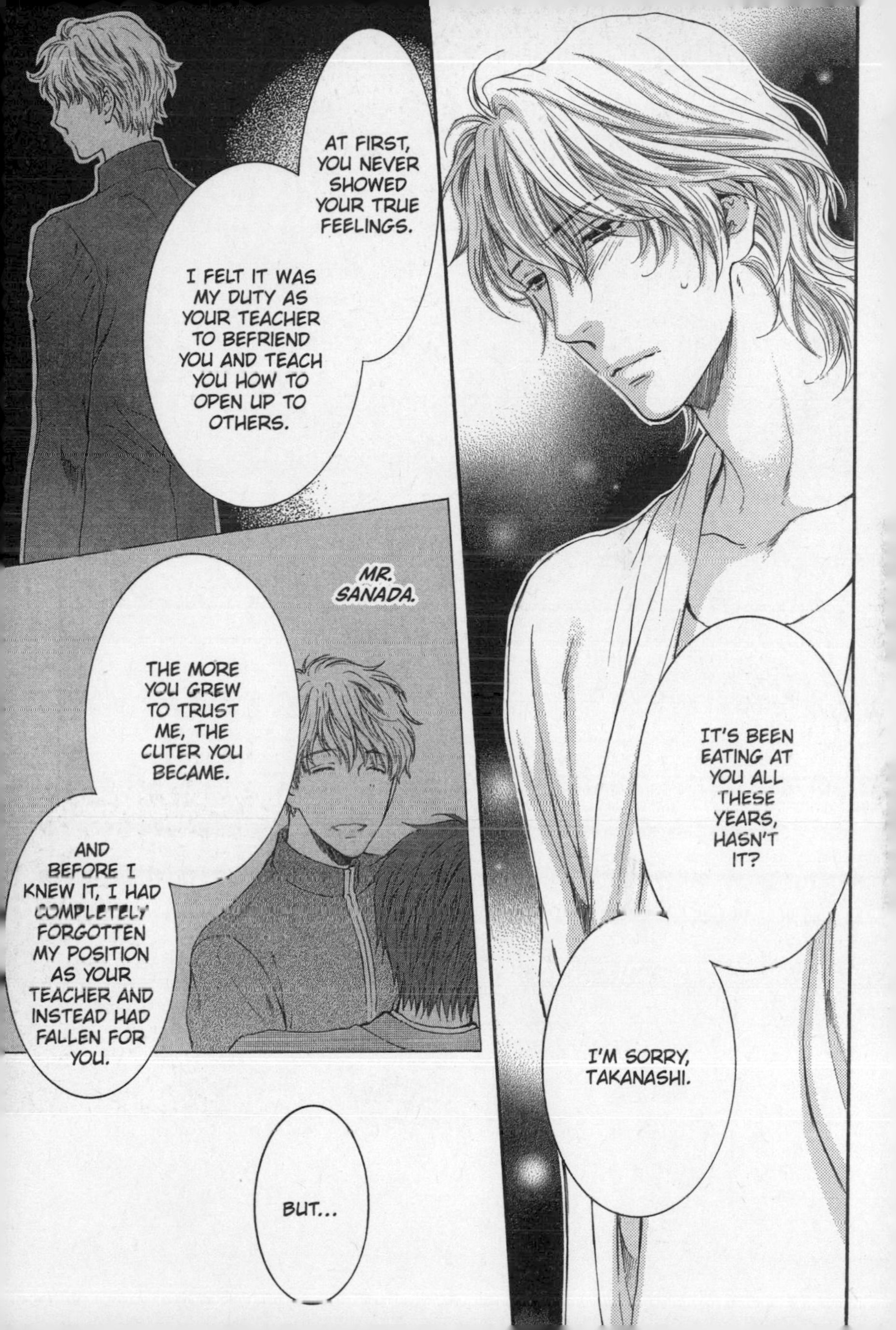
IT'S BEEN EATING AT YOU ALL THESE YEARS, HASN'T IT?
I'M SORRY, TAKANASHI.
AT FIRST, YOU NEVER SHOWED YOUR TRUE FEELINGS.
I FELT IT WAS MY DUTY AS YOUR TEACHER TO BEFRIEND YOU AND TEACH YOU HOW TO OPEN UP TO OTHERS.
MR. SANADA.
THE MORE YOU GREW TO TRUST ME, THE CUTER YOU BECAME.
AND BEFORE I KNEW IT, I HAD COMPLETELY FORGOTTEN MY POSITION AS YOUR TEACHER AND INSTEAD HAD FALLEN FOR YOU.
BUT...

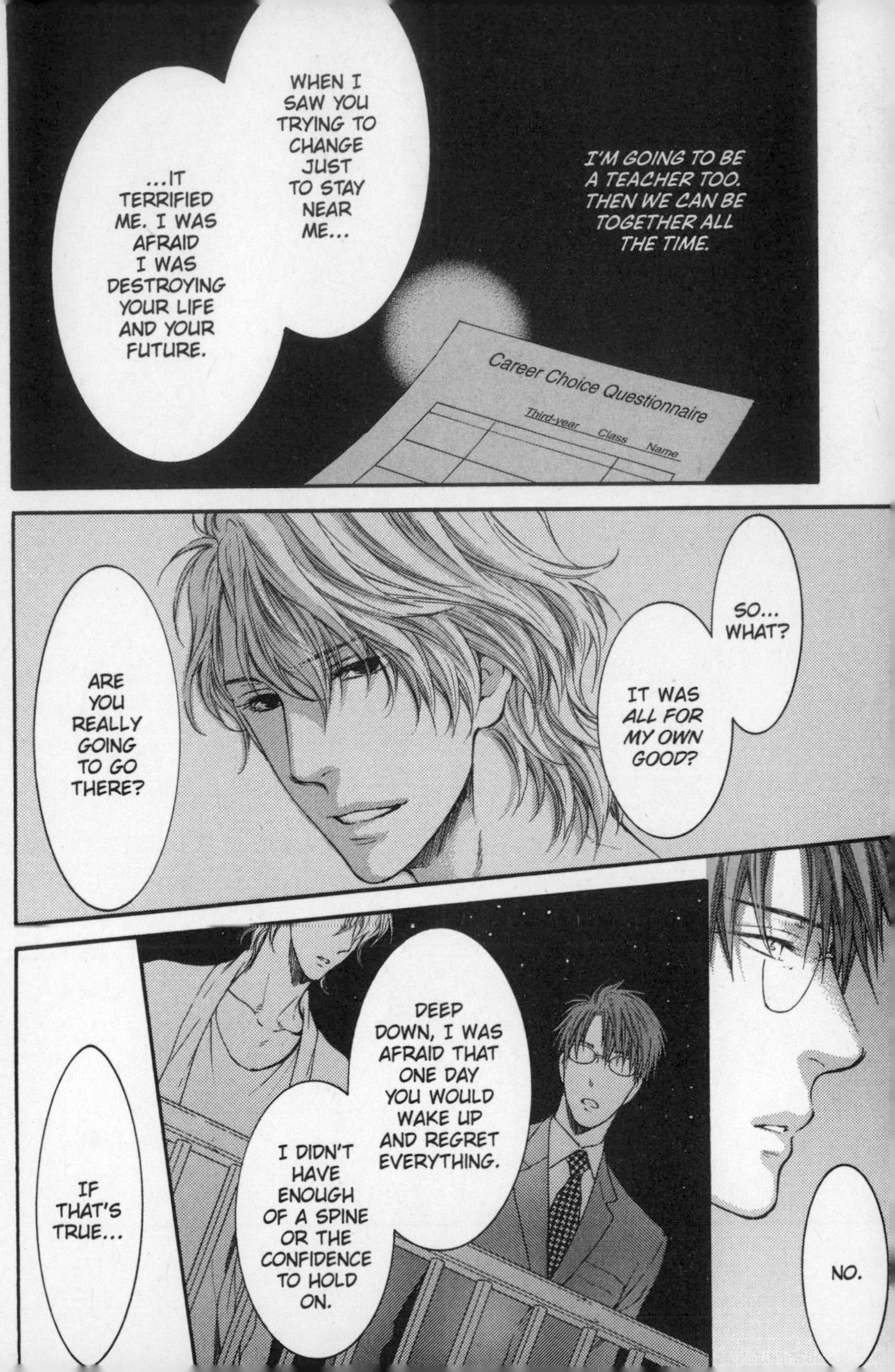
I'M GOING TO BE A TEACHER TOO. THEN WE CAN BE TOGETHER ALL THE TIME.
WHEN I SAW YOU TRYING TO CHANGE JUST TO STAY NEAR ME...
...IT TERRIFIED ME. I WAS AFRAID I WAS DESTROYING YOUR LIFE AND YOUR FUTURE.
Career Choice Questionnaire
Third-year Class Name
SO... WHAT?
IT WAS ALL FOR MY OWN GOOD?
ARE YOU REALLY GOING TO GO THERE?
NO.
DEEP DOWN, I WAS AFRAID THAT ONE DAY YOU WOULD WAKE UP AND REGRET EVERYTHING.
I DIDN'T HAVE ENOUGH OF A SPINE OR THE CONFIDENCE TO HOLD ON.
IF THAT'S TRUE...

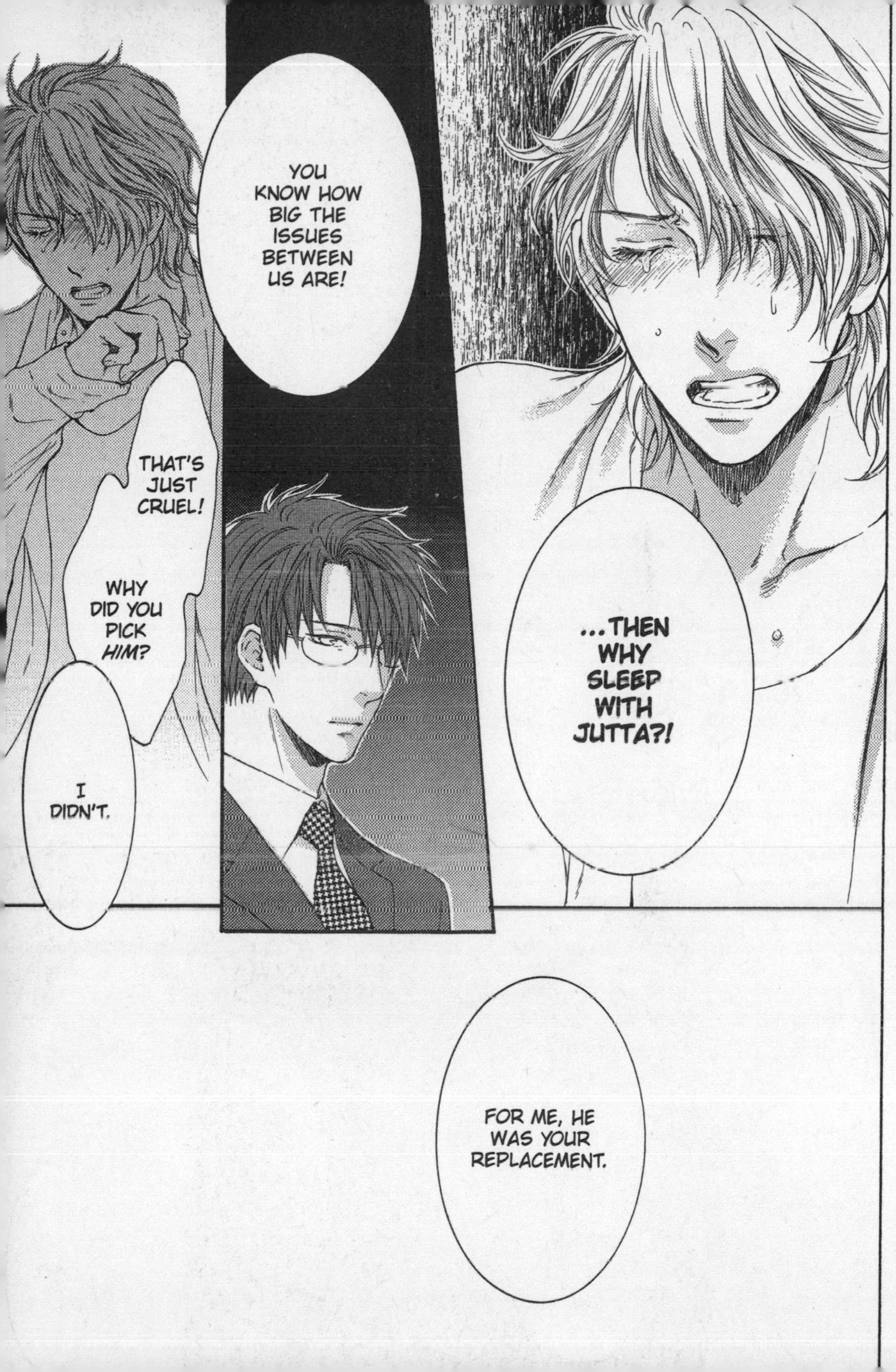
...THEN WHY SLEEP WITH JUTTA?!
YOU KNOW HOW BIG THE ISSUES BETWEEN US ARE!
THAT'S JUST CRUEL!
WHY DID YOU PICK *HIM*?
I DIDN'T.
FOR ME, HE WAS YOUR REPLACEMENT.

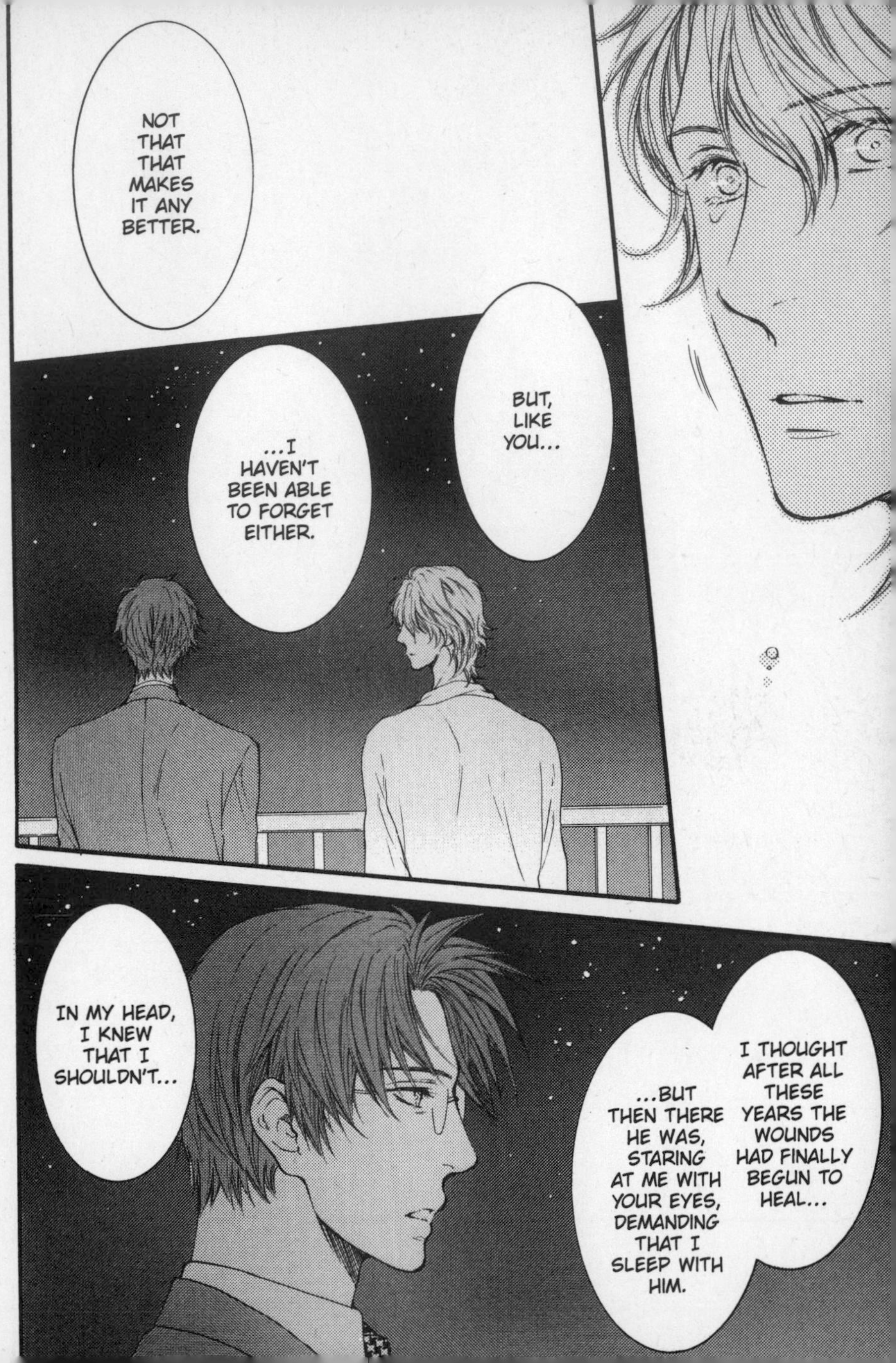
NOT THAT THAT MAKES IT ANY BETTER.
BUT, LIKE YOU...
...I HAVEN'T BEEN ABLE TO FORGET EITHER.
I THOUGHT AFTER ALL THESE YEARS THE WOUNDS HAD FINALLY BEGUN TO HEAL...
...BUT THEN THERE HE WAS, STARING AT ME WITH YOUR EYES, DEMANDING THAT I SLEEP WITH HIM.
IN MY HEAD, I KNEW THAT I SHOULDN'T...

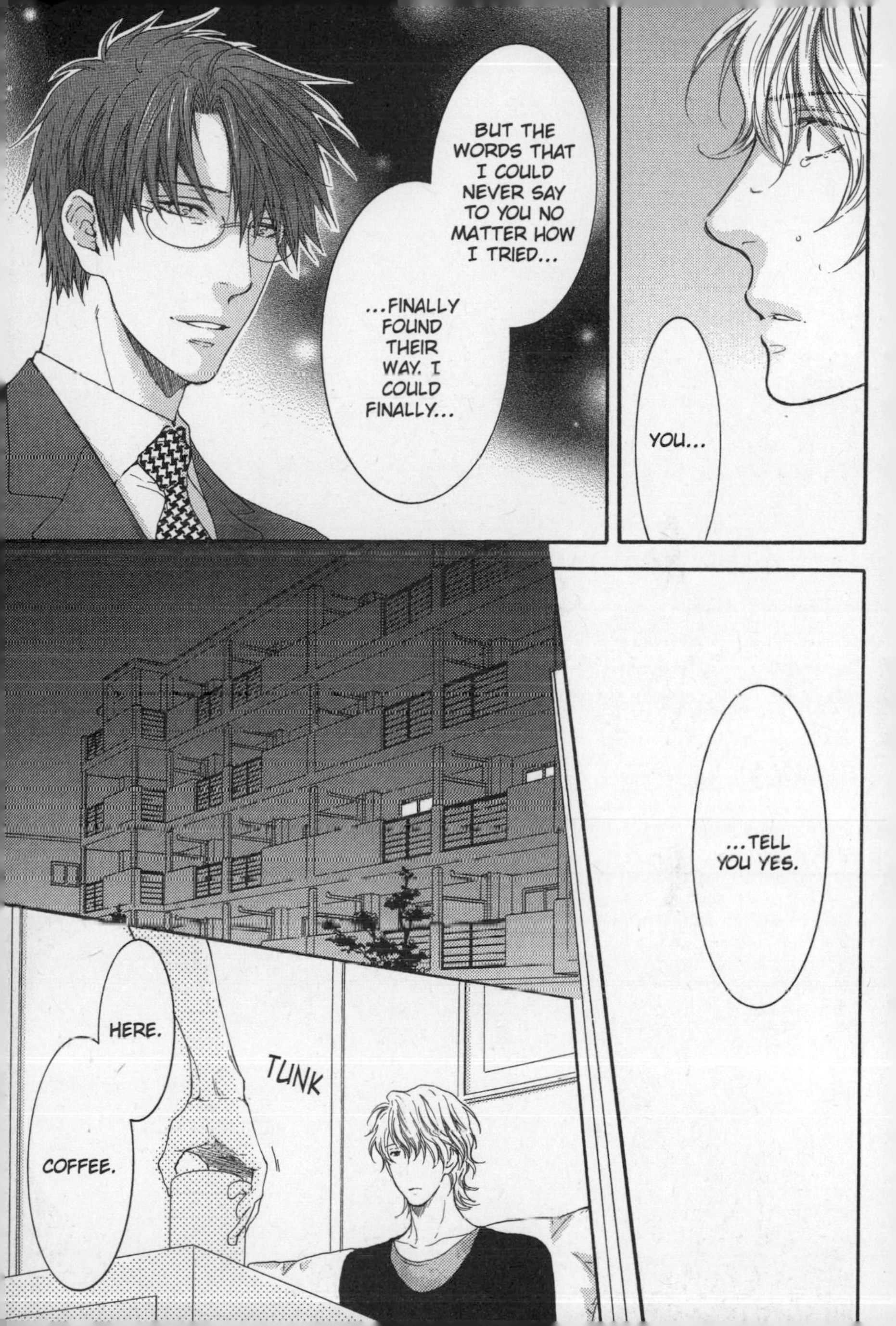
YOU...
BUT THE WORDS THAT I COULD NEVER SAY TO YOU NO MATTER HOW I TRIED...
...FINALLY FOUND THEIR WAY. I COULD FINALLY...
...TELL YOU YES.
HERE.
COFFEE.
TUNK

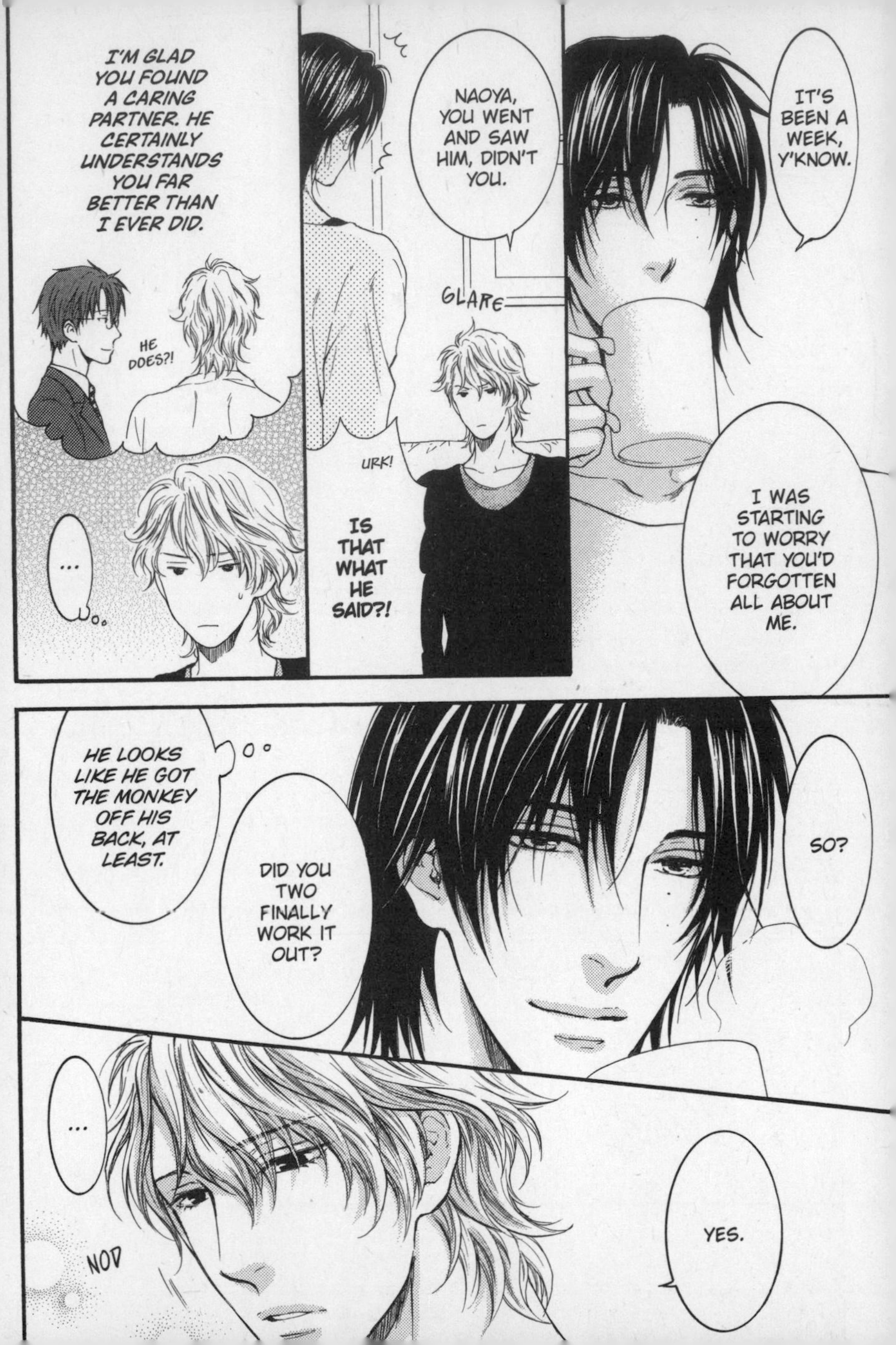
IT'S BEEN A WEEK, Y'KNOW.
I WAS STARTING TO WORRY THAT YOU'D FORGOTTEN ALL ABOUT ME.
NAOYA, YOU WENT AND SAW HIM, DIDN'T YOU.
GLARE
URK!
IS THAT WHAT HE SAID?!
I'M GLAD YOU FOUND A CARING PARTNER. HE CERTAINLY UNDERSTANDS YOU FAR BETTER THAN I EVER DID.
HE DOES?!
...
SO?
DID YOU TWO FINALLY WORK IT OUT?
HE LOOKS LIKE HE GOT THE MONKEY OFF HIS BACK, AT LEAST.
YES.
NOD
...

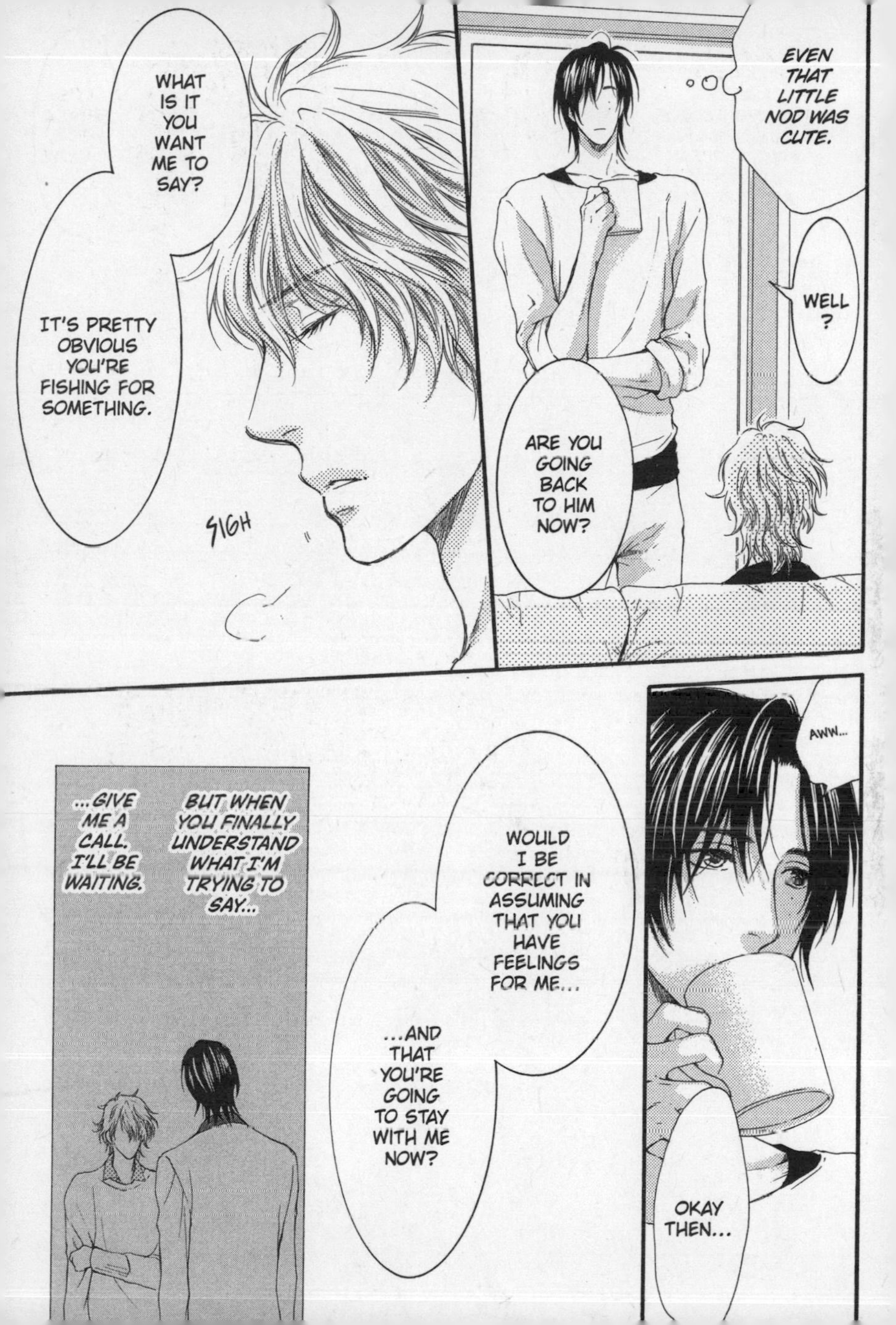
EVEN THAT LITTLE NOD WAS CUTE.
WELL?
ARE YOU GOING BACK TO HIM NOW?
WHAT IS IT YOU WANT ME TO SAY?
IT'S PRETTY OBVIOUS YOU'RE FISHING FOR SOMETHING.
SIGH
AWW...
WOULD I BE CORRECT IN ASSUMING THAT YOU HAVE FEELINGS FOR ME...
...AND THAT YOU'RE GOING TO STAY WITH ME NOW?
OKAY THEN...
BUT WHEN YOU FINALLY UNDERSTAND WHAT I'M TRYING TO SAY...
...GIVE ME A CALL. I'LL BE WAITING.

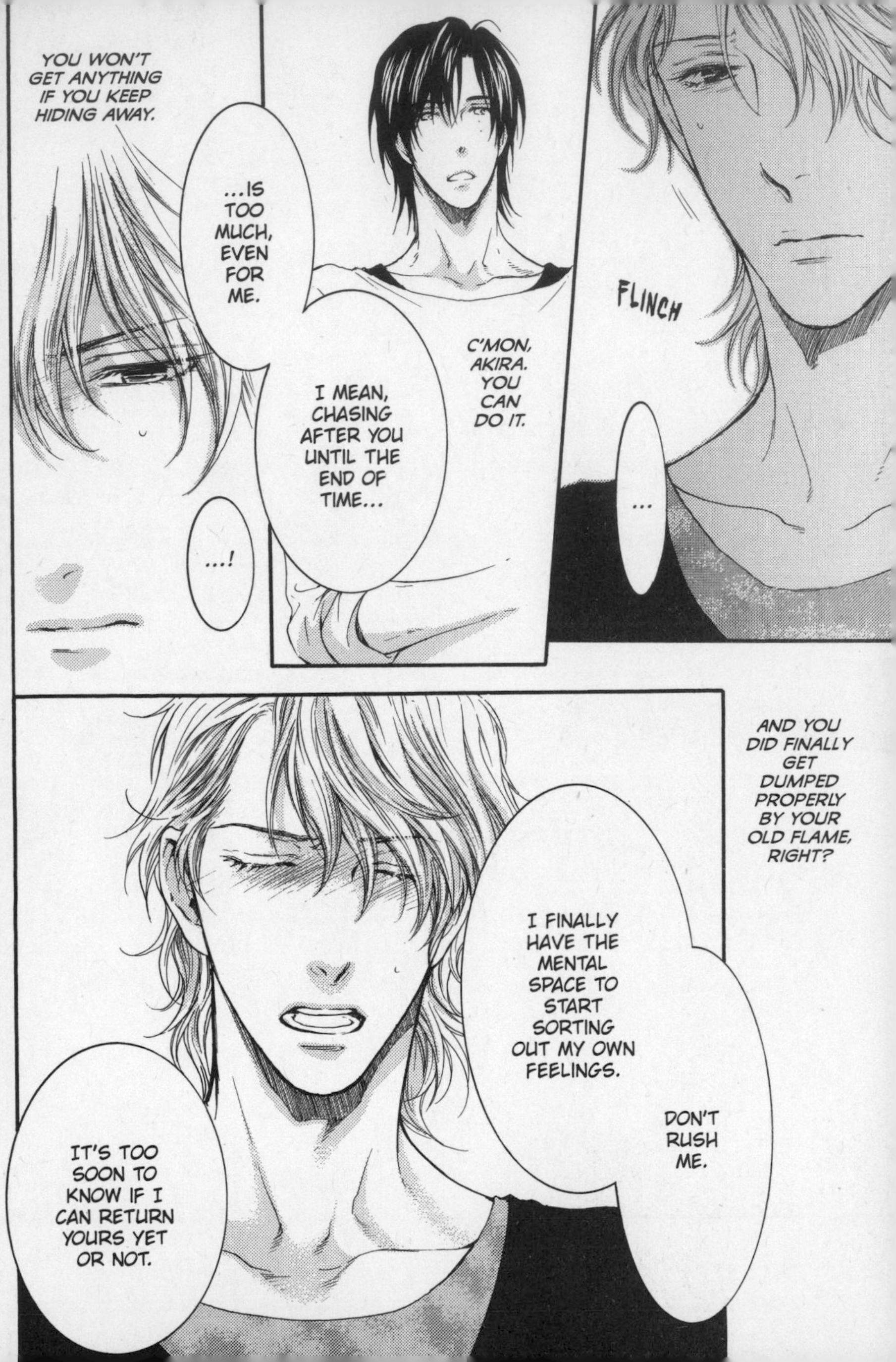
FLINCH
...
C'MON, AKIRA. YOU CAN DO IT.
I MEAN, CHASING AFTER YOU UNTIL THE END OF TIME...
...IS TOO MUCH, EVEN FOR ME.
YOU WON'T GET ANYTHING IF YOU KEEP HIDING AWAY.
...!
AND YOU DID FINALLY GET DUMPED PROPERLY BY YOUR OLD FLAME, RIGHT?
I FINALLY HAVE THE MENTAL SPACE TO START SORTING OUT MY OWN FEELINGS.
DON'T RUSH ME.
IT'S TOO SOON TO KNOW IF I CAN RETURN YOURS YET OR NOT.

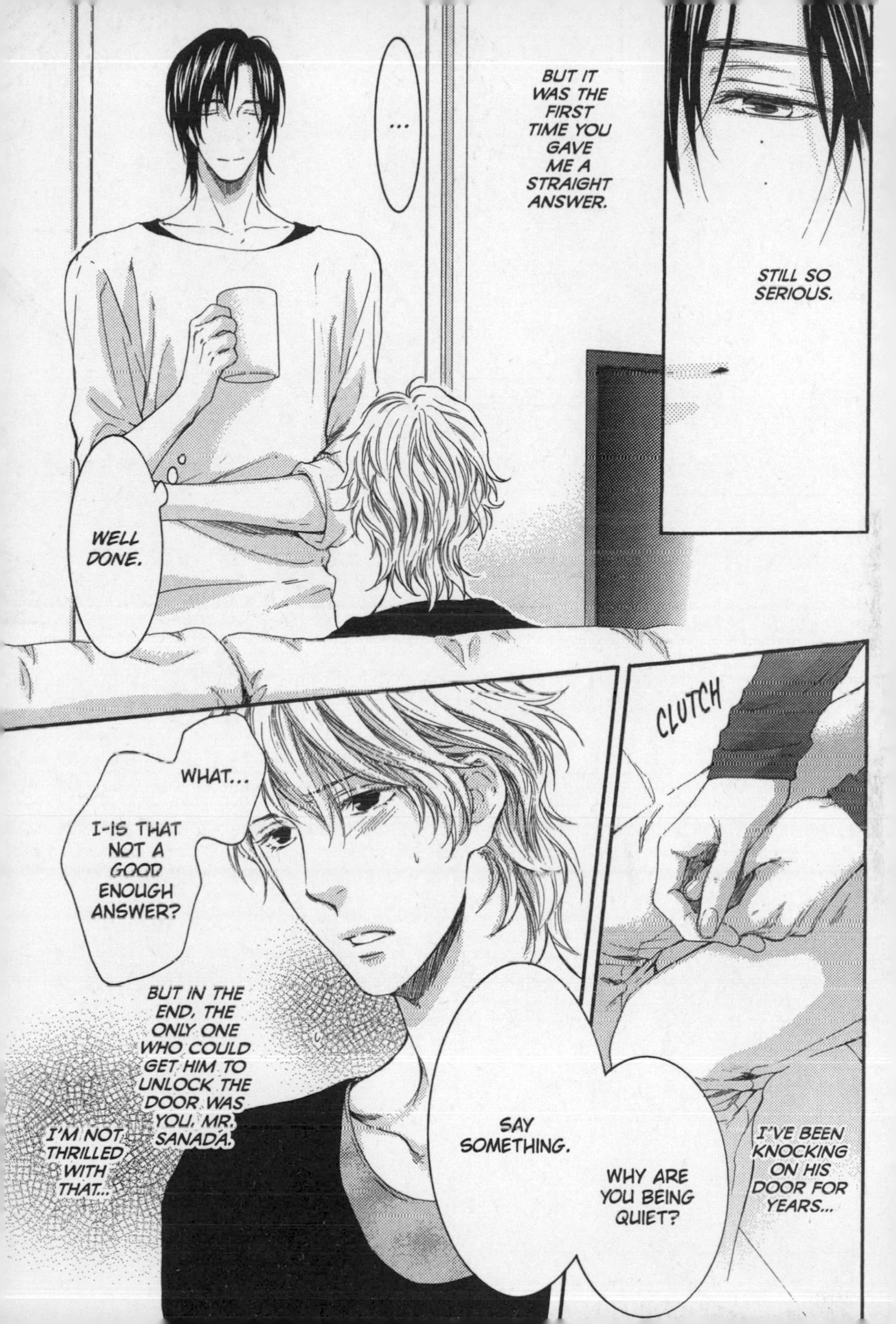
STILL SO SERIOUS.
BUT IT WAS THE FIRST TIME YOU GAVE ME A STRAIGHT ANSWER.
...
WELL DONE.
CLUTCH
I'VE BEEN KNOCKING ON HIS DOOR FOR YEARS...
SAY SOMETHING.
WHY ARE YOU BEING QUIET?
WHAT...
I-IS THAT NOT A GOOD ENOUGH ANSWER?
BUT IN THE END, THE ONLY ONE WHO COULD GET HIM TO UNLOCK THE DOOR WAS YOU, MR. SANADA.
I'M NOT THRILLED WITH THAT...

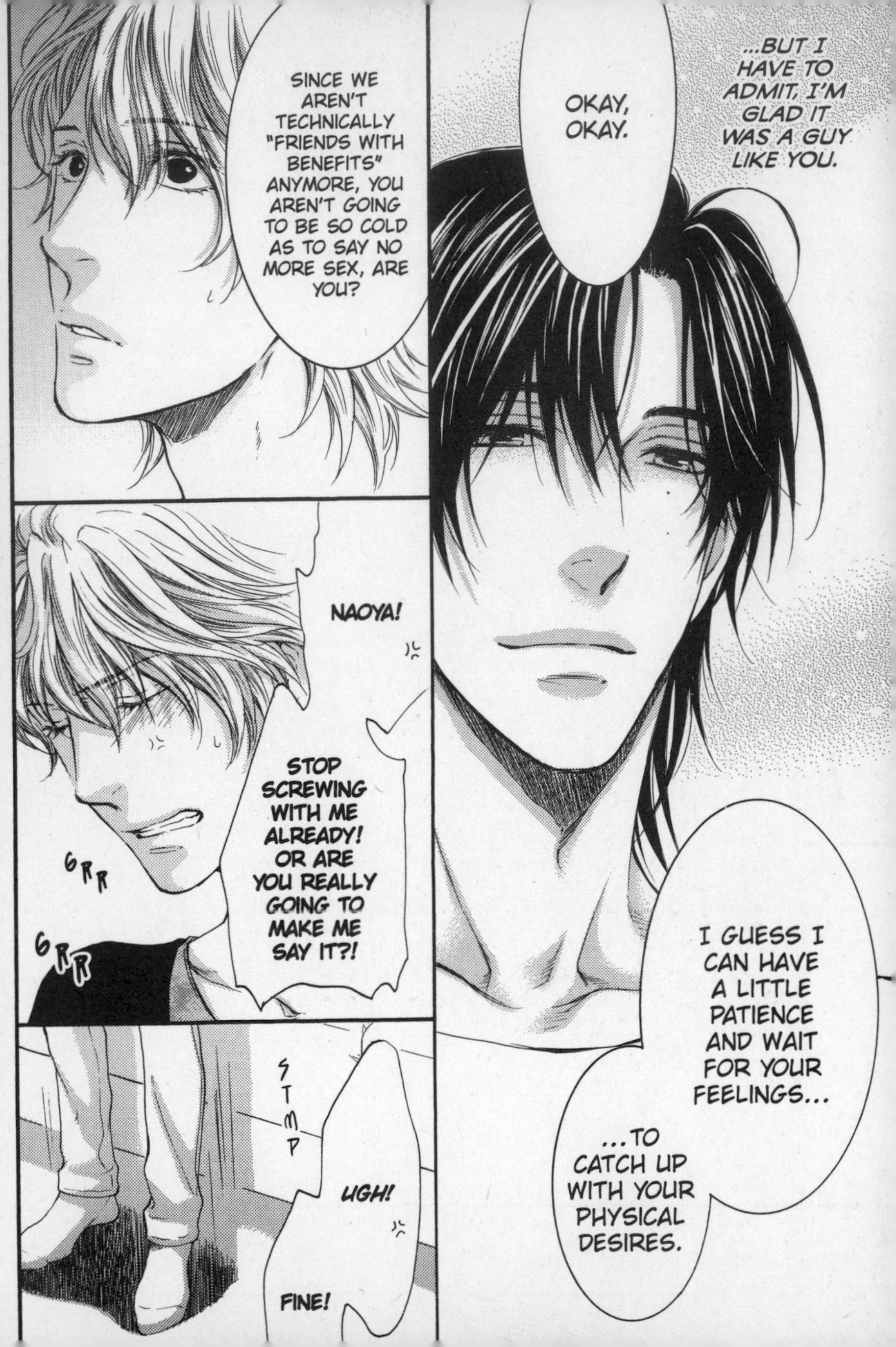
...BUT I HAVE TO ADMIT, I'M GLAD IT WAS A GUY LIKE YOU.
OKAY, OKAY.
I GUESS I CAN HAVE A LITTLE PATIENCE AND WAIT FOR YOUR FEELINGS...
...TO CATCH UP WITH YOUR PHYSICAL DESIRES.
SINCE WE AREN'T TECHNICALLY "FRIENDS WITH BENEFITS" ANYMORE, YOU AREN'T GOING TO BE SO COLD AS TO SAY NO MORE SEX, ARE YOU?
NAOYA!
STOP SCREWING WITH ME ALREADY! OR ARE YOU REALLY GOING TO MAKE ME SAY IT?!
GRR
GRR
STMP
UGH!
FINE!

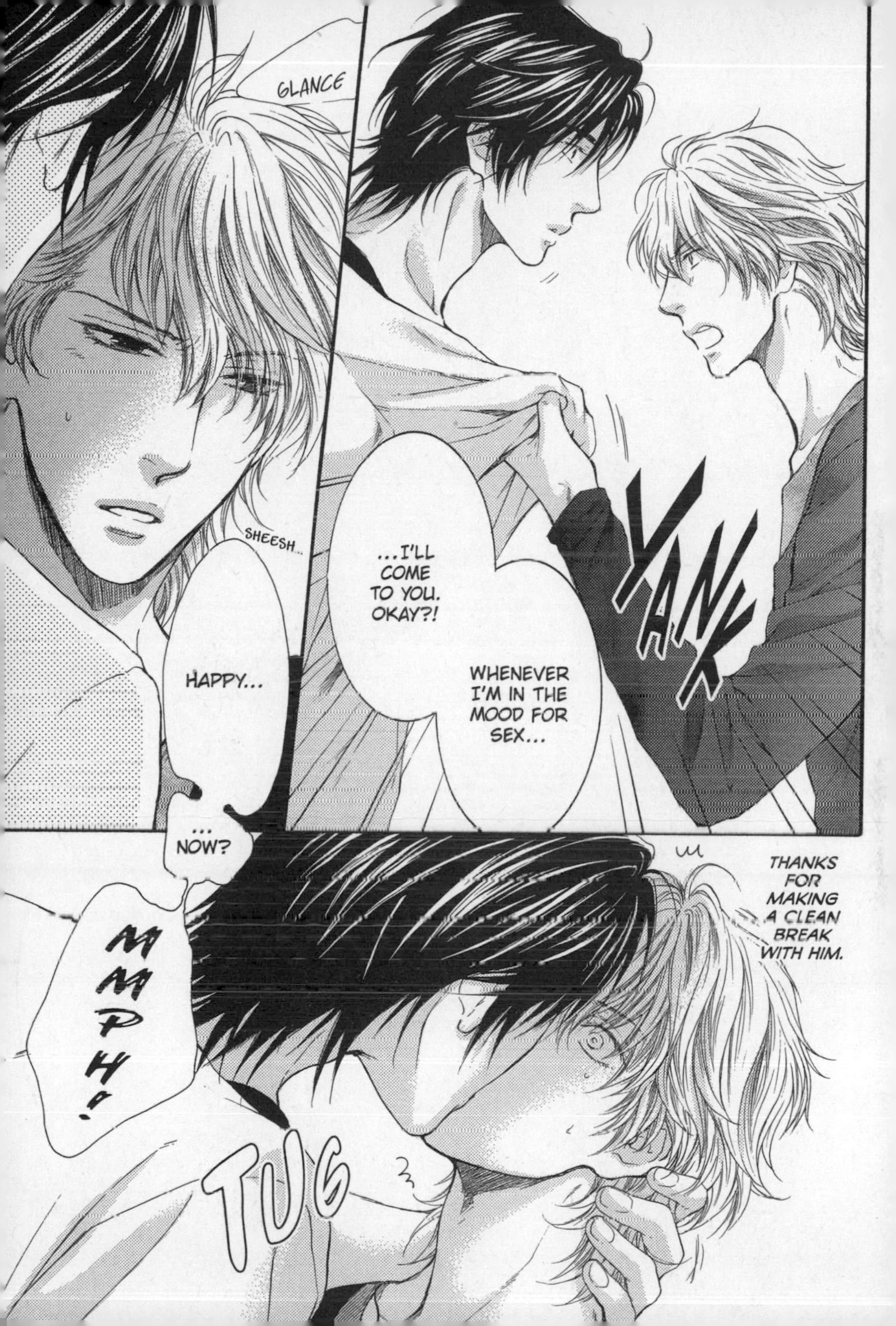
YANK
WHENEVER I'M IN THE MOOD FOR SEX...
...I'LL COME TO YOU. OKAY?!
GLANCE
SHEESH...
HAPPY...
...NOW?
THANKS FOR MAKING A CLEAN BREAK WITH HIM.
MMPH!
TUG

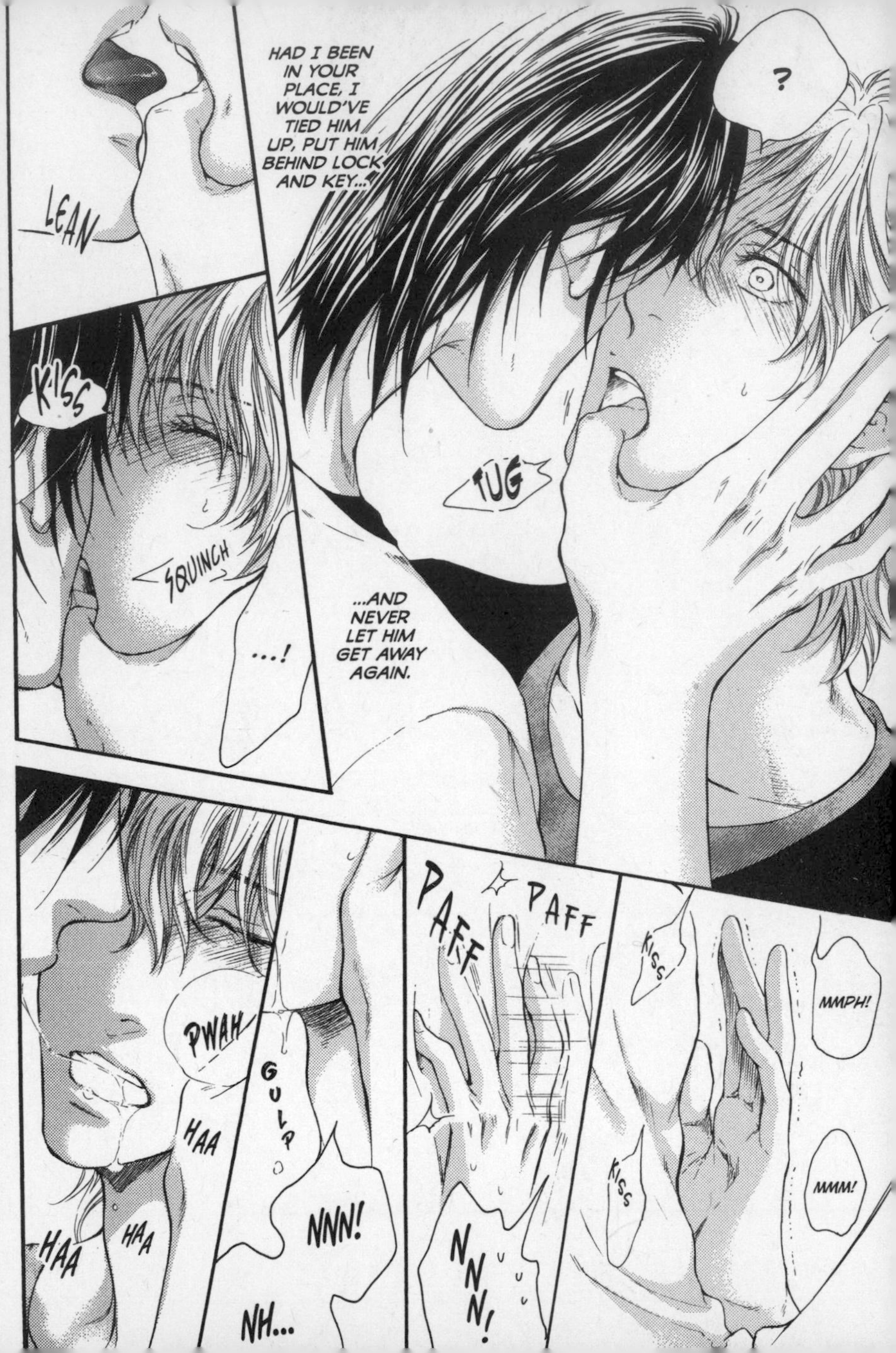
?
HAD I BEEN IN YOUR PLACE, I WOULD'VE TIED HIM UP, PUT HIM BEHIND LOCK AND KEY...
TUG
...AND NEVER LET HIM GET AWAY AGAIN.
LEAN
KISS
SQUINCH
...!
MMPH!
KISS
MMM!
KISS
PAFF
PAFF
NNN!
GULP
NNN!
PWAH
HAA
HAA
HAA
NH...

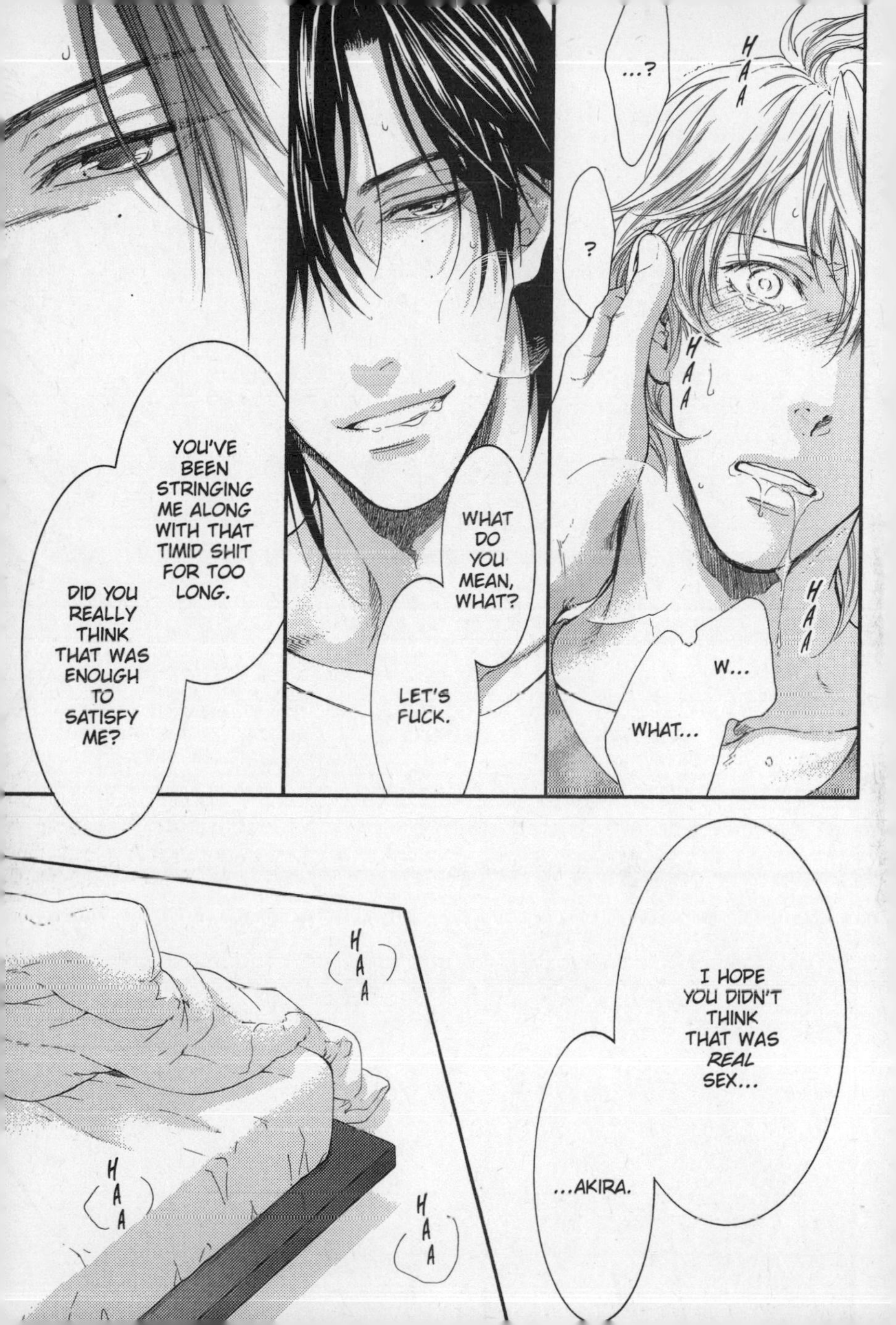
...?
HAA
?
HAA
HAA
W...
WHAT...
WHAT DO YOU MEAN, WHAT?
LET'S FUCK.
YOU'VE BEEN STRINGING ME ALONG WITH THAT TIMID SHIT FOR TOO LONG.
DID YOU REALLY THINK THAT WAS ENOUGH TO SATISFY ME?
I HOPE YOU DIDN'T THINK THAT WAS *REAL* SEX...
...AKIRA.
HAA
HAA
HAA

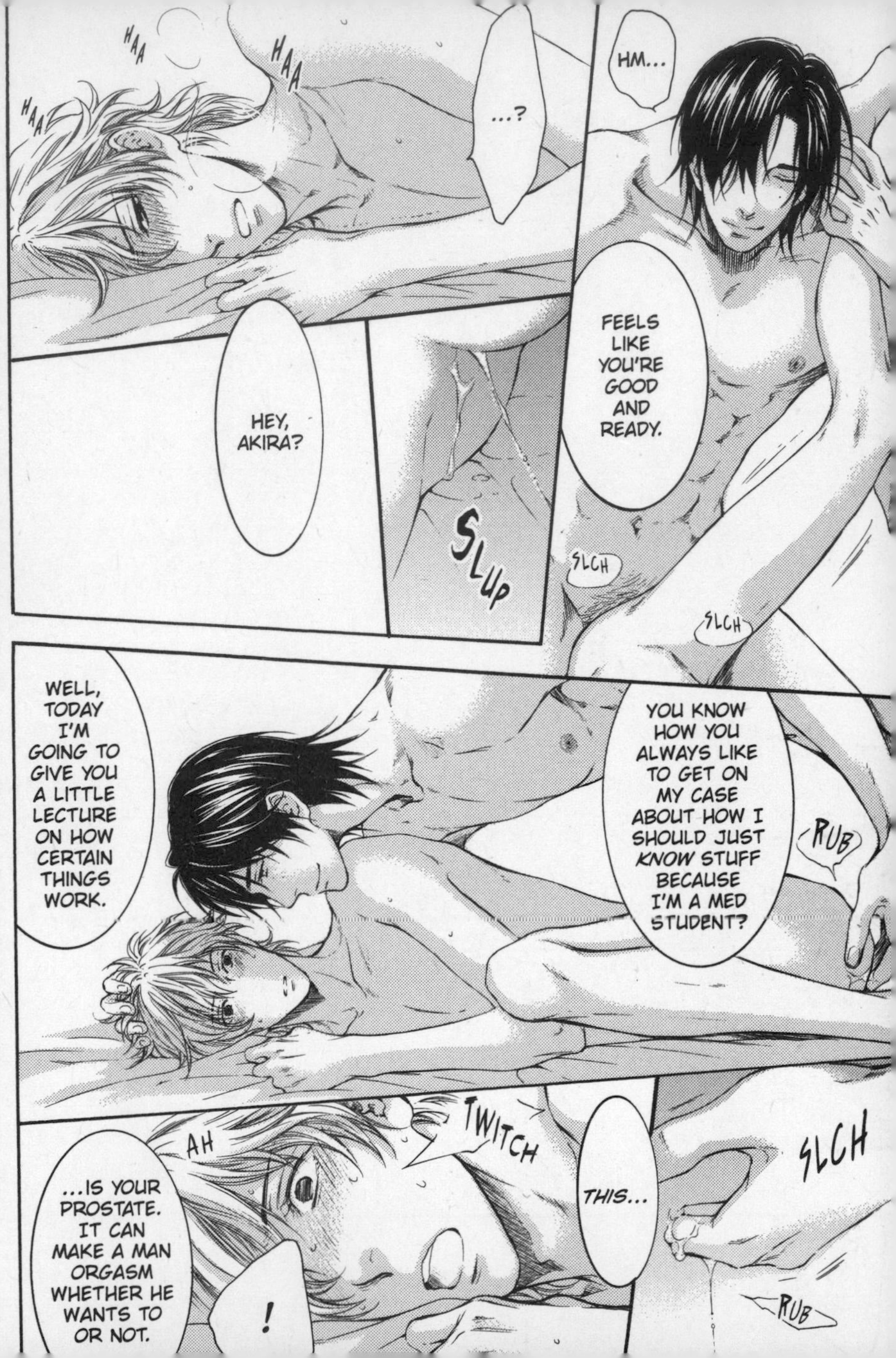
HM...
FEELS LIKE YOU'RE GOOD AND READY.
SLCH
SLCH
...?
HAA
HAA
HAA
SLUP
HEY, AKIRA?
YOU KNOW HOW YOU ALWAYS LIKE TO GET ON MY CASE ABOUT HOW I SHOULD JUST *KNOW* STUFF BECAUSE I'M A MED STUDENT?
RUB
WELL, TODAY I'M GOING TO GIVE YOU A LITTLE LECTURE ON HOW CERTAIN THINGS WORK.
SLCH
RUB
THIS...
TWITCH
AH
!
...IS YOUR PROSTATE. IT CAN MAKE A MAN ORGASM WHETHER HE WANTS TO OR NOT.

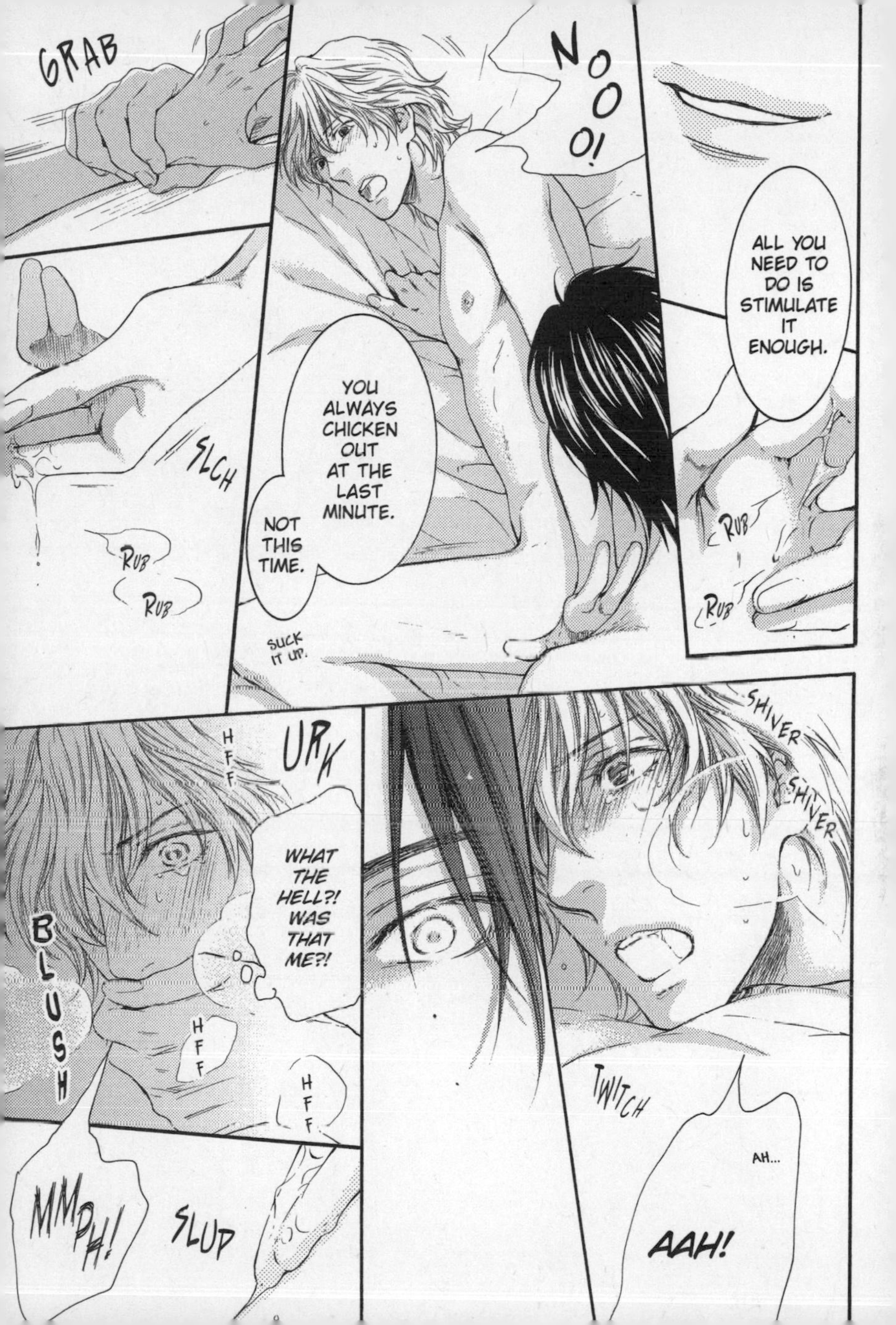

ALL YOU NEED TO DO IS STIMULATE IT ENOUGH.
RUB
RUB
NOOOO!
YOU ALWAYS CHICKEN OUT AT THE LAST MINUTE.
NOT THIS TIME.
SUCK IT UP.
GRAB
SLCH
RUB
RUB
SHIVER
SHIVER
TWITCH
AH...
AAH!
HFF
URK
WHAT THE HELL?! WAS THAT ME?!
BLUSH
HFF
HFF
MMPH!
SLUP

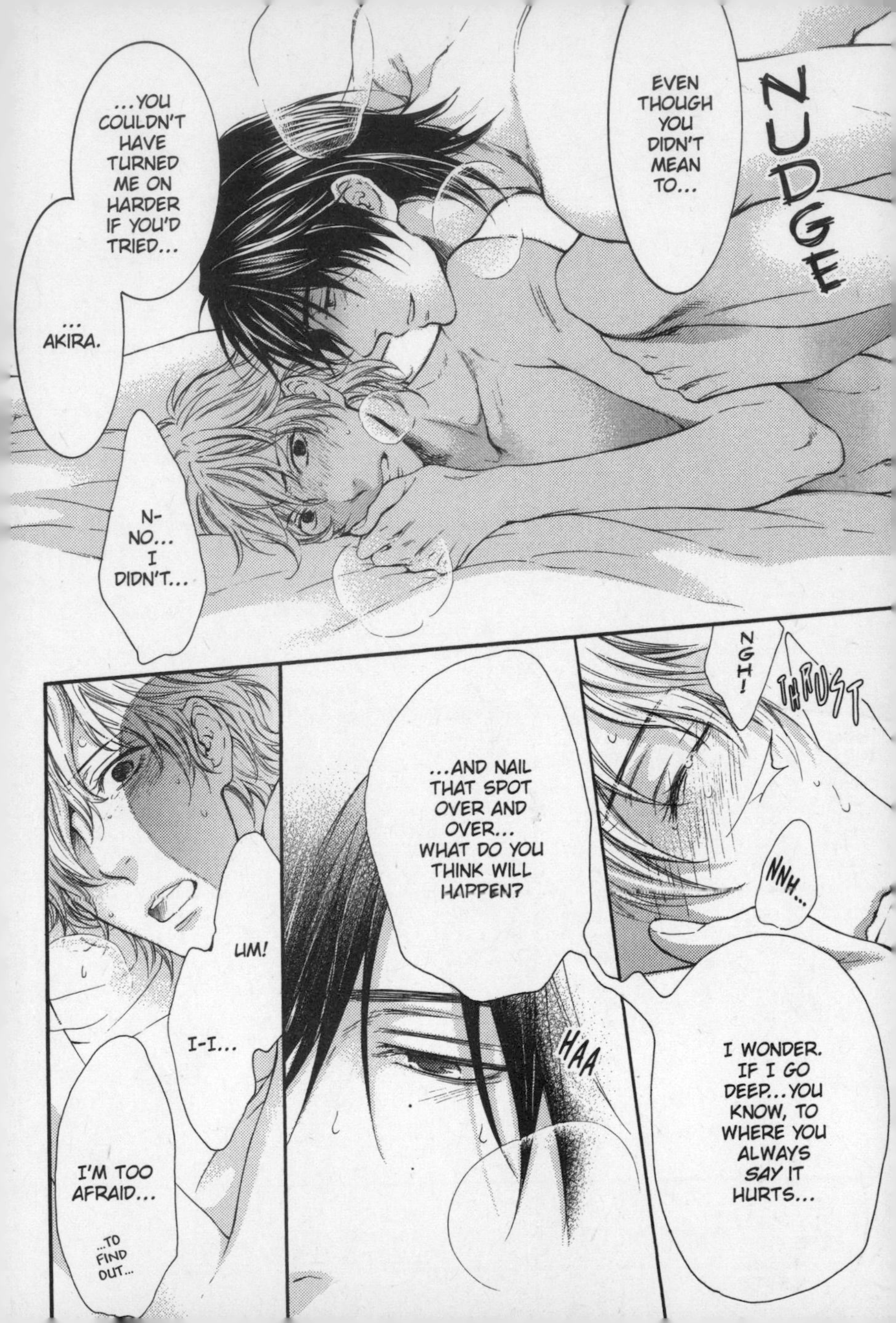
EVEN THOUGH YOU DIDN'T MEAN TO...
NUDGE
...YOU COULDN'T HAVE TURNED ME ON HARDER IF YOU'D TRIED...
... AKIRA.
N-NO... I DIDN'T...
NGH!
THRUST
NNH...
I WONDER. IF I GO DEEP...YOU KNOW, TO WHERE YOU ALWAYS SAY IT HURTS...
...AND NAIL THAT SPOT OVER AND OVER... WHAT DO YOU THINK WILL HAPPEN?
HAA
UM!
I-I...
I'M TOO AFRAID...
...TO FIND OUT...

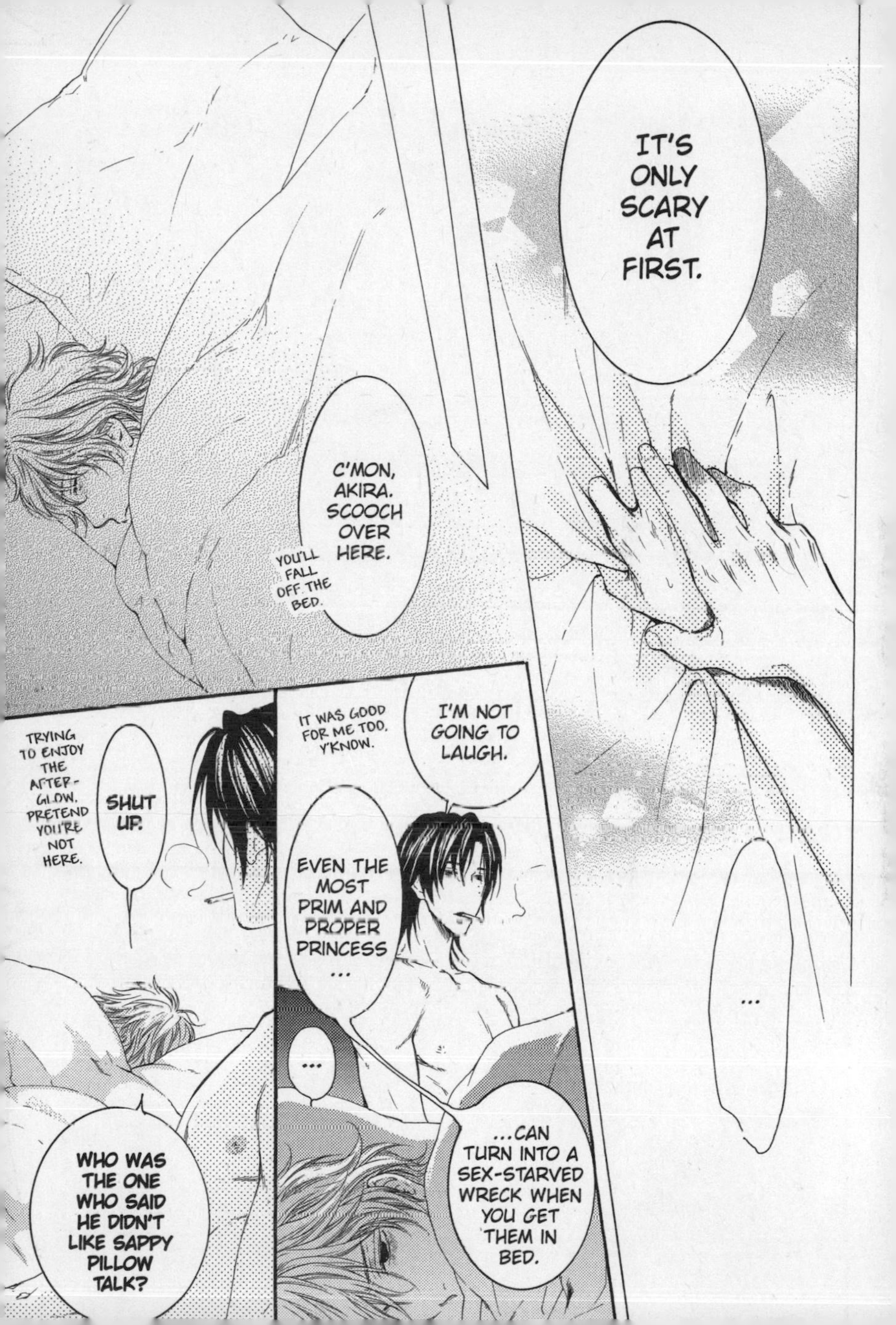
IT'S ONLY SCARY AT FIRST.
...
C'MON, AKIRA. SCOOCH OVER HERE.
YOU'LL FALL OFF THE BED.
I'M NOT GOING TO LAUGH.
IT WAS GOOD FOR ME TOO, Y'KNOW.
EVEN THE MOST PRIM AND PROPER PRINCESS...
...
...CAN TURN INTO A SEX-STARVED WRECK WHEN YOU GET THEM IN BED.
SHUT UP.
TRYING TO ENJOY THE AFTER-GLOW. PRETEND YOU'RE NOT HERE.
WHO WAS THE ONE WHO SAID HE DIDN'T LIKE SAPPY PILLOW TALK?

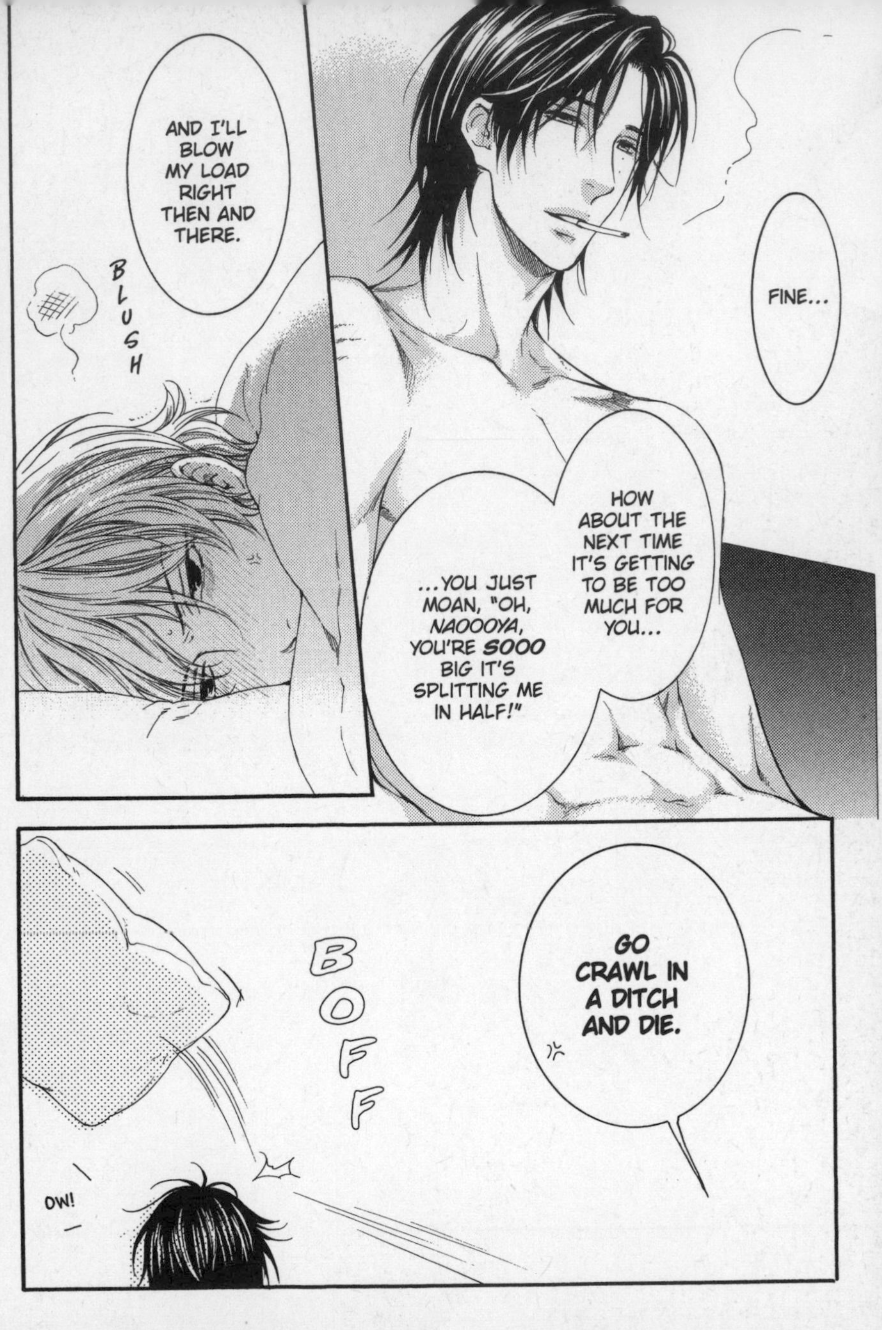
FINE...
HOW ABOUT THE NEXT TIME IT'S GETTING TO BE TOO MUCH FOR YOU...
...YOU JUST MOAN, "OH, NAOOOYA, YOU'RE SOOO BIG IT'S SPLITTING ME IN HALF!"
AND I'LL BLOW MY LOAD RIGHT THEN AND THERE.
BLUSH
GO CRAWL IN A DITCH AND DIE.
BOFF
OW!

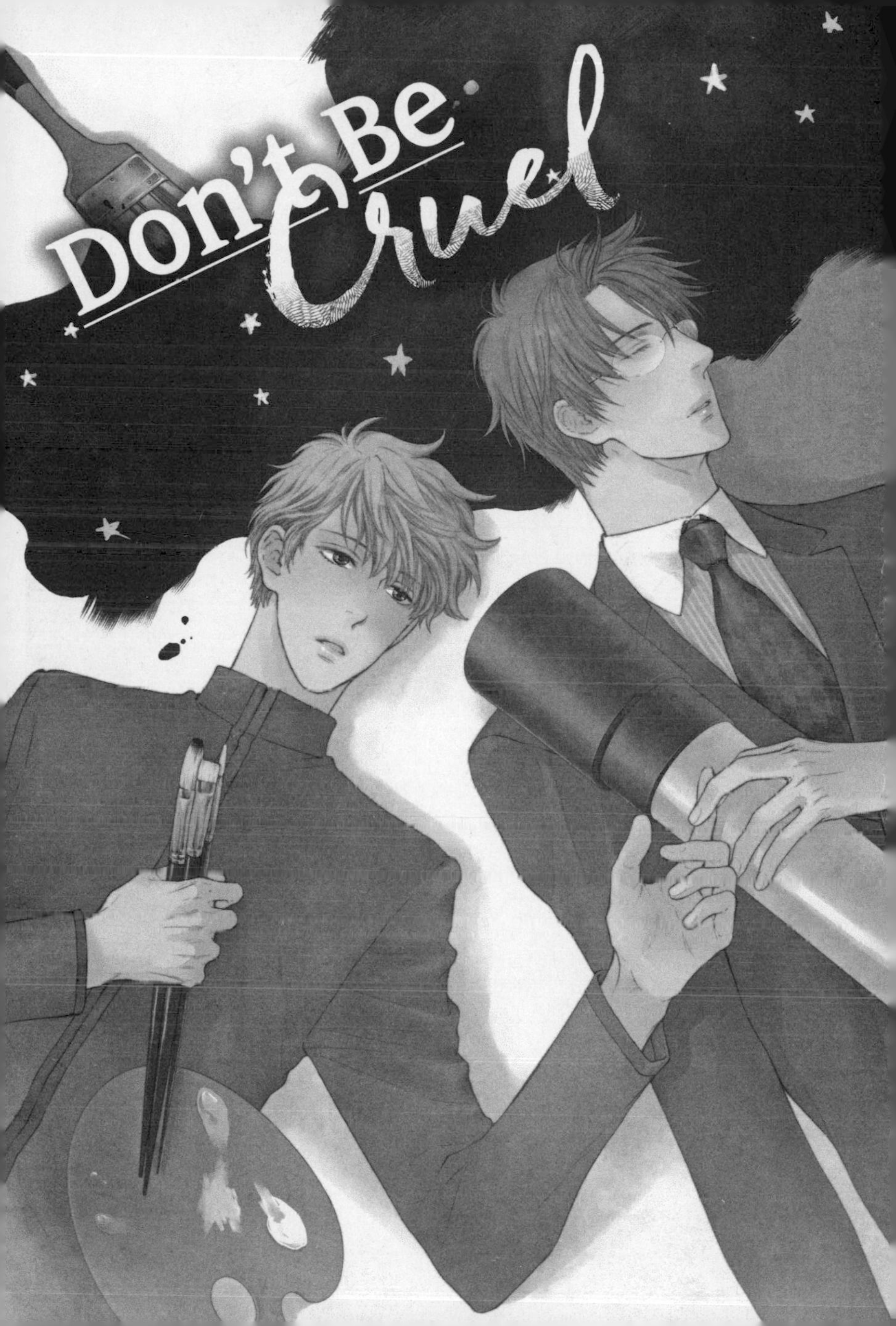
Don't Be Cruel

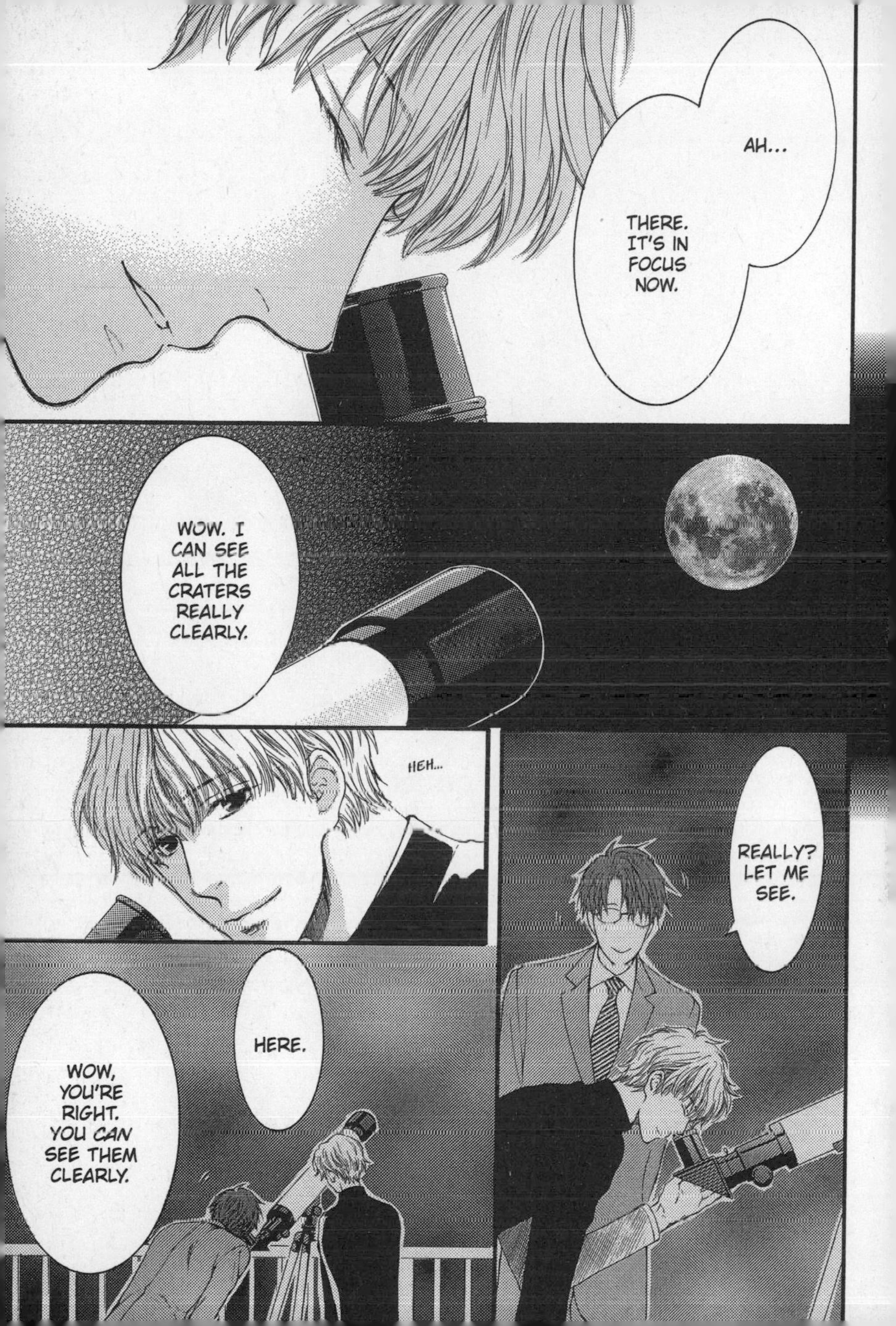
AH...
THERE. IT'S IN FOCUS NOW.
WOW. I CAN SEE ALL THE CRATERS REALLY CLEARLY.
REALLY? LET ME SEE.
HEH...
HERE.
WOW, YOU'RE RIGHT. YOU CAN SEE THEM CLEARLY.

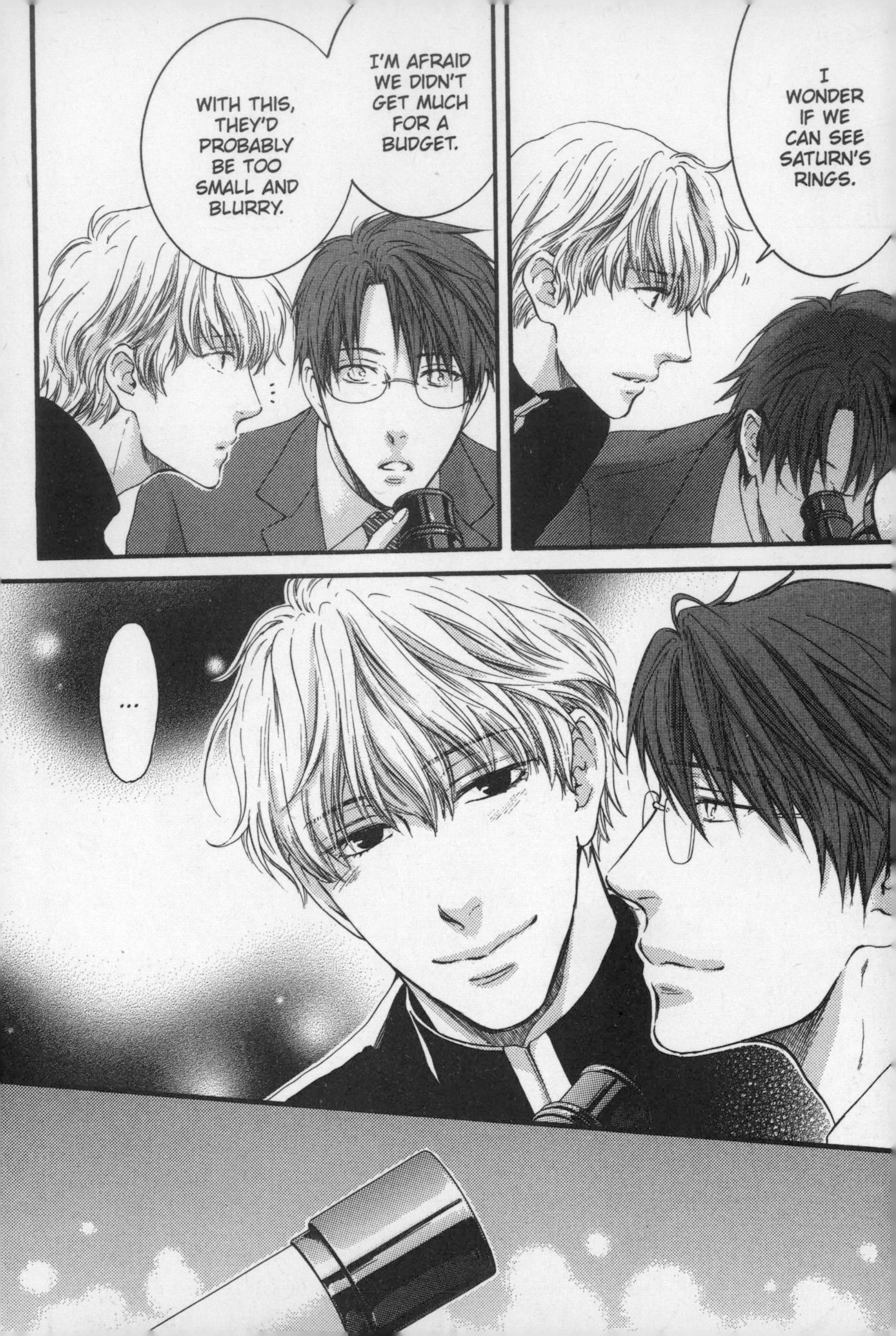
I WONDER IF WE CAN SEE SATURN'S RINGS.
I'M AFRAID WE DIDN'T GET MUCH FOR A BUDGET.
WITH THIS, THEY'D PROBABLY BE TOO SMALL AND BLURRY.
...
...

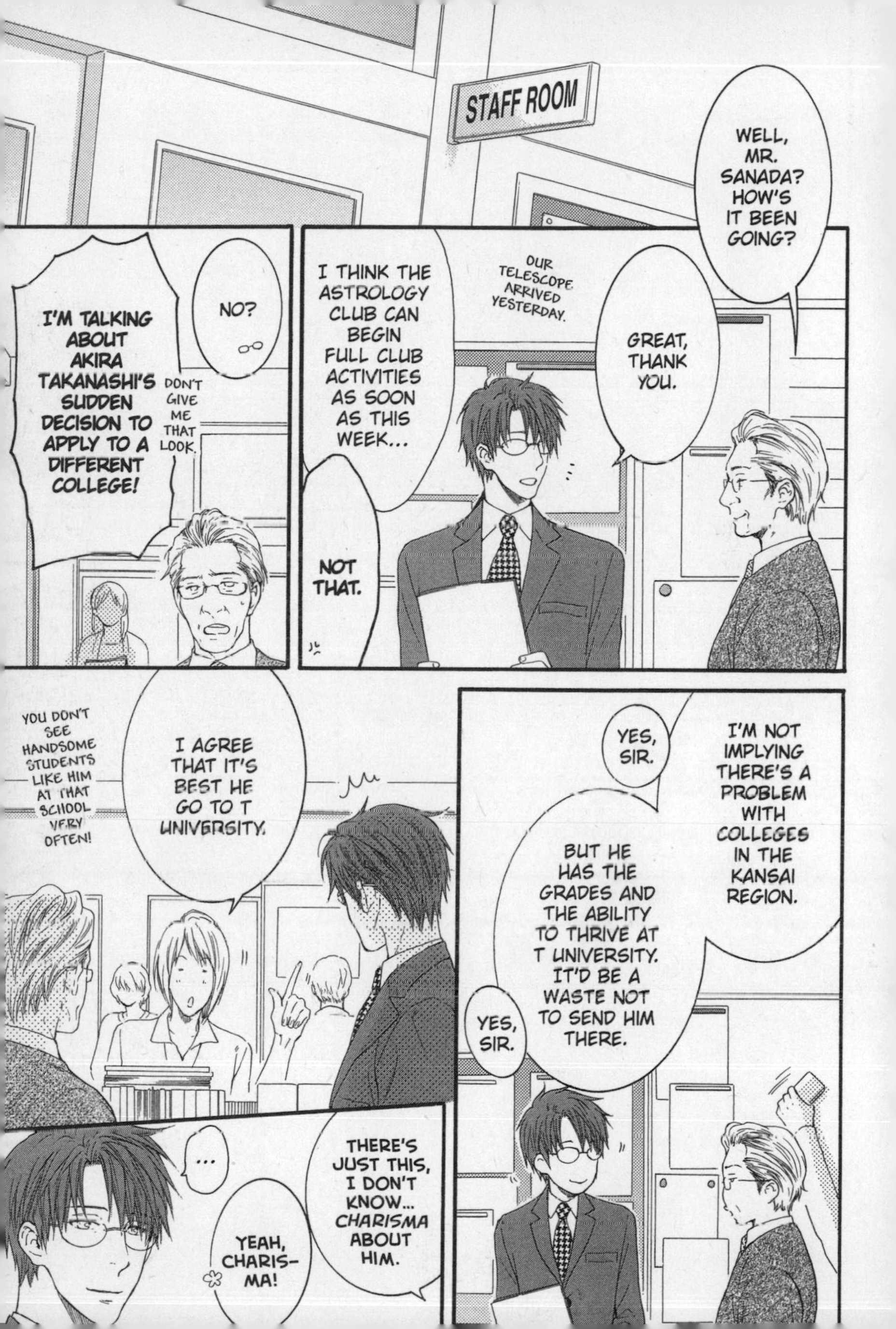
STAFF ROOM
WELL, MR. SANADA? HOW'S IT BEEN GOING?
GREAT, THANK YOU.
OUR TELESCOPE ARRIVED YESTERDAY.
I THINK THE ASTROLOGY CLUB CAN BEGIN FULL CLUB ACTIVITIES AS SOON AS THIS WEEK...
NOT THAT.
NO?
I'M TALKING ABOUT AKIRA TAKANASHI'S SUDDEN DECISION TO APPLY TO A DIFFERENT COLLEGE!
DON'T GIVE ME THAT LOOK.
I'M NOT IMPLYING THERE'S A PROBLEM WITH COLLEGES IN THE KANSAI REGION.
YES, SIR.
BUT HE HAS THE GRADES AND THE ABILITY TO THRIVE AT T UNIVERSITY. IT'D BE A WASTE NOT TO SEND HIM THERE.
YES, SIR.
I AGREE THAT IT'S BEST HE GO TO T UNIVERSITY.
YOU DON'T SEE HANDSOME STUDENTS LIKE HIM AT THAT SCHOOL VERY OFTEN!
THERE'S JUST THIS, I DON'T KNOW... CHARISMA ABOUT HIM.
...
YEAH, CHARIS-MA!

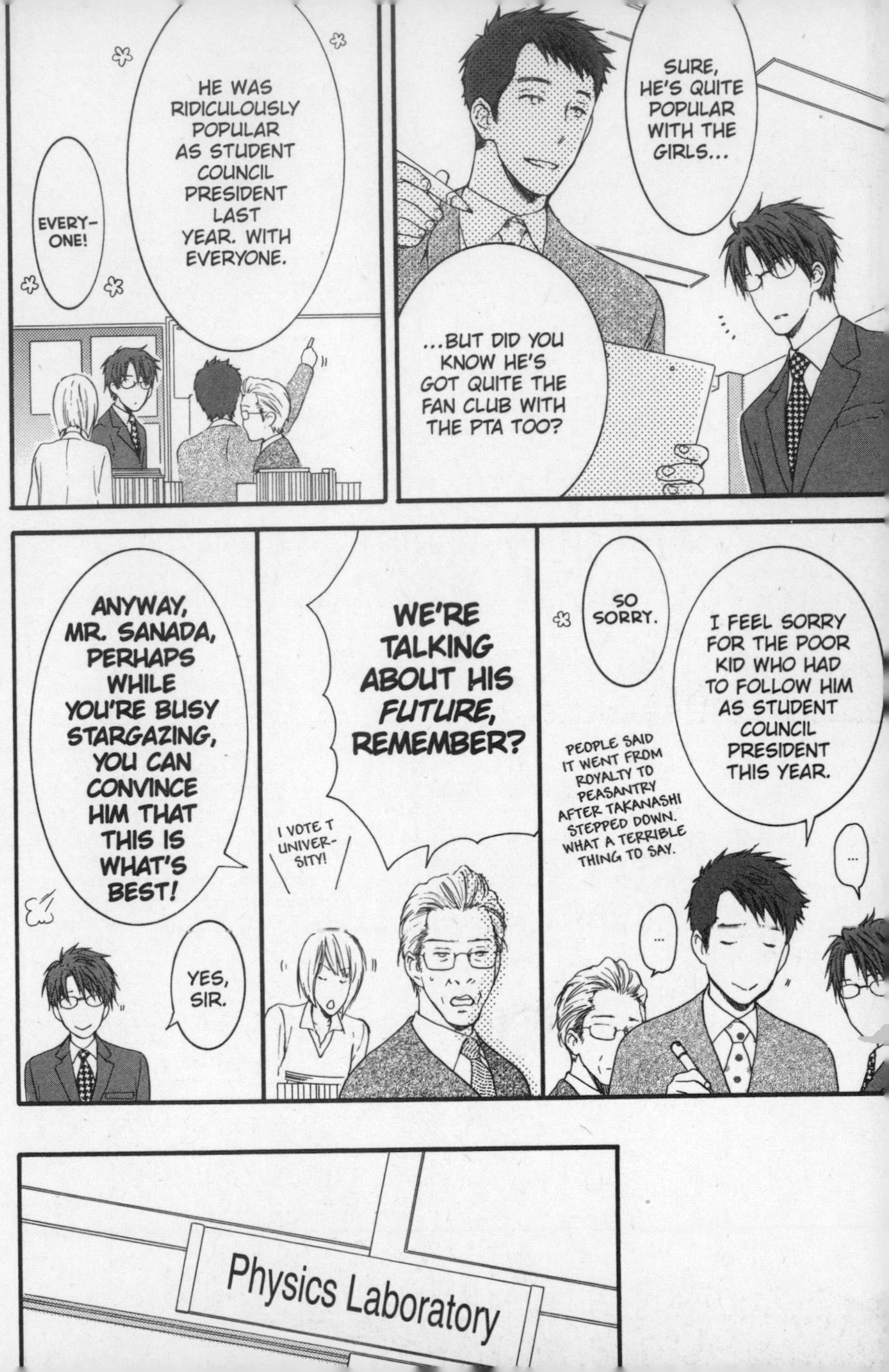
SURE, HE'S QUITE POPULAR WITH THE GIRLS...
...BUT DID YOU KNOW HE'S GOT QUITE THE FAN CLUB WITH THE PTA TOO?
...
HE WAS RIDICULOUSLY POPULAR AS STUDENT COUNCIL PRESIDENT LAST YEAR. WITH EVERYONE.
EVERY-ONE!
I FEEL SORRY FOR THE POOR KID WHO HAD TO FOLLOW HIM AS STUDENT COUNCIL PRESIDENT THIS YEAR.
SO SORRY.
PEOPLE SAID IT WENT FROM ROYALTY TO PEASANTRY AFTER TAKANASHI STEPPED DOWN. WHAT A TERRIBLE THING TO SAY.
...
...
WE'RE TALKING ABOUT HIS *FUTURE*, REMEMBER?
I VOTE T UNIVER-SITY!
ANYWAY, MR. SANADA, PERHAPS WHILE YOU'RE BUSY STARGAZING, YOU CAN CONVINCE HIM THAT THIS IS WHAT'S BEST!
YES, SIR.
Physics Laboratory

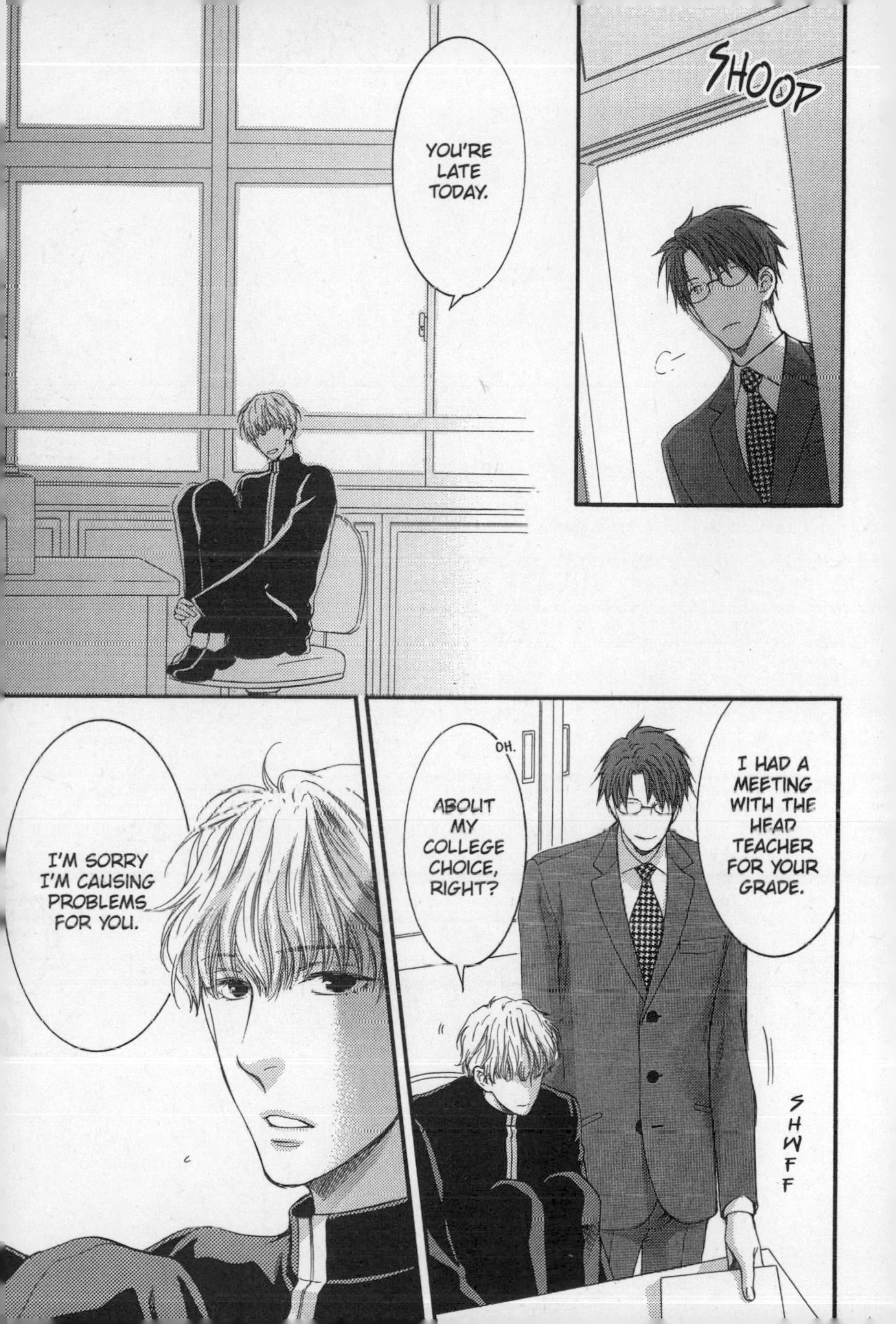
SHOOP
YOU'RE LATE TODAY.
I HAD A MEETING WITH THE HEAD TEACHER FOR YOUR GRADE.
SHWFF
OH.
ABOUT MY COLLEGE CHOICE, RIGHT?
I'M SORRY I'M CAUSING PROBLEMS FOR YOU.

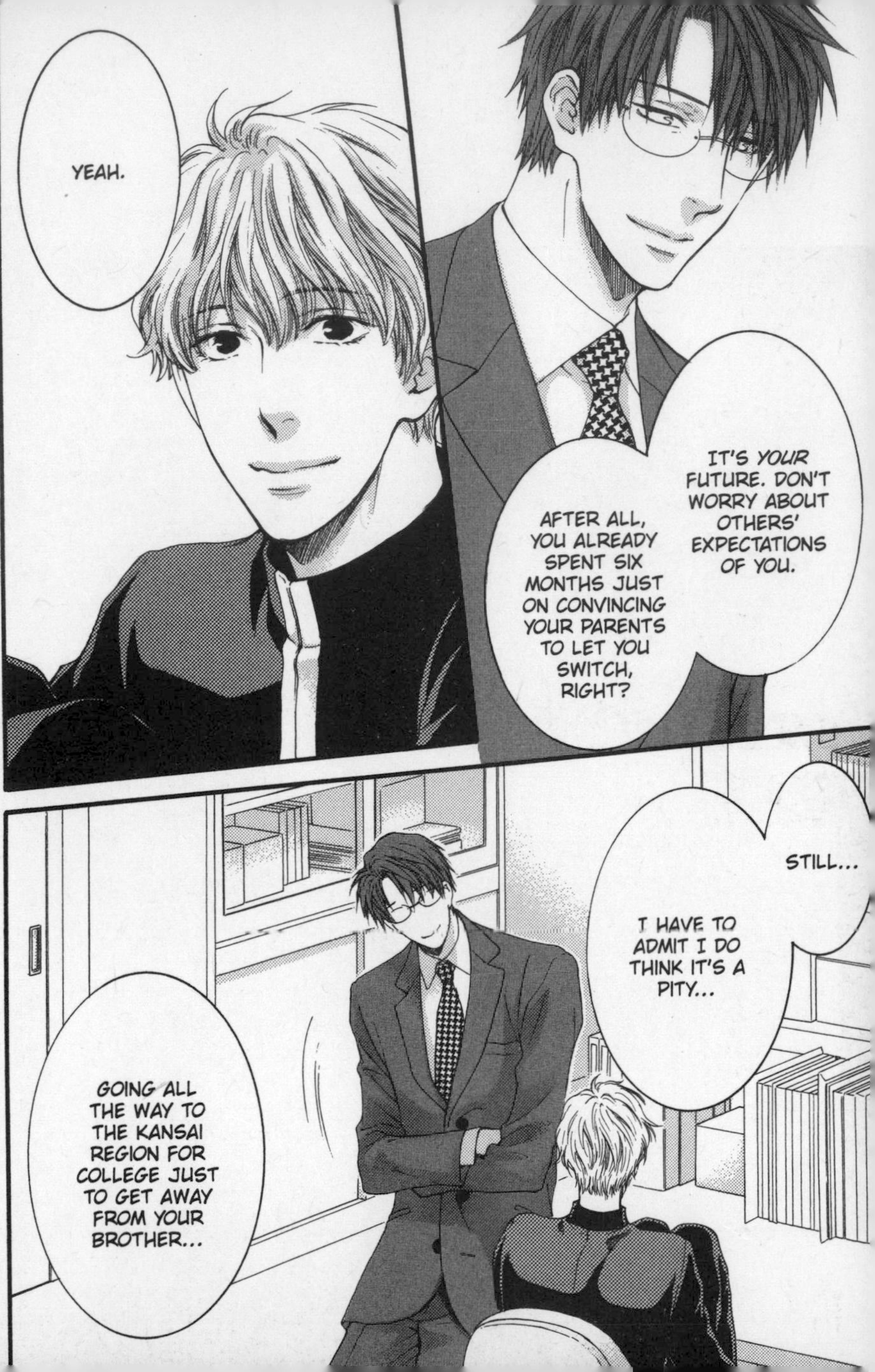
IT'S *YOUR* FUTURE. DON'T WORRY ABOUT OTHERS' EXPECTATIONS OF YOU.
AFTER ALL, YOU ALREADY SPENT SIX MONTHS JUST ON CONVINCING YOUR PARENTS TO LET YOU SWITCH, RIGHT?
YEAH.
STILL...
I HAVE TO ADMIT I DO THINK IT'S A PITY...
GOING ALL THE WAY TO THE KANSAI REGION FOR COLLEGE JUST TO GET AWAY FROM YOUR BROTHER...

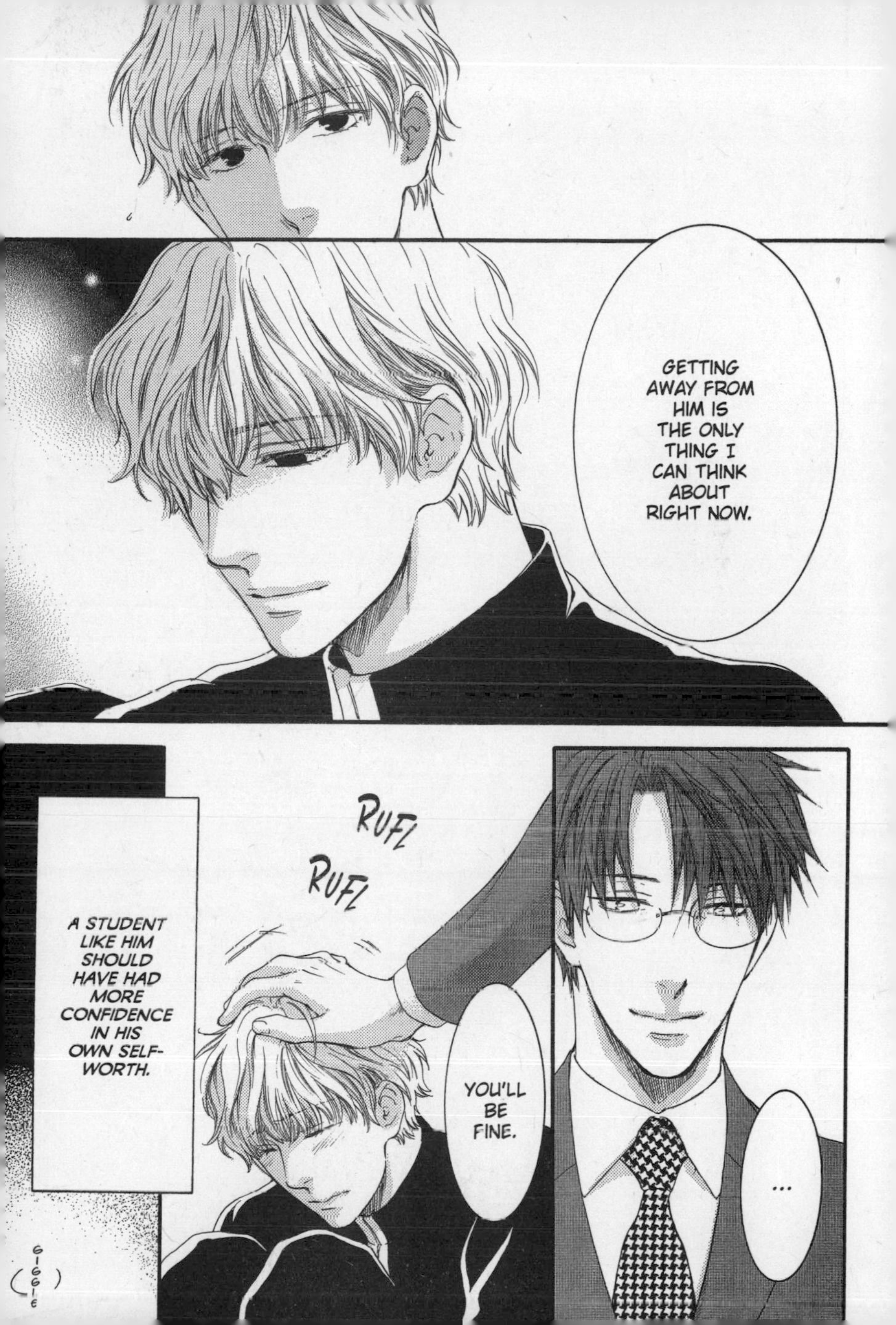
GETTING AWAY FROM HIM IS THE ONLY THING I CAN THINK ABOUT RIGHT NOW.
...
RUFL
RUFL
YOU'LL BE FINE.
A STUDENT LIKE HIM SHOULD HAVE HAD MORE CONFIDENCE IN HIS OWN SELF-WORTH.
(GIGGLE)

KCHAK

BUT IF GETTING AWAY FROM HIS BROTHER WAS WHAT IT WAS GOING TO TAKE FOR HIM TO GET OVER HIS INFERIORITY COMPLEX...

HEE HEE!

STOP IT! AKIRA WILL COME BACK!

OH, WE'LL BE FINE.

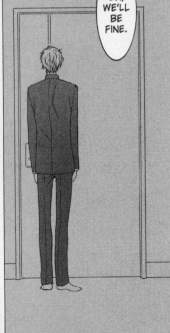

...I WAS WILLING TO DO WHATEVER IT TOOK.

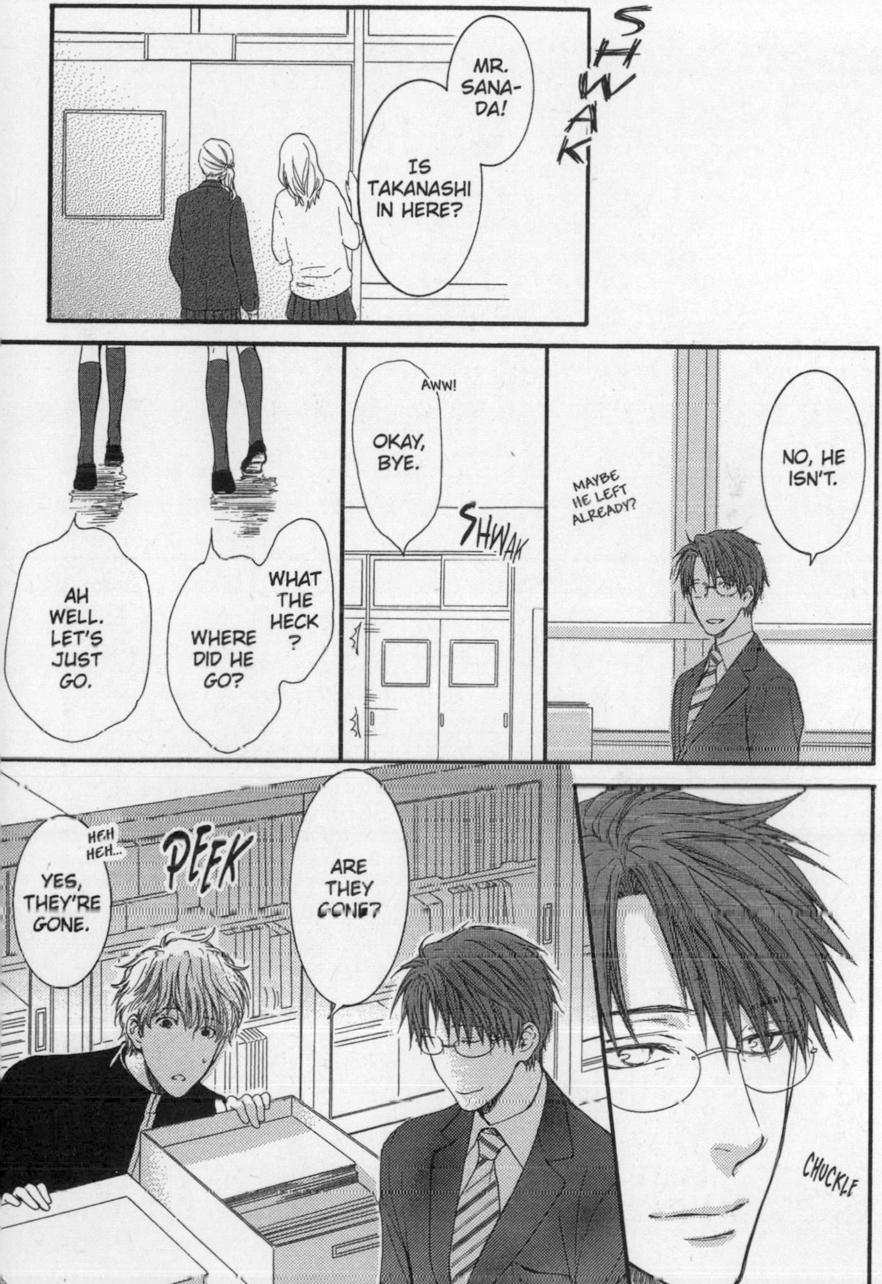
SHWAK
MR. SANADA!
IS TAKANASHI IN HERE?
NO, HE ISN'T.
MAYBE HE LEFT ALREADY?
AWW!
OKAY, BYE.
SHWAK
WHAT THE HECK?
WHERE DID HE GO?
AH WELL. LET'S JUST GO.
CHUCKLE
ARE THEY GONE?
PEEK
HEH HEH...
YES, THEY'RE GONE.

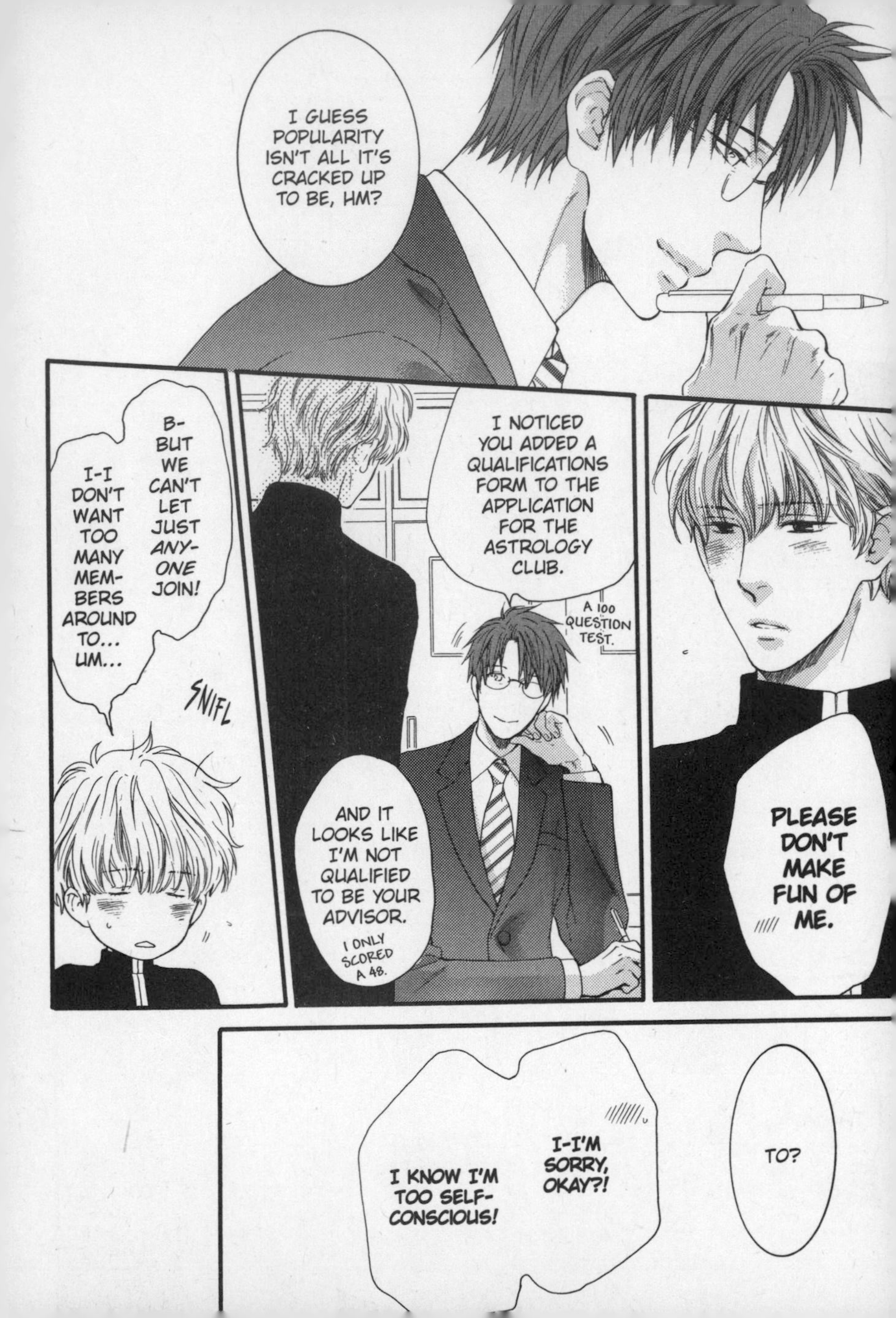
I GUESS POPULARITY ISN'T ALL IT'S CRACKED UP TO BE, HM?
PLEASE DON'T MAKE FUN OF ME.
I NOTICED YOU ADDED A QUALIFICATIONS FORM TO THE APPLICATION FOR THE ASTROLOGY CLUB.
A 100 QUESTION TEST.
AND IT LOOKS LIKE I'M NOT QUALIFIED TO BE YOUR ADVISOR.
I ONLY SCORED A 48.
B-BUT WE CAN'T LET JUST ANY-ONE JOIN!
I-I DON'T WANT TOO MANY MEM-BERS AROUND TO... UM...
SNIFL
TO?
I-I'M SORRY, OKAY?!
I KNOW I'M TOO SELF-CONSCIOUS!

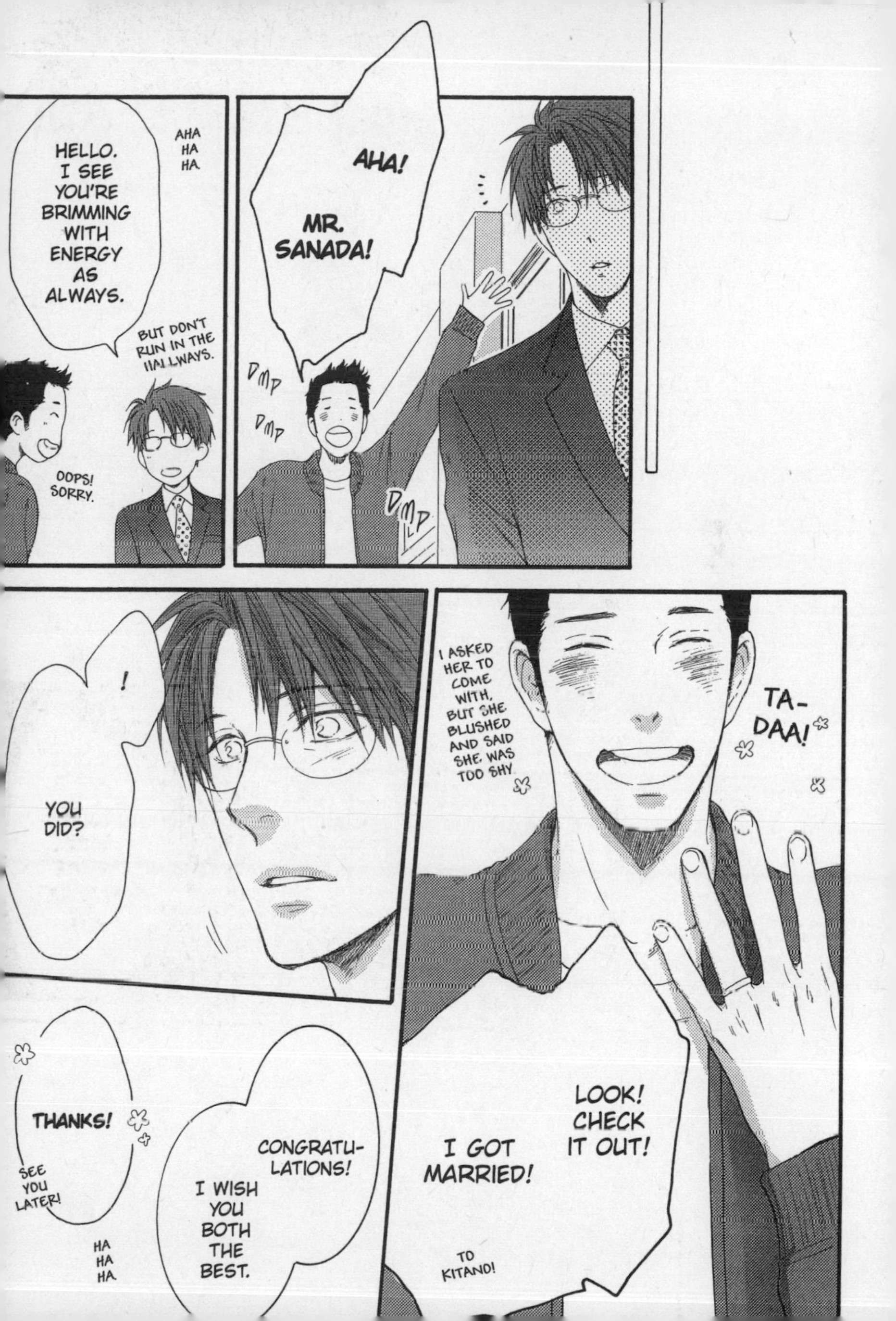
AHA!
MR. SANADA!
DMP
DMP
DMP
HELLO. I SEE YOU'RE BRIMMING WITH ENERGY AS ALWAYS.
AHA HA HA.
BUT DON'T RUN IN THE HALLWAYS.
OOPS! SORRY.
TA-DAA!
I ASKED HER TO COME WITH, BUT SHE BLUSHED AND SAID SHE WAS TOO SHY.
LOOK! CHECK IT OUT!
I GOT MARRIED!
TO KITANO!
!
YOU DID?
CONGRATULATIONS!
I WISH YOU BOTH THE BEST.
THANKS!
SEE YOU LATER!
HA HA HA.

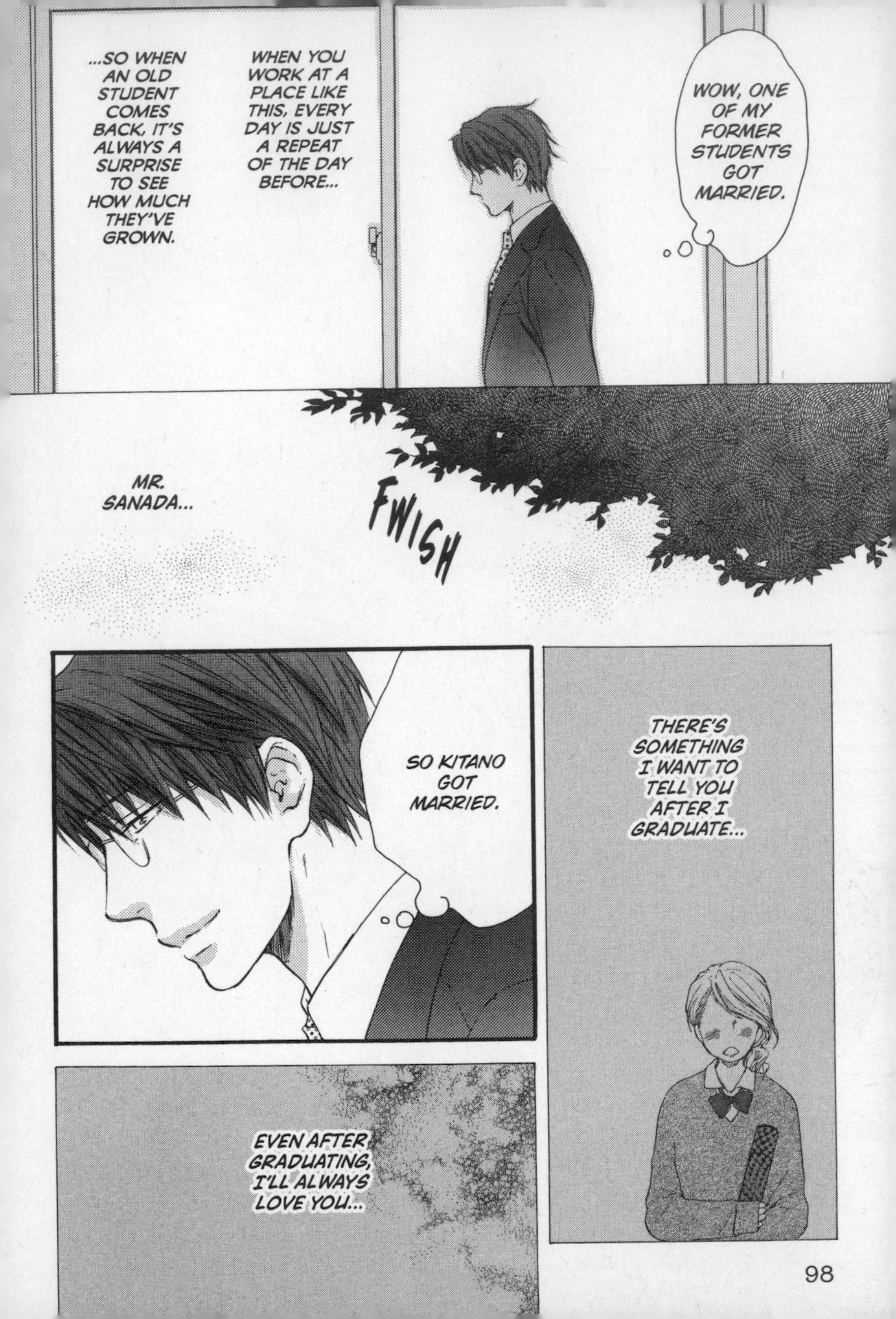
WOW, ONE OF MY FORMER STUDENTS GOT MARRIED.
WHEN YOU WORK AT A PLACE LIKE THIS, EVERY DAY IS JUST A REPEAT OF THE DAY BEFORE...
...SO WHEN AN OLD STUDENT COMES BACK, IT'S ALWAYS A SURPRISE TO SEE HOW MUCH THEY'VE GROWN.
FWISH
MR. SANADA...
THERE'S SOMETHING I WANT TO TELL YOU AFTER I GRADUATE...
SO KITANO GOT MARRIED.
EVEN AFTER GRADUATING, I'LL ALWAYS LOVE YOU...

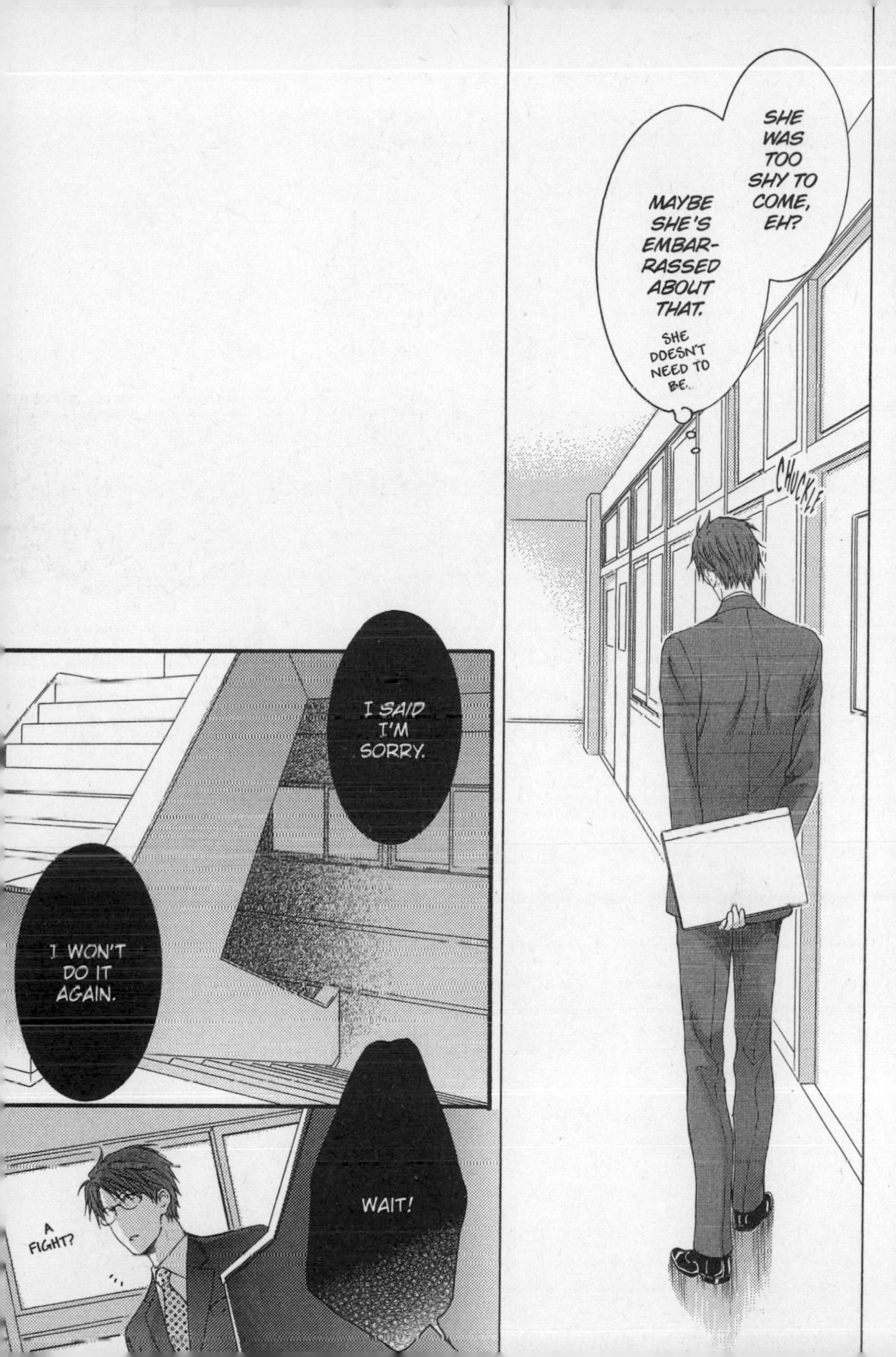
SHE WAS TOO SHY TO COME, EH?
MAYBE SHE'S EMBAR-RASSED ABOUT THAT.
SHE DOESN'T NEED TO BE...
CHUCKLE
I SAID I'M SORRY.
I WON'T DO IT AGAIN.
WAIT!
A FIGHT?
...

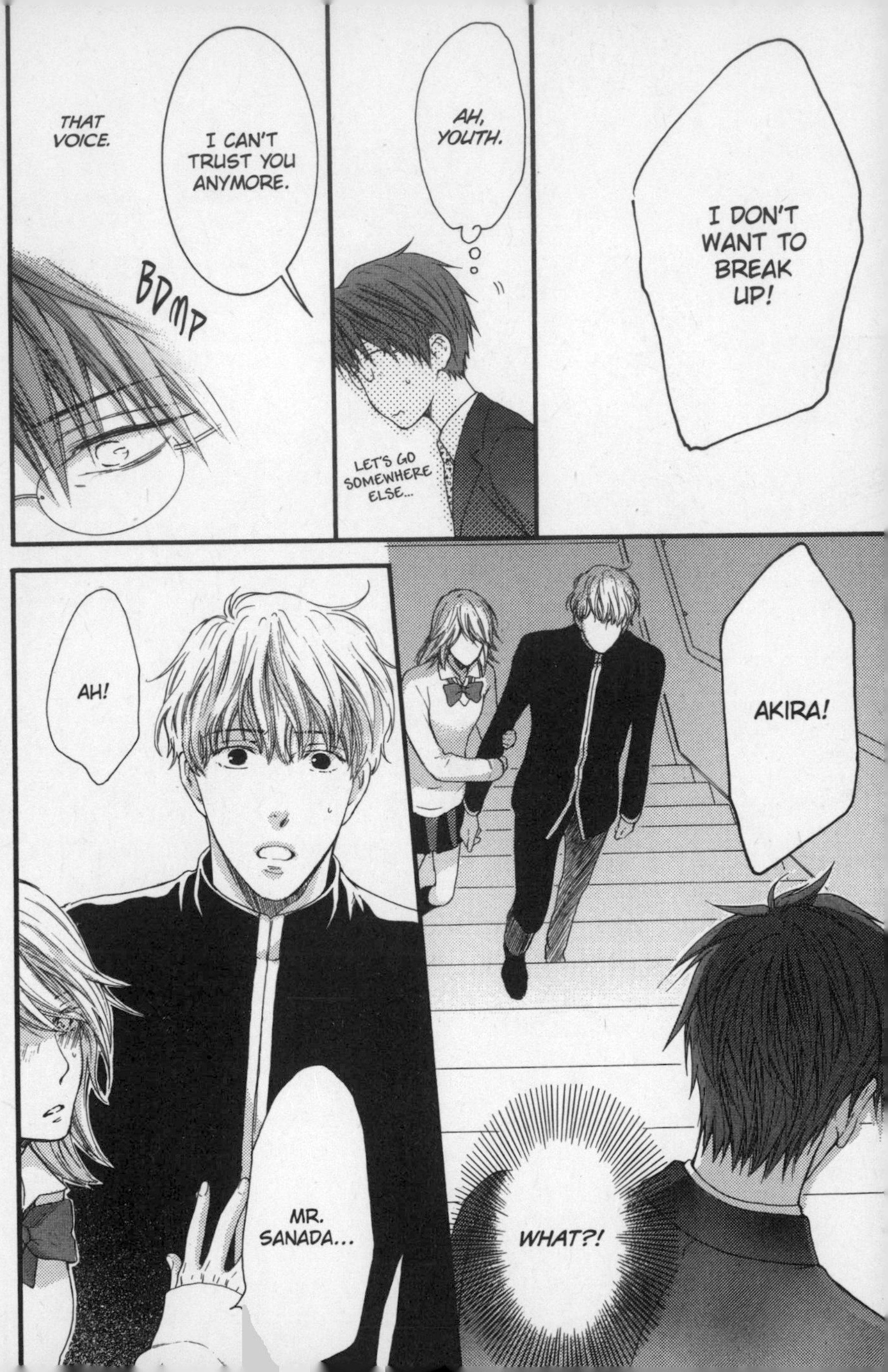
I DON'T WANT TO BREAK UP!
AH, YOUTH.
LET'S GO SOMEWHERE ELSE...
I CAN'T TRUST YOU ANYMORE.
THAT VOICE.
BDMP
AKIRA!
WHAT?!
AH!
MR. SANADA...

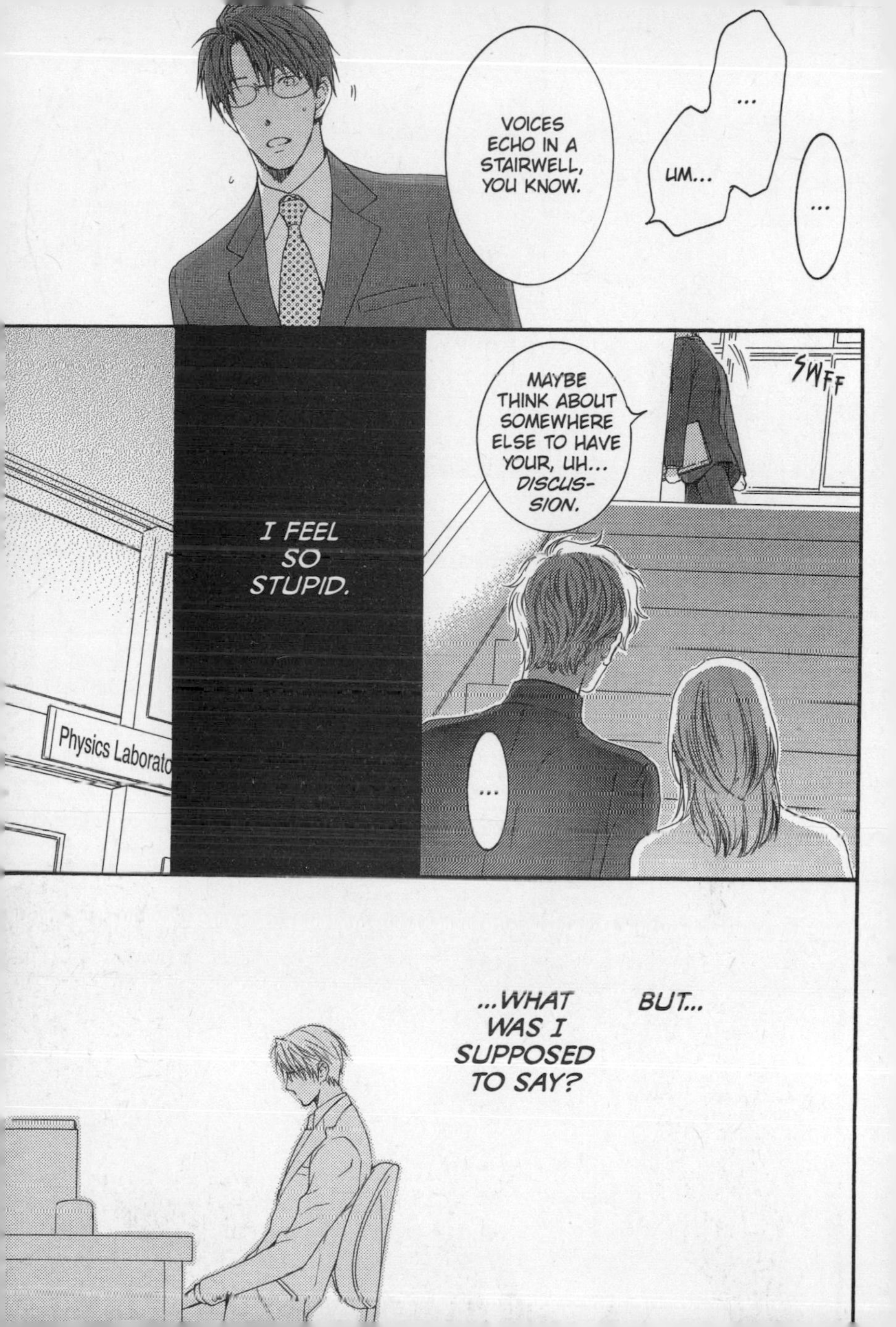
...
... UM...
VOICES ECHO IN A STAIRWELL, YOU KNOW.
SWFF
MAYBE THINK ABOUT SOMEWHERE ELSE TO HAVE YOUR, UH... DISCUSSION.
...
I FEEL SO STUPID.
Physics Laborato
BUT...
...WHAT WAS I SUPPOSED TO SAY?

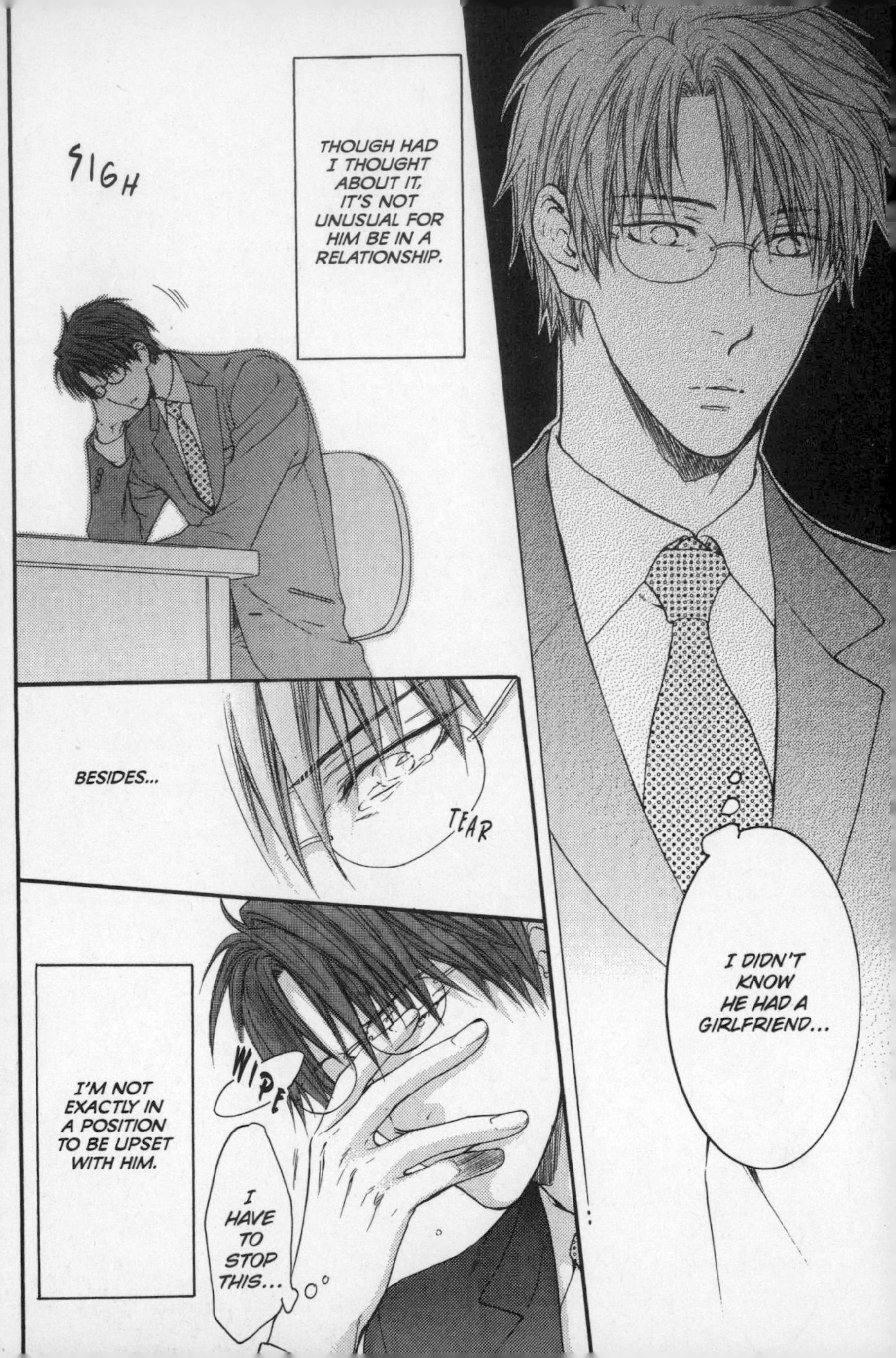
I DIDN'T KNOW HE HAD A GIRLFRIEND...
THOUGH HAD I THOUGHT ABOUT IT, IT'S NOT UNUSUAL FOR HIM BE IN A RELATIONSHIP.
SIGH
BESIDES...
TEAR
WIPE
I'M NOT EXACTLY IN A POSITION TO BE UPSET WITH HIM.
I HAVE TO STOP THIS...

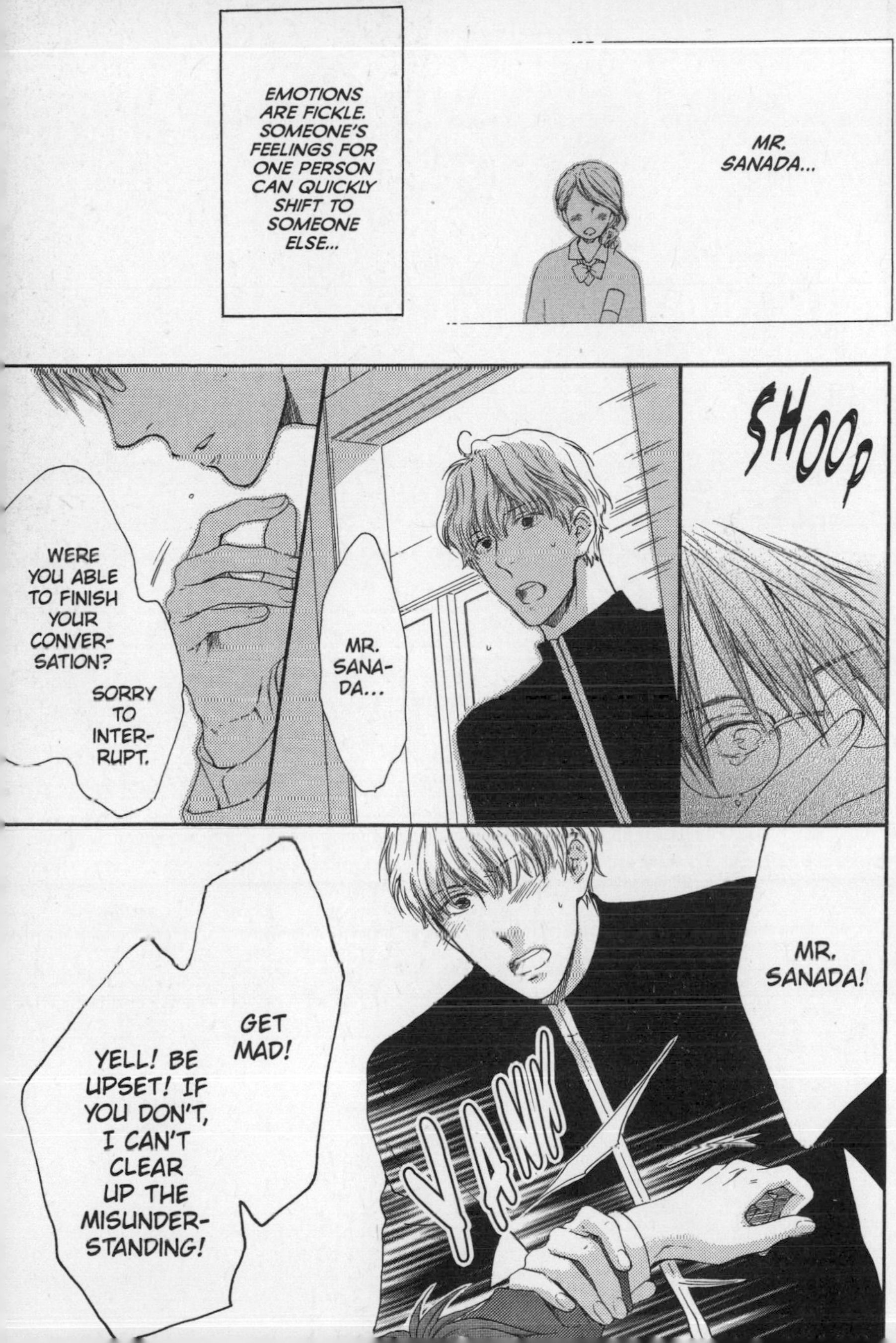
MR. SANADA...
EMOTIONS ARE FICKLE. SOMEONE'S FEELINGS FOR ONE PERSON CAN QUICKLY SHIFT TO SOMEONE ELSE...
SHOOP
MR. SANADA...
WERE YOU ABLE TO FINISH YOUR CONVERSATION?
SORRY TO INTERRUPT.
MR. SANADA!
GET MAD!
YELL! BE UPSET! IF YOU DON'T, I CAN'T CLEAR UP THE MISUNDERSTANDING!
YANK

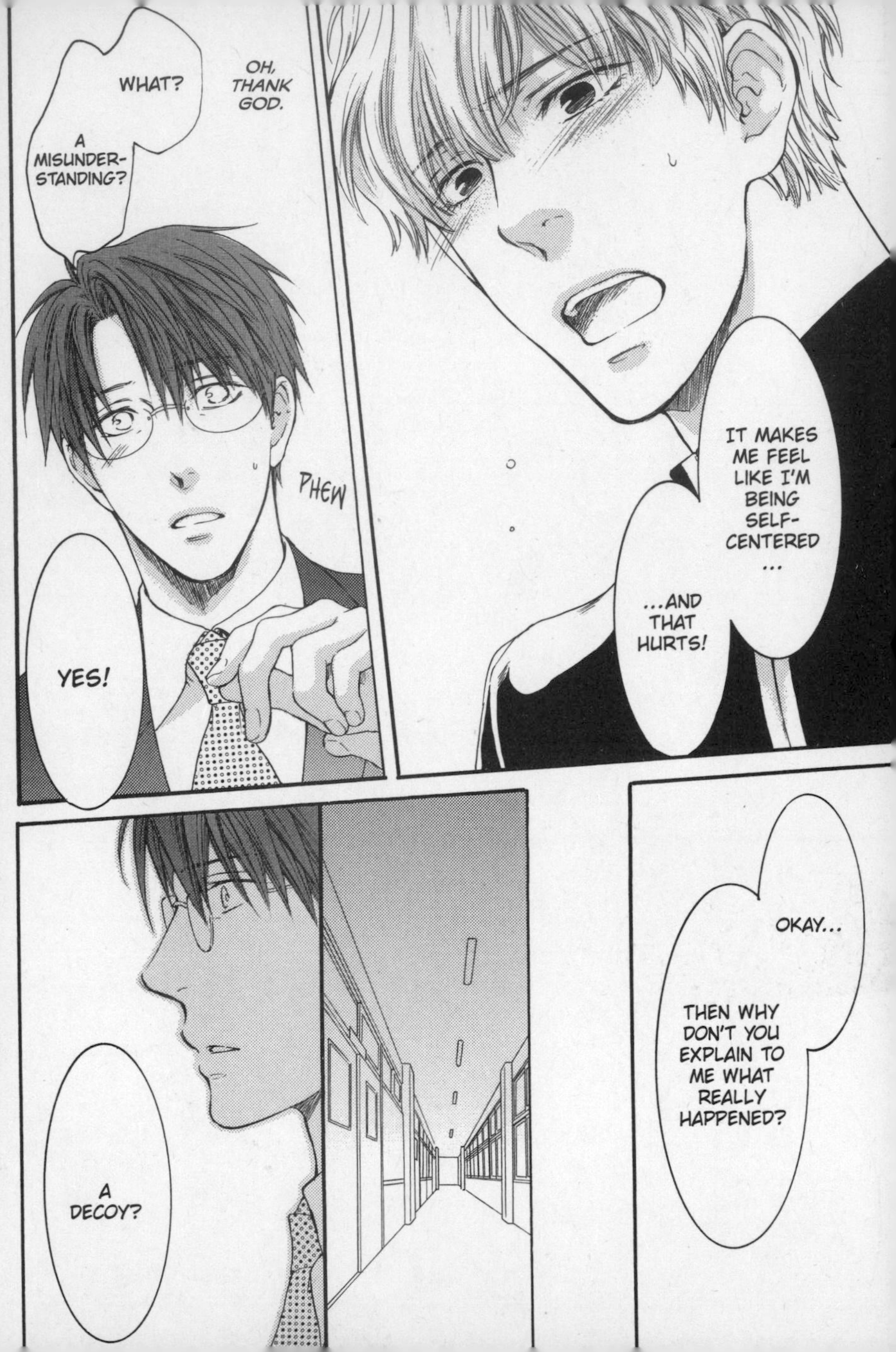
IT MAKES ME FEEL LIKE I'M BEING SELF-CENTERED...
...AND THAT HURTS!
OH, THANK GOD.
WHAT?
A MISUNDERSTANDING?
PHEW
YES!
OKAY...
THEN WHY DON'T YOU EXPLAIN TO ME WHAT REALLY HAPPENED?
A DECOY?

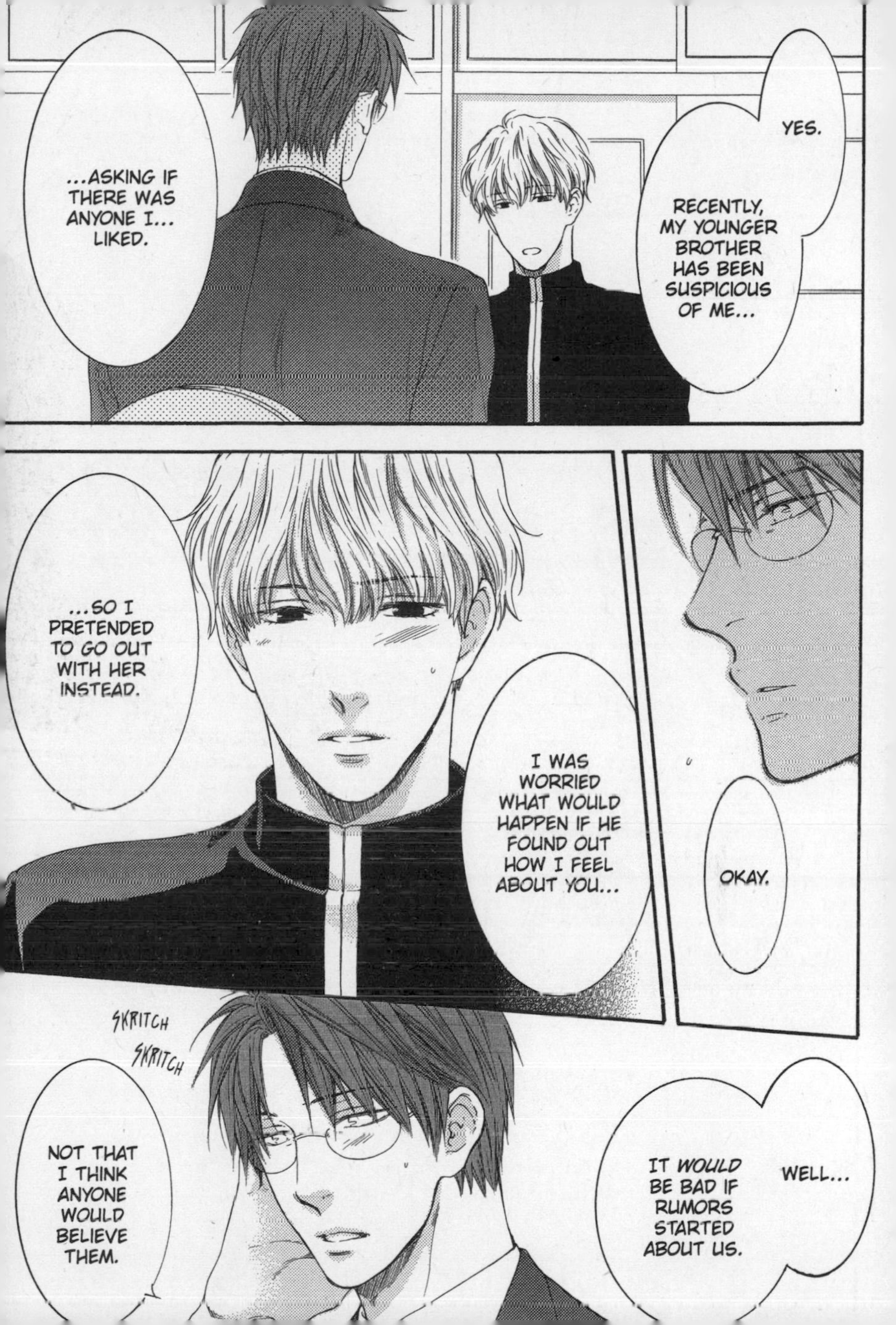
YES.
RECENTLY, MY YOUNGER BROTHER HAS BEEN SUSPICIOUS OF ME...
...ASKING IF THERE WAS ANYONE I... LIKED.
...SO I PRETENDED TO GO OUT WITH HER INSTEAD.
I WAS WORRIED WHAT WOULD HAPPEN IF HE FOUND OUT HOW I FEEL ABOUT YOU...
OKAY.
WELL...
IT *WOULD* BE BAD IF RUMORS STARTED ABOUT US.
SKRITCH
SKRITCH
NOT THAT I THINK ANYONE WOULD BELIEVE THEM.

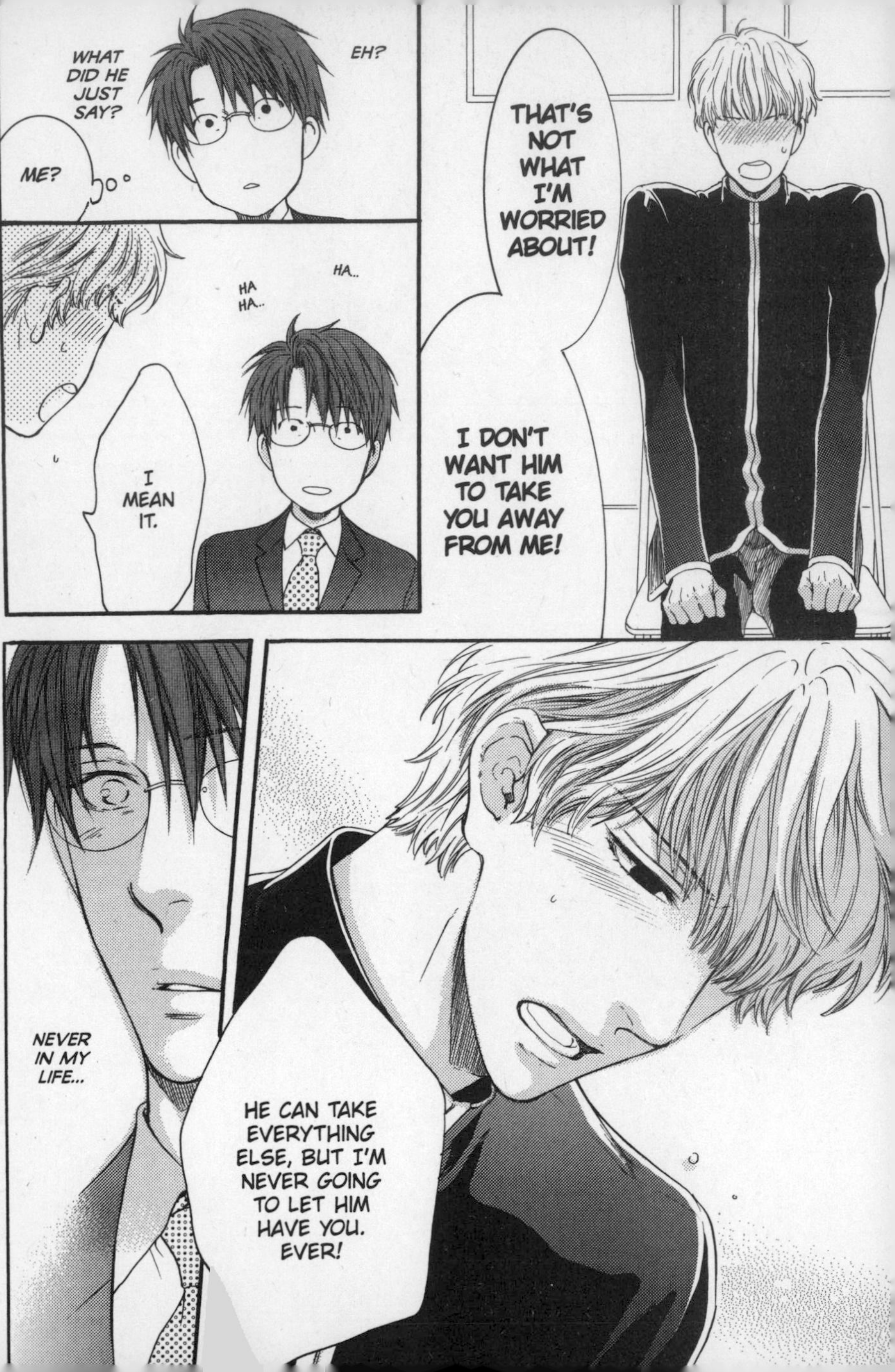
THAT'S NOT WHAT I'M WORRIED ABOUT!
I DON'T WANT HIM TO TAKE YOU AWAY FROM ME!
EH?
WHAT DID HE JUST SAY?
ME?
HA...
HA HA...
I MEAN IT.
HE CAN TAKE EVERYTHING ELSE, BUT I'M NEVER GOING TO LET HIM HAVE YOU. EVER!
NEVER IN MY LIFE...

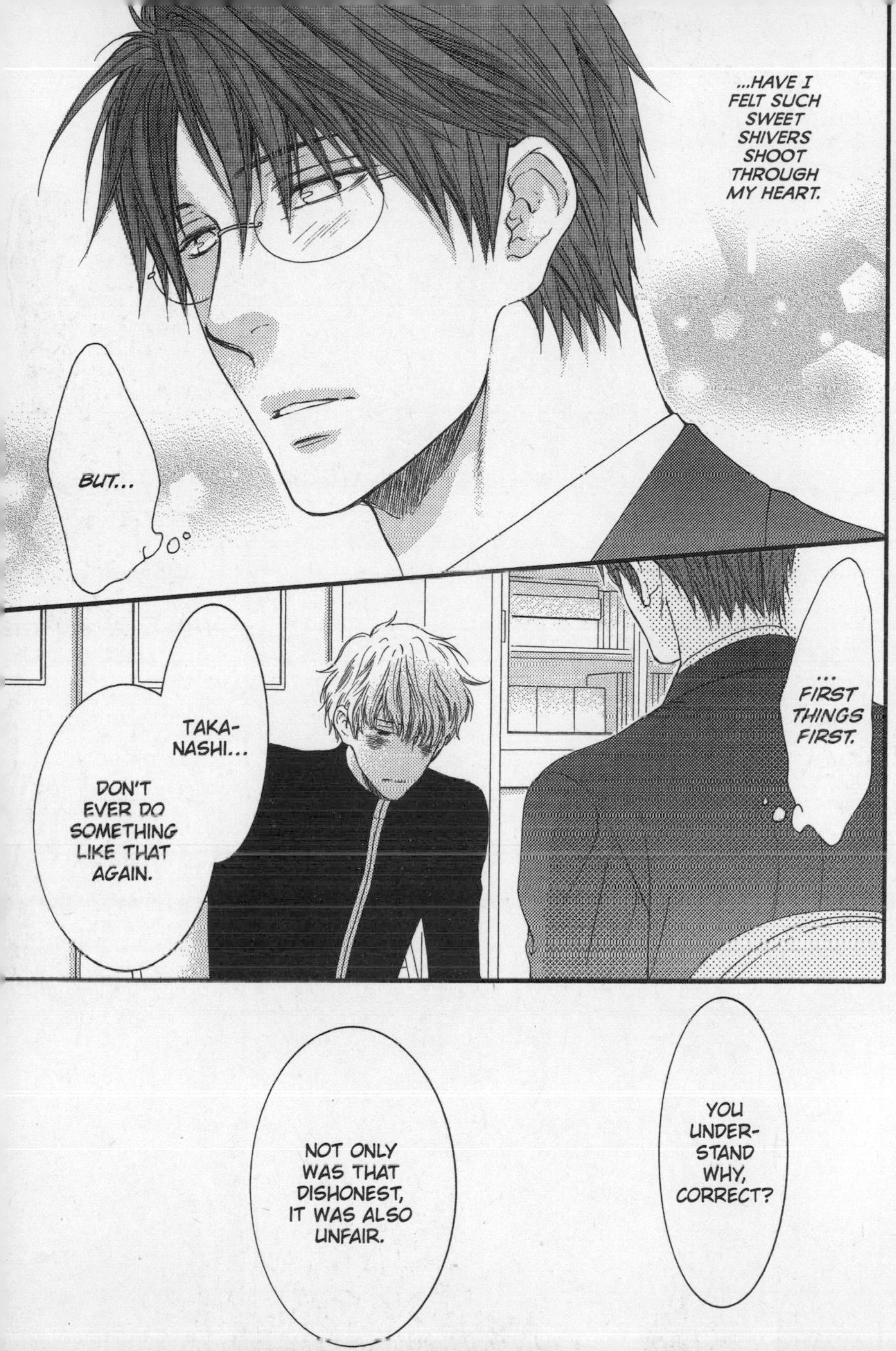
...HAVE I FELT SUCH SWEET SHIVERS SHOOT THROUGH MY HEART.
BUT...
...FIRST THINGS FIRST.
TAKA-NASHI...
DON'T EVER DO SOMETHING LIKE THAT AGAIN.
YOU UNDER-STAND WHY, CORRECT?
NOT ONLY WAS THAT DISHONEST, IT WAS ALSO UNFAIR.

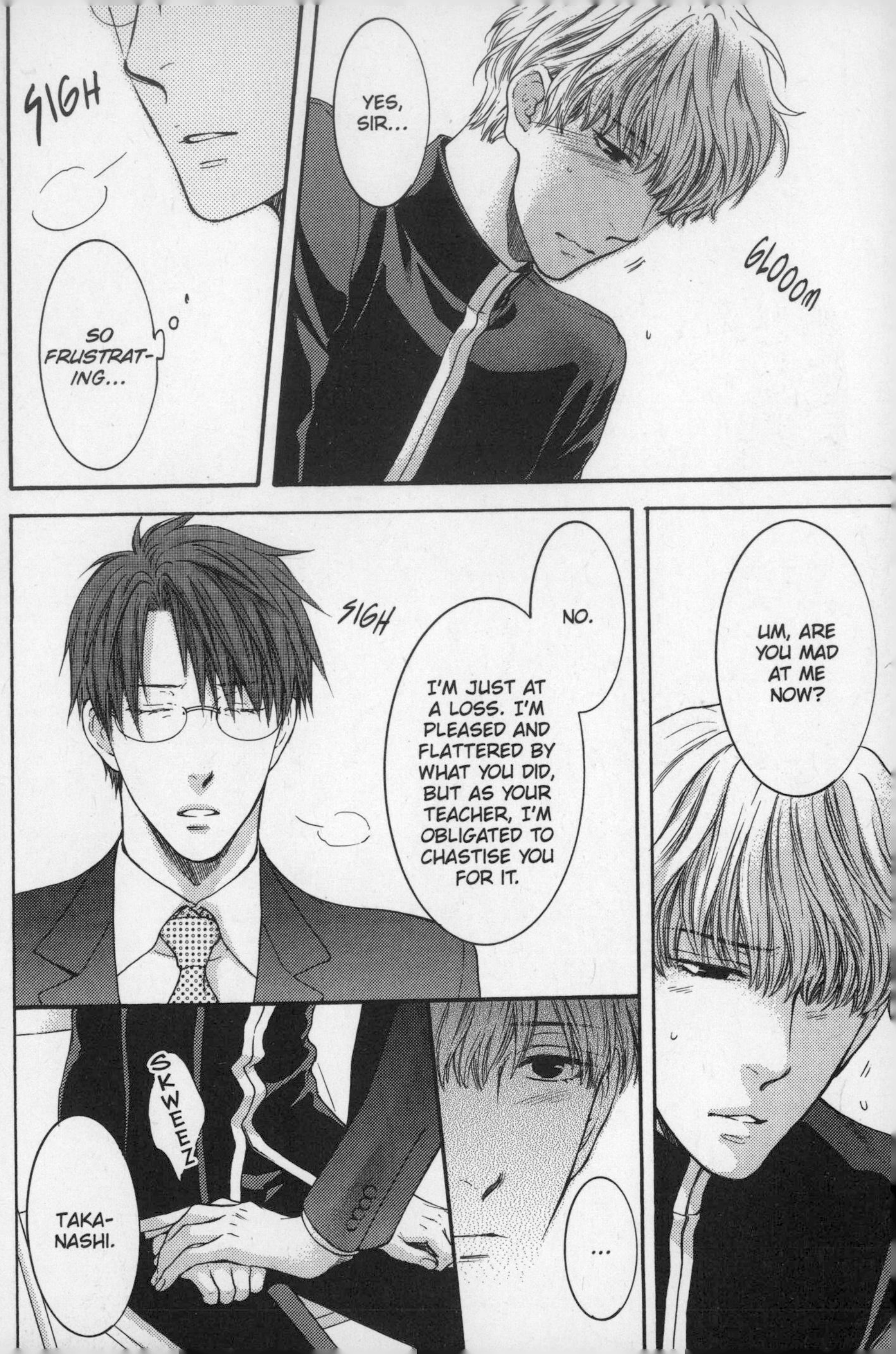
YES, SIR...
GLOOOM
SIGH
SO FRUSTRAT-ING...
UM, ARE YOU MAD AT ME NOW?
NO.
I'M JUST AT A LOSS. I'M PLEASED AND FLATTERED BY WHAT YOU DID, BUT AS YOUR TEACHER, I'M OBLIGATED TO CHASTISE YOU FOR IT.
SIGH
...
SKWEEZ
TAKA-NASHI.

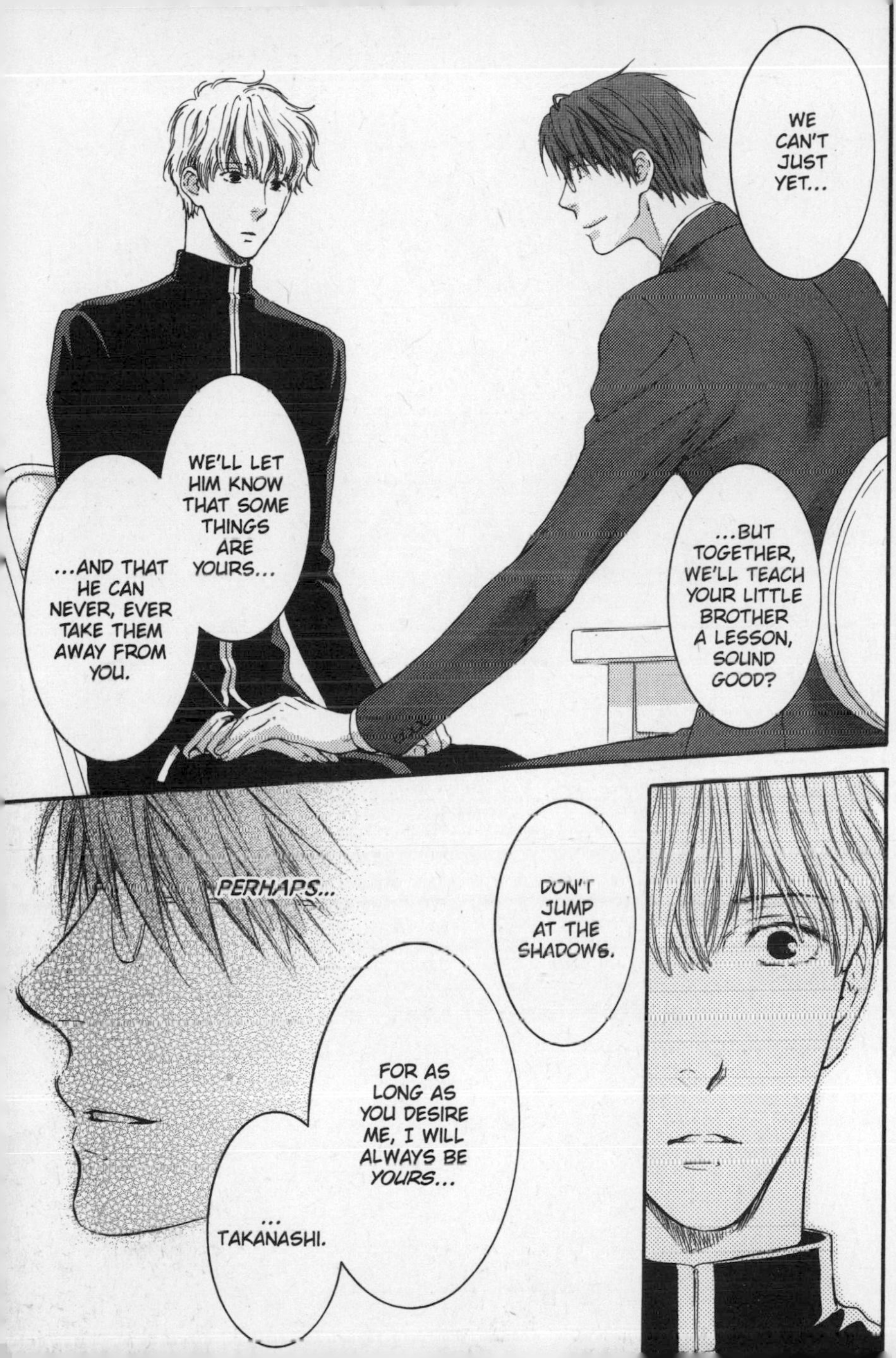
WE CAN'T JUST YET...
...BUT TOGETHER, WE'LL TEACH YOUR LITTLE BROTHER A LESSON, SOUND GOOD?
WE'LL LET HIM KNOW THAT SOME THINGS ARE YOURS...
...AND THAT HE CAN NEVER, EVER TAKE THEM AWAY FROM YOU.
DON'T JUMP AT THE SHADOWS.
PERHAPS...
FOR AS LONG AS YOU DESIRE ME, I WILL ALWAYS BE *YOURS*...
... TAKANASHI.

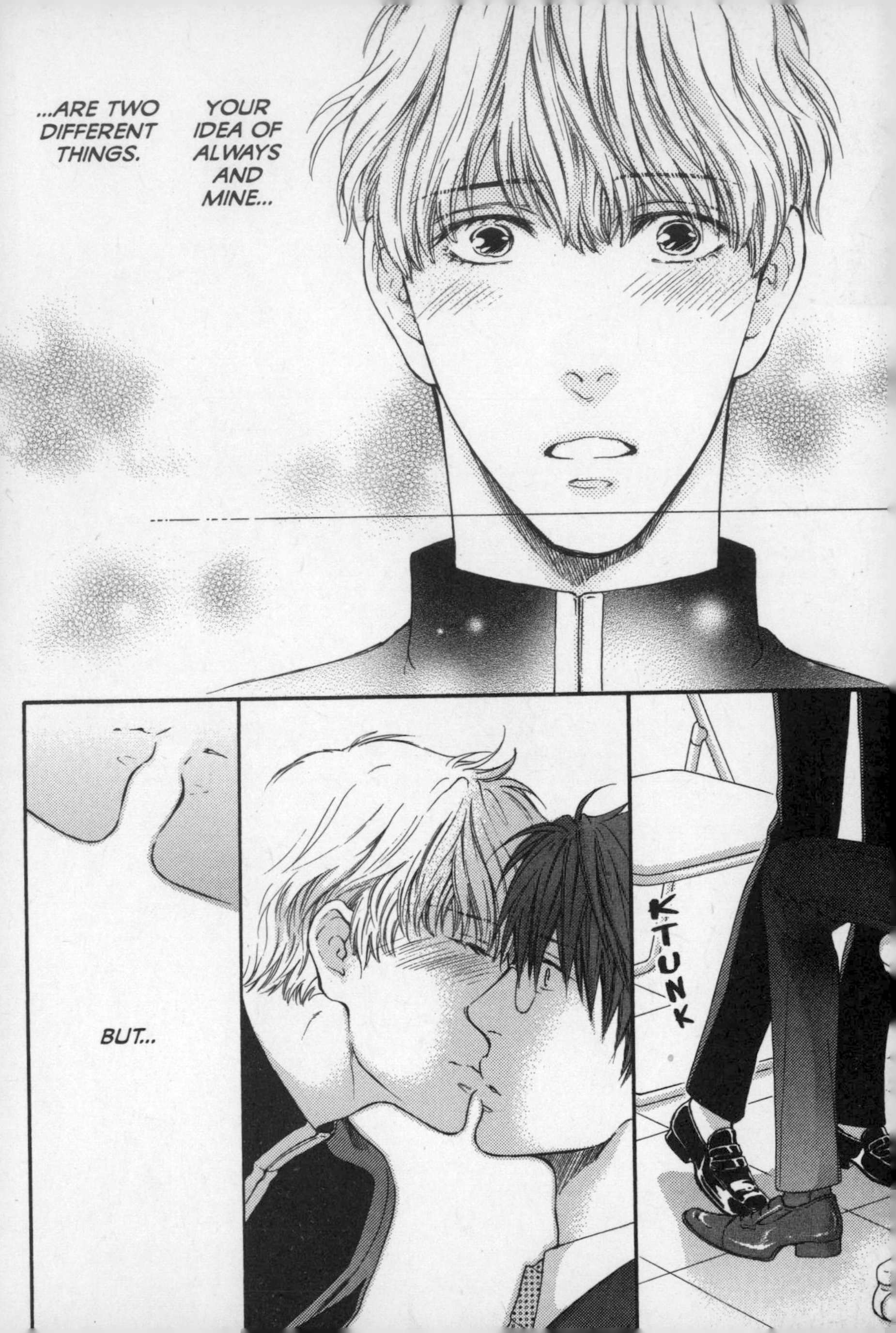
YOUR IDEA OF ALWAYS AND MINE...
...ARE TWO DIFFERENT THINGS.
KTUNK
BUT...

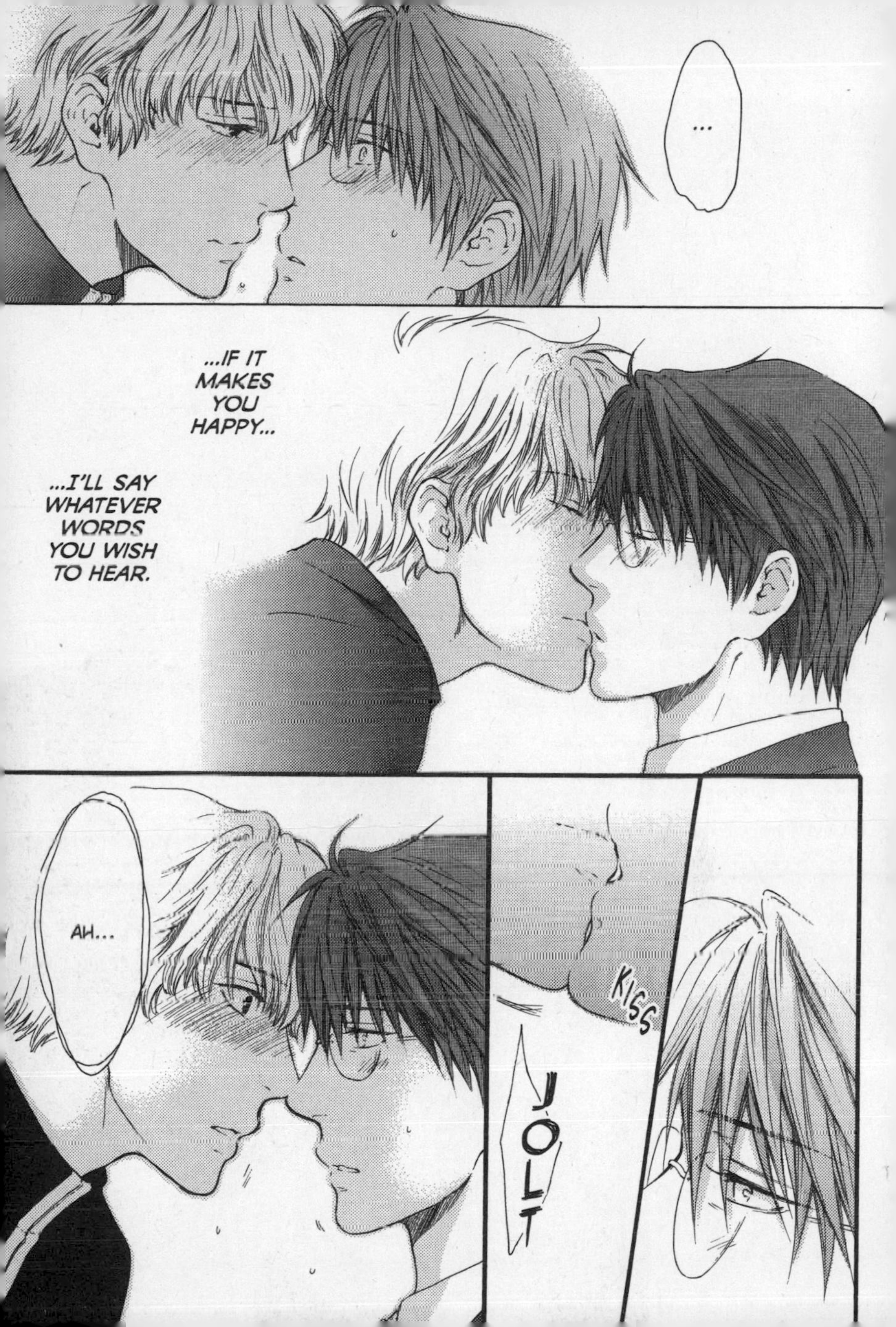
...
...IF IT MAKES YOU HAPPY...
...I'LL SAY WHATEVER WORDS YOU WISH TO HEAR.
KISS
JOLT
AH...

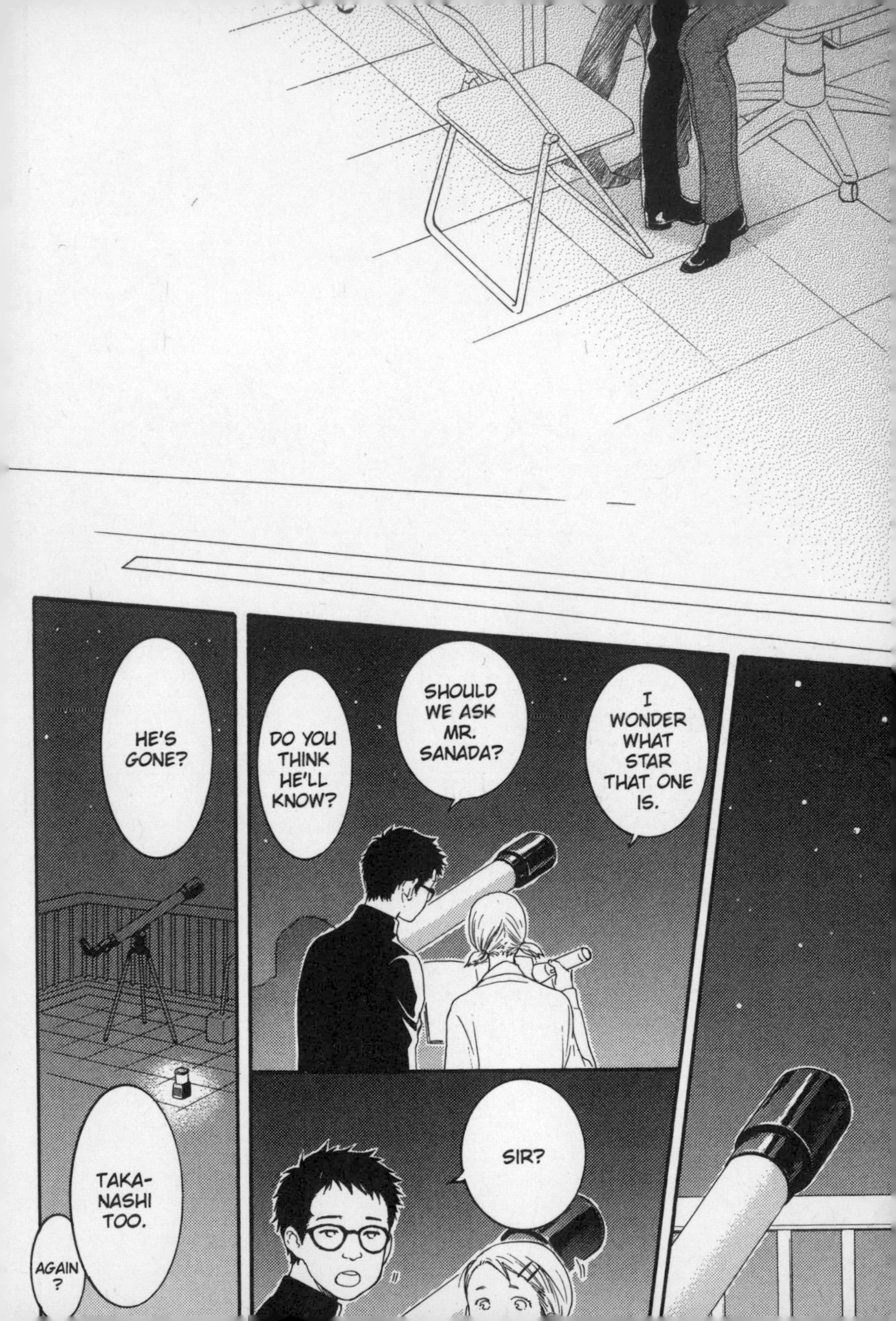
I WONDER WHAT STAR THAT ONE IS.
SHOULD WE ASK MR. SANADA?
DO YOU THINK HE'LL KNOW?
SIR?
HE'S GONE?
TAKA-NASHI TOO.
AGAIN?

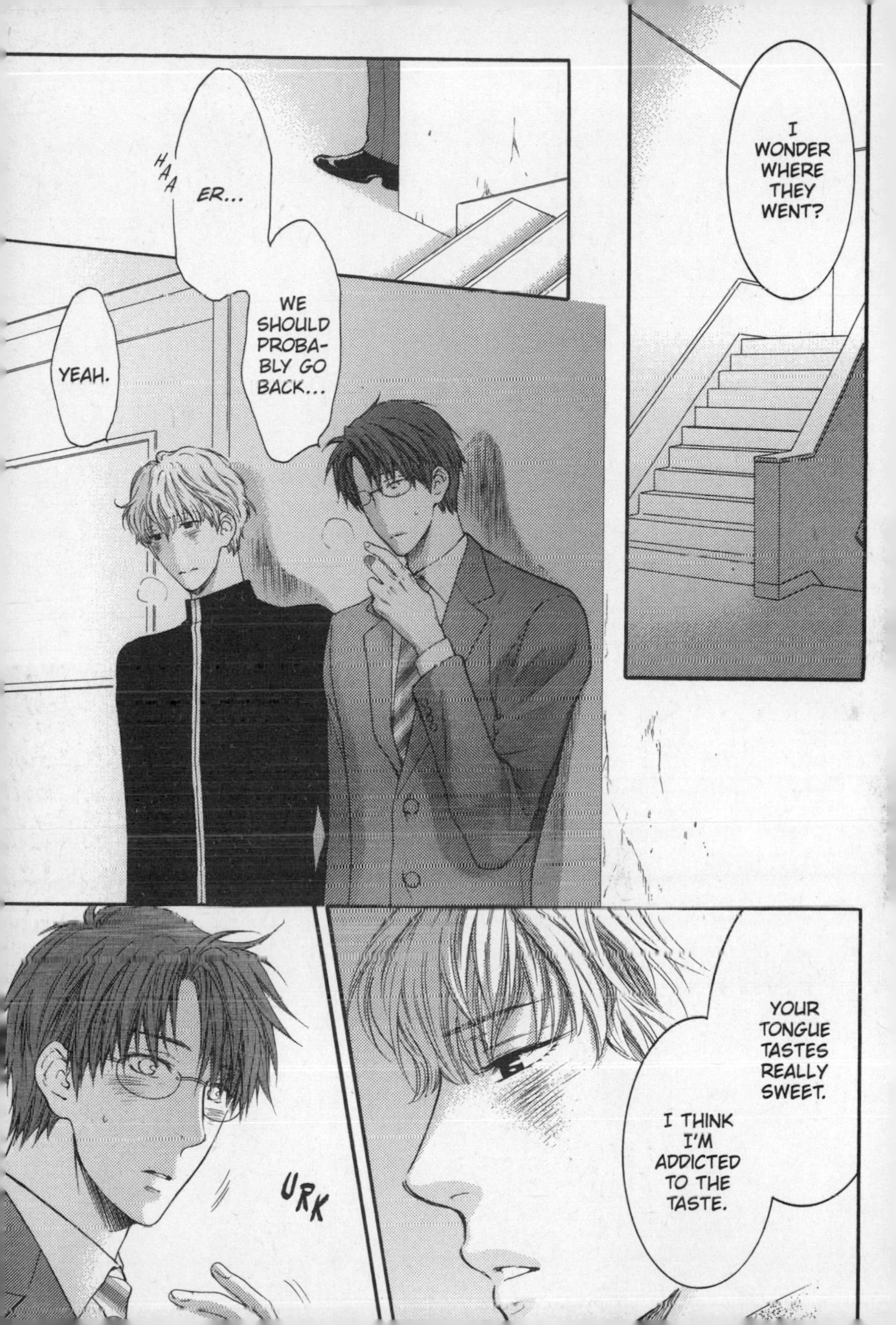
I WONDER WHERE THEY WENT?
HAA
ER...
WE SHOULD PROBA-BLY GO BACK...
YEAH.
YOUR TONGUE TASTES REALLY SWEET.
I THINK I'M ADDICTED TO THE TASTE.
URK

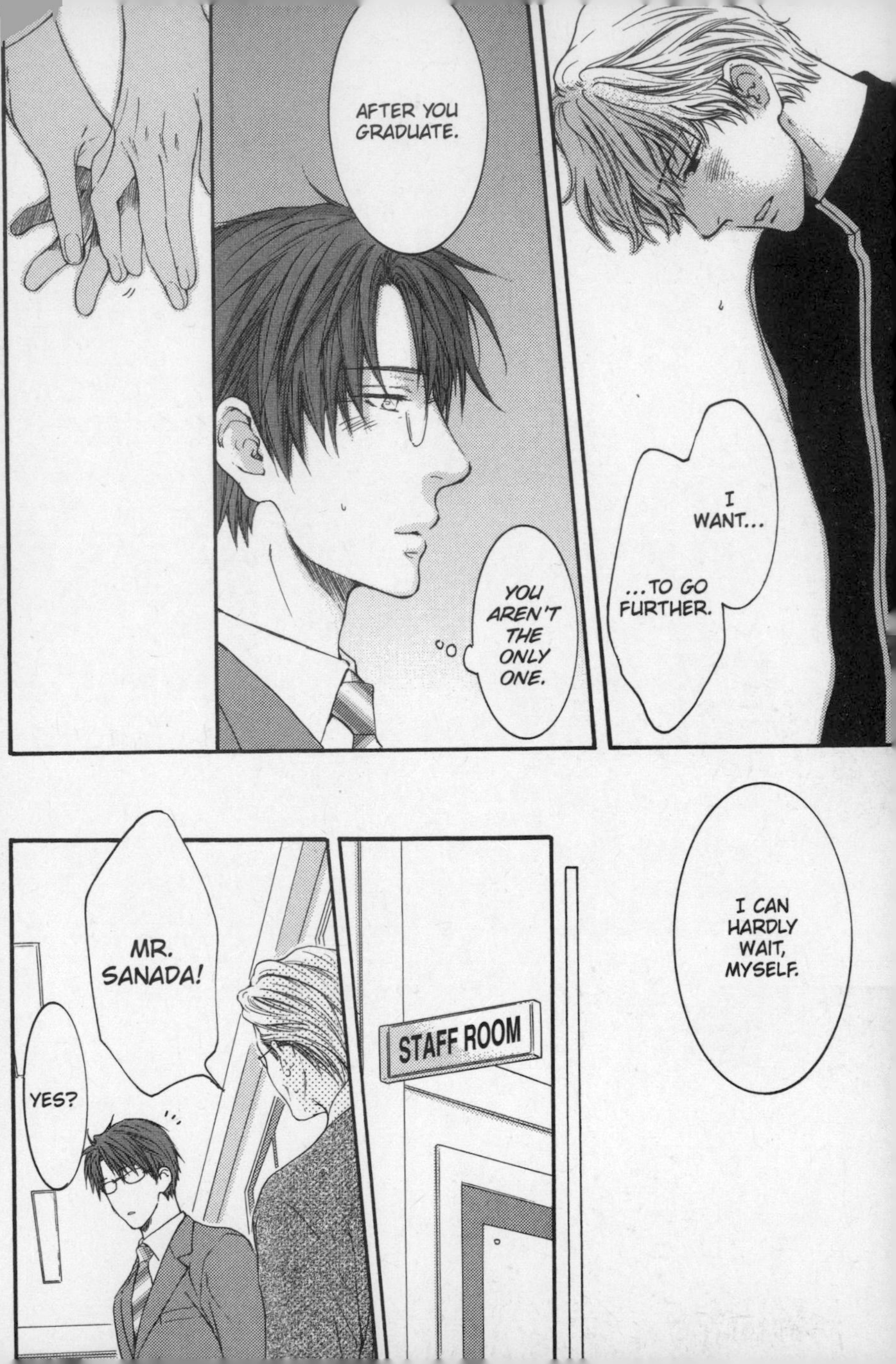
I WANT...
...TO GO FURTHER.
AFTER YOU GRADUATE.
YOU AREN'T THE ONLY ONE.
I CAN HARDLY WAIT, MYSELF.
STAFF ROOM
MR. SANADA!
YES?

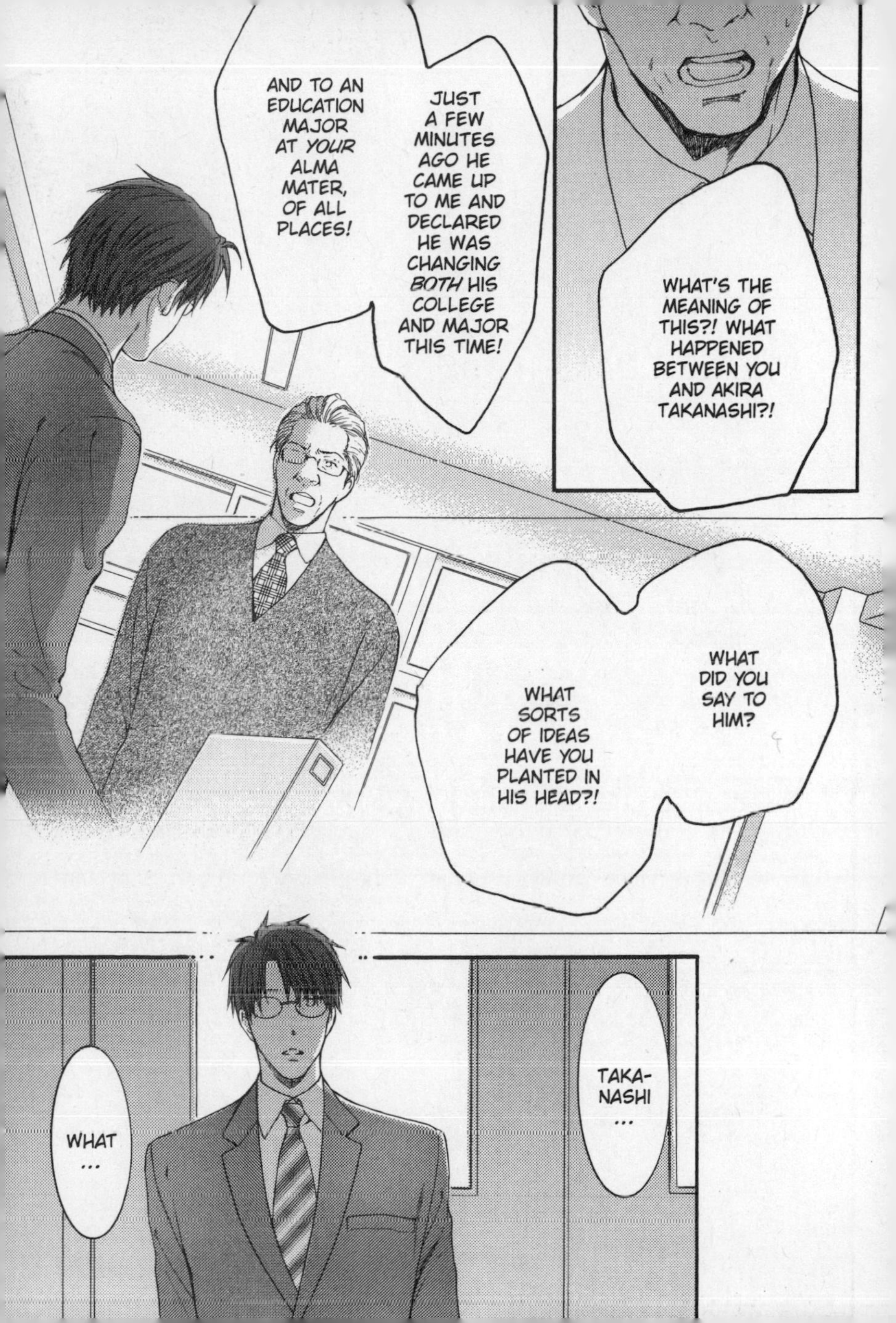
WHAT'S THE MEANING OF THIS?! WHAT HAPPENED BETWEEN YOU AND AKIRA TAKANASHI?!
JUST A FEW MINUTES AGO HE CAME UP TO ME AND DECLARED HE WAS CHANGING *BOTH* HIS COLLEGE AND MAJOR THIS TIME!
AND TO AN EDUCATION MAJOR AT *YOUR* ALMA MATER, OF ALL PLACES!
WHAT DID YOU SAY TO HIM?
WHAT SORTS OF IDEAS HAVE YOU PLANTED IN HIS HEAD?!
...
...
TAKA-NASHI ...
WHAT ...

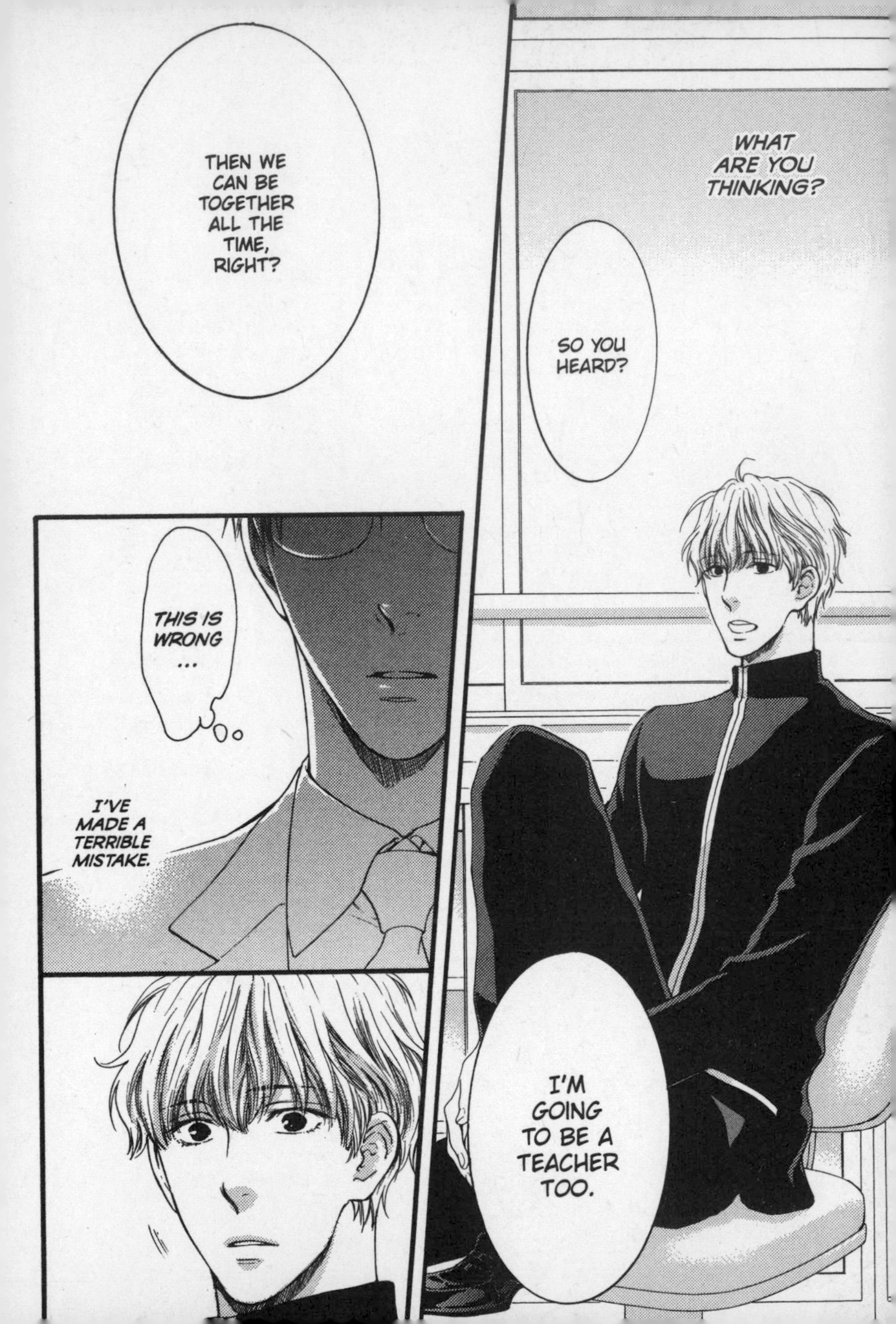
WHAT ARE YOU THINKING?
SO YOU HEARD?
I'M GOING TO BE A TEACHER TOO.
THEN WE CAN BE TOGETHER ALL THE TIME, RIGHT?
THIS IS WRONG ...
I'VE MADE A TERRIBLE MISTAKE.

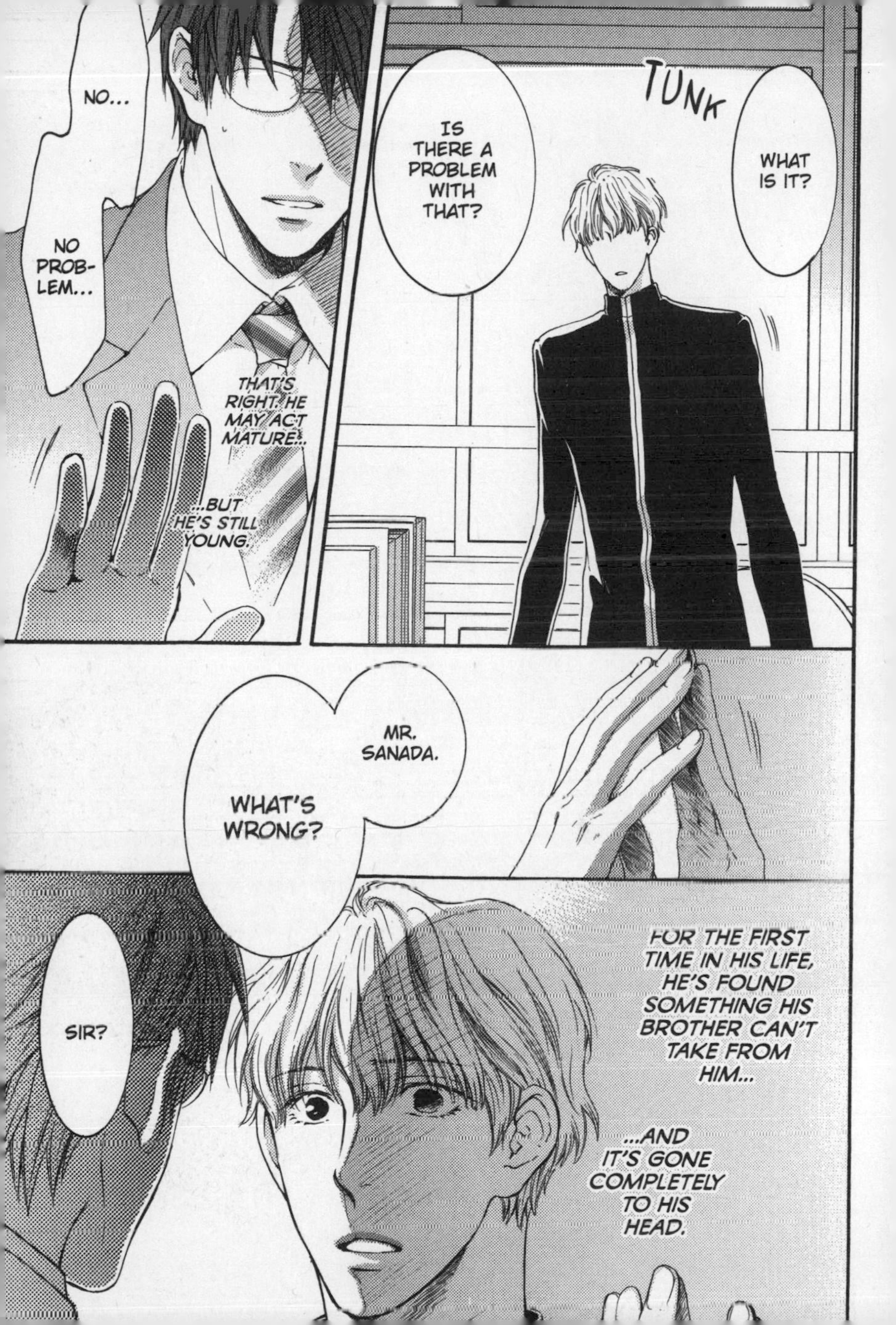
TUNK
WHAT IS IT?
IS THERE A PROBLEM WITH THAT?
NO...
NO PROBLEM...
THAT'S RIGHT. HE MAY ACT MATURE...
...BUT HE'S STILL YOUNG.
MR. SANADA.
WHAT'S WRONG?
FOR THE FIRST TIME IN HIS LIFE, HE'S FOUND SOMETHING HIS BROTHER CAN'T TAKE FROM HIM...
...AND IT'S GONE COMPLETELY TO HIS HEAD.
SIR?

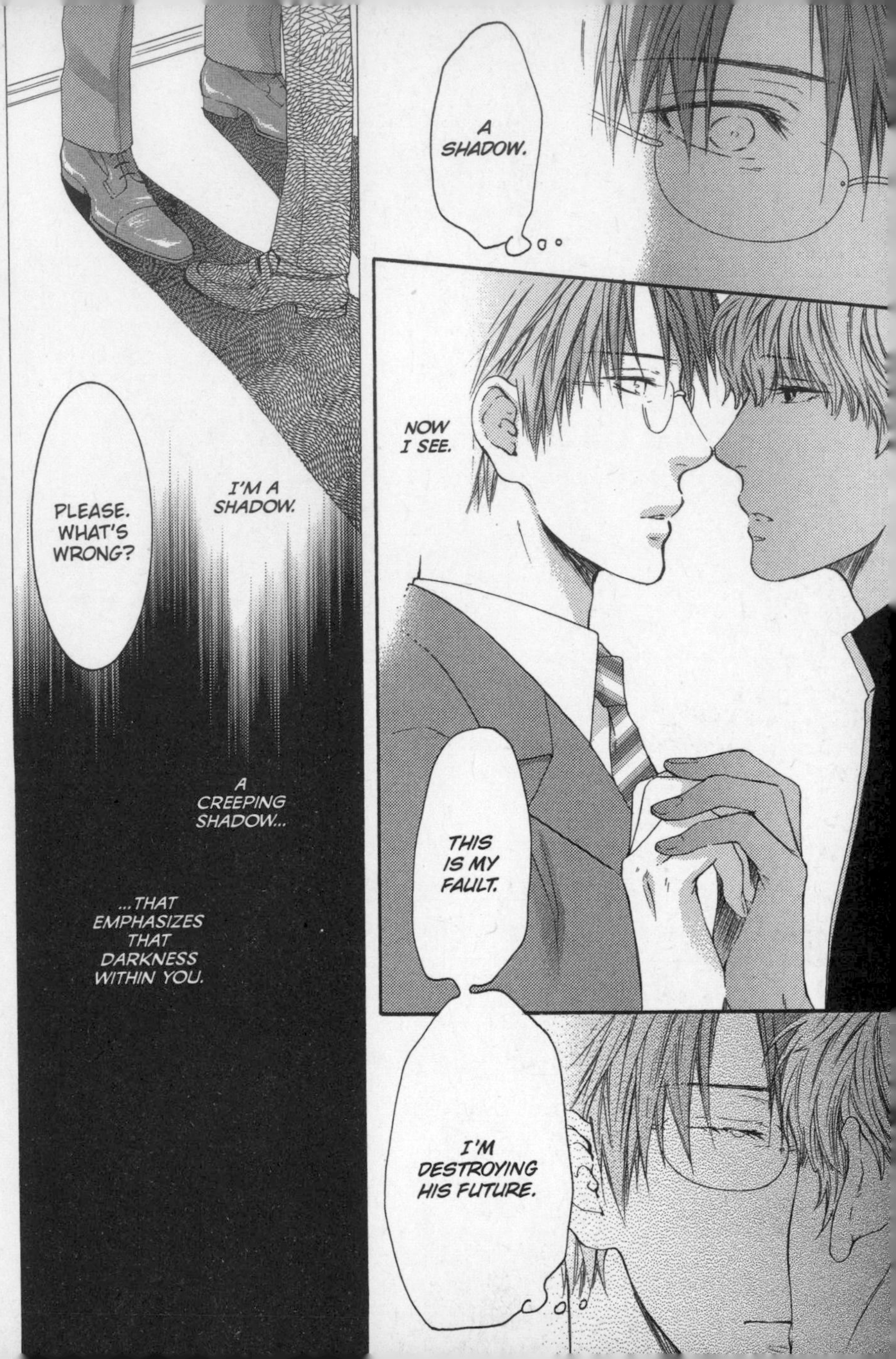
A SHADOW.
NOW I SEE.
THIS IS MY FAULT.
I'M DESTROYING HIS FUTURE.
I'M A SHADOW.
PLEASE. WHAT'S WRONG?
A CREEPING SHADOW...
...THAT EMPHASIZES THAT DARKNESS WITHIN YOU.

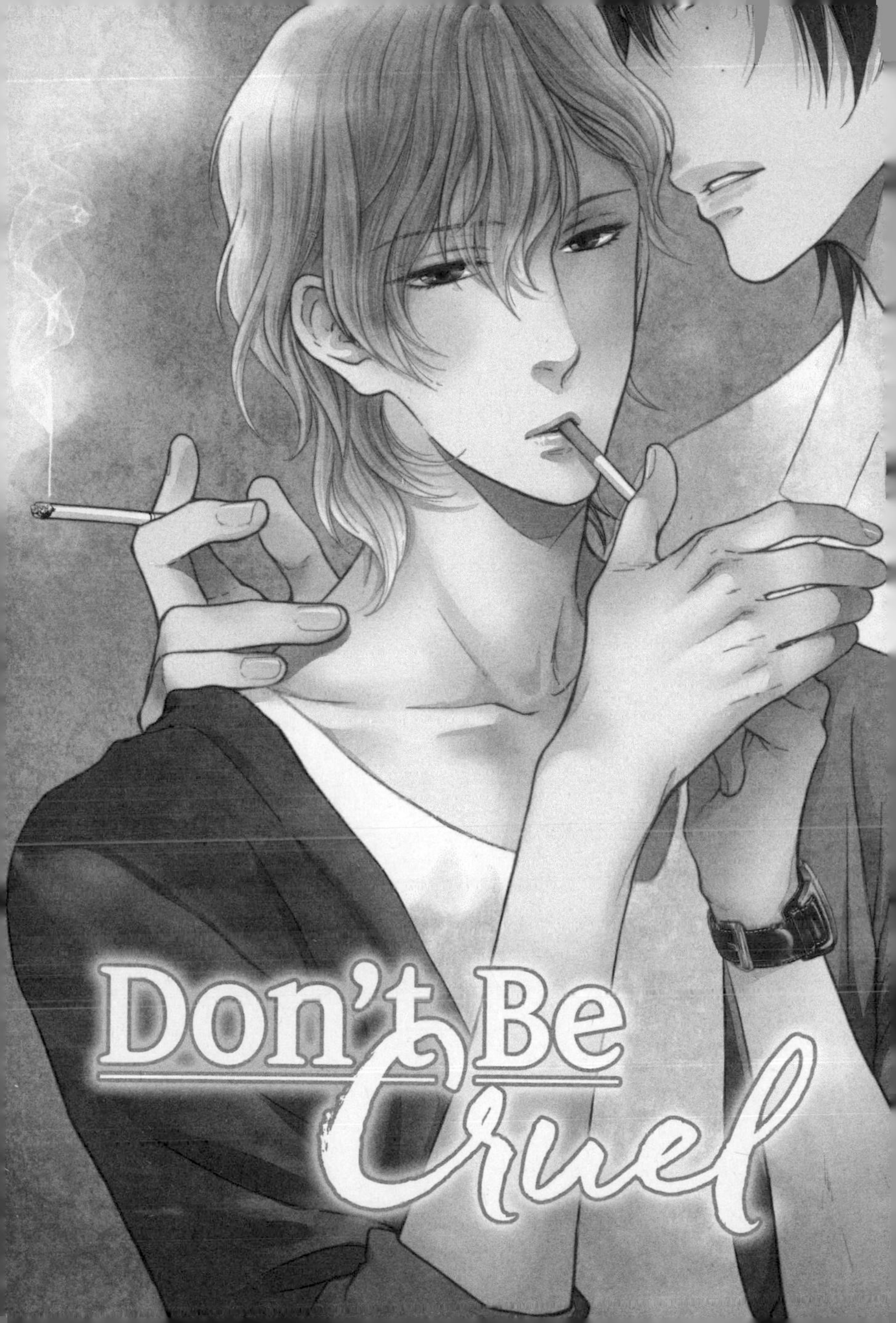
Don’t Be
Cruel

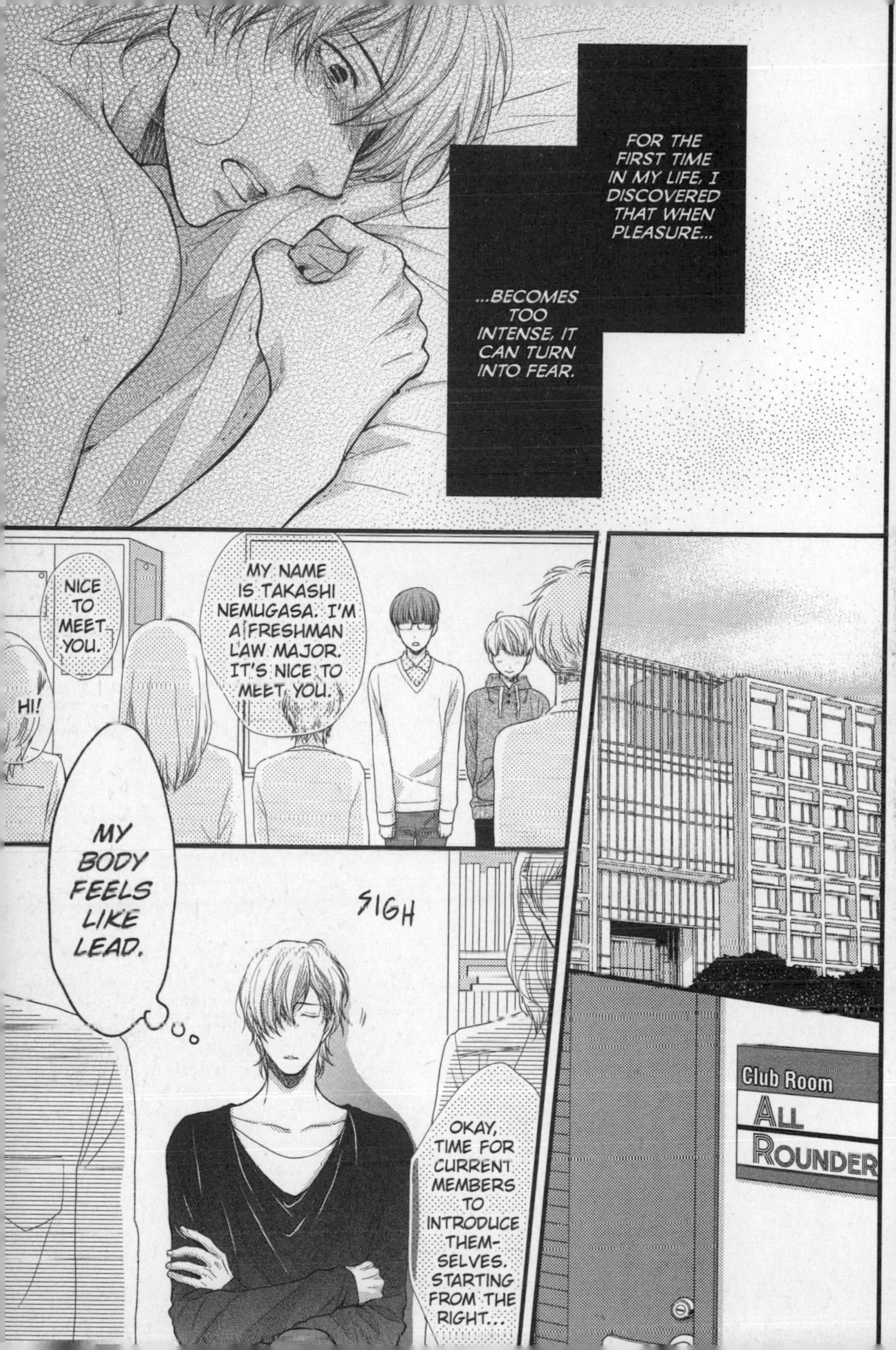
FOR THE FIRST TIME IN MY LIFE, I DISCOVERED THAT WHEN PLEASURE...
...BECOMES TOO INTENSE, IT CAN TURN INTO FEAR.
Club Room
ALL ROUNDER
MY NAME IS TAKASHI NEMUGASA. I'M A FRESHMAN LAW MAJOR. IT'S NICE TO MEET YOU.
NICE TO MEET YOU.
HI!
OKAY, TIME FOR CURRENT MEMBERS TO INTRODUCE THEM-SELVES. STARTING FROM THE RIGHT...
SIGH
MY BODY FEELS LIKE LEAD.

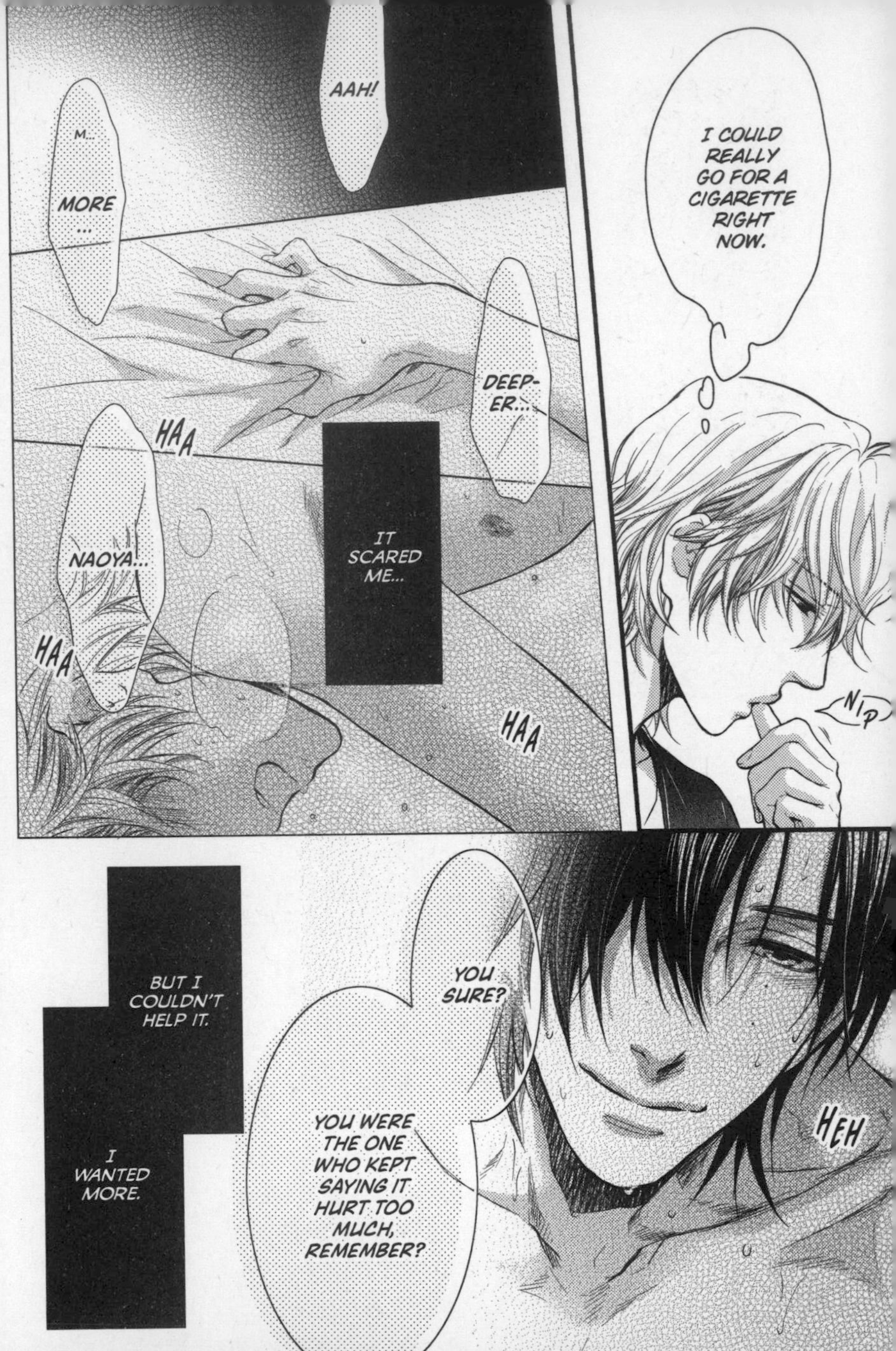
I COULD REALLY GO FOR A CIGARETTE RIGHT NOW.
NIP
AAH!
M... MORE...
DEEPER...
IT SCARED ME...
HAA
NAOYA...
HAA
HAA
YOU SURE?
HEH
YOU WERE THE ONE WHO KEPT SAYING IT HURT TOO MUCH, REMEMBER?
BUT I COULDN'T HELP IT.
I WANTED MORE.

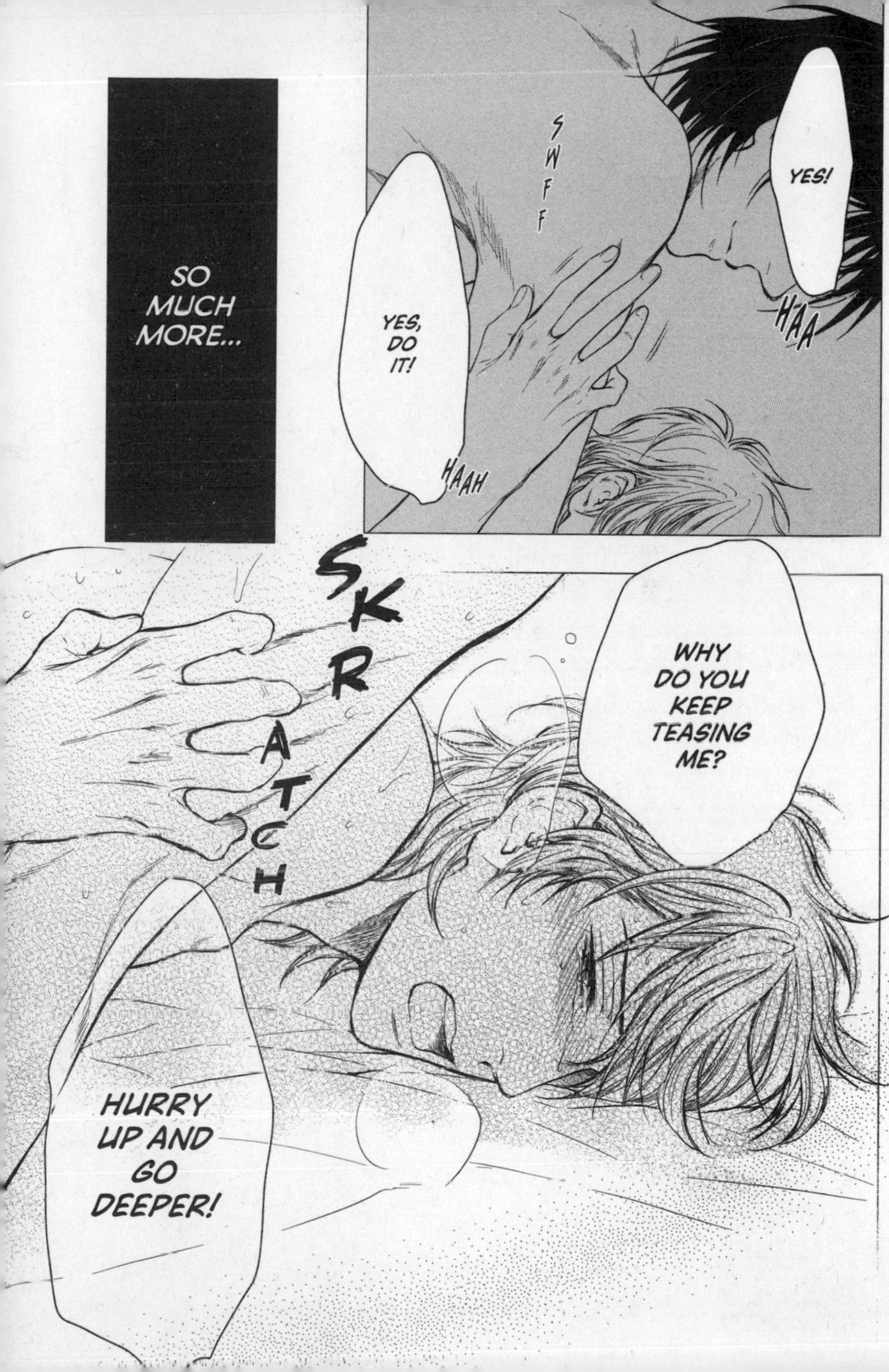
YES!
SWFF
HAA
YES, DO IT!
HAAH
SO MUCH MORE...
WHY DO YOU KEEP TEASING ME?
SKRATCH
HURRY UP AND GO DEEPER!

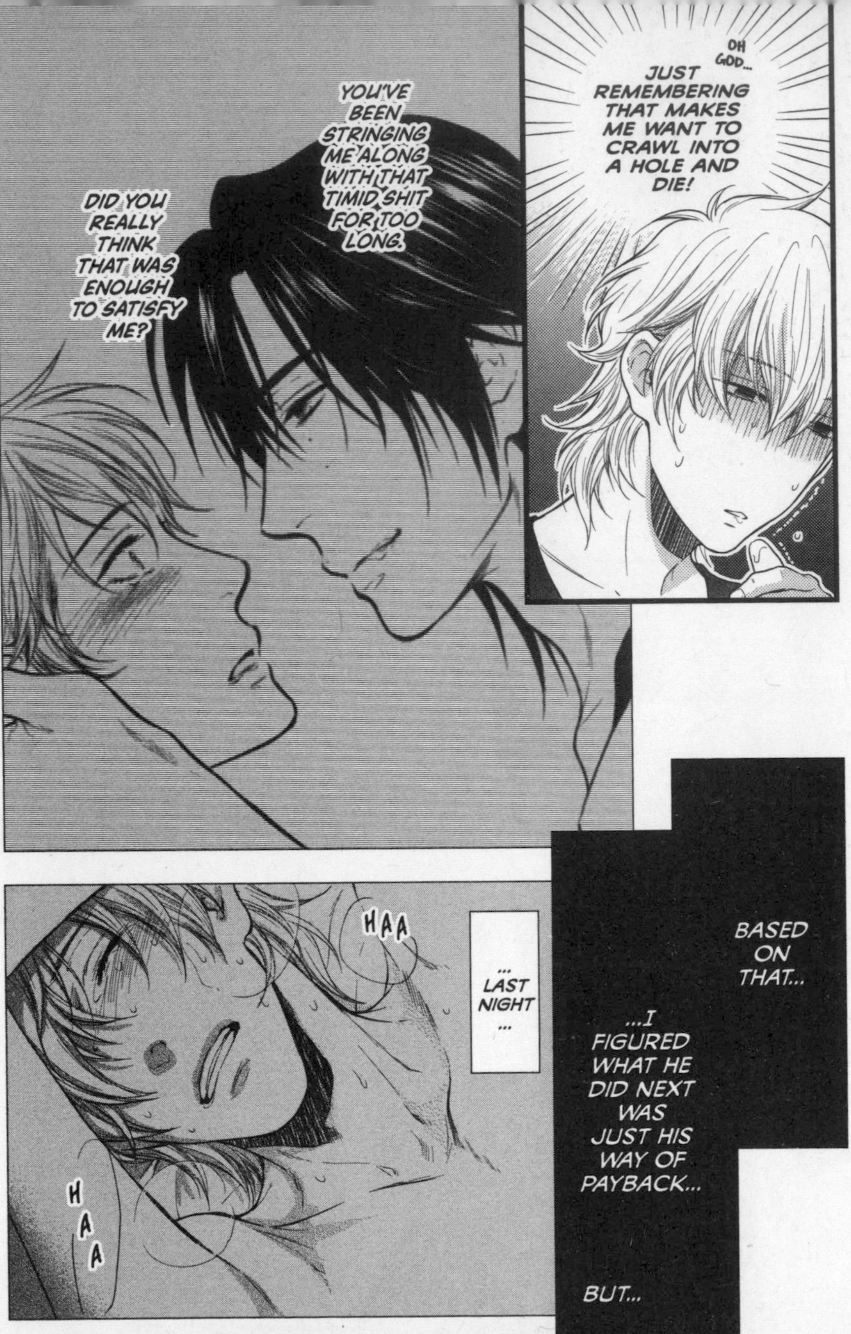
OH GOD...
JUST REMEMBERING THAT MAKES ME WANT TO CRAWL INTO A HOLE AND DIE!
YOU'VE BEEN STRINGING ME ALONG WITH THAT TIMID SHIT FOR TOO LONG.
DID YOU REALLY THINK THAT WAS ENOUGH TO SATISFY ME?
BASED ON THAT...
...I FIGURED WHAT HE DID NEXT WAS JUST HIS WAY OF PAYBACK...
BUT...
...LAST NIGHT...
HAA
HAA

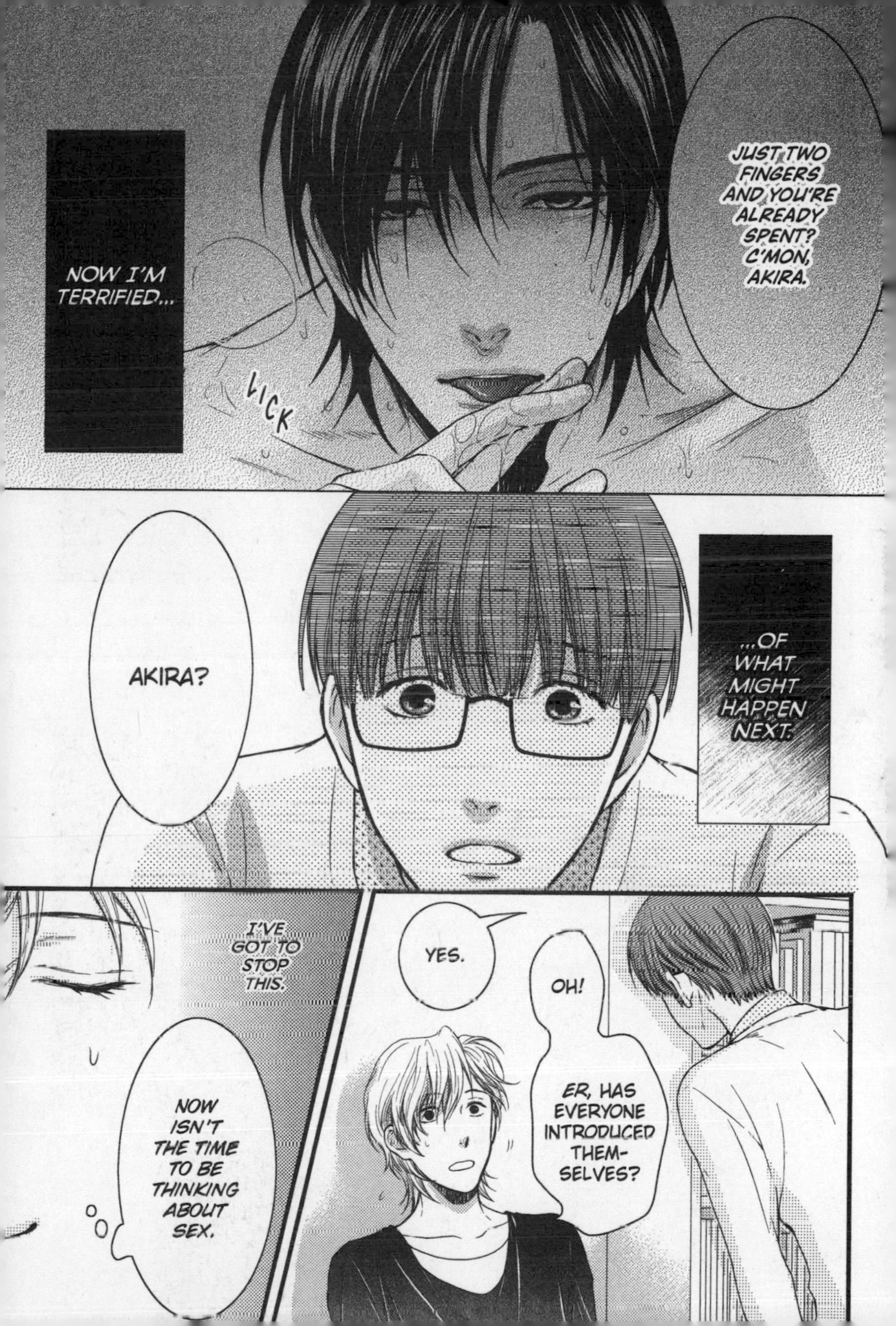
JUST TWO FINGERS AND YOU'RE ALREADY SPENT? C'MON, AKIRA.
LICK
NOW I'M TERRIFIED...
...OF WHAT MIGHT HAPPEN NEXT.
AKIRA?
YES.
OH!
ER, HAS EVERYONE INTRODUCED THEM-SELVES?
I'VE GOT TO STOP THIS.
NOW ISN'T THE TIME TO BE THINKING ABOUT SEX.

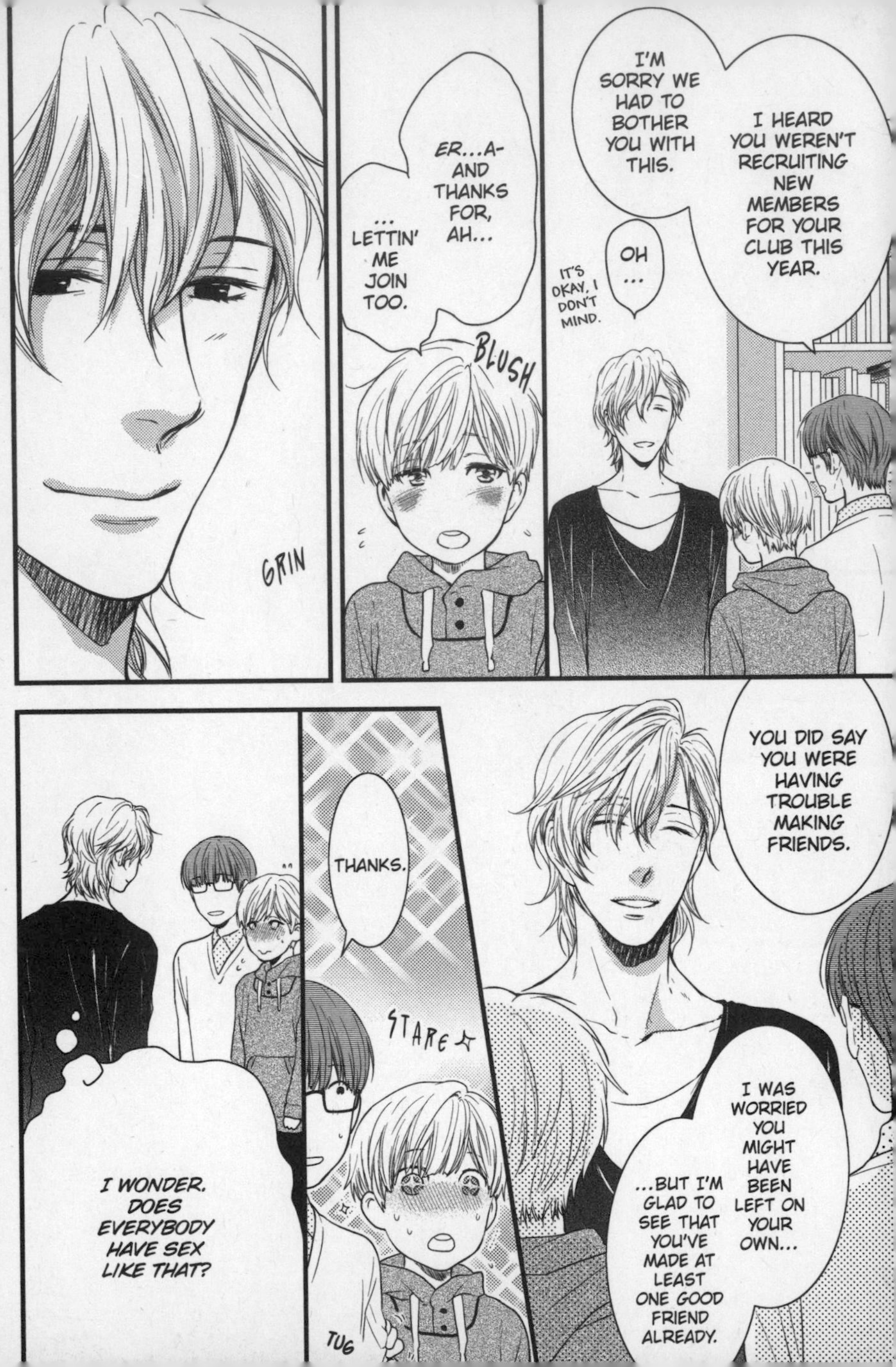
I HEARD YOU WEREN'T RECRUITING NEW MEMBERS FOR YOUR CLUB THIS YEAR.
I'M SORRY WE HAD TO BOTHER YOU WITH THIS.
OH ...
IT'S OKAY, I DON'T MIND.
ER...A-AND THANKS FOR, AH...
...LETTIN' ME JOIN TOO.
BLUSH
GRIN
YOU DID SAY YOU WERE HAVING TROUBLE MAKING FRIENDS.
I WAS WORRIED YOU MIGHT HAVE BEEN LEFT ON YOUR OWN...
...BUT I'M GLAD TO SEE THAT YOU'VE MADE AT LEAST ONE GOOD FRIEND ALREADY.
THANKS.
STARE
TUG
I WONDER. DOES EVERYBODY HAVE SEX LIKE THAT?

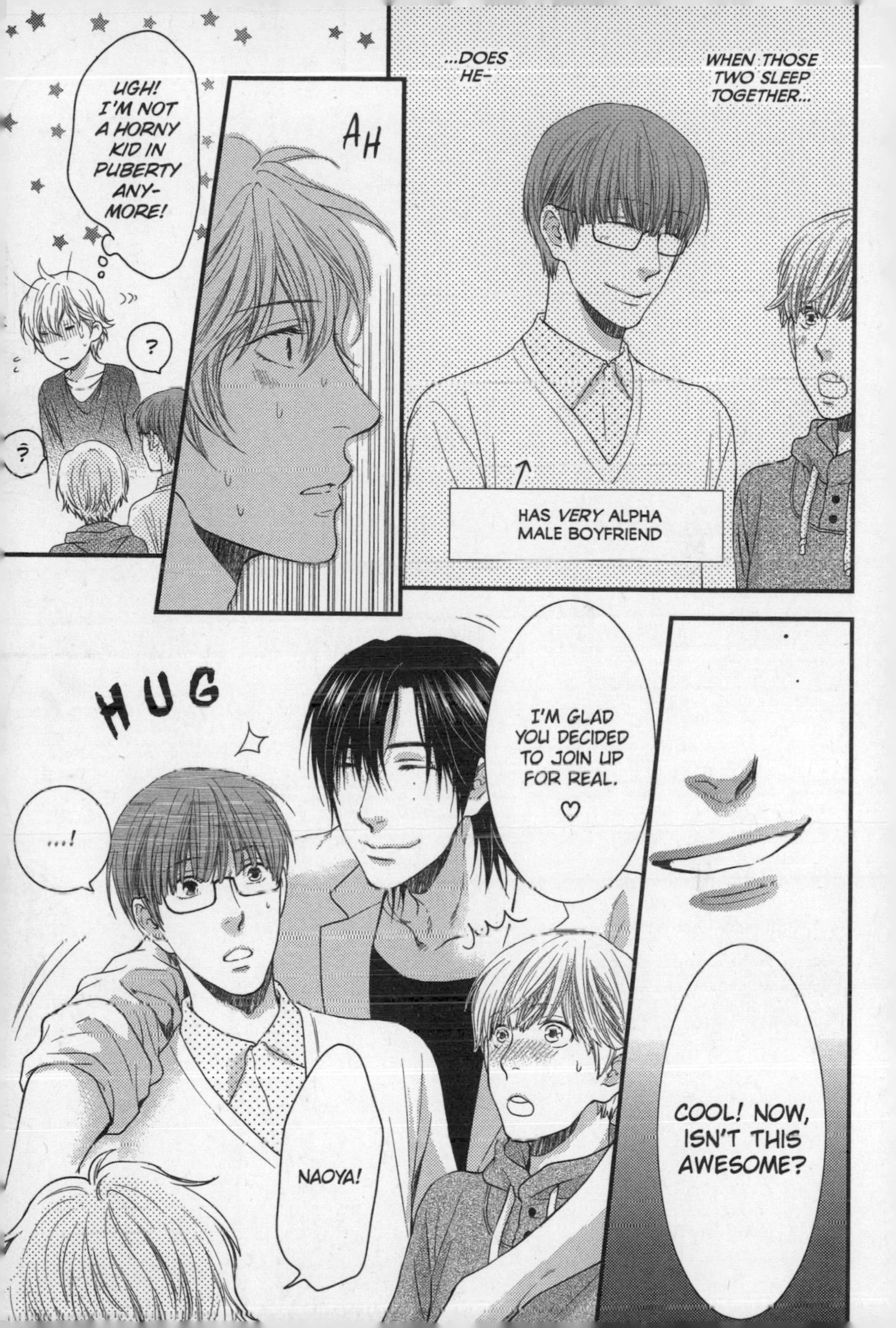
WHEN THOSE TWO SLEEP TOGETHER...
...DOES HE-
HAS VERY ALPHA MALE BOYFRIEND
AH
UGH! I'M NOT A HORNY KID IN PUBERTY ANYMORE!
?
?
COOL! NOW, ISN'T THIS AWESOME?
I'M GLAD YOU DECIDED TO JOIN UP FOR REAL. ♡
HUG
...!
NAOYA!

AKIRA CONSIDERS YOU ONE OF HIS FAVORITE UNDER-CLASSMEN, AFTER ALL.

DON'T WORRY ABOUT IT.

UM, A LOT OF PEOPLE TELL ME THAT I CAN BE DENSE AT TIMES, SO...

...THAT DAY I'M AFRAID I TOOK IT ALL AT FACE VALUE...

OH...

THAT?

I'M SORRY.

NERVOUS SMILE

BY THE WAY, DOES HIDEYUKI KNOW YOU'VE JOINED OUR CLUB?

YEAH.

HE TRIED TO STOP ME THOUGH.

AHA HA! FIG- URED.

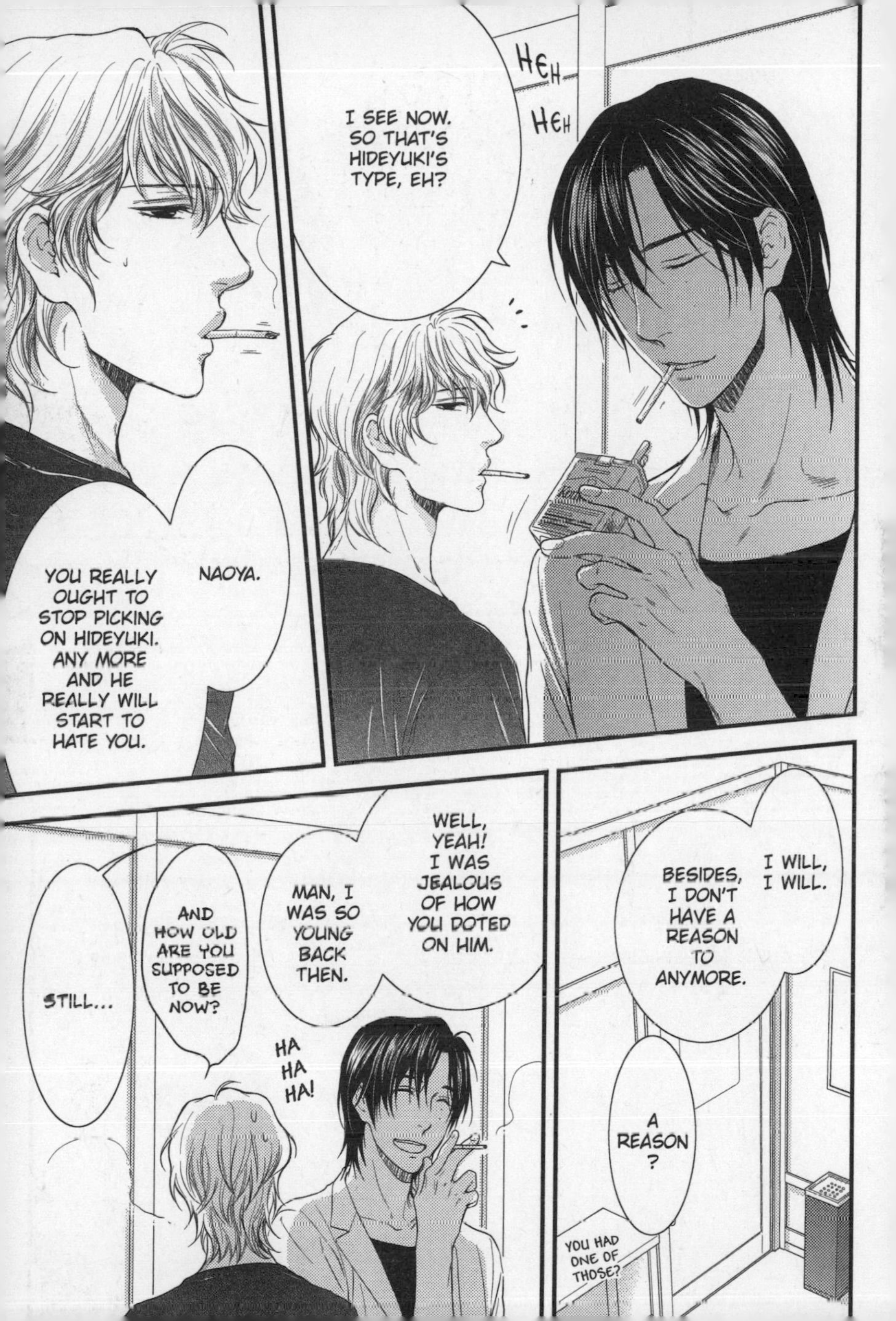
HEH
HEH
I SEE NOW. SO THAT'S HIDEYUKI'S TYPE, EH?
NAOYA.
YOU REALLY OUGHT TO STOP PICKING ON HIDEYUKI. ANY MORE AND HE REALLY WILL START TO HATE YOU.
I WILL, I WILL.
BESIDES, I DON'T HAVE A REASON TO ANYMORE.
A REASON?
YOU HAD ONE OF THOSE?
WELL, YEAH! I WAS JEALOUS OF HOW YOU DOTED ON HIM.
MAN, I WAS SO YOUNG BACK THEN.
HA HA HA!
AND HOW OLD ARE YOU SUPPOSED TO BE NOW?
STILL...

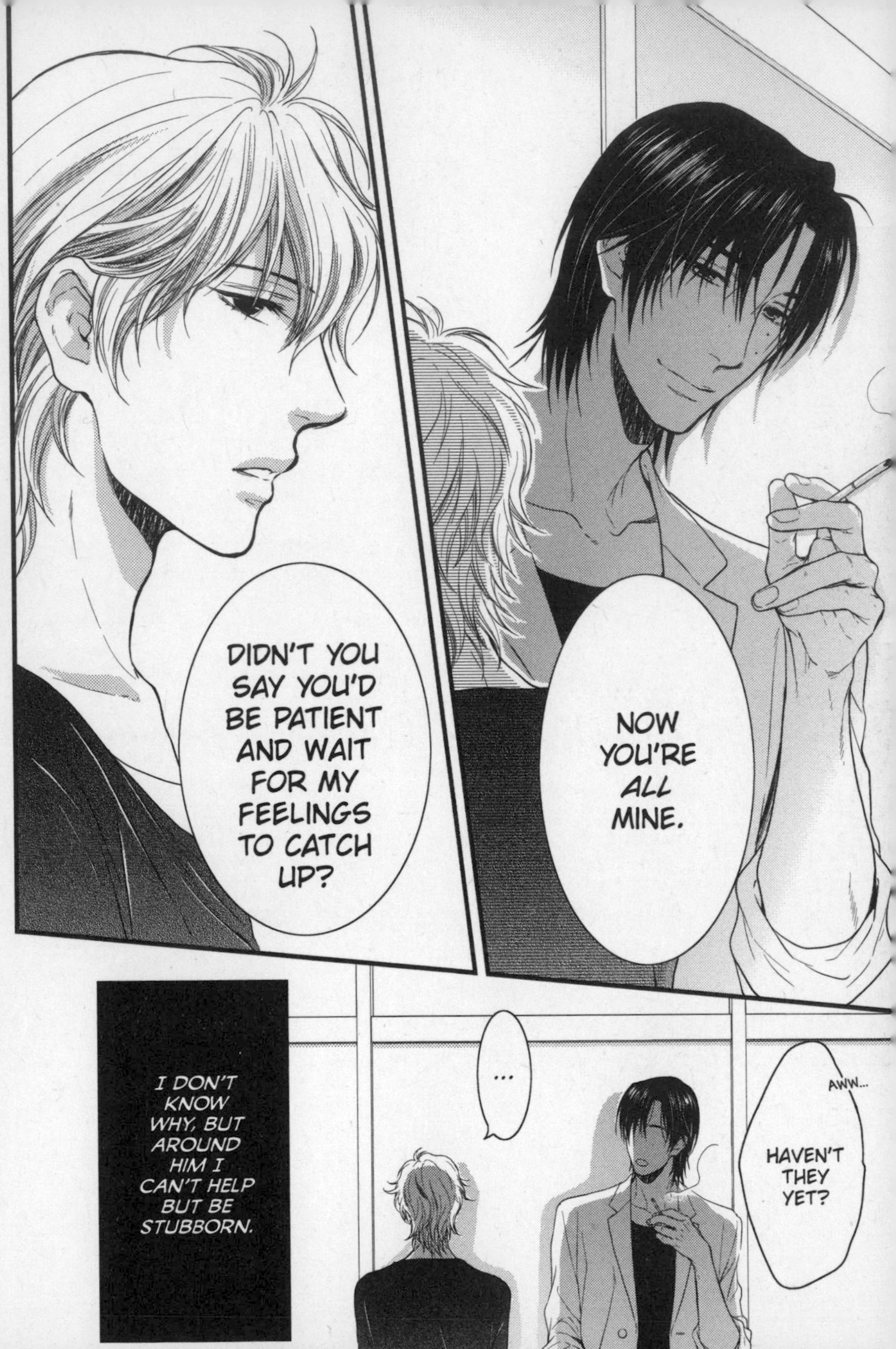
NOW YOU'RE ALL MINE.
DIDN'T YOU SAY YOU'D BE PATIENT AND WAIT FOR MY FEELINGS TO CATCH UP?
AWW...
HAVEN'T THEY YET?
...
I DON'T KNOW WHY, BUT AROUND HIM I CAN'T HELP BUT BE STUBBORN.

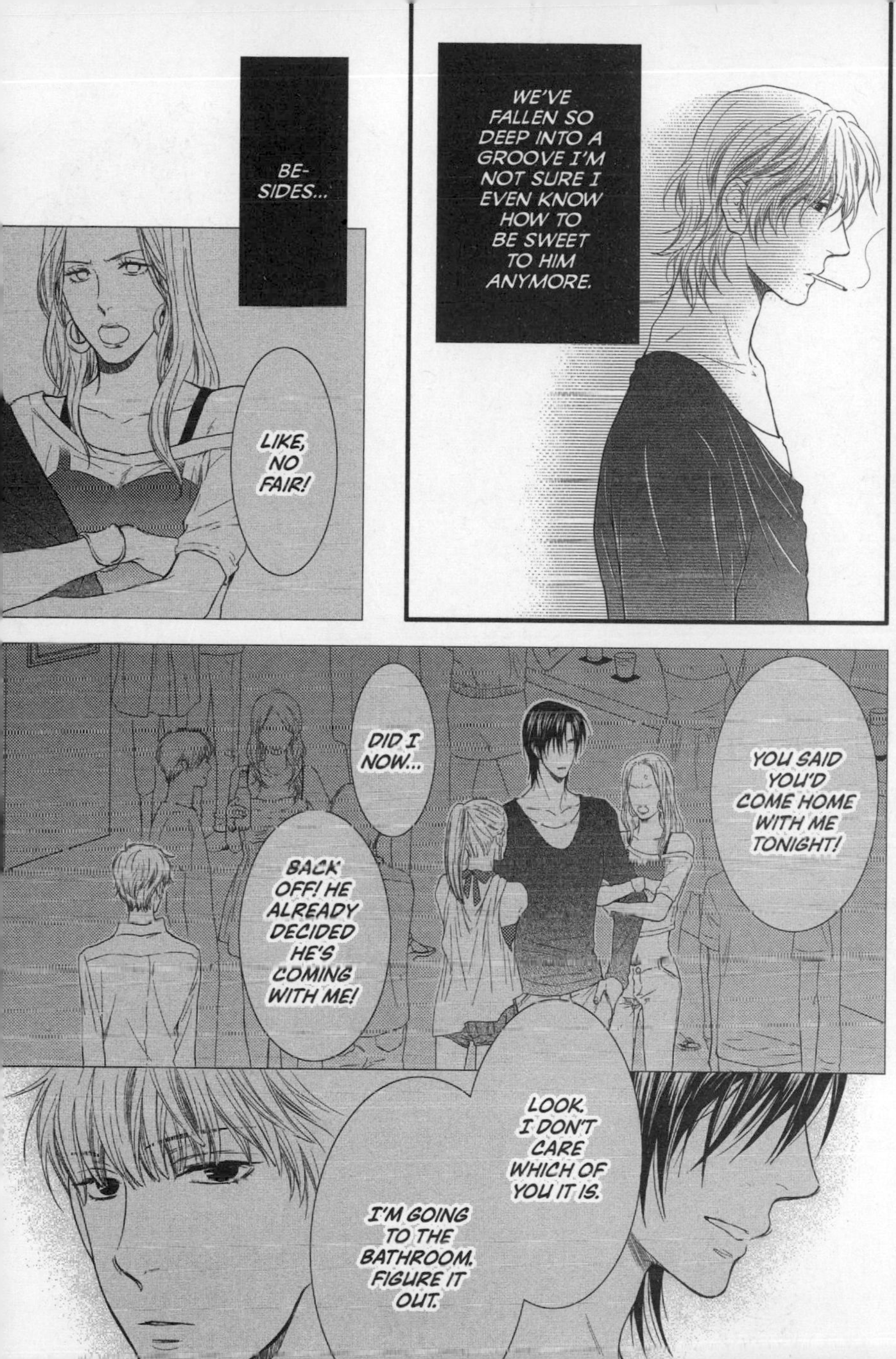
WE'VE FALLEN SO DEEP INTO A GROOVE I'M NOT SURE I EVEN KNOW HOW TO BE SWEET TO HIM ANYMORE.
BE-SIDES...
LIKE, NO FAIR!
YOU SAID YOU'D COME HOME WITH ME TONIGHT!
DID I NOW...
BACK OFF! HE ALREADY DECIDED HE'S COMING WITH ME!
LOOK. I DON'T CARE WHICH OF YOU IT IS.
I'M GOING TO THE BATHROOM. FIGURE IT OUT.

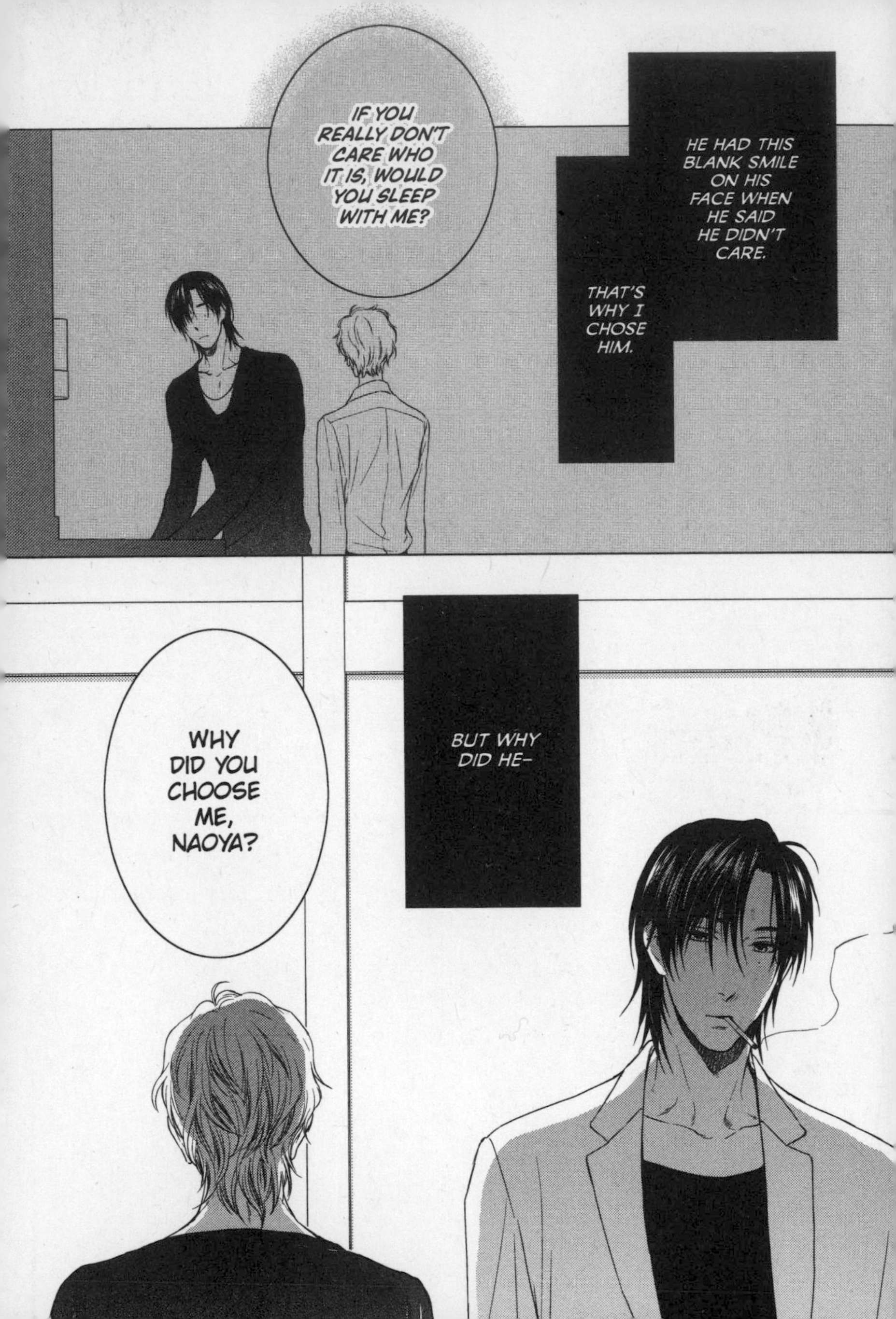
HE HAD THIS BLANK SMILE ON HIS FACE WHEN HE SAID HE DIDN'T CARE.
THAT'S WHY I CHOSE HIM.
IF YOU REALLY DON'T CARE WHO IT IS, WOULD YOU SLEEP WITH ME?
BUT WHY DID HE–
WHY DID YOU CHOOSE ME, NAOYA?

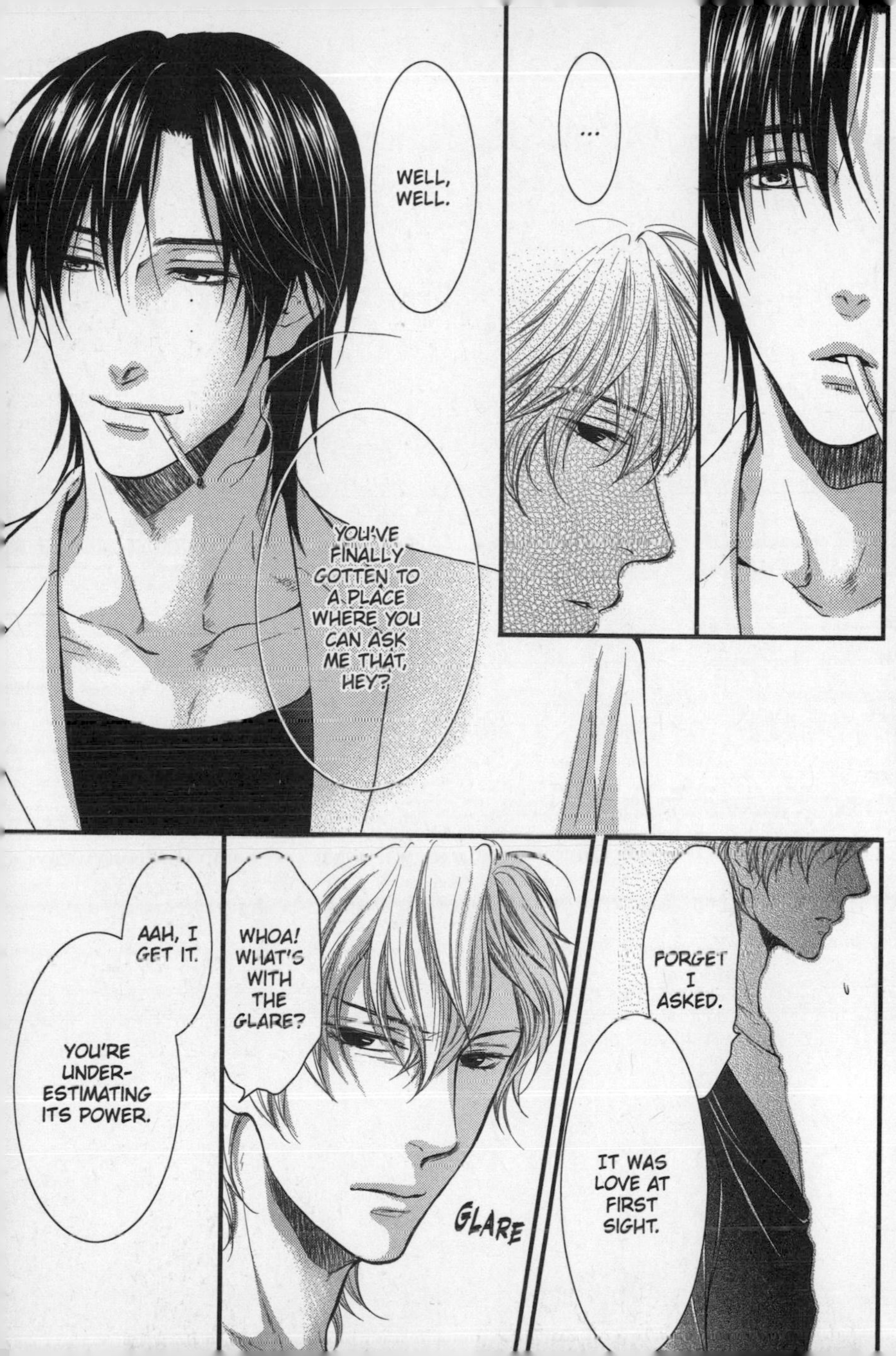
...
WELL, WELL.
YOU'VE FINALLY GOTTEN TO A PLACE WHERE YOU CAN ASK ME THAT, HEY?
FORGET I ASKED.
IT WAS LOVE AT FIRST SIGHT.
WHOA! WHAT'S WITH THE GLARE?
GLARE
AAH, I GET IT.
YOU'RE UNDER-ESTIMATING ITS POWER.

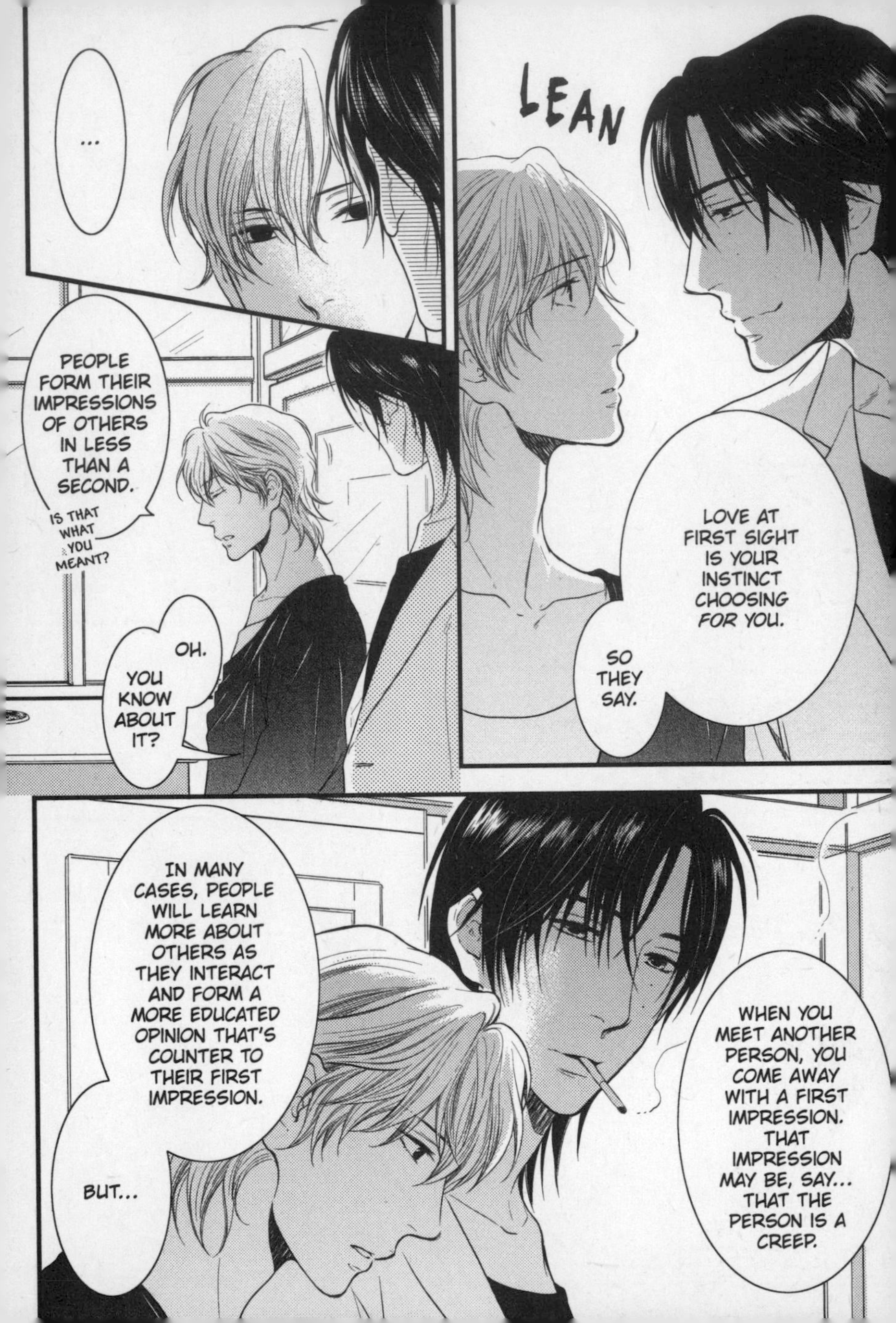
LEAN
LOVE AT FIRST SIGHT IS YOUR INSTINCT CHOOSING FOR YOU.
SO THEY SAY.
...
PEOPLE FORM THEIR IMPRESSIONS OF OTHERS IN LESS THAN A SECOND.
IS THAT WHAT YOU MEANT?
OH. YOU KNOW ABOUT IT?
WHEN YOU MEET ANOTHER PERSON, YOU COME AWAY WITH A FIRST IMPRESSION. THAT IMPRESSION MAY BE, SAY... THAT THE PERSON IS A CREEP.
...
IN MANY CASES, PEOPLE WILL LEARN MORE ABOUT OTHERS AS THEY INTERACT AND FORM A MORE EDUCATED OPINION THAT'S COUNTER TO THEIR FIRST IMPRESSION.
BUT...

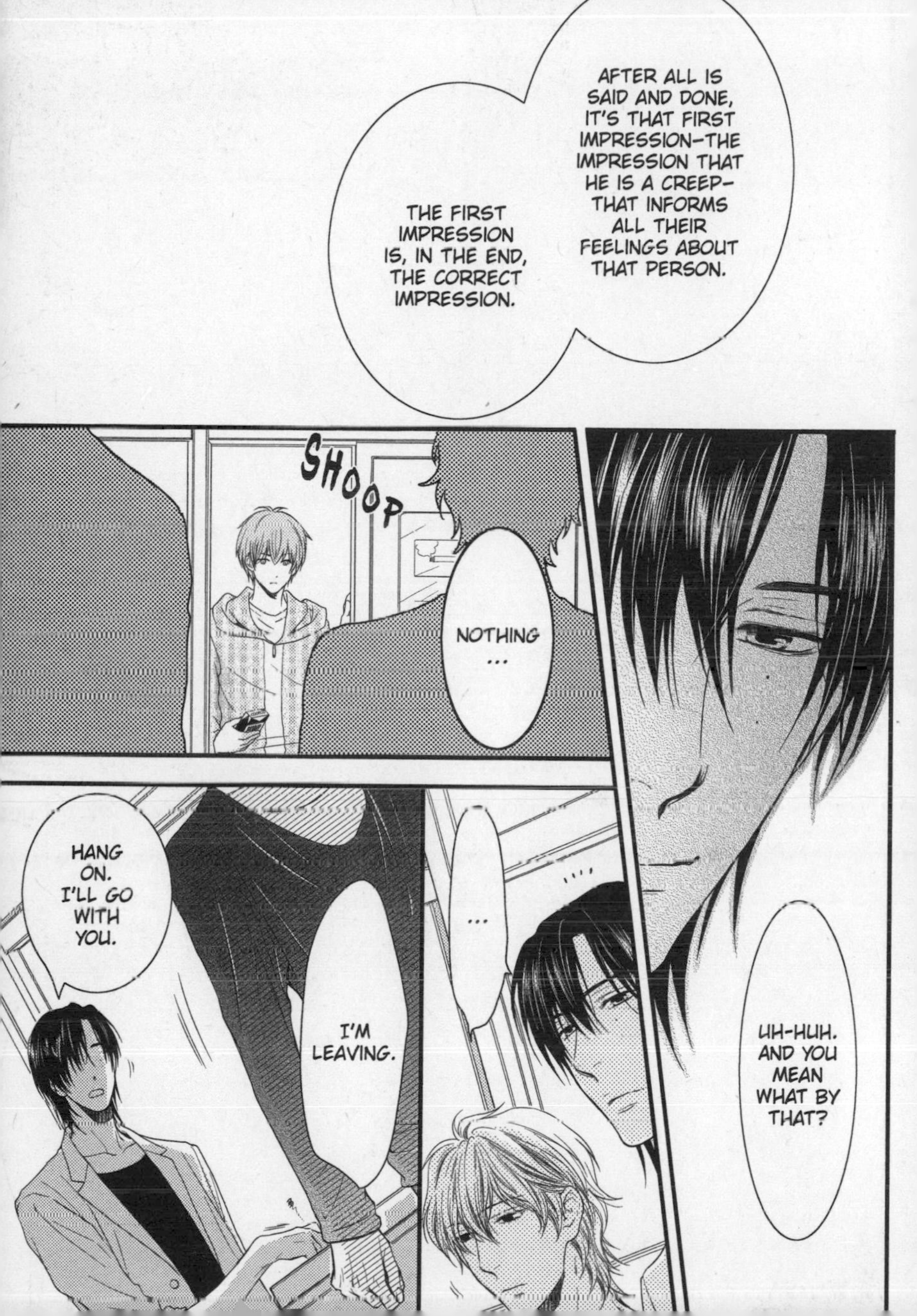
AFTER ALL IS SAID AND DONE, IT'S THAT FIRST IMPRESSION—THE IMPRESSION THAT HE IS A CREEP—THAT INFORMS ALL THEIR FEELINGS ABOUT THAT PERSON.
THE FIRST IMPRESSION IS, IN THE END, THE CORRECT IMPRESSION.
UH-HUH. AND YOU MEAN WHAT BY THAT?
SHOOP
NOTHING ...
...
I'M LEAVING.
HANG ON. I'LL GO WITH YOU.

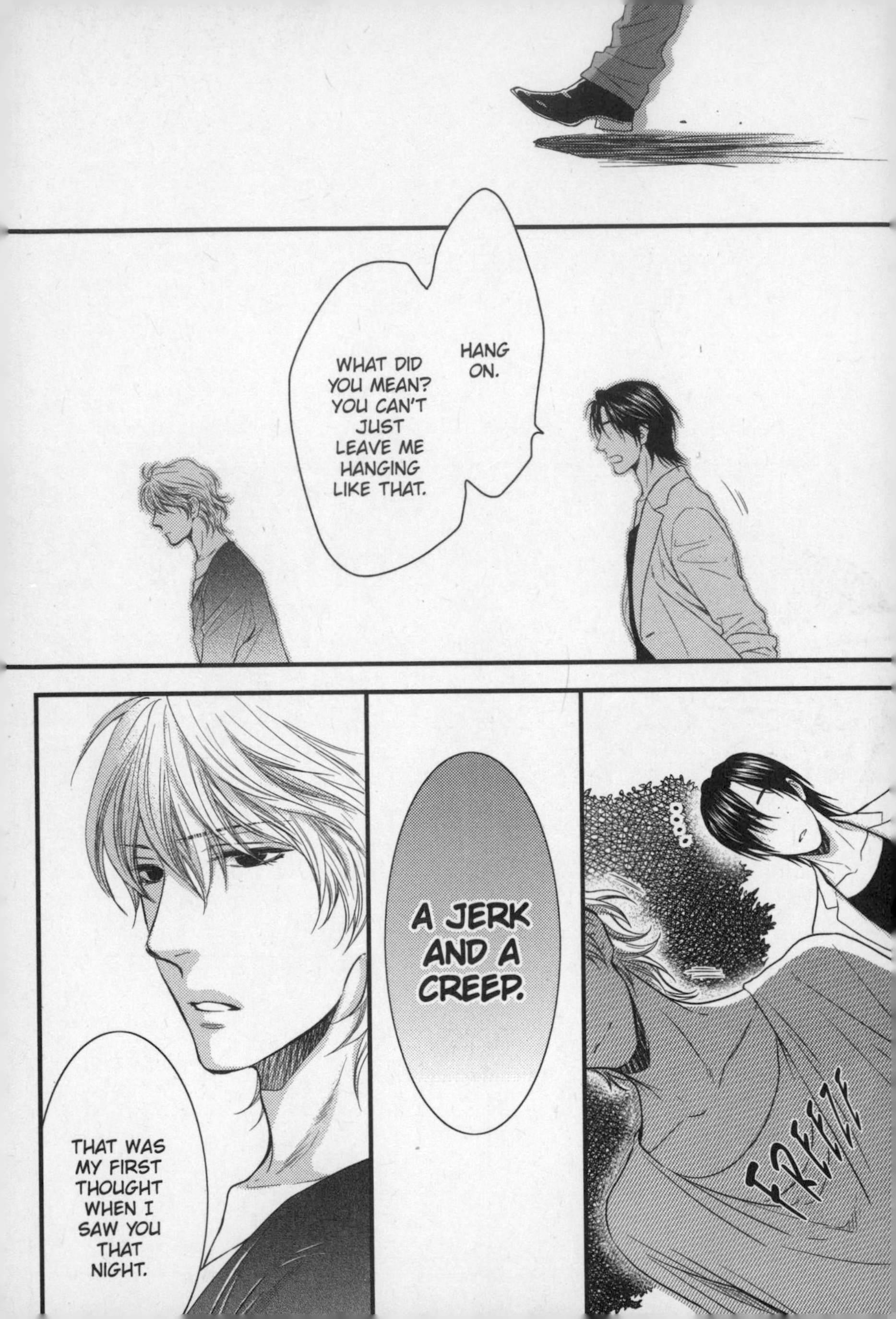
HANG ON.
WHAT DID YOU MEAN? YOU CAN'T JUST LEAVE ME HANGING LIKE THAT.
FREEZE
A JERK AND A CREEP.
THAT WAS MY FIRST THOUGHT WHEN I SAW YOU THAT NIGHT.

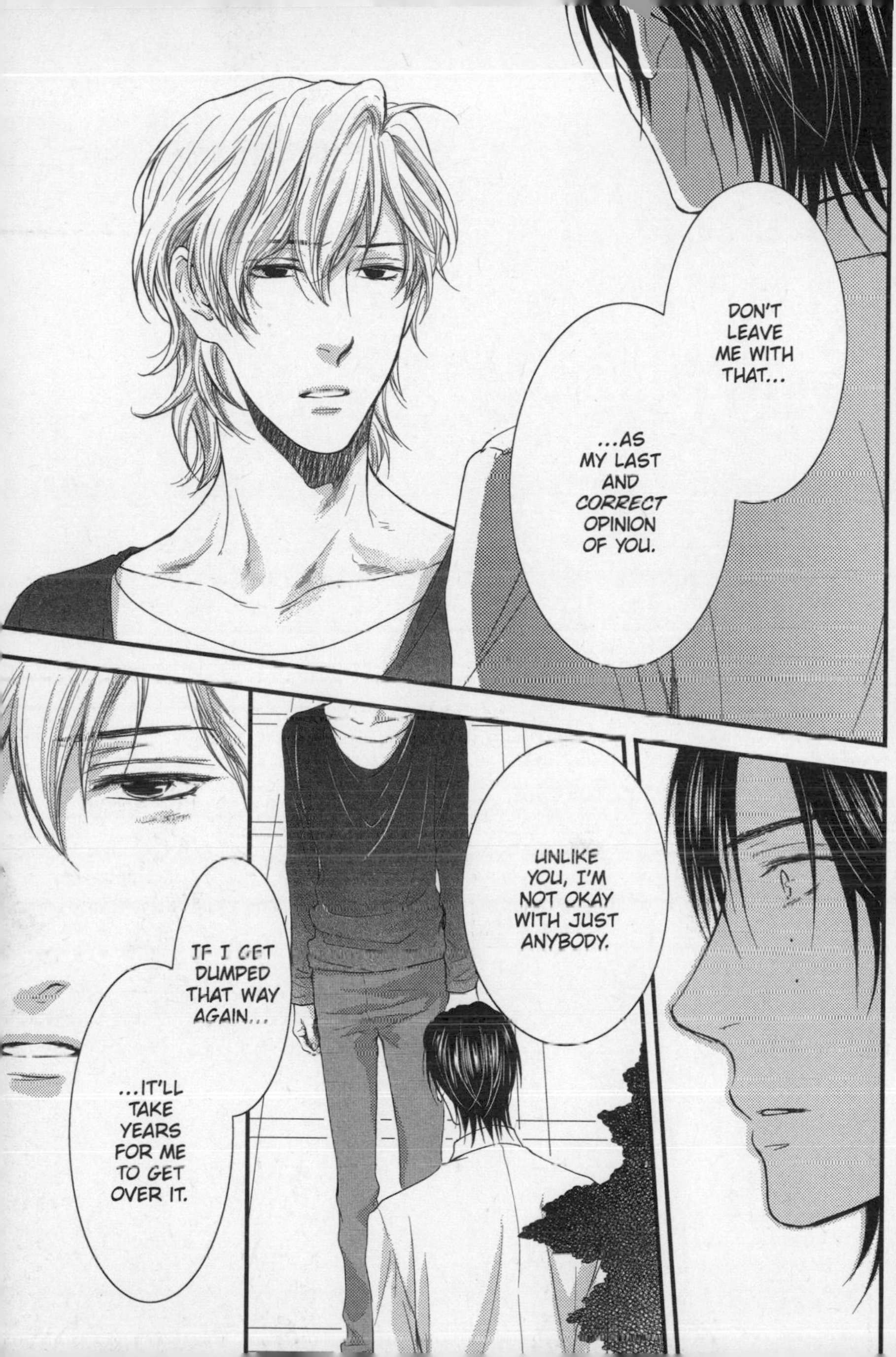
DON'T LEAVE ME WITH THAT...
...AS MY LAST AND CORRECT OPINION OF YOU.
UNLIKE YOU, I'M NOT OKAY WITH JUST ANYBODY.
IF I GET DUMPED THAT WAY AGAIN...
...IT'LL TAKE YEARS FOR ME TO GET OVER IT.

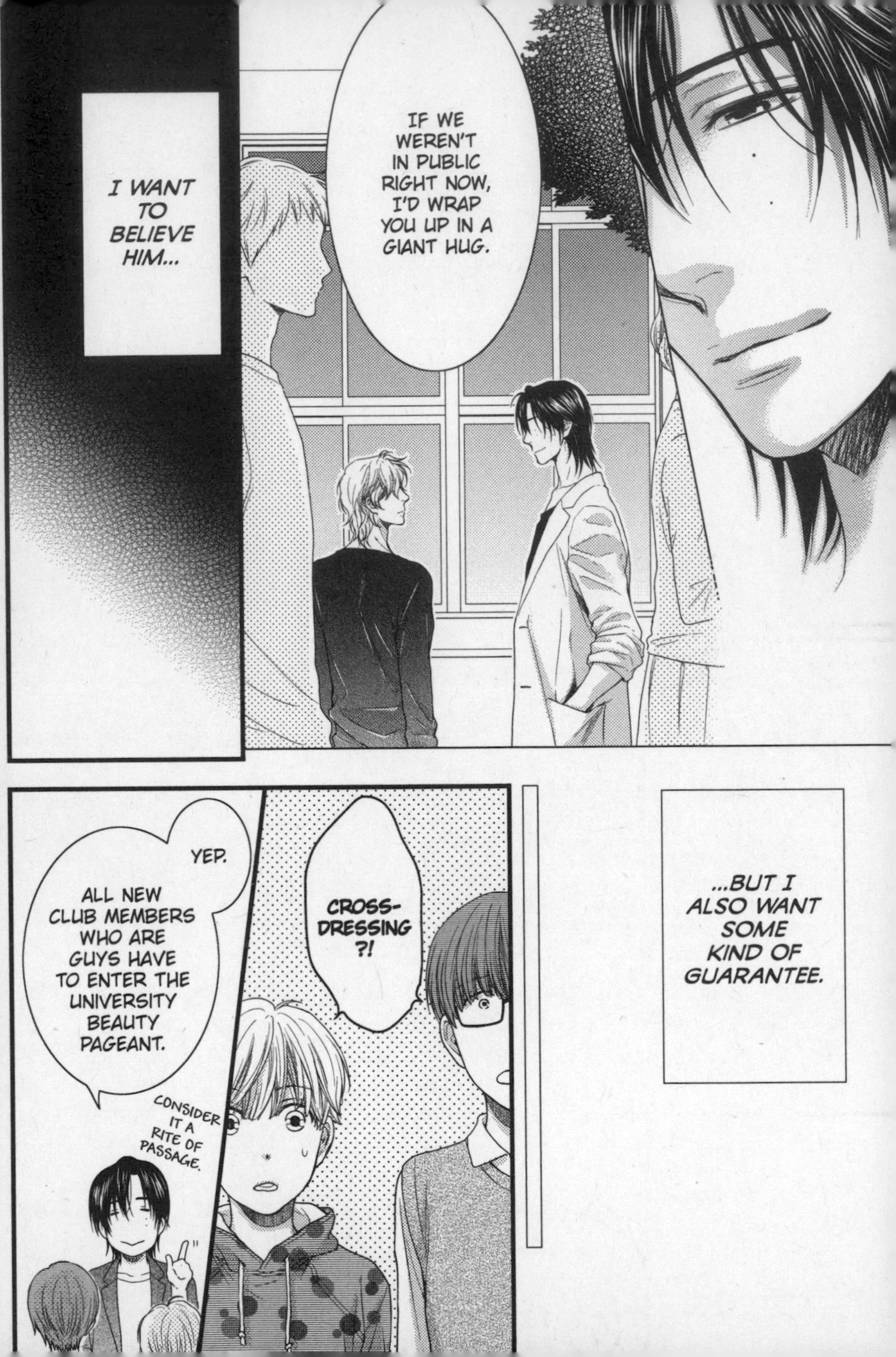
IF WE WEREN'T IN PUBLIC RIGHT NOW, I'D WRAP YOU UP IN A GIANT HUG.
I WANT TO BELIEVE HIM...
...BUT I ALSO WANT SOME KIND OF GUARANTEE.
CROSS-DRESSING?!
YEP. ALL NEW CLUB MEMBERS WHO ARE GUYS HAVE TO ENTER THE UNIVERSITY BEAUTY PAGEANT.
CONSIDER IT A RITE OF PASSAGE.

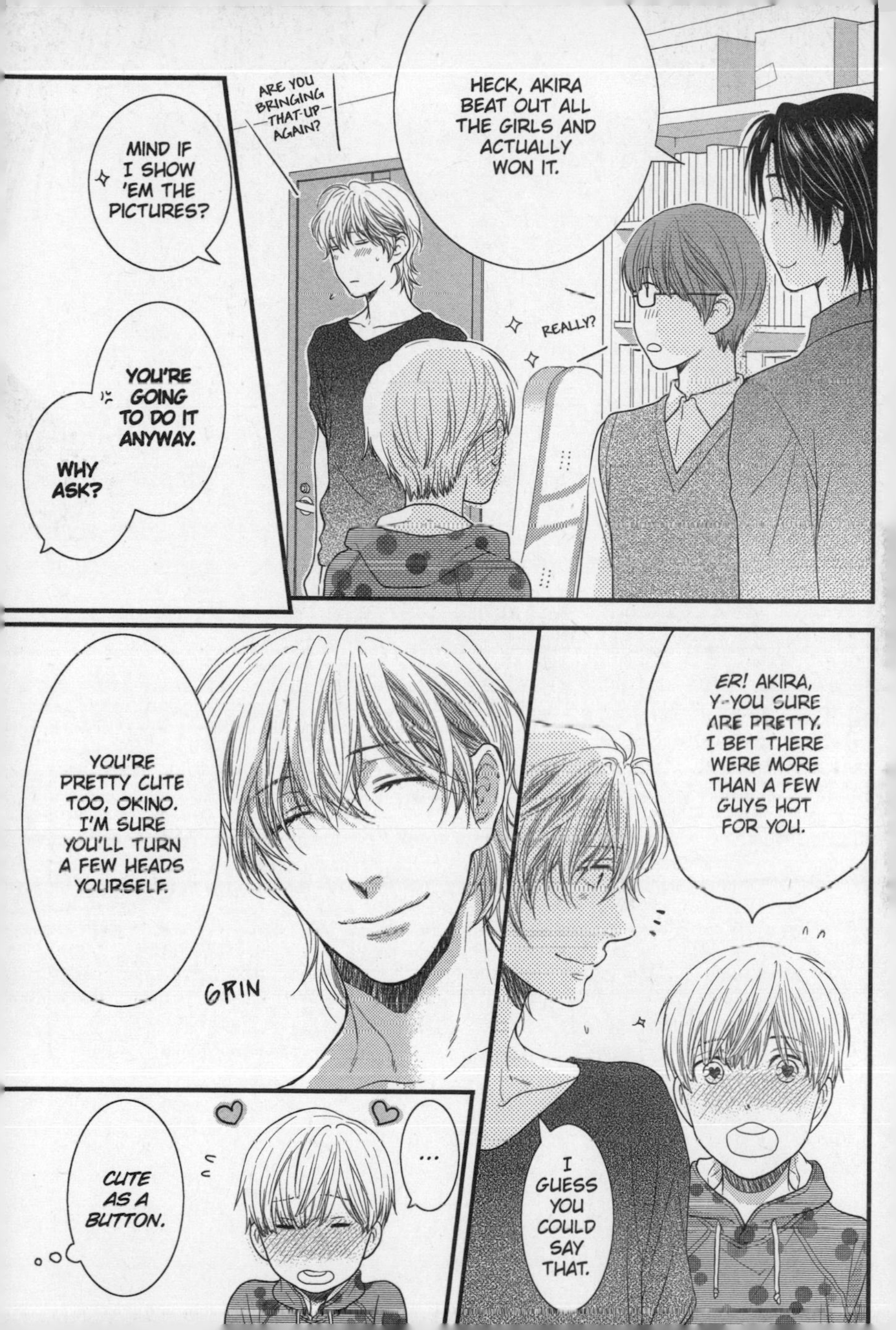
HECK, AKIRA BEAT OUT ALL THE GIRLS AND ACTUALLY WON IT.
REALLY?
ARE YOU BRINGING THAT UP AGAIN?
MIND IF I SHOW 'EM THE PICTURES?
YOU'RE GOING TO DO IT ANYWAY.
WHY ASK?
ER! AKIRA, Y-YOU SURE ARE PRETTY. I BET THERE WERE MORE THAN A FEW GUYS HOT FOR YOU.
I GUESS YOU COULD SAY THAT.
YOU'RE PRETTY CUTE TOO, OKINO. I'M SURE YOU'LL TURN A FEW HEADS YOURSELF.
GRIN
...
CUTE AS A BUTTON.

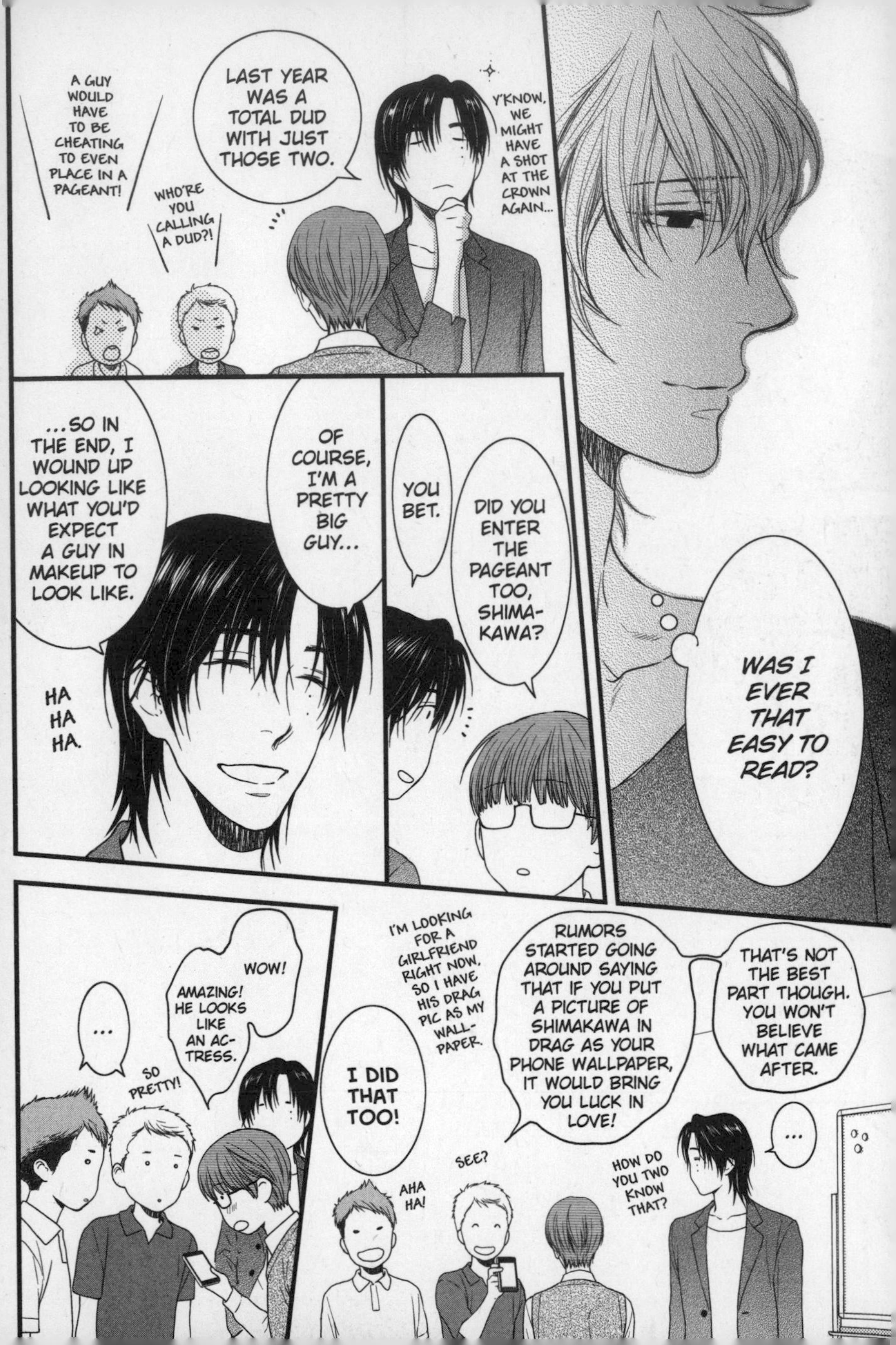
WAS I EVER THAT EASY TO READ?
Y'KNOW, WE MIGHT HAVE A SHOT AT THE CROWN AGAIN...
LAST YEAR WAS A TOTAL DUD WITH JUST THOSE TWO.
WHO'RE YOU CALLING A DUD?!
A GUY WOULD HAVE TO BE CHEATING TO EVEN PLACE IN A PAGEANT!
DID YOU ENTER THE PAGEANT TOO, SHIMAKAWA?
YOU BET.
OF COURSE, I'M A PRETTY BIG GUY...
...SO IN THE END, I WOUND UP LOOKING LIKE WHAT YOU'D EXPECT A GUY IN MAKEUP TO LOOK LIKE.
HA HA HA.
THAT'S NOT THE BEST PART THOUGH. YOU WON'T BELIEVE WHAT CAME AFTER.
...
RUMORS STARTED GOING AROUND SAYING THAT IF YOU PUT A PICTURE OF SHIMAKAWA IN DRAG AS YOUR PHONE WALLPAPER, IT WOULD BRING YOU LUCK IN LOVE!
HOW DO YOU TWO KNOW THAT?
I'M LOOKING FOR A GIRLFRIEND RIGHT NOW, SO I HAVE HIS DRAG PIC AS MY WALLPAPER.
SEE?
I DID THAT TOO!
AHA HA!
WOW!
AMAZING! HE LOOKS LIKE AN ACTRESS.
...
SO PRETTY!

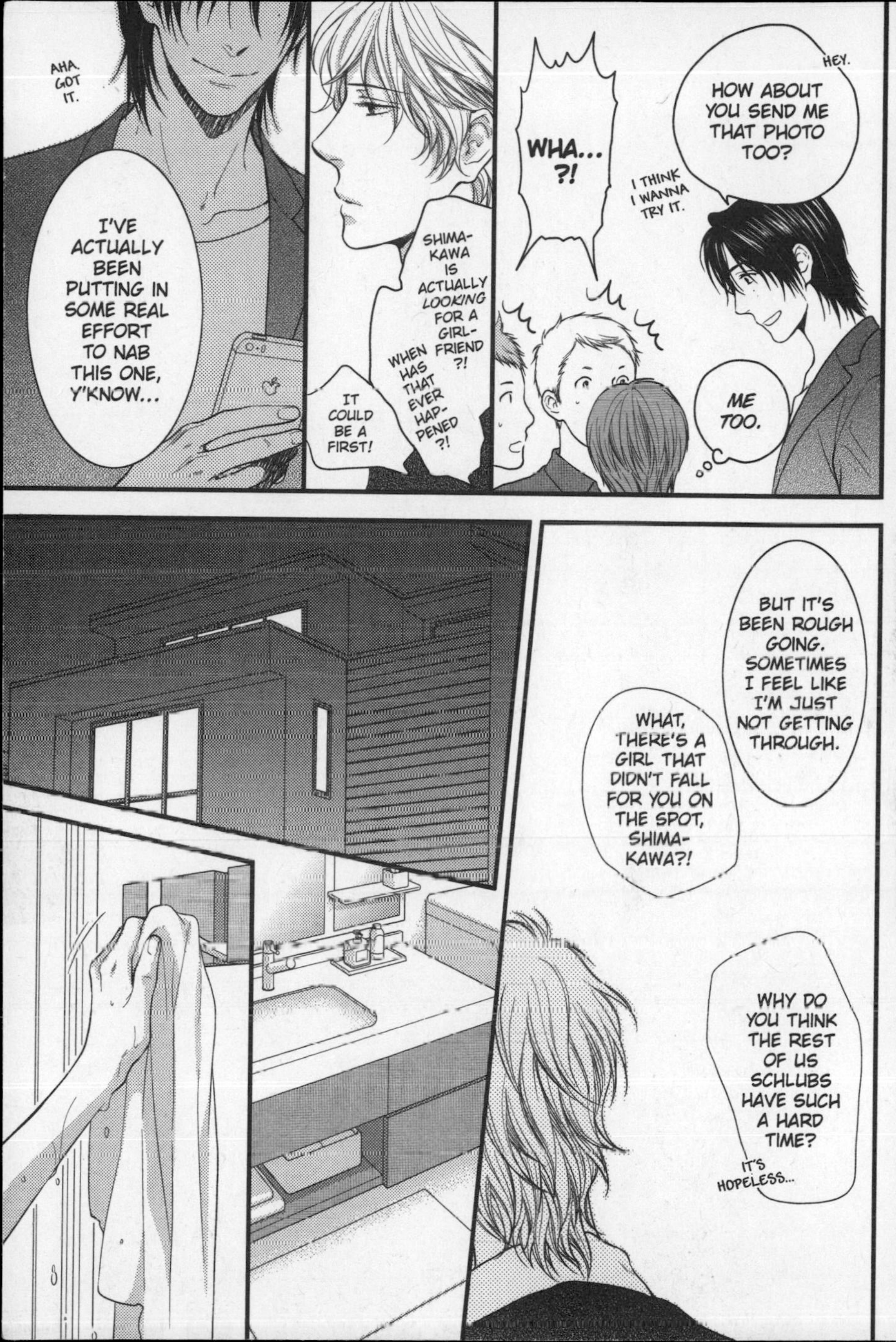
HEY.
HOW ABOUT YOU SEND ME THAT PHOTO TOO?
I THINK I WANNA TRY IT.
WHA...?!
ME TOO.
SHIMA-KAWA IS ACTUALLY LOOKING FOR A GIRL-FRIEND?!
WHEN HAS THAT EVER HAP-PENED?!
IT COULD BE A FIRST!
AHA. GOT IT.
I'VE ACTUALLY BEEN PUTTING IN SOME REAL EFFORT TO NAB THIS ONE, Y'KNOW...
BUT IT'S BEEN ROUGH GOING. SOMETIMES I FEEL LIKE I'M JUST NOT GETTING THROUGH.
WHAT, THERE'S A GIRL THAT DIDN'T FALL FOR YOU ON THE SPOT, SHIMA-KAWA?!
WHY DO YOU THINK THE REST OF US SCHLUBS HAVE SUCH A HARD TIME?
IT'S HOPELESS...

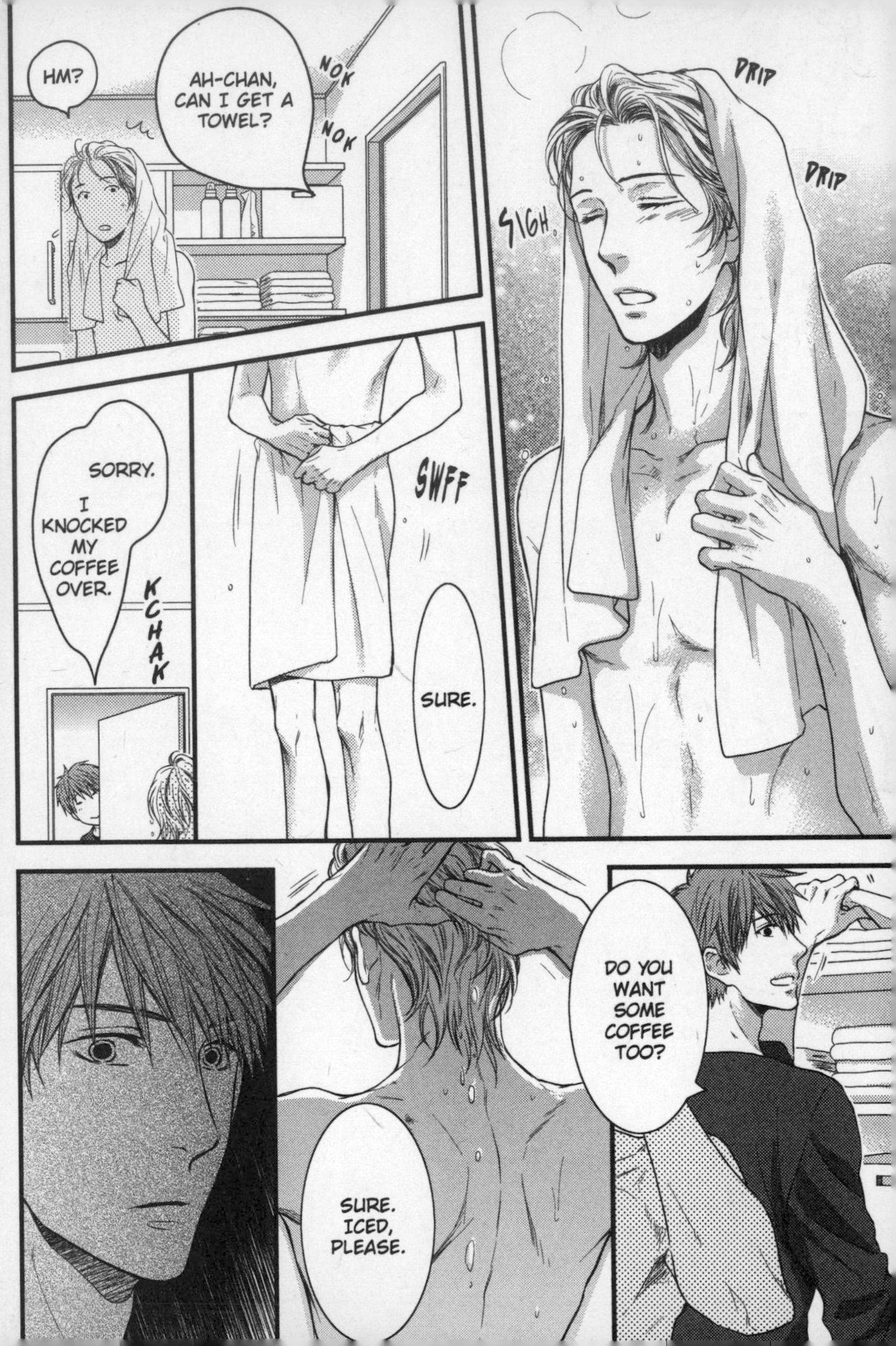
DRIP
DRIP
SIGH
NOK
NOK
AH-CHAN, CAN I GET A TOWEL?
HM?
SWFF
SURE.
SORRY. I KNOCKED MY COFFEE OVER.
KCHAK
DO YOU WANT SOME COFFEE TOO?
SURE. ICED, PLEASE.

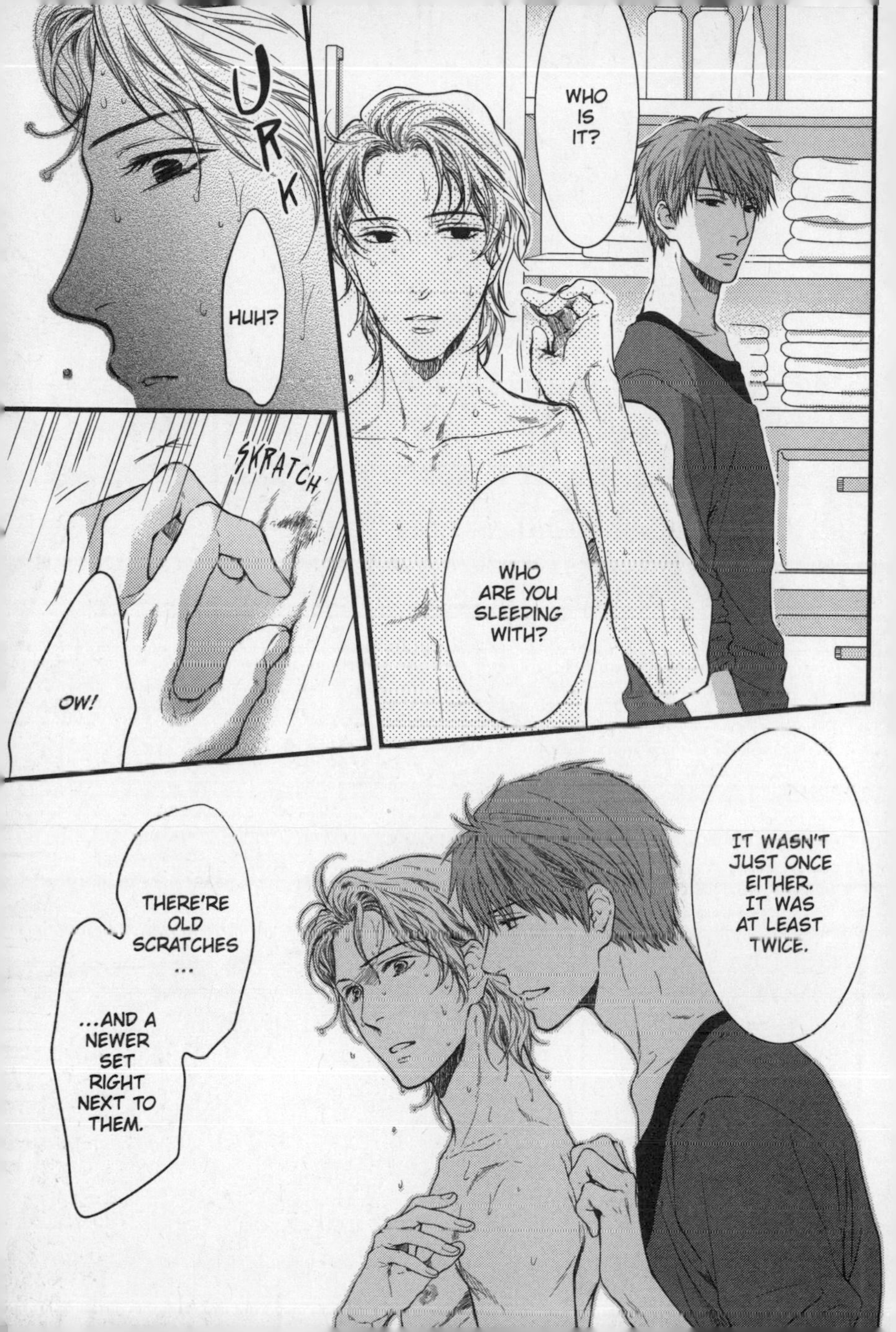
WHO IS IT?
WHO ARE YOU SLEEPING WITH?
URK
HUH?
SKRATCH
OW!
IT WASN'T JUST ONCE EITHER. IT WAS AT LEAST TWICE.
THERE'RE OLD SCRATCHES ...
...AND A NEWER SET RIGHT NEXT TO THEM.

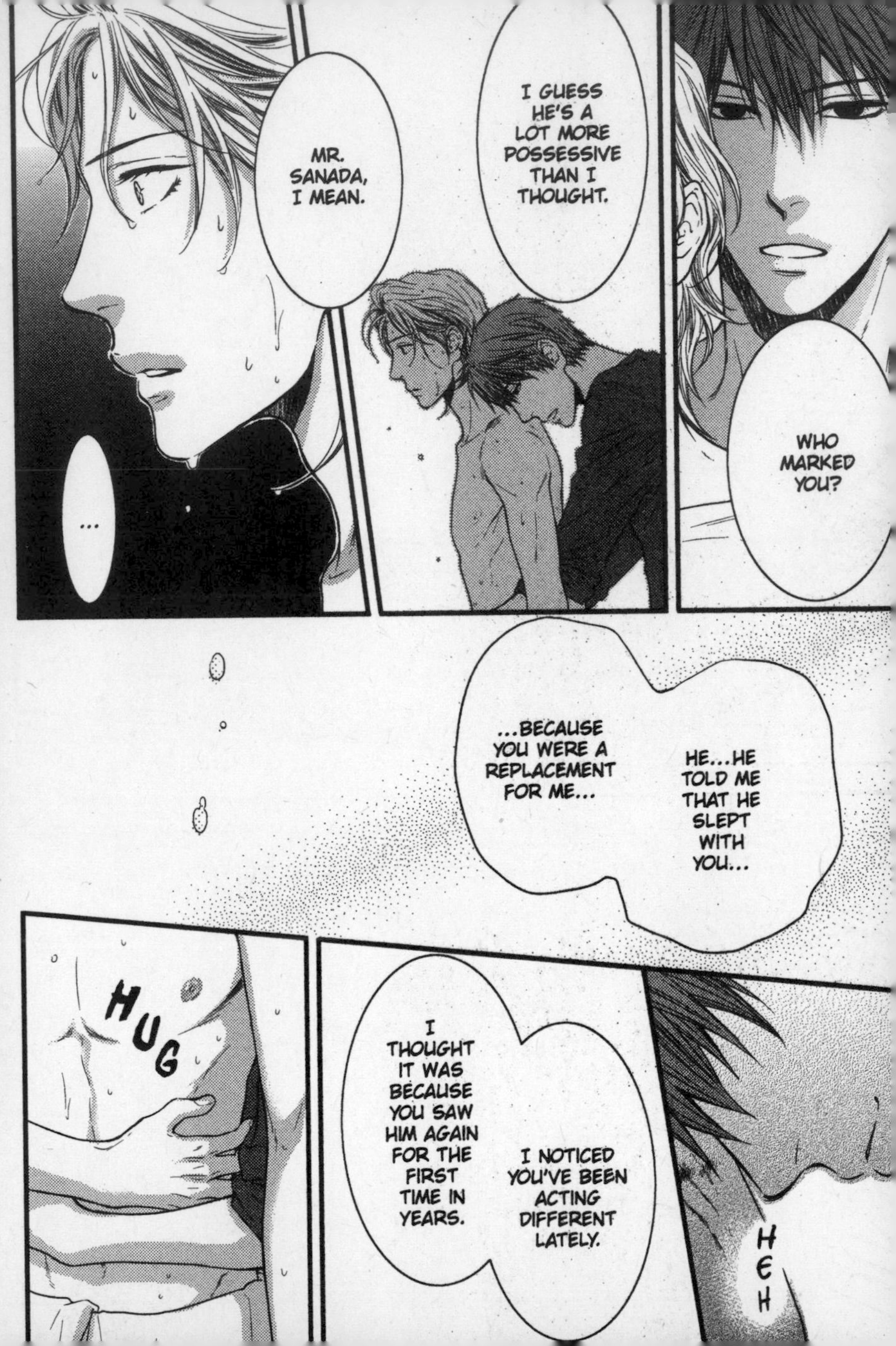
WHO MARKED YOU?
I GUESS HE'S A LOT MORE POSSESSIVE THAN I THOUGHT.
MR. SANADA, I MEAN.
...
HE...HE TOLD ME THAT HE SLEPT WITH YOU...
...BECAUSE YOU WERE A REPLACEMENT FOR ME...
HEH
I NOTICED YOU'VE BEEN ACTING DIFFERENT LATELY.
I THOUGHT IT WAS BECAUSE YOU SAW HIM AGAIN FOR THE FIRST TIME IN YEARS.
HUG

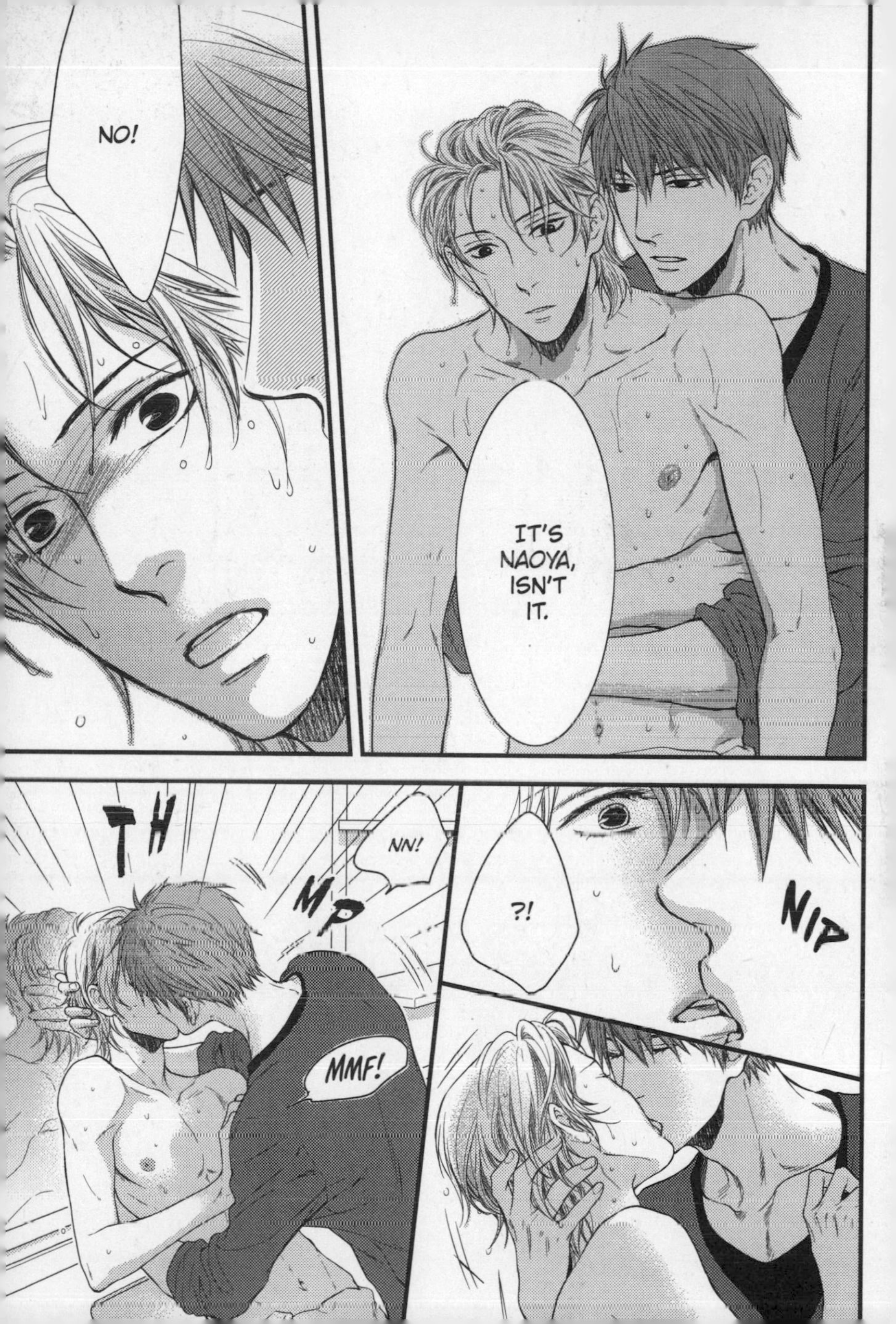
IT'S NAOYA, ISN'T IT.
NO!
?!
NIP
TH
MP
NN!
MMF!

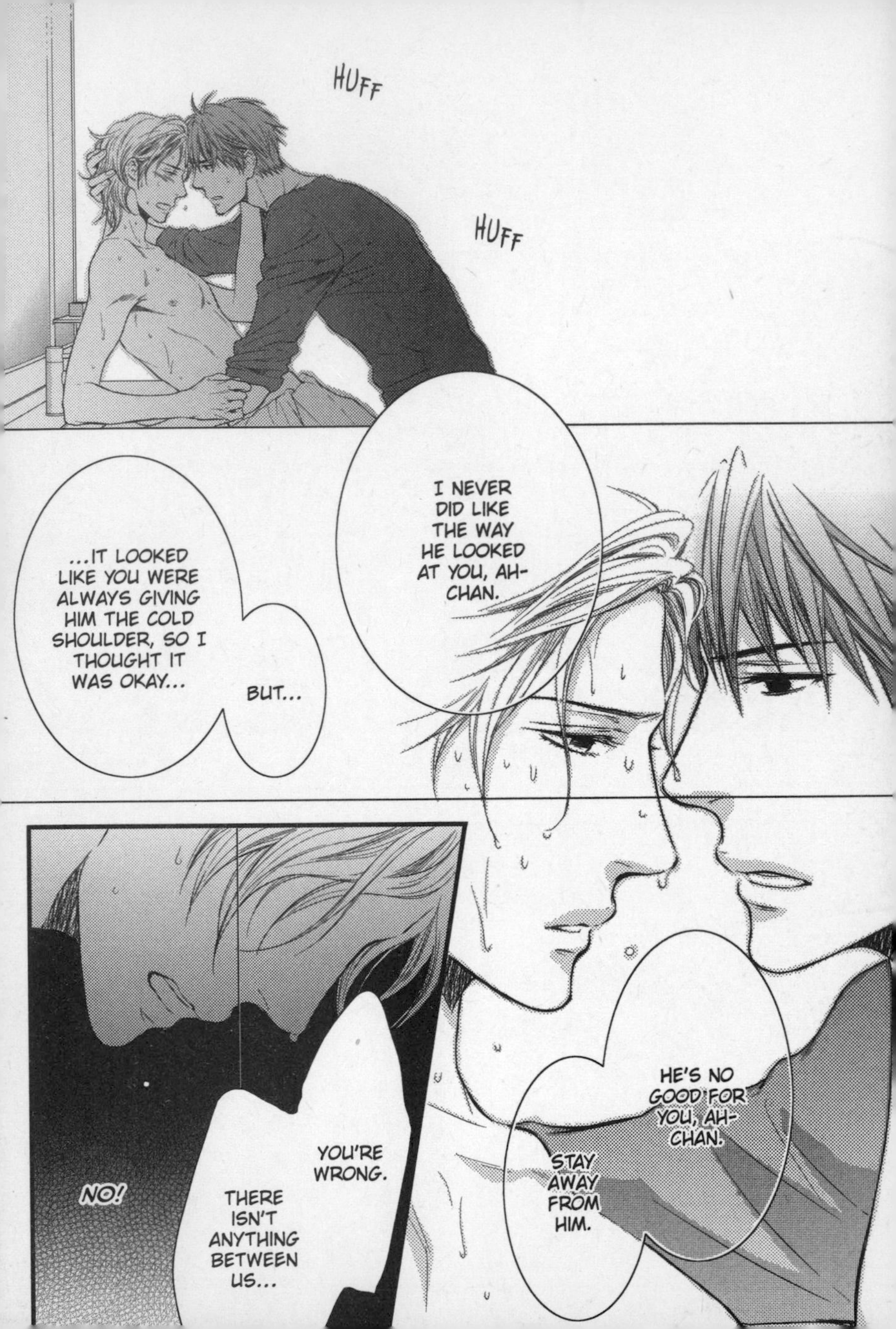
HUFF
HUFF
I NEVER DID LIKE THE WAY HE LOOKED AT YOU, AH-CHAN.
...IT LOOKED LIKE YOU WERE ALWAYS GIVING HIM THE COLD SHOULDER, SO I THOUGHT IT WAS OKAY...
BUT...
HE'S NO GOOD FOR YOU, AH-CHAN.
STAY AWAY FROM HIM.
YOU'RE WRONG.
THERE ISN'T ANYTHING BETWEEN US...
NO!

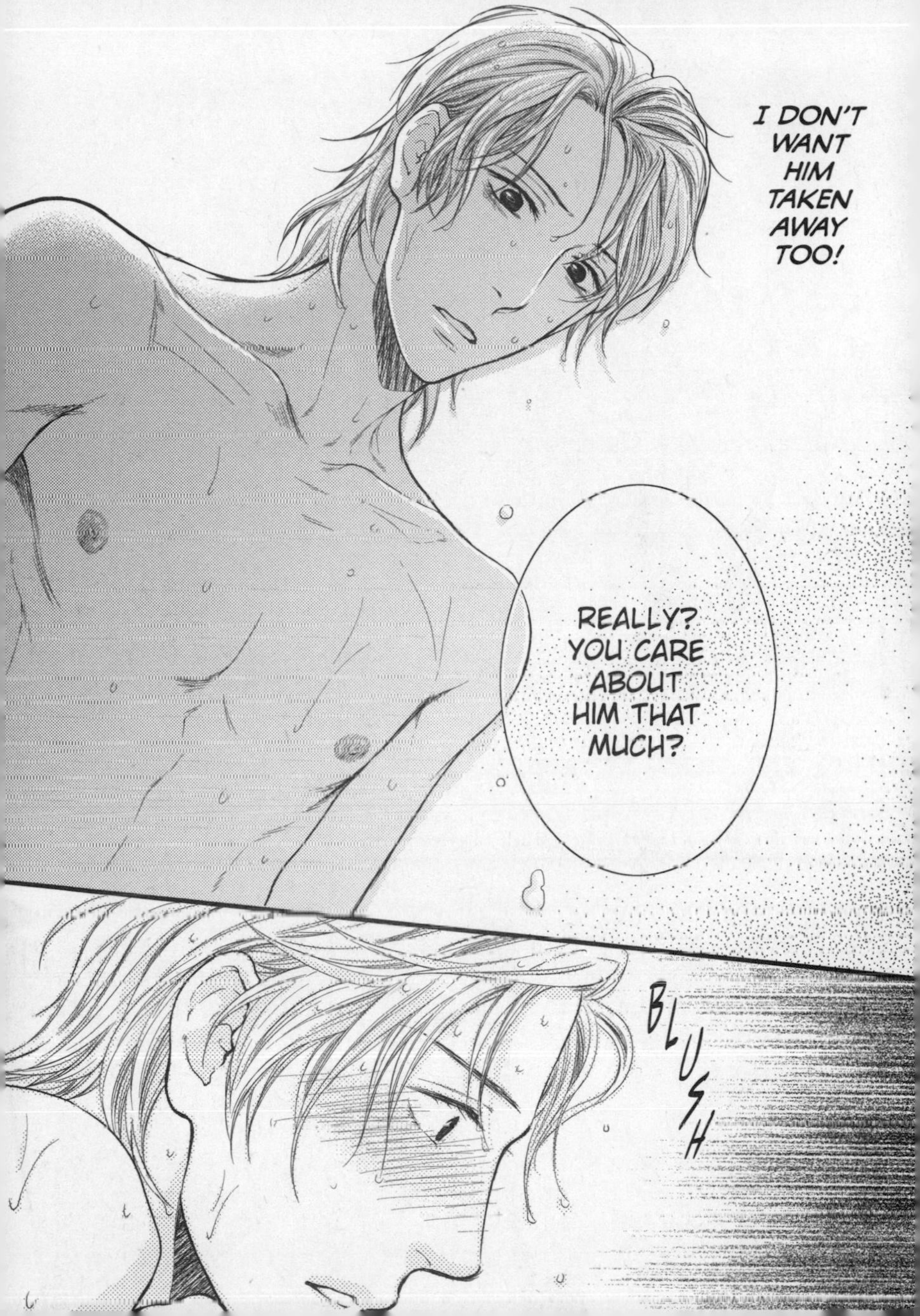
I DON'T WANT HIM TAKEN AWAY TOO!
REALLY? YOU CARE ABOUT HIM THAT MUCH?
BLUSH

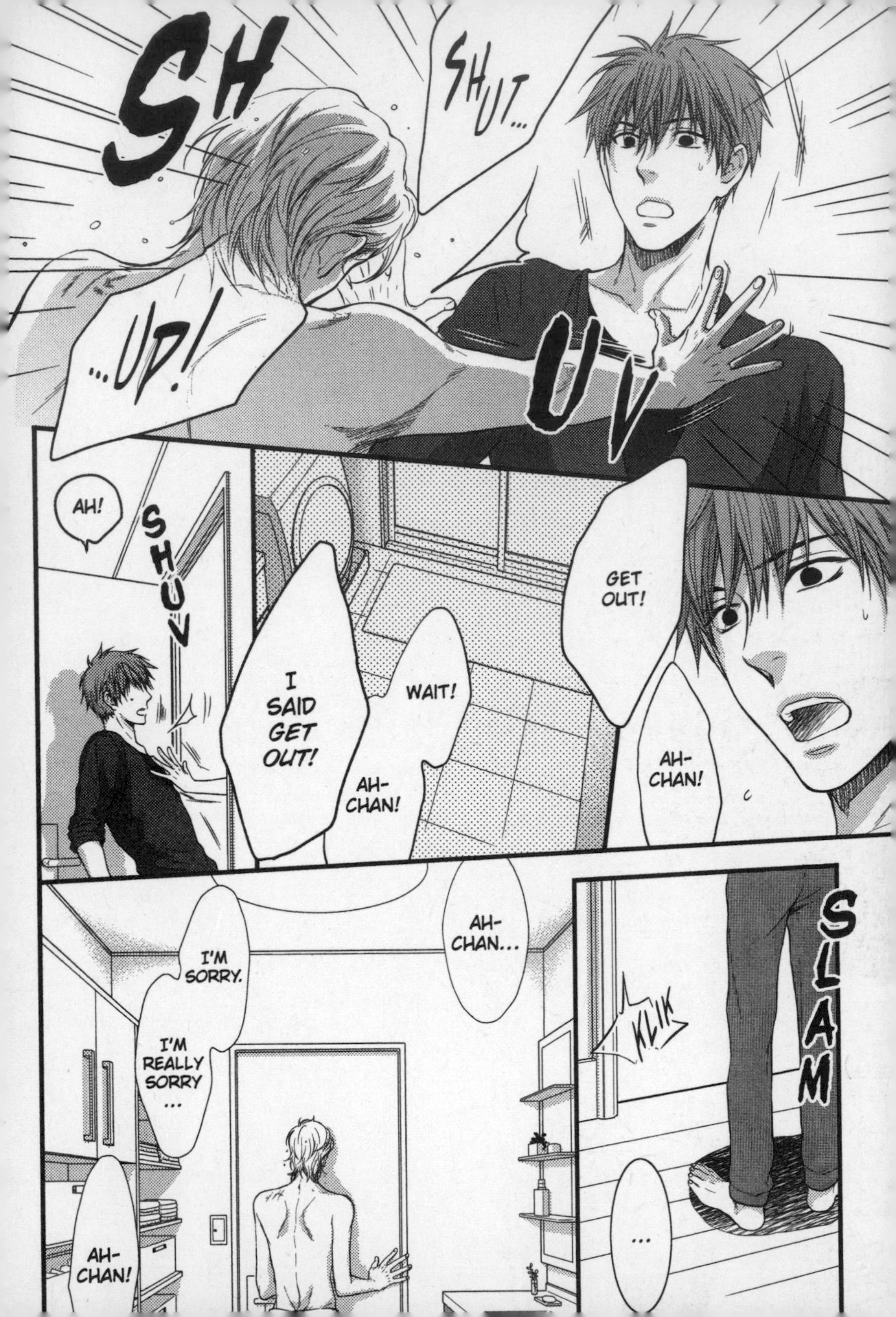
SHUT...
SH
UV
...UP!
GET OUT!
AH-CHAN!
WAIT!
I SAID GET OUT!
AH-CHAN!
AH!
SHUV
SLAM
KLIK
...
AH-CHAN...
I'M SORRY.
I'M REALLY SORRY...
AH-CHAN!

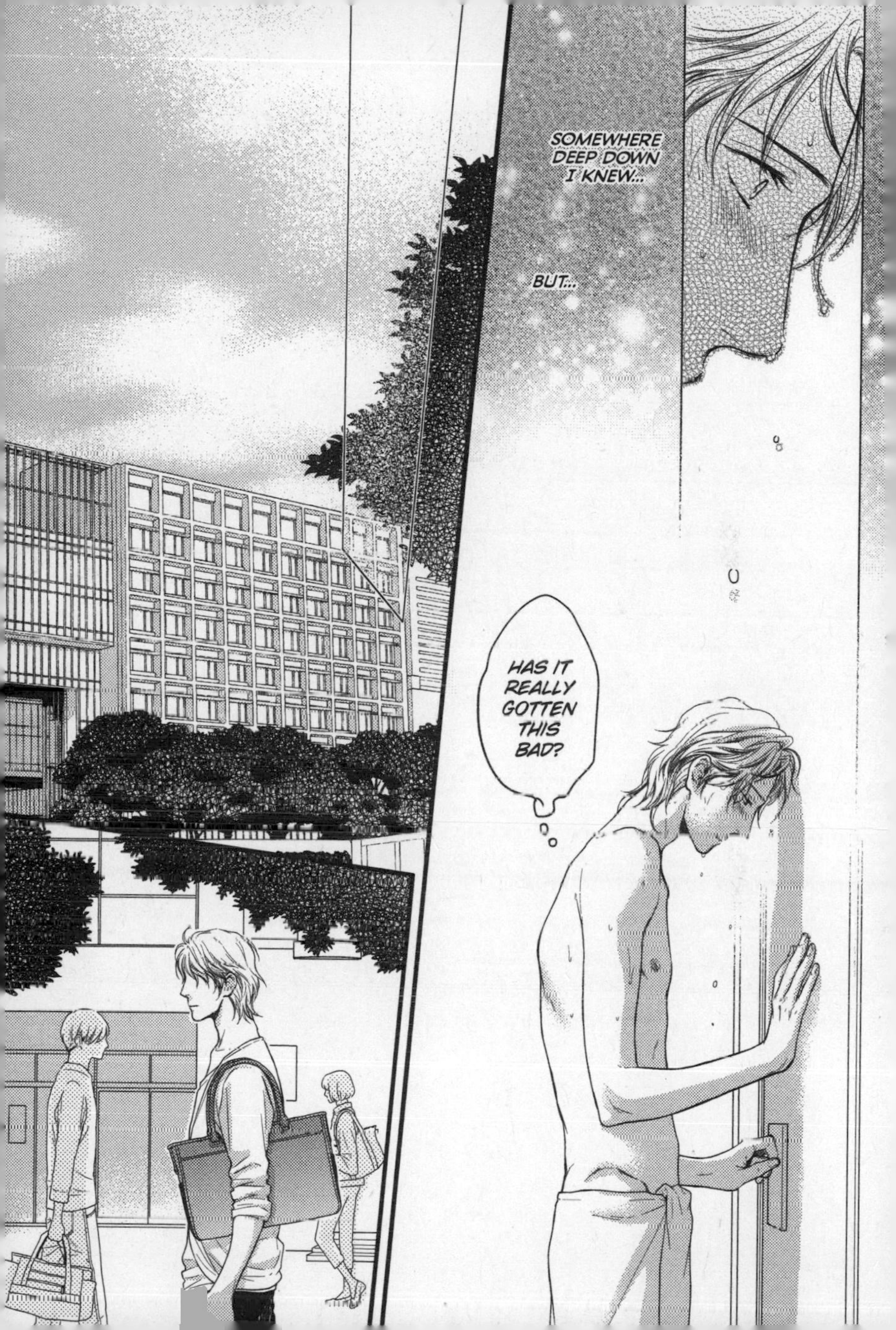
SOMEWHERE DEEP DOWN I KNEW...
BUT...
HAS IT REALLY GOTTEN THIS BAD?

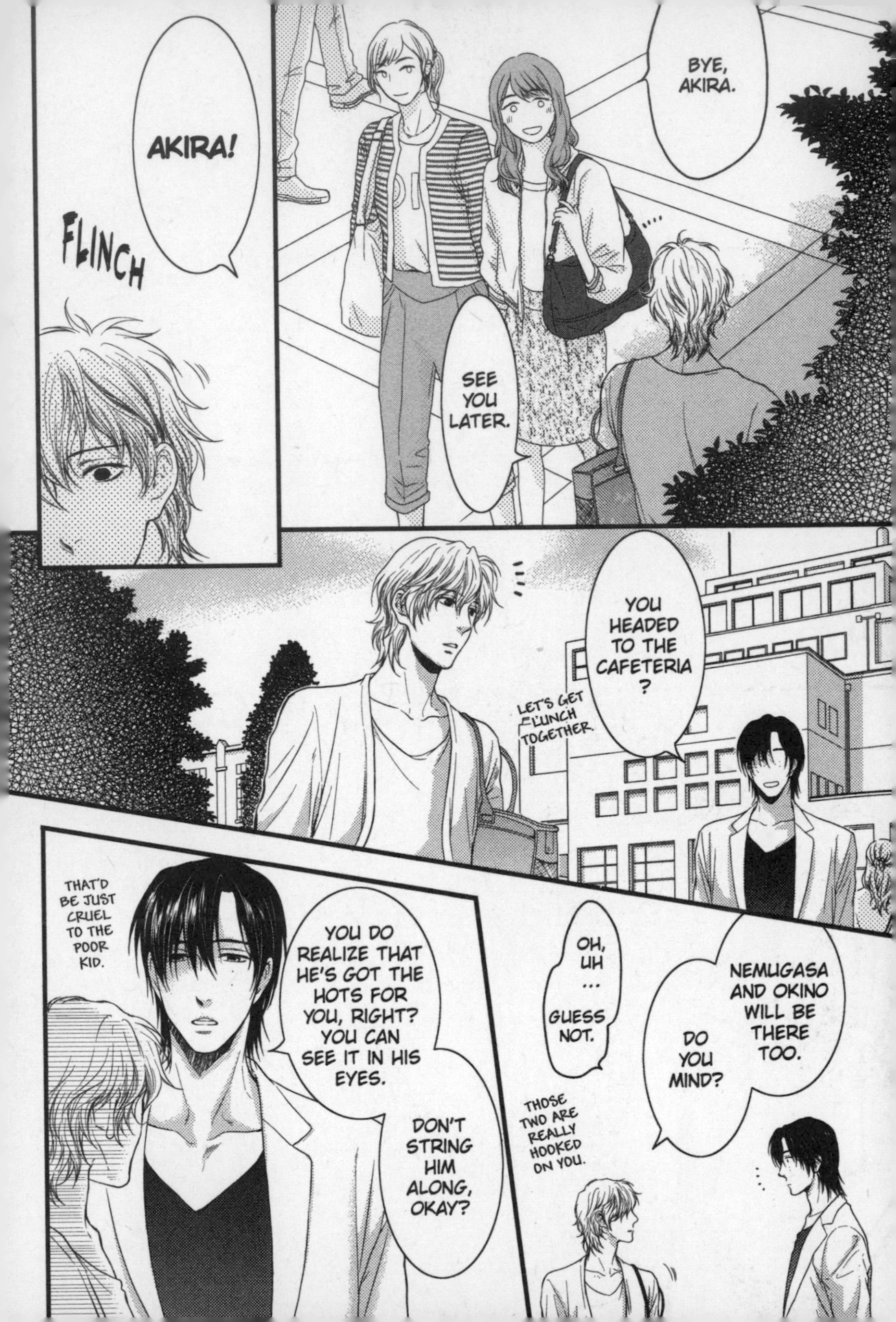
BYE, AKIRA.
....
SEE YOU LATER.
AKIRA!
FLINCH
YOU HEADED TO THE CAFETERIA?
LET'S GET LUNCH TOGETHER.
NEMUGASA AND OKINO WILL BE THERE TOO.
DO YOU MIND?
THOSE TWO ARE REALLY HOOKED ON YOU.
OH, UH ... GUESS NOT.
YOU DO REALIZE THAT HE'S GOT THE HOTS FOR YOU, RIGHT? YOU CAN SEE IT IN HIS EYES.
DON'T STRING HIM ALONG, OKAY?
THAT'D BE JUST CRUEL TO THE POOR KID.

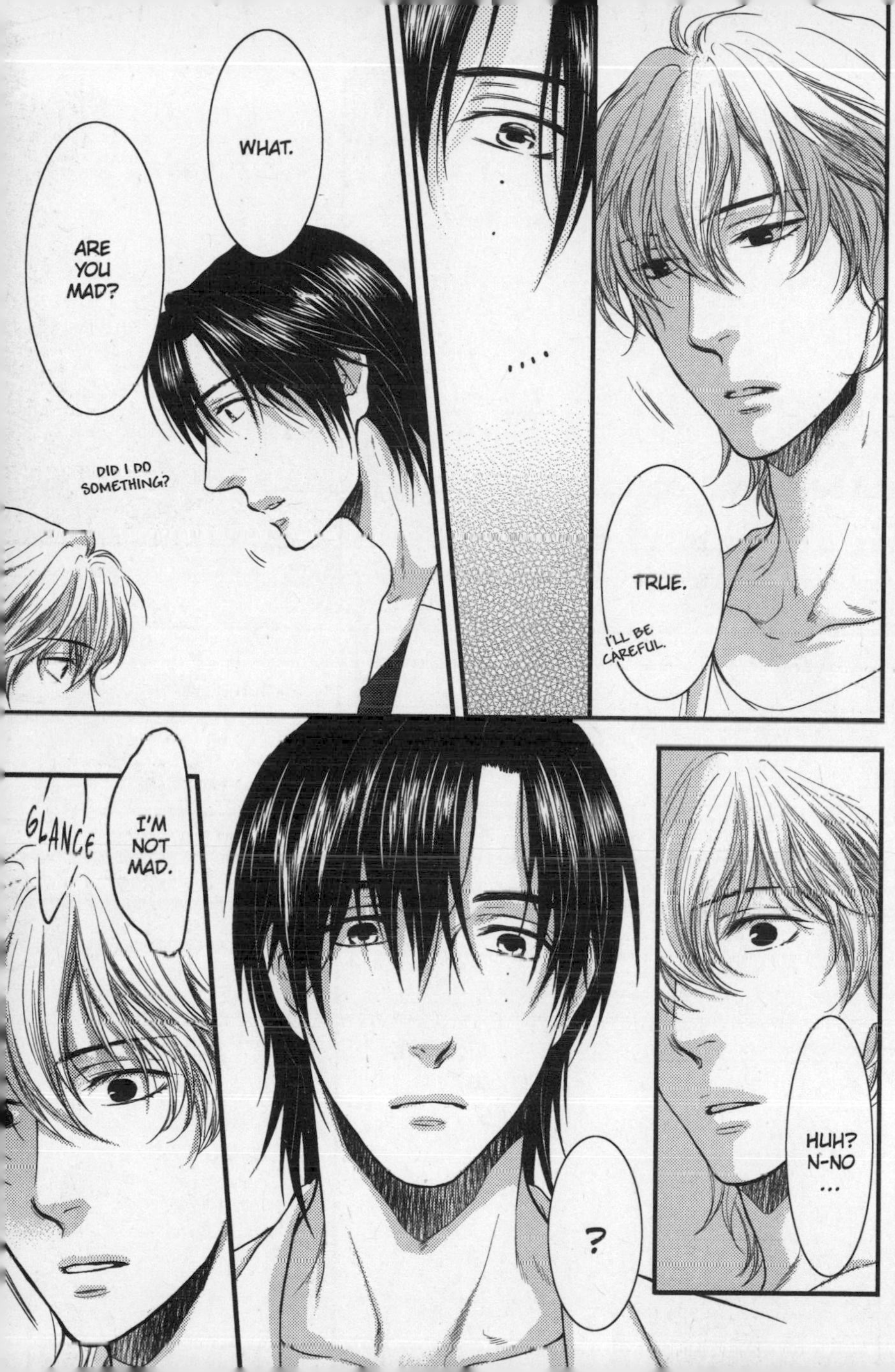
TRUE.
I'LL BE CAREFUL.
....
WHAT.
ARE YOU MAD?
DID I DO SOMETHING?
HUH? N-NO ...
?
I'M NOT MAD.
GLANCE

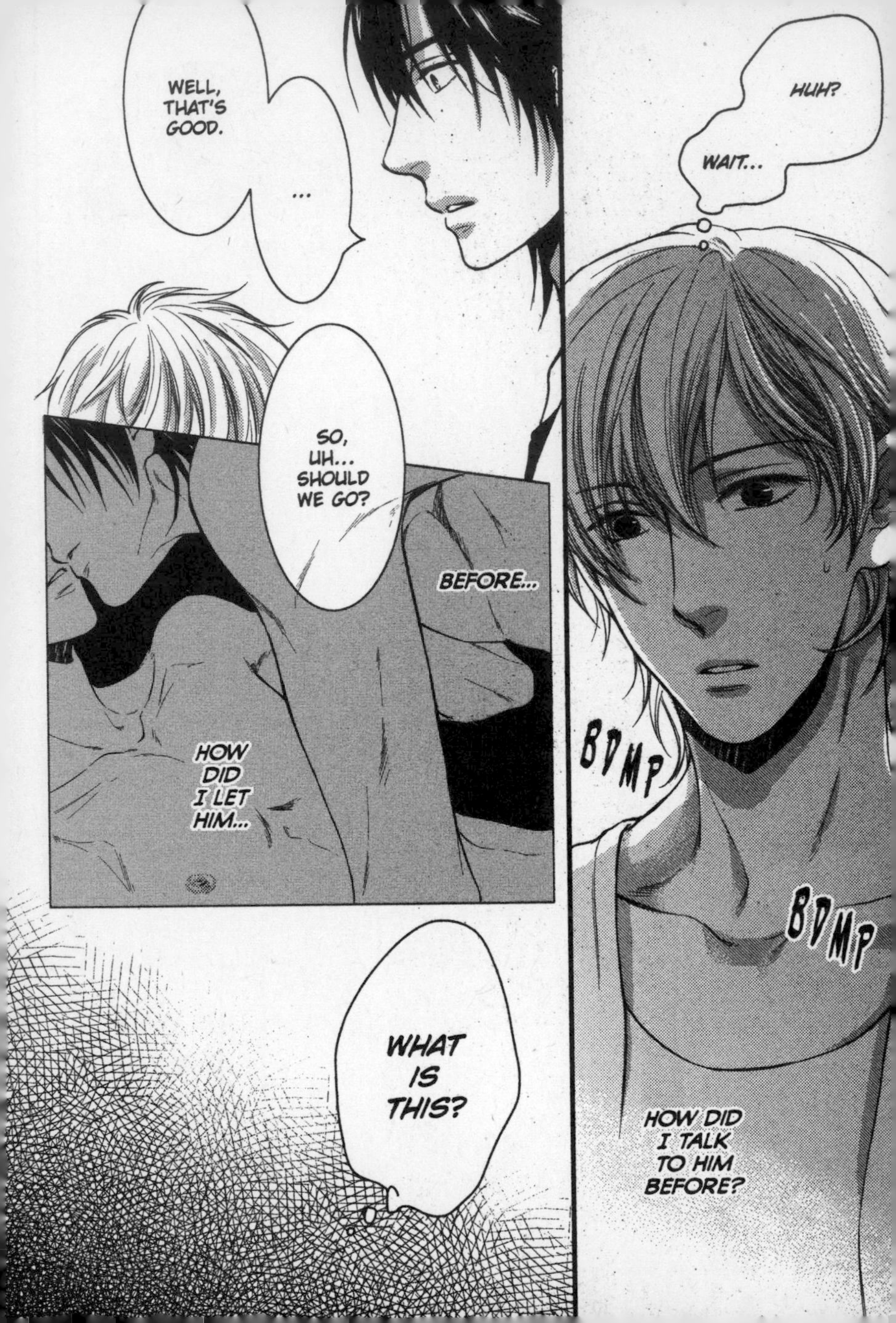
HUH?
WAIT...
BDMP
BDMP
HOW DID I TALK TO HIM BEFORE?
WELL, THAT'S GOOD.
...
SO, UH... SHOULD WE GO?
BEFORE...
HOW DID I LET HIM...
WHAT IS THIS?

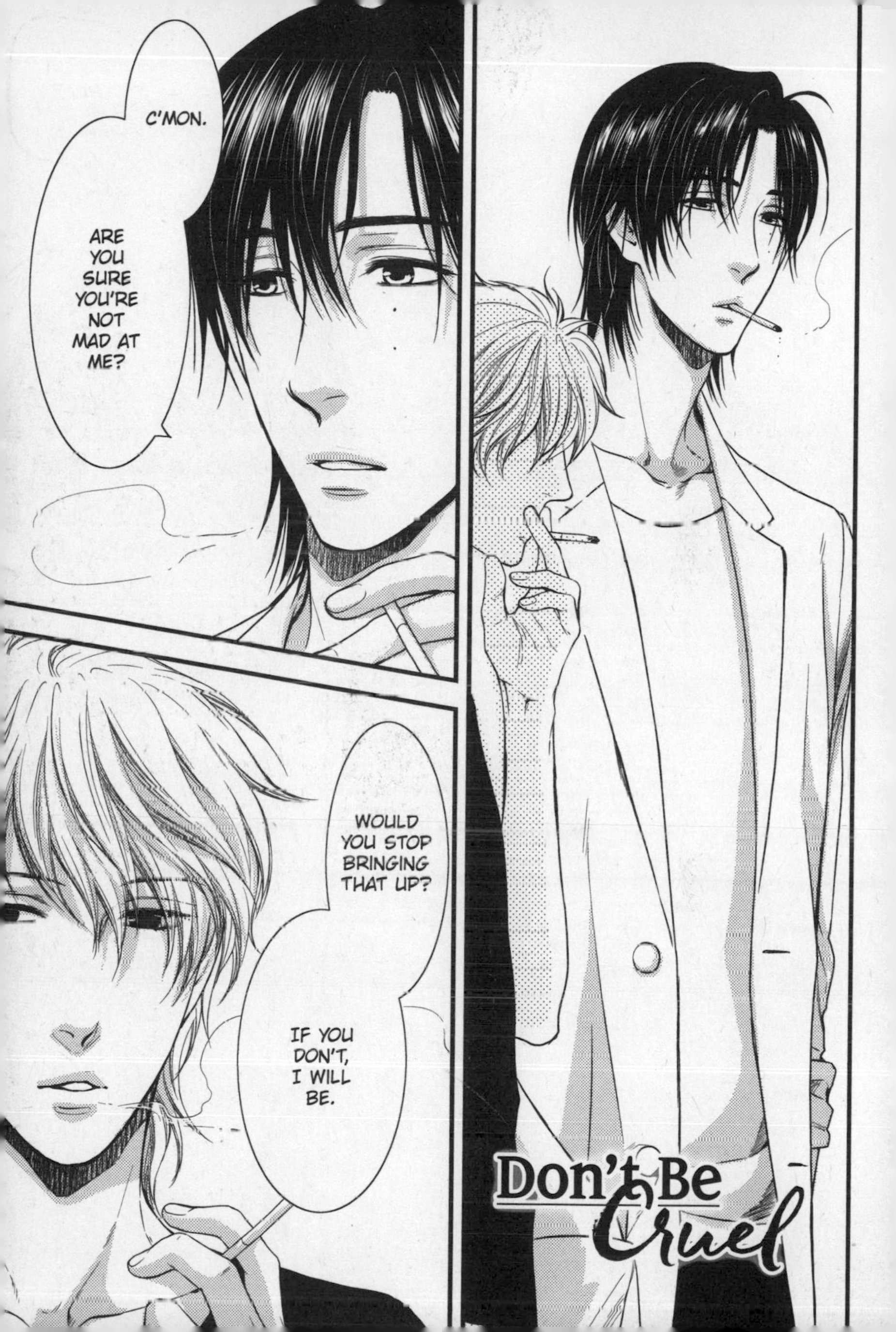
Don't Be Cruel
C'MON.
ARE YOU SURE YOU'RE NOT MAD AT ME?
WOULD YOU STOP BRINGING THAT UP?
IF YOU DON'T, I WILL BE.

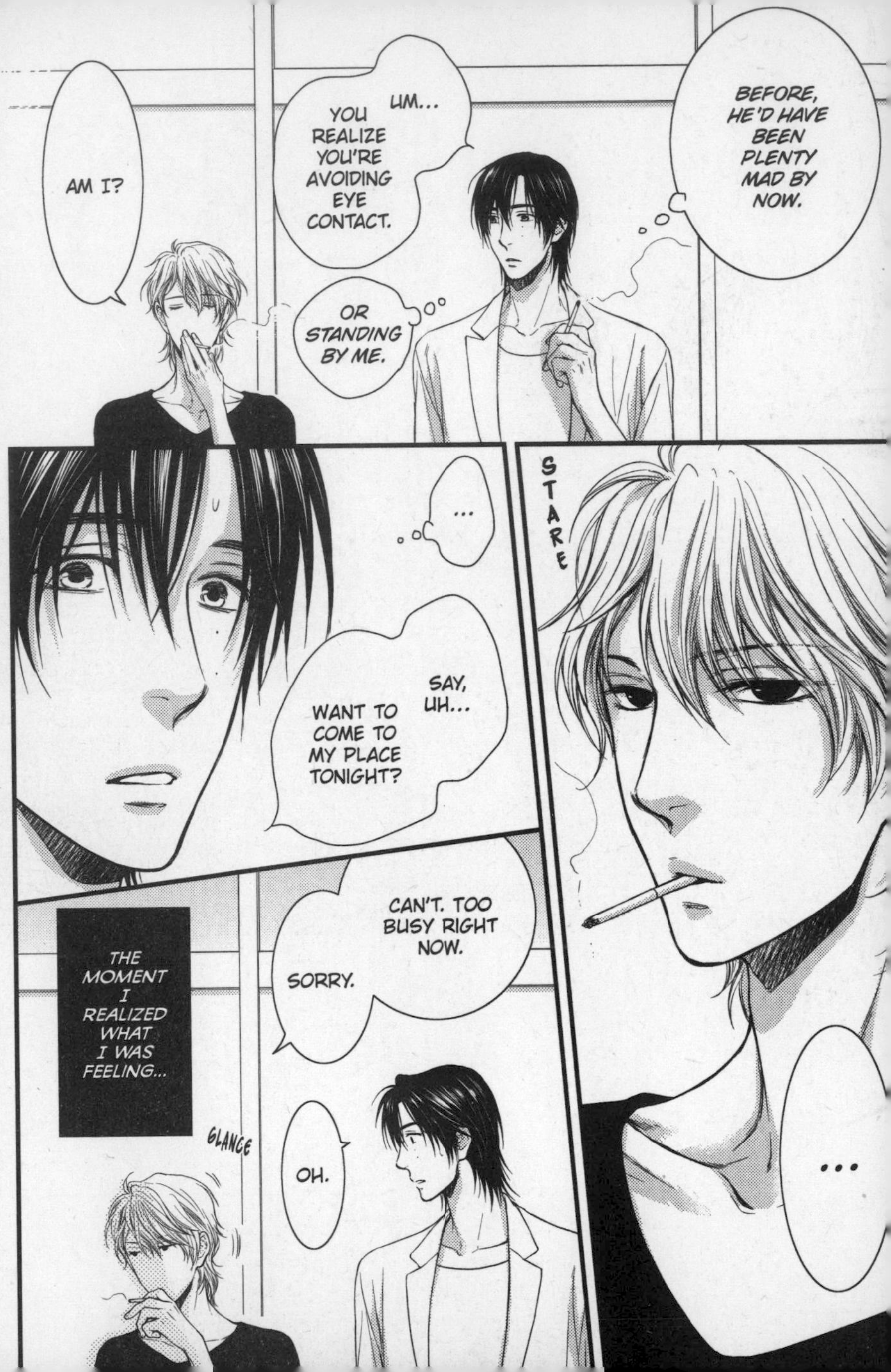
BEFORE, HE'D HAVE BEEN PLENTY MAD BY NOW.
UM... YOU REALIZE YOU'RE AVOIDING EYE CONTACT.
OR STANDING BY ME.
AM I?
STARE
...
...
SAY, UH... WANT TO COME TO MY PLACE TONIGHT?
CAN'T. TOO BUSY RIGHT NOW.
SORRY.
THE MOMENT I REALIZED WHAT I WAS FEELING...
OH.
GLANCE

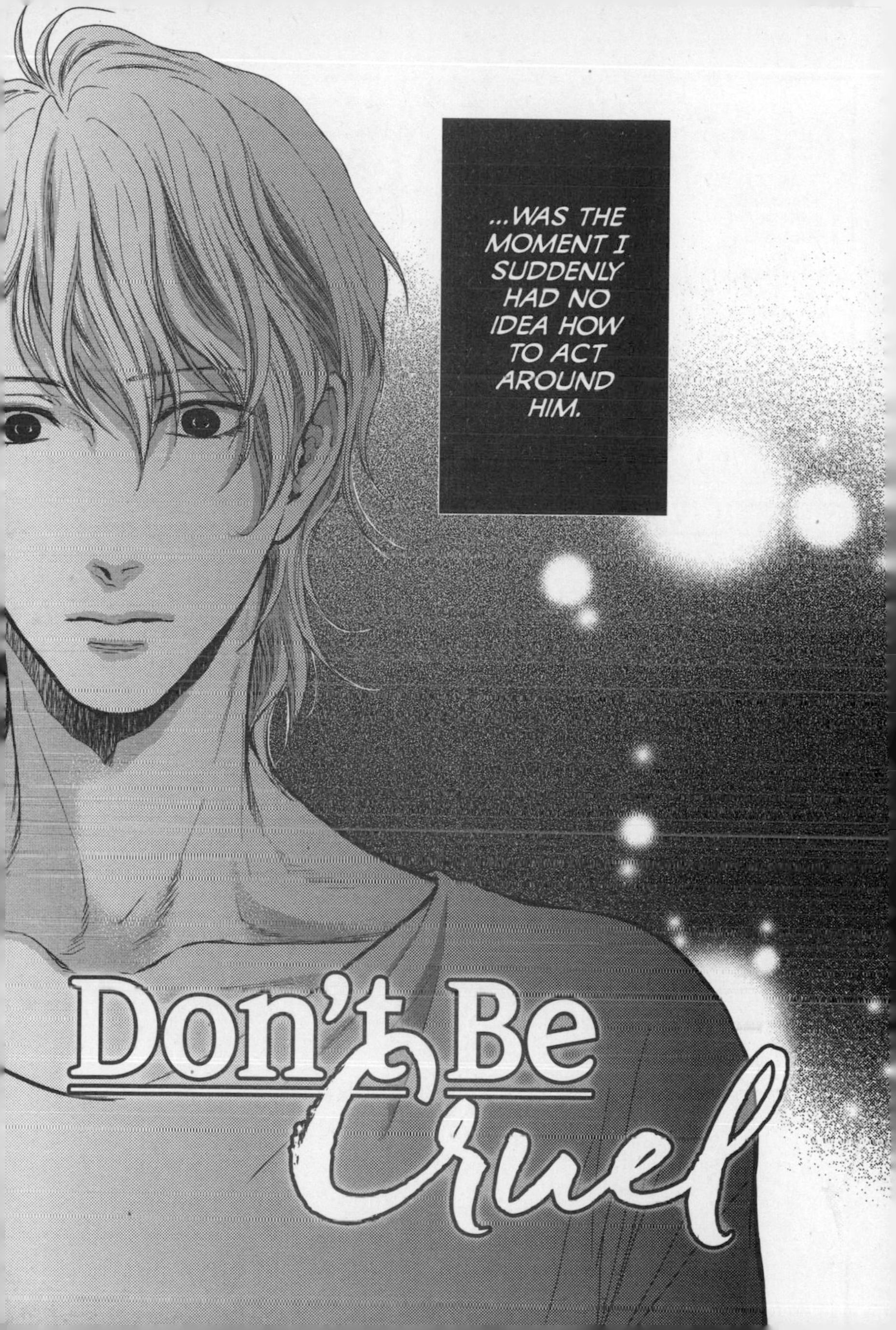
...WAS THE MOMENT I SUDDENLY HAD NO IDEA HOW TO ACT AROUND HIM.
Don't Be Cruel

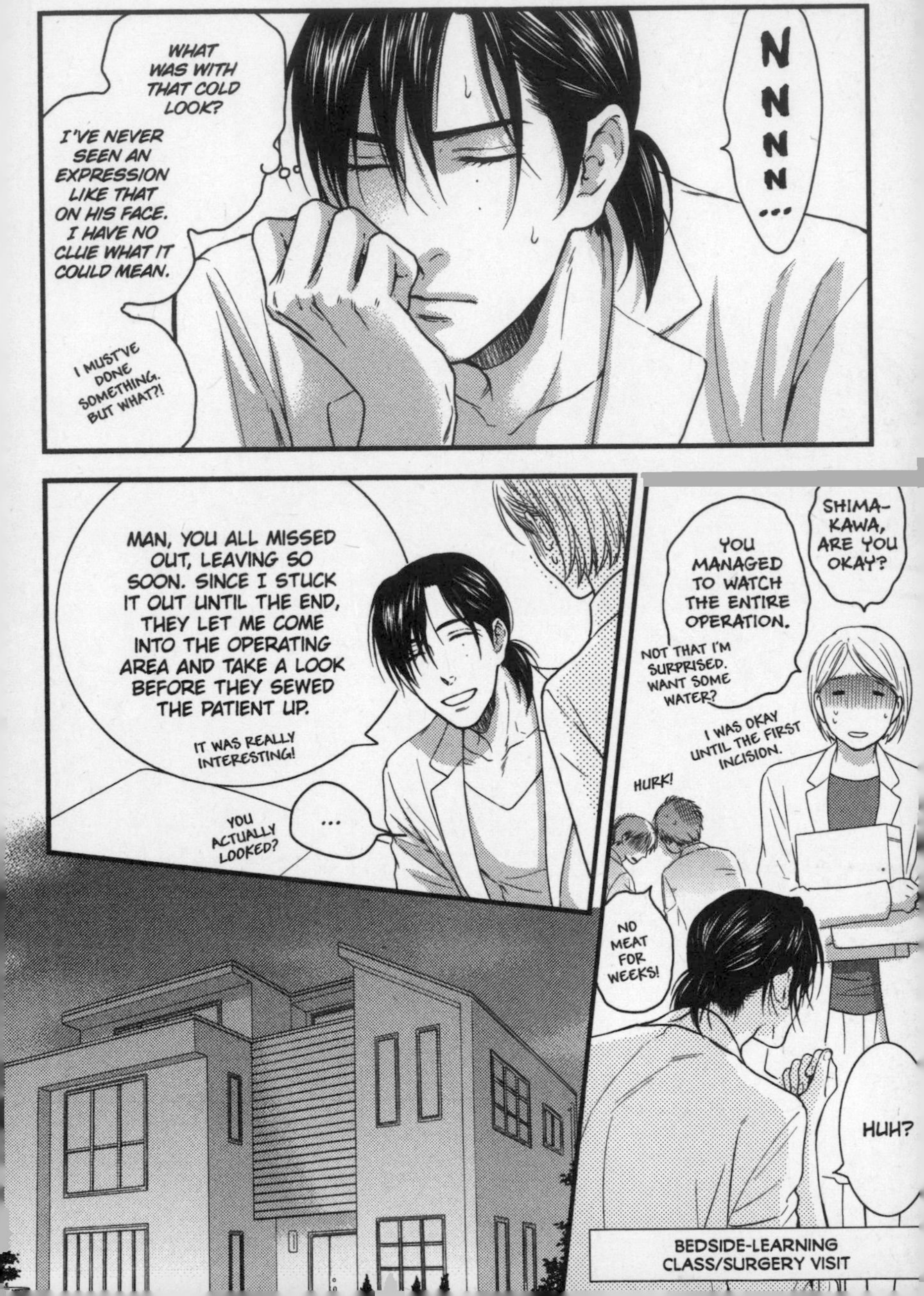
NNNN...
WHAT WAS WITH THAT COLD LOOK?
I'VE NEVER SEEN AN EXPRESSION LIKE THAT ON HIS FACE. I HAVE NO CLUE WHAT IT COULD MEAN.
I MUST'VE DONE SOMETHING. BUT WHAT?!
SHIMA-KAWA, ARE YOU OKAY?
YOU MANAGED TO WATCH THE ENTIRE OPERATION.
NOT THAT I'M SURPRISED. WANT SOME WATER?
I WAS OKAY UNTIL THE FIRST INCISION.
HURK!
NO MEAT FOR WEEKS!
HUH?
BEDSIDE-LEARNING CLASS/SURGERY VISIT
MAN, YOU ALL MISSED OUT, LEAVING SO SOON. SINCE I STUCK IT OUT UNTIL THE END, THEY LET ME COME INTO THE OPERATING AREA AND TAKE A LOOK BEFORE THEY SEWED THE PATIENT UP.
IT WAS REALLY INTERESTING!
...
YOU ACTUALLY LOOKED?

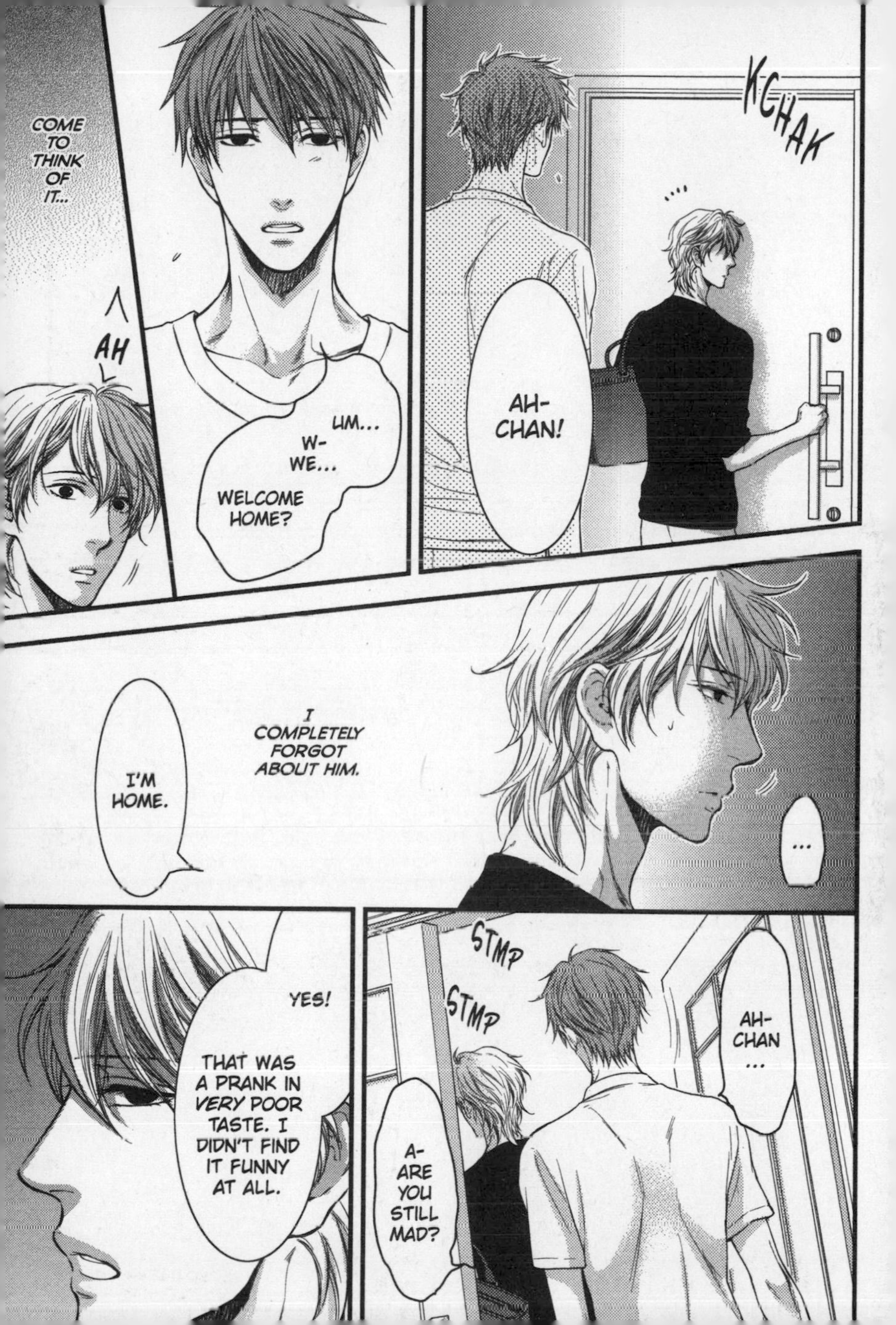
KCHAK
...
AH-CHAN!
COME TO THINK OF IT...
AH
UM...
W- WE...
WELCOME HOME?
...
I COMPLETELY FORGOT ABOUT HIM.
I'M HOME.
AH-CHAN...
STMP
STMP
A-ARE YOU STILL MAD?
YES!
THAT WAS A PRANK IN VERY POOR TASTE. I DIDN'T FIND IT FUNNY AT ALL.

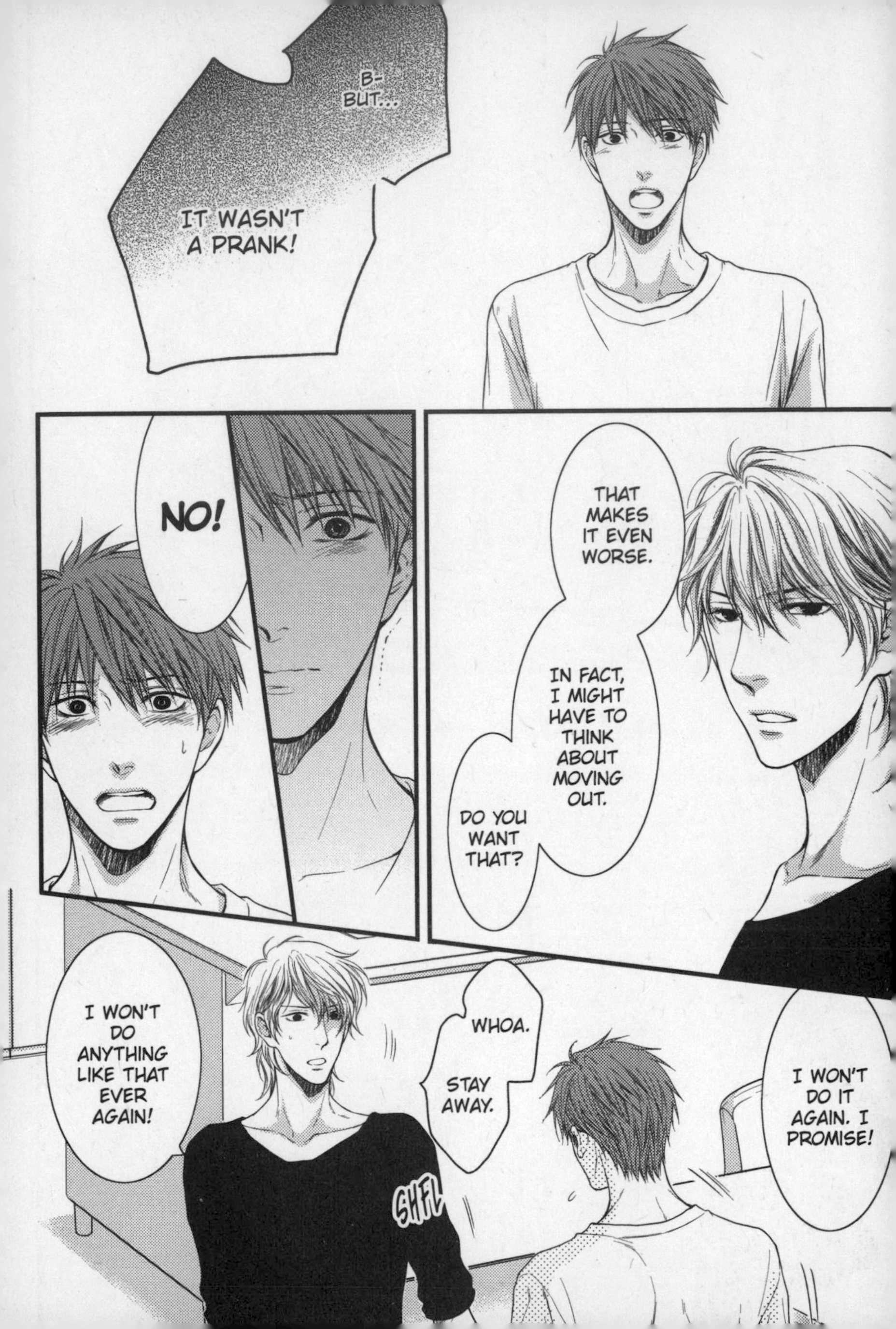
B-BUT...
IT WASN'T A PRANK!
THAT MAKES IT EVEN WORSE.
IN FACT, I MIGHT HAVE TO THINK ABOUT MOVING OUT.
DO YOU WANT THAT?
NO!
I WON'T DO IT AGAIN. I PROMISE!
WHOA.
STAY AWAY.
SHFL
I WON'T DO ANYTHING LIKE THAT EVER AGAIN!

AH-CHAN...

PLIP

AH-CHAN...

RUFL

SHEESH. YOU'VE CERTAINLY GOTTEN BETTER AT THE CROCODILE TEARS.

RING

Mr. Sanada
090-XXXX-XX

...I SHOULD PROBABLY GET IN TOUCH WITH MR. SANADA.

COME TO THINK OF IT...

THERE, THERE.

I'M SORRY!

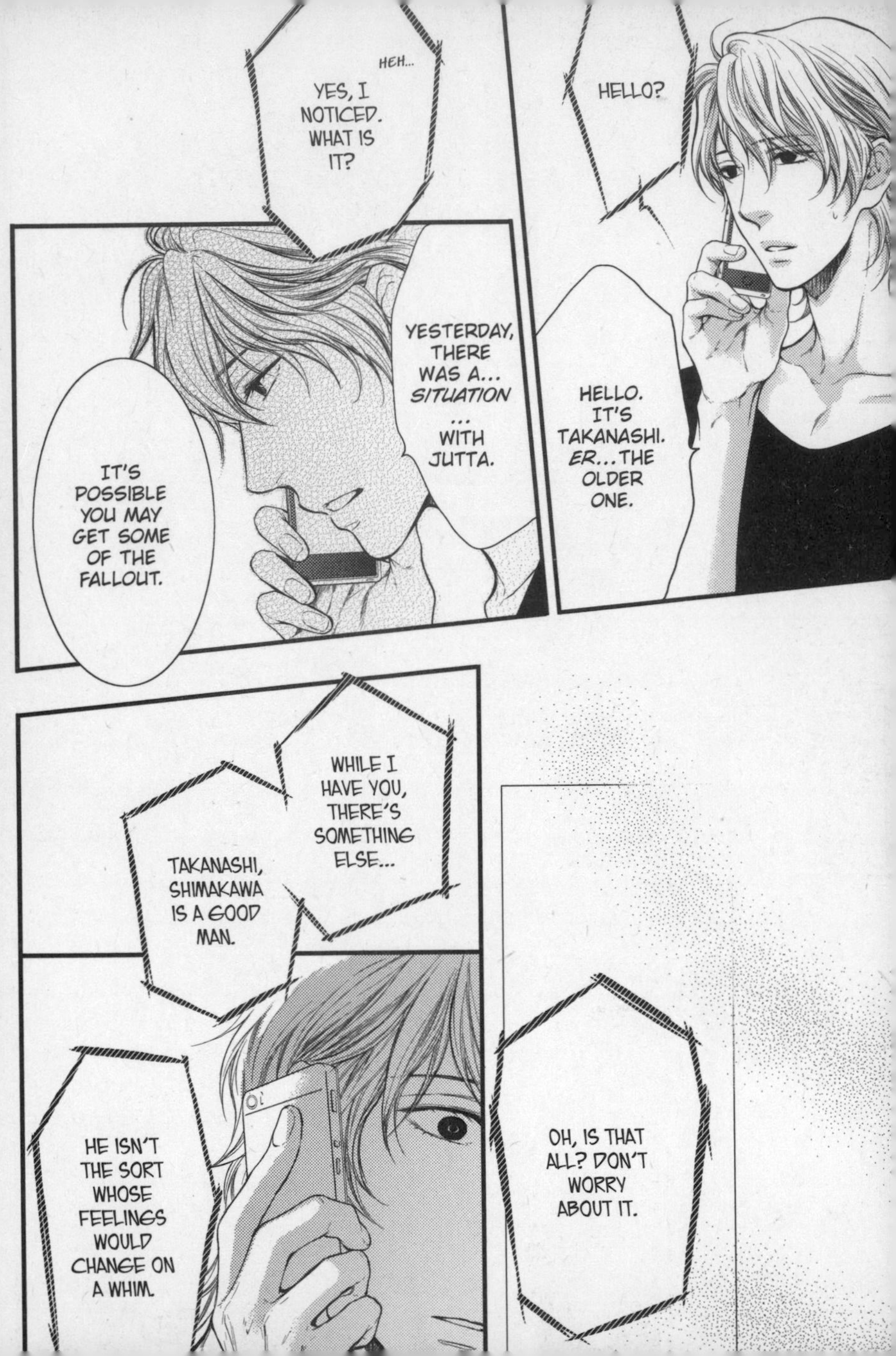
HELLO?
HELLO. IT'S TAKANASHI. ER...THE OLDER ONE.
HEH...
YES, I NOTICED. WHAT IS IT?
YESTERDAY, THERE WAS A... SITUATION ... WITH JUTTA.
IT'S POSSIBLE YOU MAY GET SOME OF THE FALLOUT.
OH, IS THAT ALL? DON'T WORRY ABOUT IT.
WHILE I HAVE YOU, THERE'S SOMETHING ELSE...
TAKANASHI, SHIMAKAWA IS A GOOD MAN.
HE ISN'T THE SORT WHOSE FEELINGS WOULD CHANGE ON A WHIM.

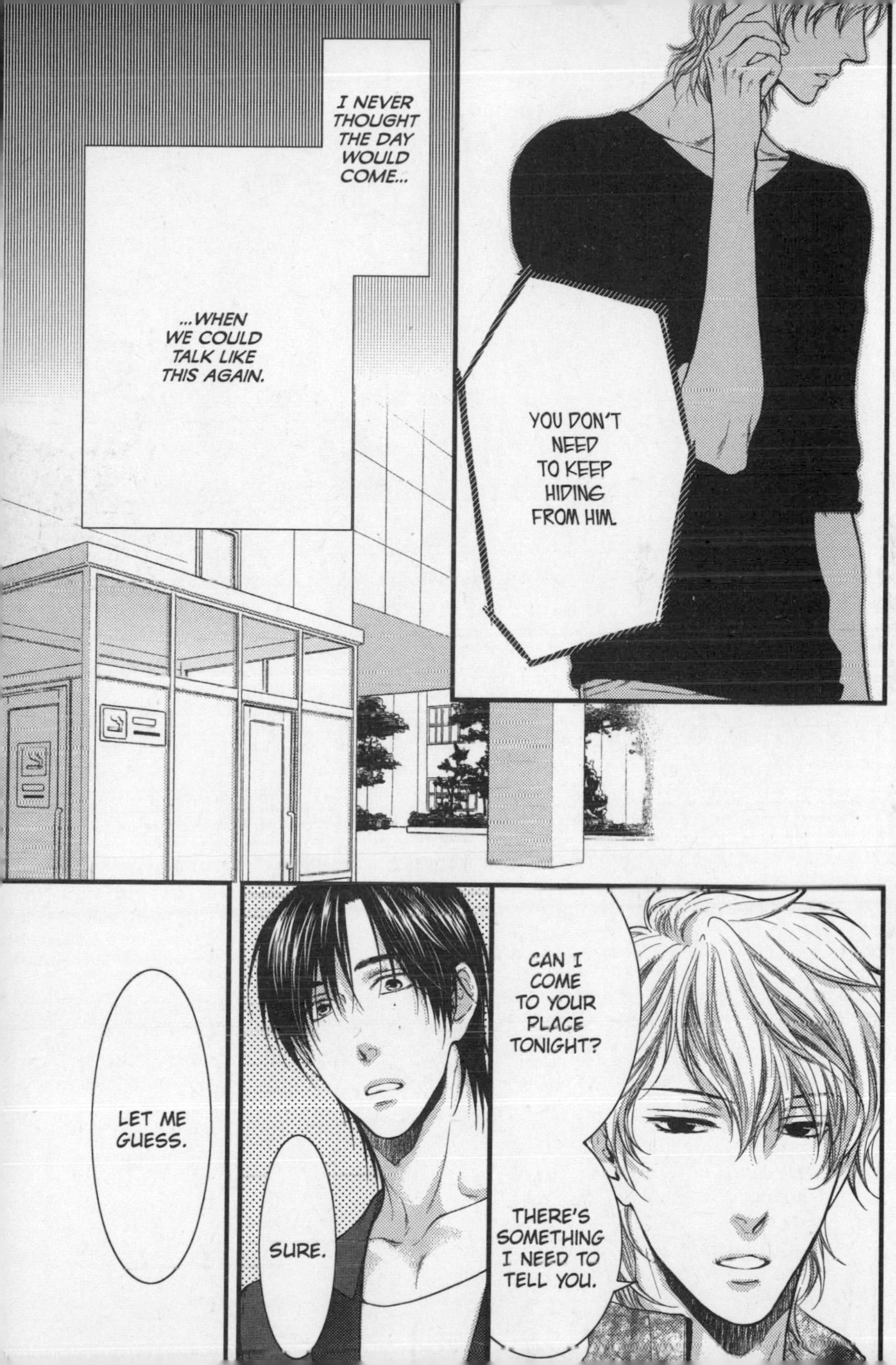
YOU DON'T NEED TO KEEP HIDING FROM HIM.
I NEVER THOUGHT THE DAY WOULD COME...
...WHEN WE COULD TALK LIKE THIS AGAIN.
CAN I COME TO YOUR PLACE TONIGHT?
THERE'S SOMETHING I NEED TO TELL YOU.
SURE.
LET ME GUESS.

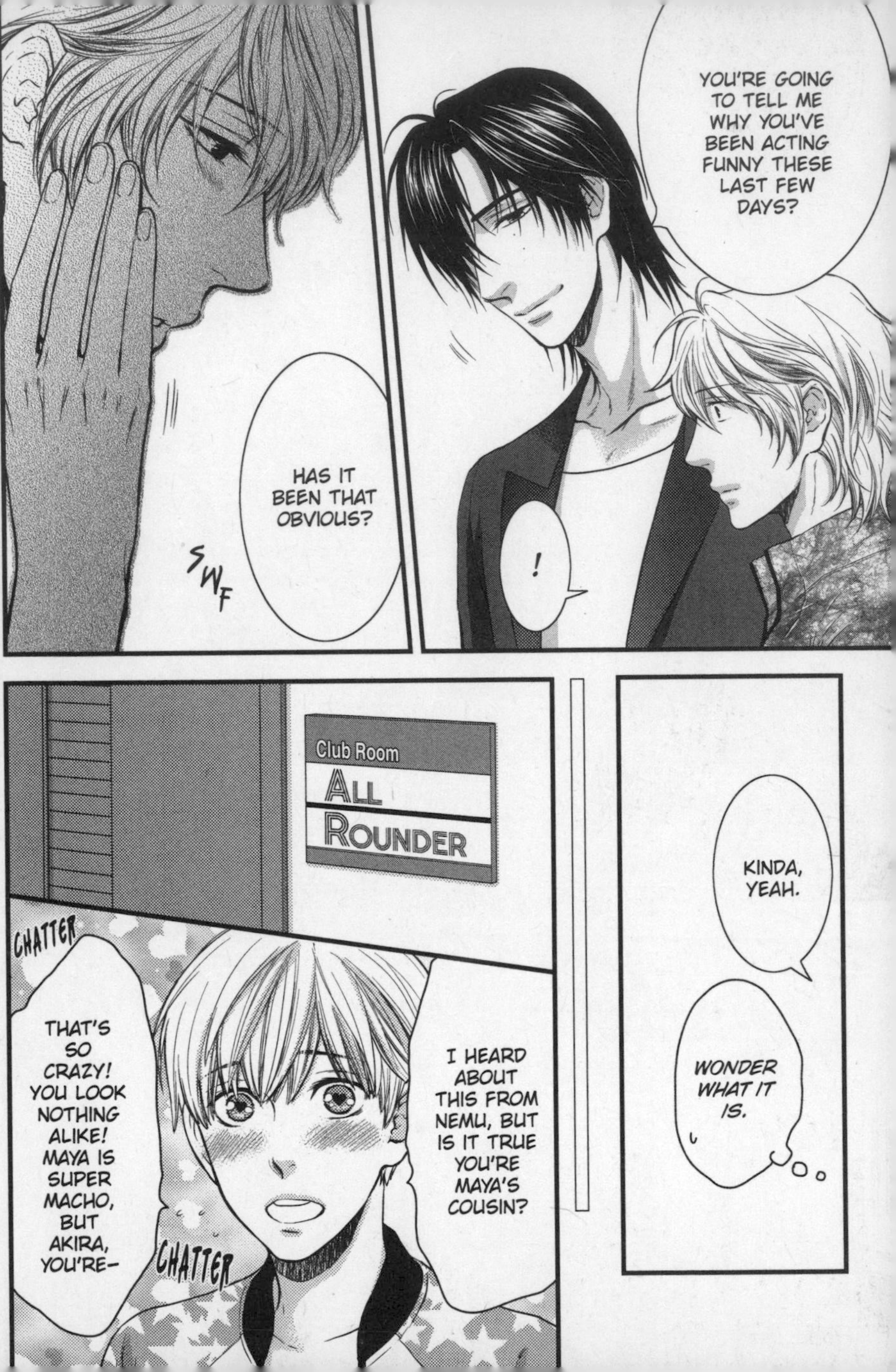
YOU'RE GOING TO TELL ME WHY YOU'VE BEEN ACTING FUNNY THESE LAST FEW DAYS?
!
HAS IT BEEN THAT OBVIOUS?
SWF
KINDA, YEAH.
WONDER WHAT IT IS.
Club Room
ALL ROUNDER
I HEARD ABOUT THIS FROM NEMU, BUT IS IT TRUE YOU'RE MAYA'S COUSIN?
CHATTER
THAT'S SO CRAZY! YOU LOOK NOTHING ALIKE! MAYA IS SUPER MACHO, BUT AKIRA, YOU'RE–
CHATTER

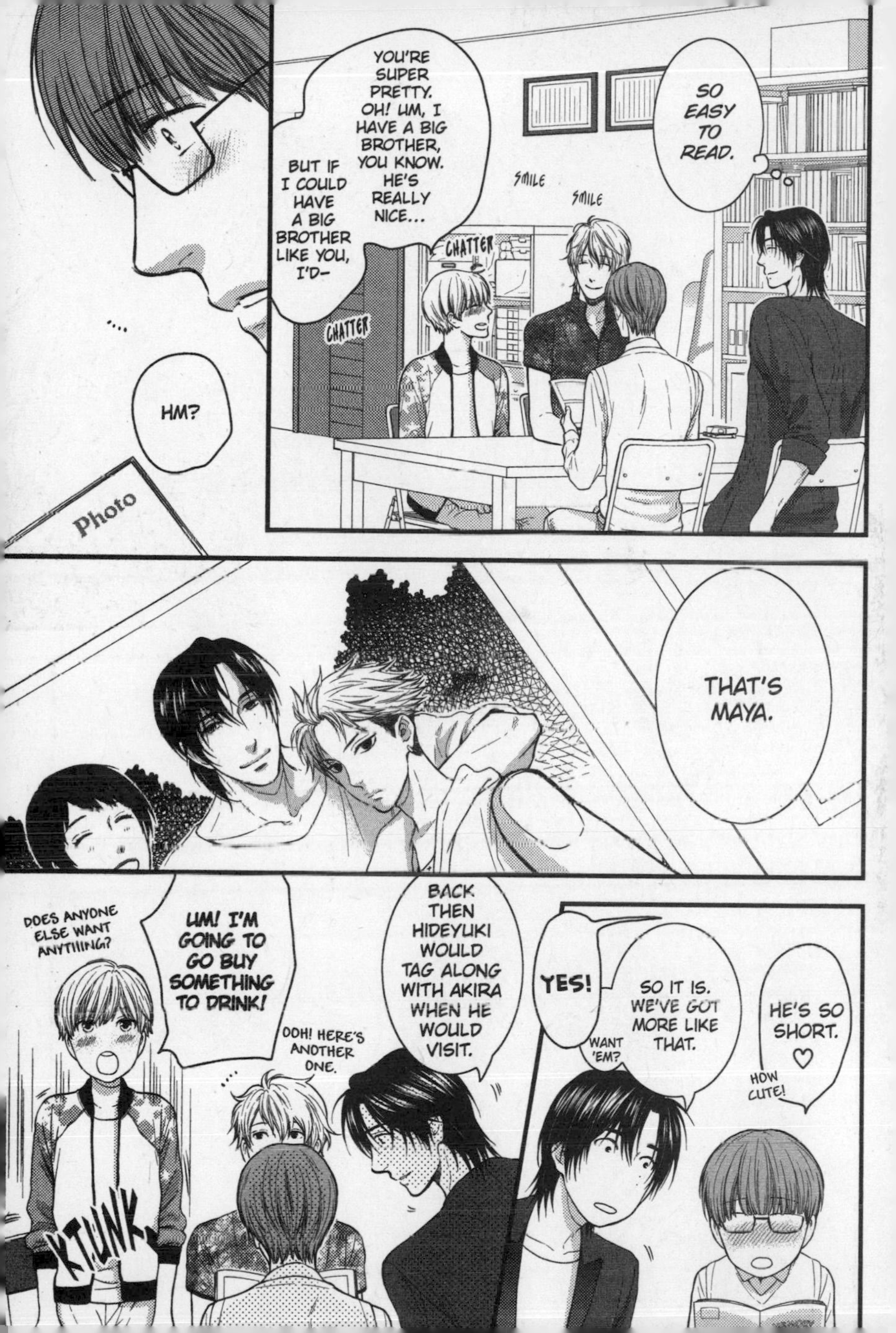
SO EASY TO READ.
SMILE
SMILE
YOU'RE SUPER PRETTY. OH! UM, I HAVE A BIG BROTHER, YOU KNOW. HE'S REALLY NICE...
BUT IF I COULD HAVE A BIG BROTHER LIKE YOU, I'D–
CHATTER
CHATTER
....
HM?
Photo
THAT'S MAYA.
HE'S SO SHORT. ♥
HOW CUTE!
SO IT IS. WE'VE GOT MORE LIKE THAT.
WANT 'EM?
YES!
BACK THEN HIDEYUKI WOULD TAG ALONG WITH AKIRA WHEN HE WOULD VISIT.
OOH! HERE'S ANOTHER ONE.
...
UM! I'M GOING TO GO BUY SOMETHING TO DRINK!
DOES ANYONE ELSE WANT ANYTHING?
KTUNK

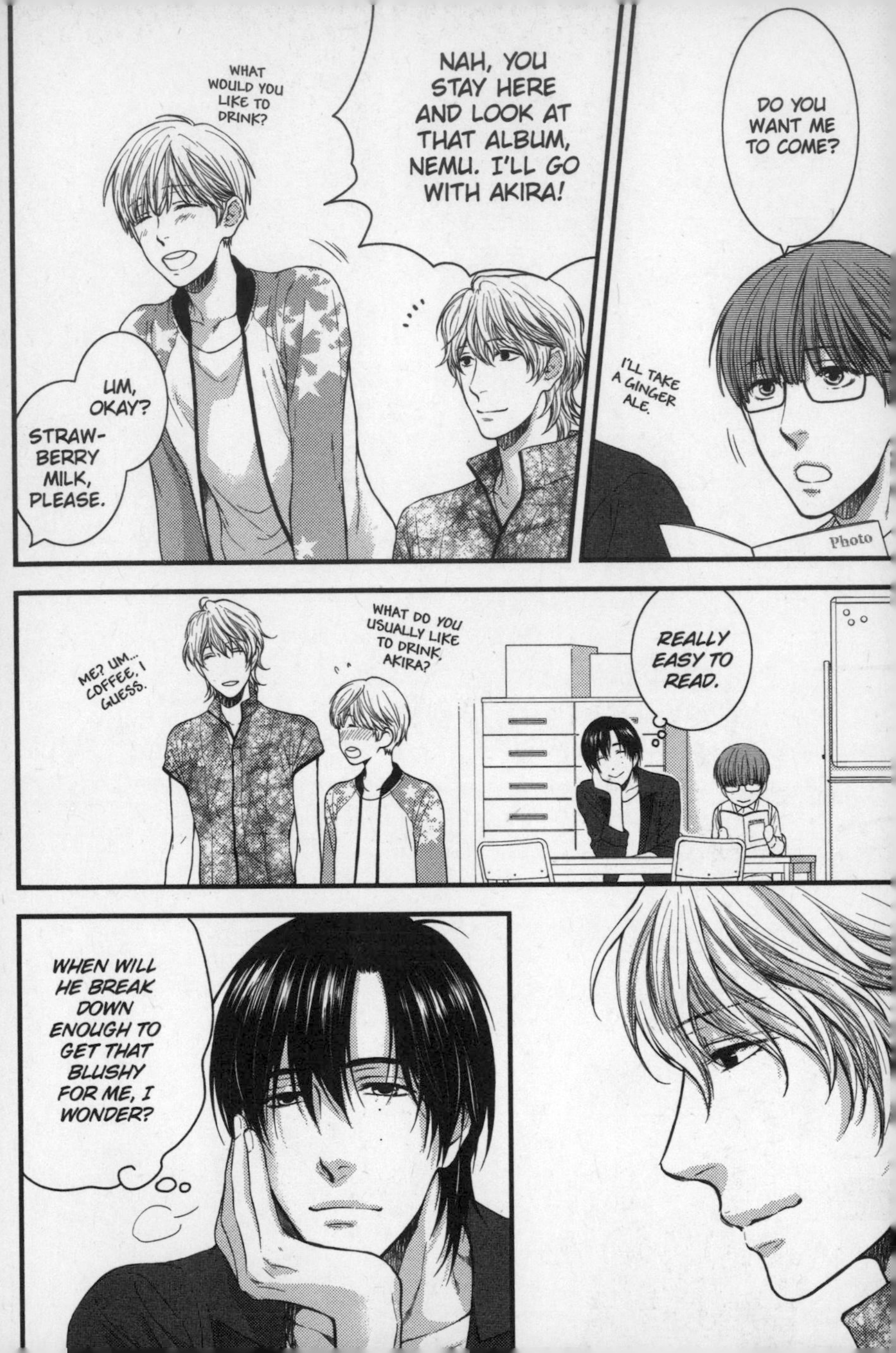
DO YOU WANT ME TO COME?
Photo
I'LL TAKE A GINGER ALE.
NAH, YOU STAY HERE AND LOOK AT THAT ALBUM, NEMU. I'LL GO WITH AKIRA!
WHAT WOULD YOU LIKE TO DRINK?
UM, OKAY?
STRAW-BERRY MILK, PLEASE.
REALLY EASY TO READ.
WHAT DO YOU USUALLY LIKE TO DRINK, AKIRA?
ME? UM... COFFEE, I GUESS.
WHEN WILL HE BREAK DOWN ENOUGH TO GET THAT BLUSHY FOR ME, I WONDER?

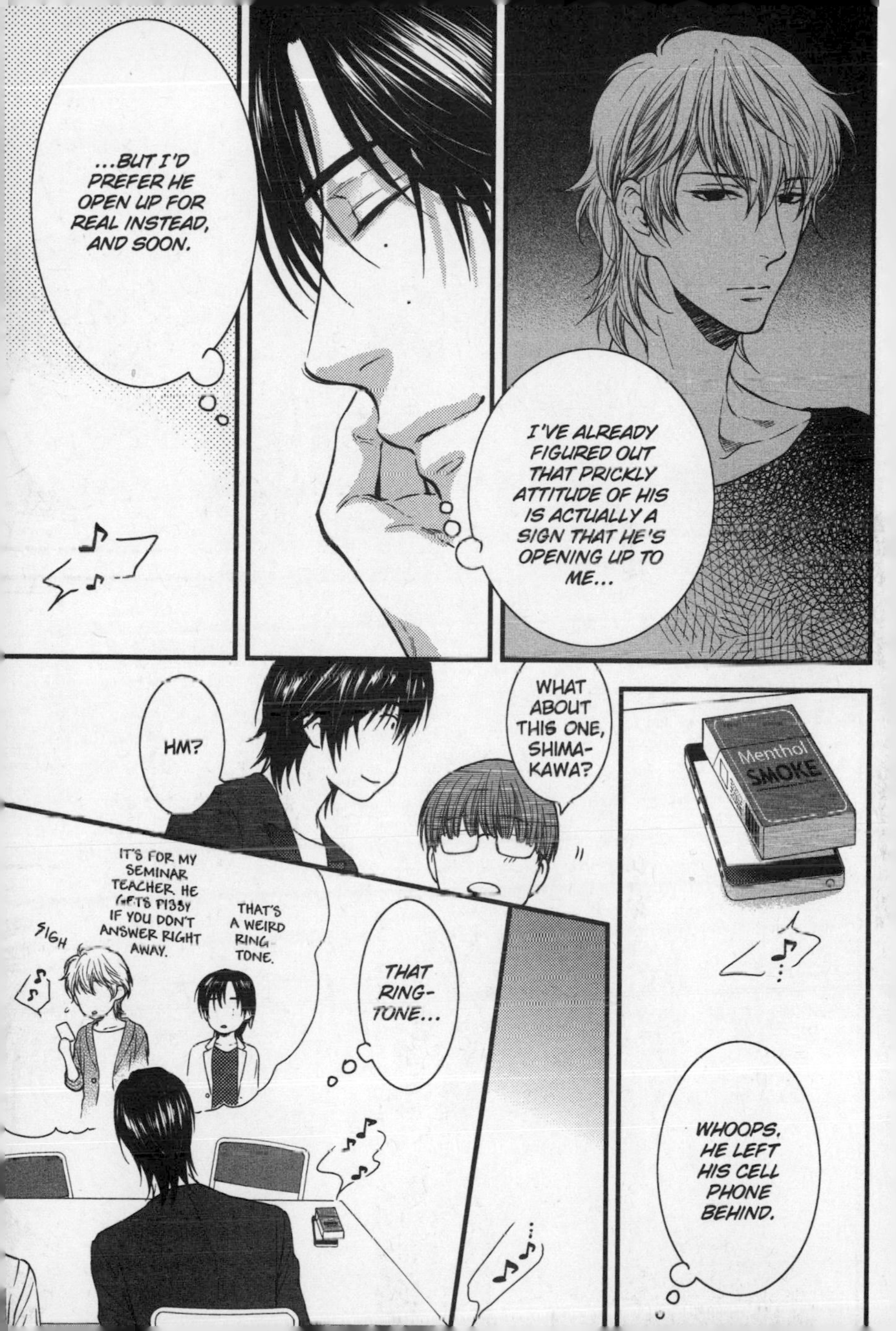
I'VE ALREADY FIGURED OUT THAT PRICKLY ATTITUDE OF HIS IS ACTUALLY A SIGN THAT HE'S OPENING UP TO ME...
...BUT I'D PREFER HE OPEN UP FOR REAL INSTEAD, AND SOON.
Menthol SMOKE
WHOOPS. HE LEFT HIS CELL PHONE BEHIND.
WHAT ABOUT THIS ONE, SHIMA-KAWA?
HM?
THAT RING-TONE...
THAT'S A WEIRD RING-TONE.
IT'S FOR MY SEMINAR TEACHER. HE GETS PISSY IF YOU DON'T ANSWER RIGHT AWAY.
SIGH

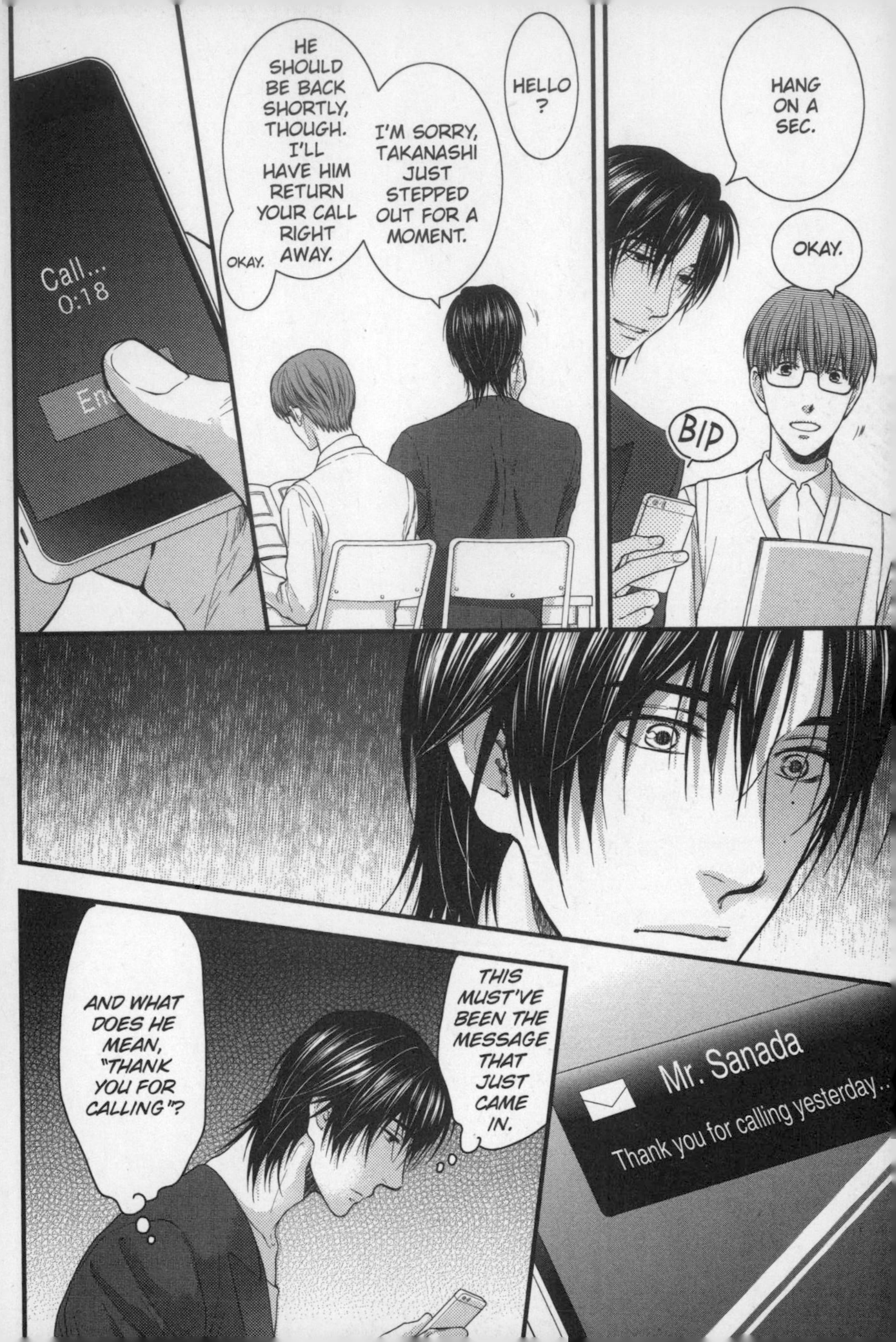
HANG ON A SEC.
OKAY.
BIP
HELLO?
I'M SORRY, TAKANASHI JUST STEPPED OUT FOR A MOMENT.
HE SHOULD BE BACK SHORTLY, THOUGH. I'LL HAVE HIM RETURN YOUR CALL RIGHT AWAY.
OKAY.
Call... 0:18
Mr. Sanada
Thank you for calling yesterday...
THIS MUST'VE BEEN THE MESSAGE THAT JUST CAME IN.
AND WHAT DOES HE MEAN, "THANK YOU FOR CALLING"?

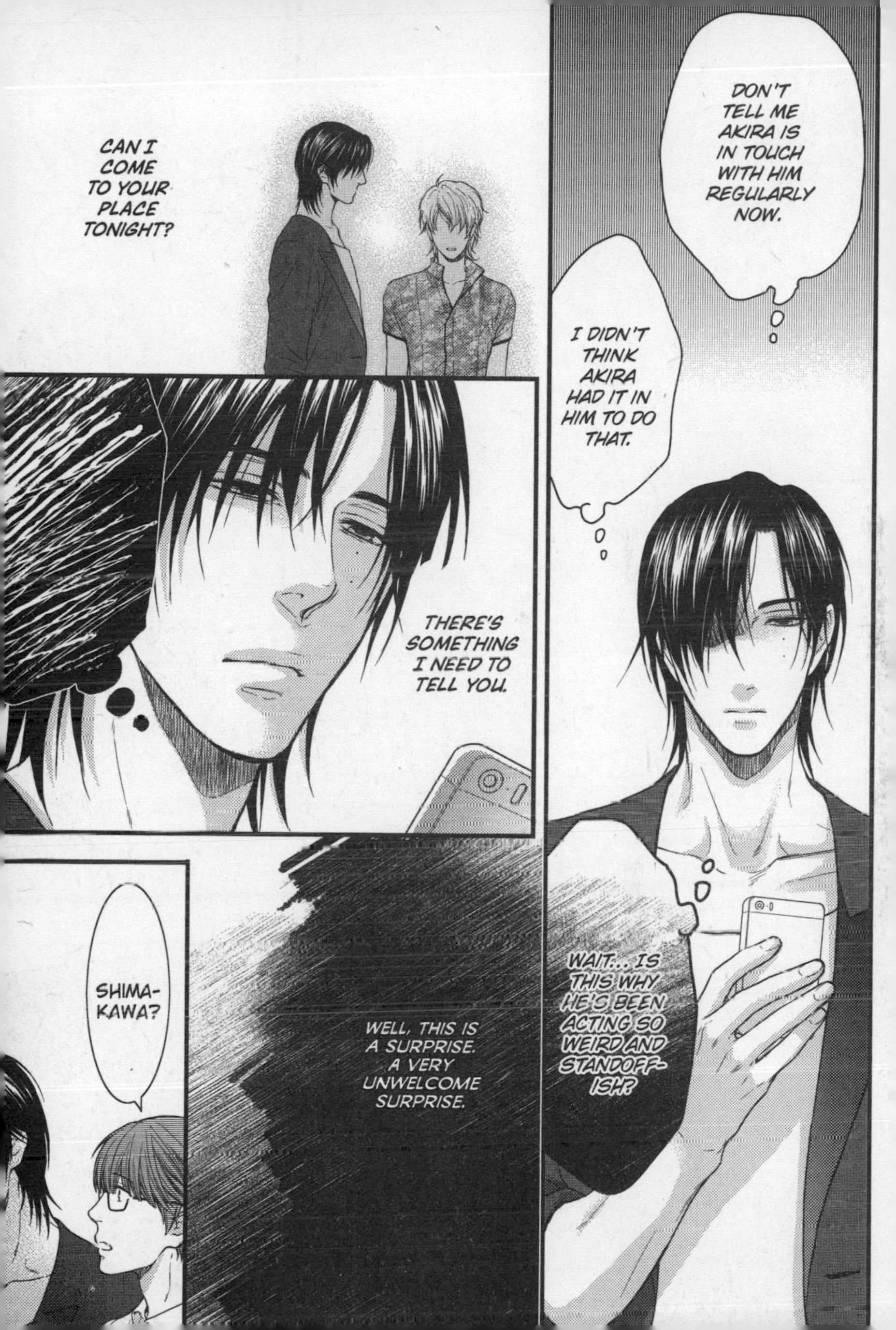
DON'T TELL ME AKIRA IS IN TOUCH WITH HIM REGULARLY NOW.
I DIDN'T THINK AKIRA HAD IT IN HIM TO DO THAT.
WAIT... IS THIS WHY HE'S BEEN ACTING SO WEIRD AND STANDOFF-ISH?
CAN I COME TO YOUR PLACE TONIGHT?
THERE'S SOMETHING I NEED TO TELL YOU.
WELL, THIS IS A SURPRISE. A VERY UNWELCOME SURPRISE.
SHIMA-KAWA?

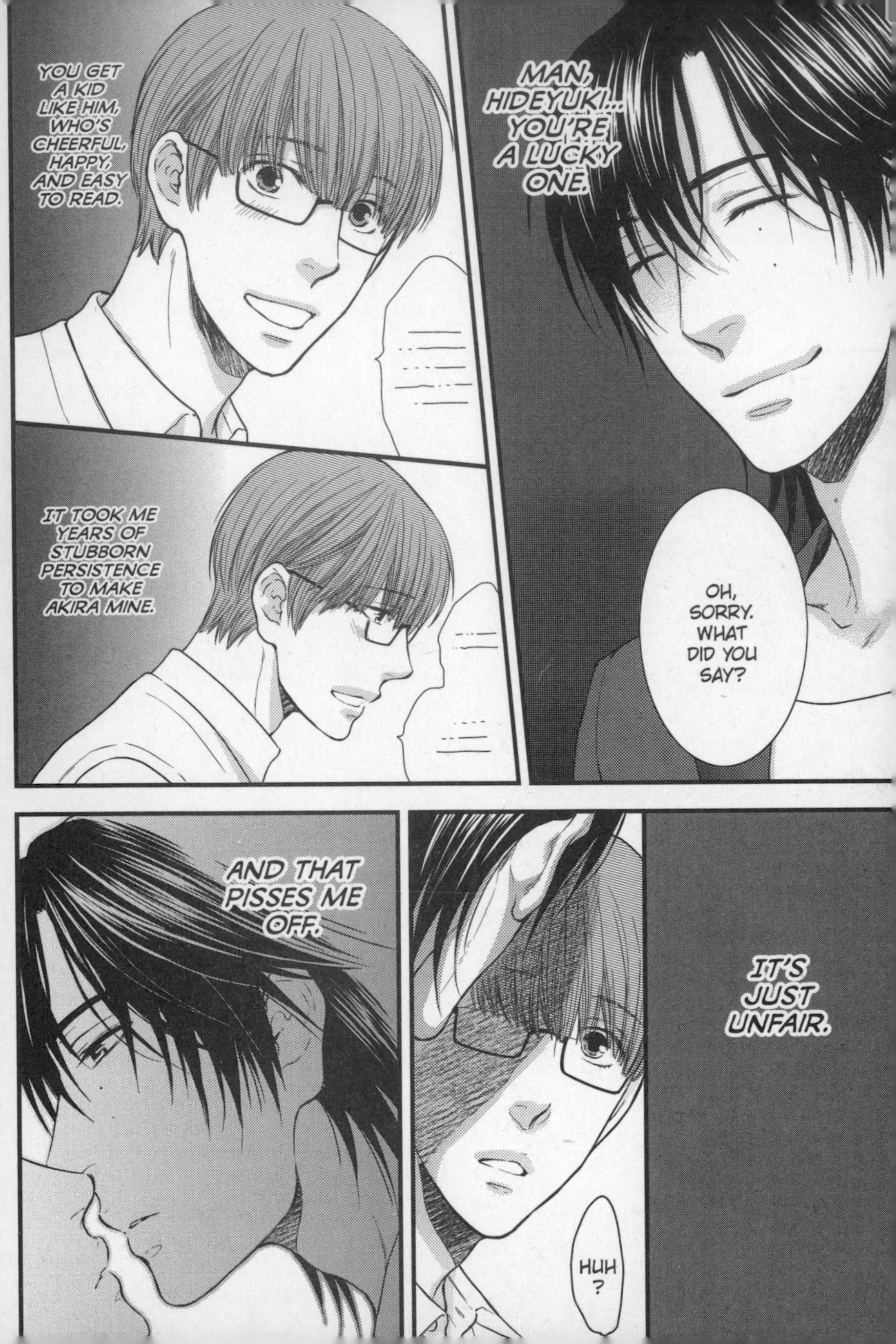
MAN, HIDEYUKI... YOU'RE A LUCKY ONE.
OH, SORRY. WHAT DID YOU SAY?
YOU GET A KID LIKE HIM, WHO'S CHEERFUL, HAPPY, AND EASY TO READ.
IT TOOK ME YEARS OF STUBBORN PERSISTENCE TO MAKE AKIRA MINE.
IT'S JUST UNFAIR.
HUH?
AND THAT PISSES ME OFF.

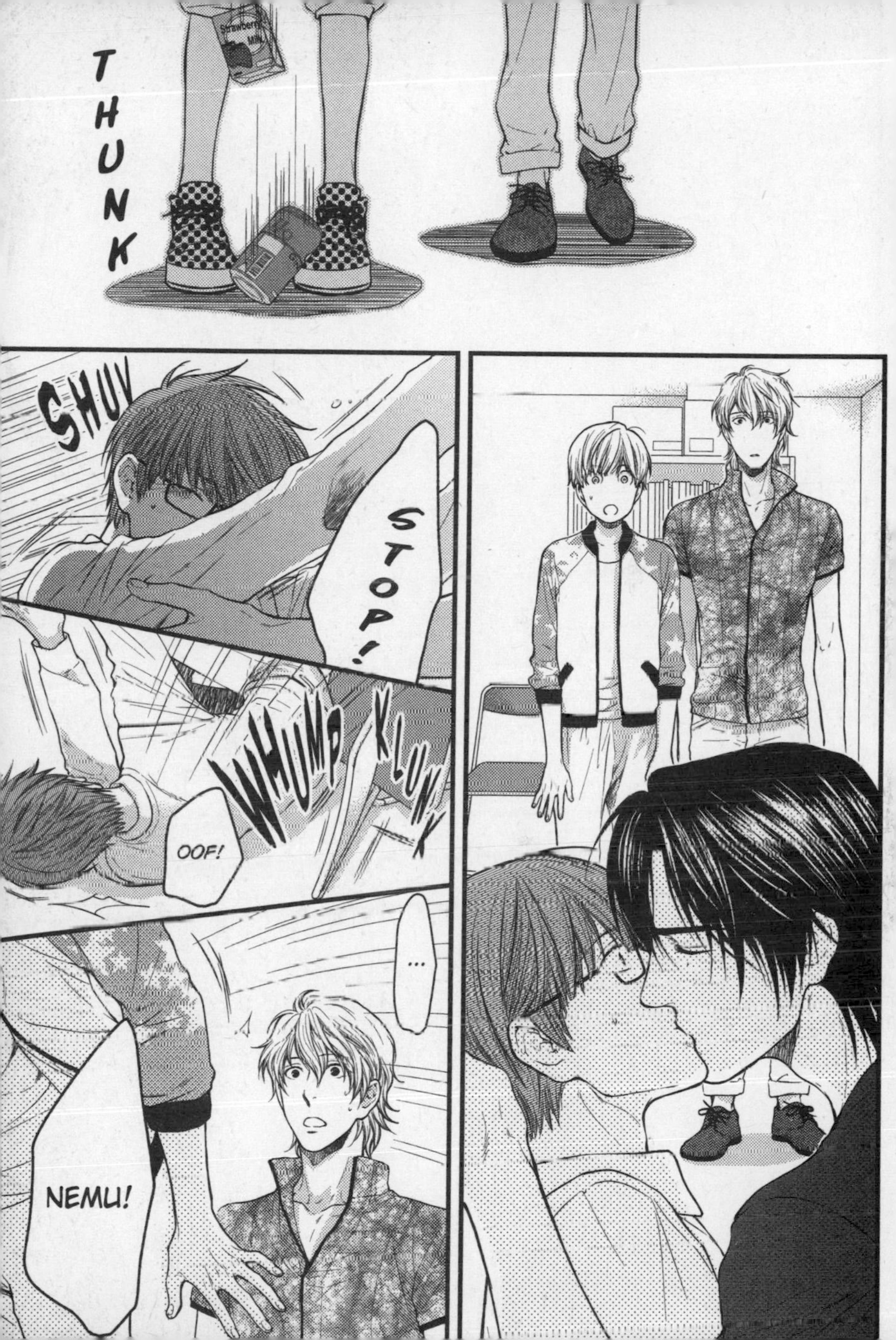
THUNK
SHUV
STOP!
KLUNK
WHUMP
OOF!
...
NEMU!

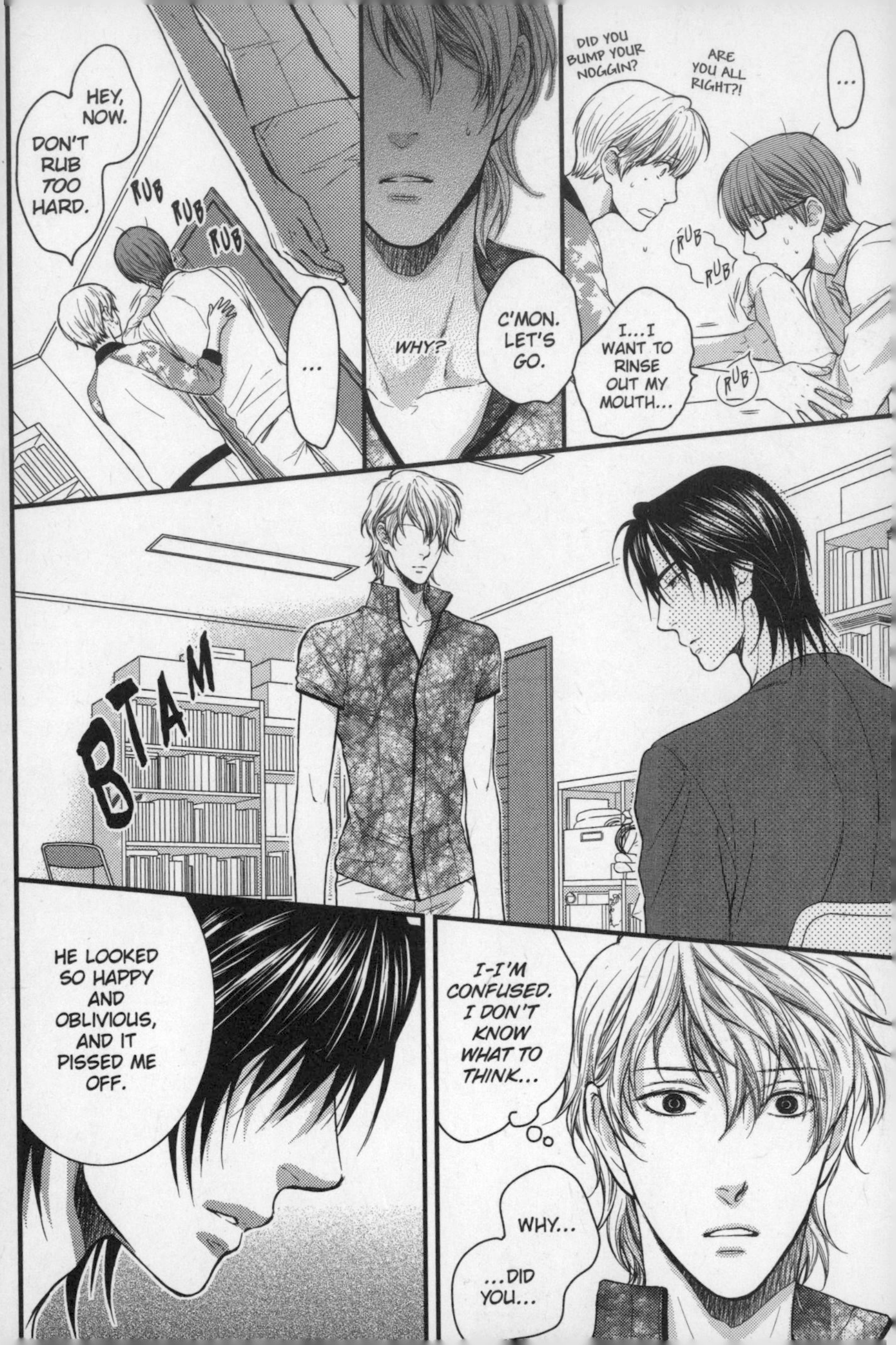
...
ARE YOU ALL RIGHT?!
DID YOU BUMP YOUR NOGGIN?
RUB RUB
I...I WANT TO RINSE OUT MY MOUTH...
RUB
C'MON. LET'S GO.
WHY?
...
HEY, NOW.
DON'T RUB TOO HARD.
RUB RUB RUB
BTAM
I-I'M CONFUSED. I DON'T KNOW WHAT TO THINK...
WHY...
...DID YOU...
HE LOOKED SO HAPPY AND OBLIVIOUS, AND IT PISSED ME OFF.

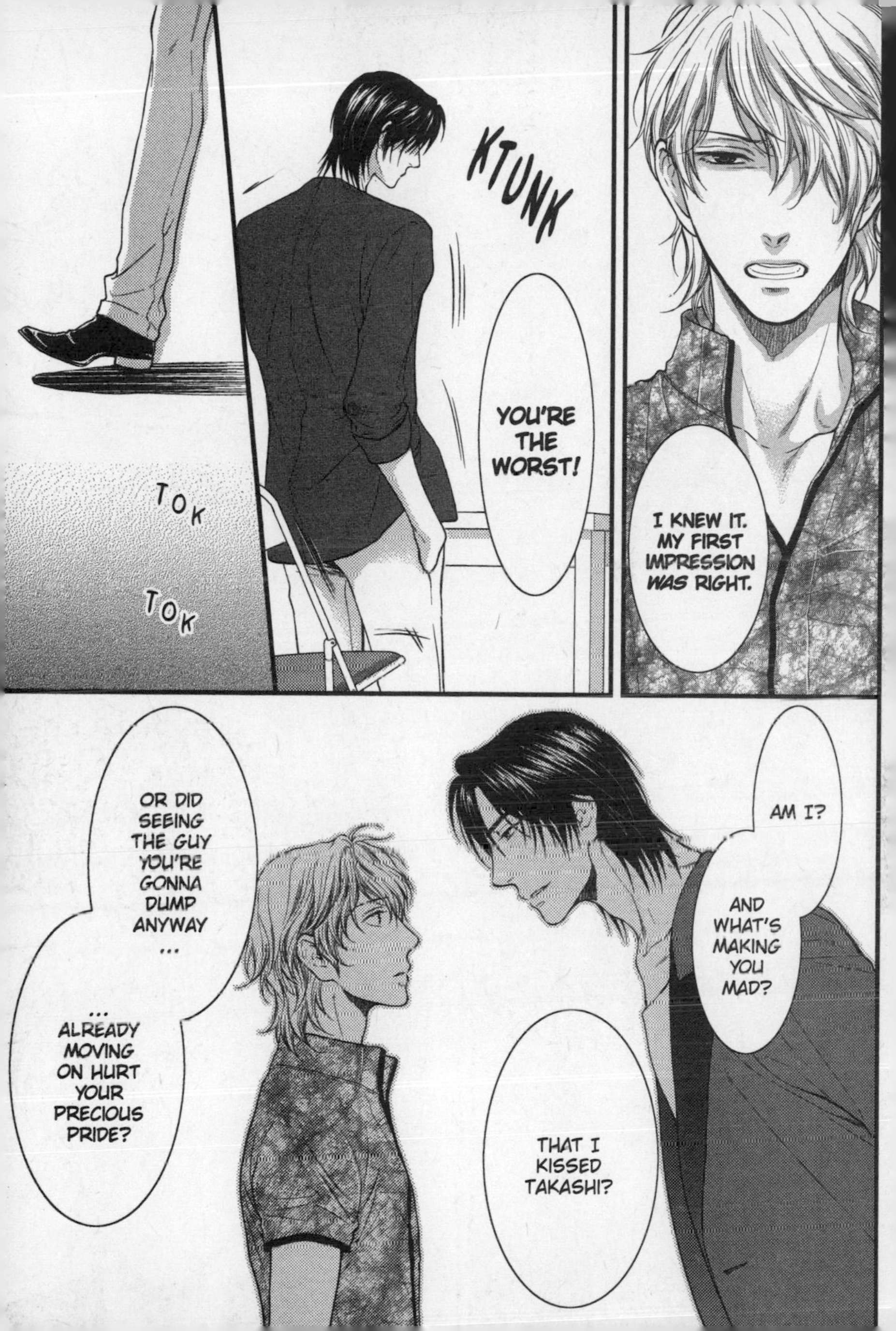
I KNEW IT. MY FIRST IMPRESSION WAS RIGHT.
KTUNK
YOU'RE THE WORST!
TOK
TOK
AM I?
AND WHAT'S MAKING YOU MAD?
THAT I KISSED TAKASHI?
OR DID SEEING THE GUY YOU'RE GONNA DUMP ANYWAY ...
... ALREADY MOVING ON HURT YOUR PRECIOUS PRIDE?

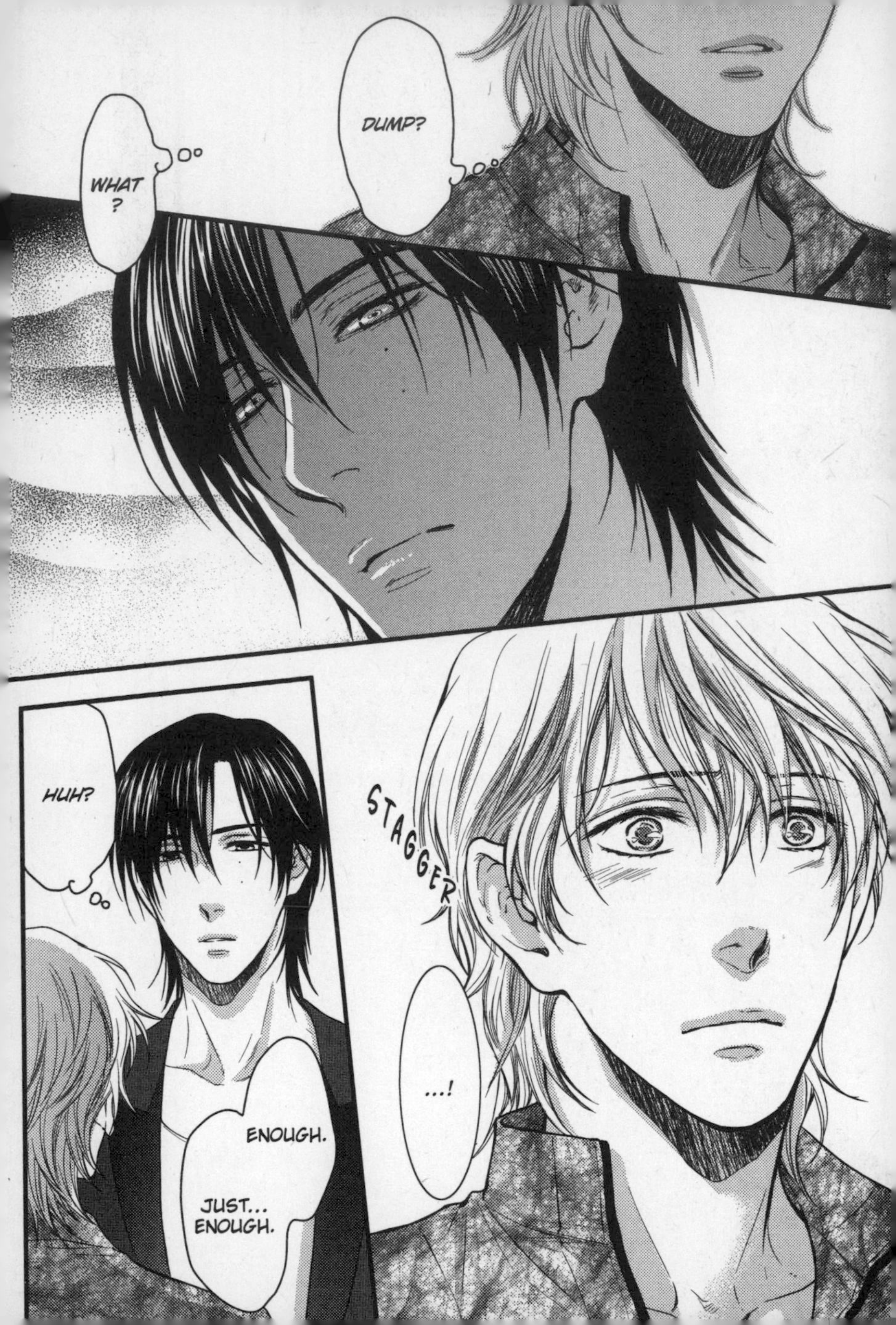
DUMP?
WHAT?
STAGGER
...!
HUH?
ENOUGH.
JUST... ENOUGH.

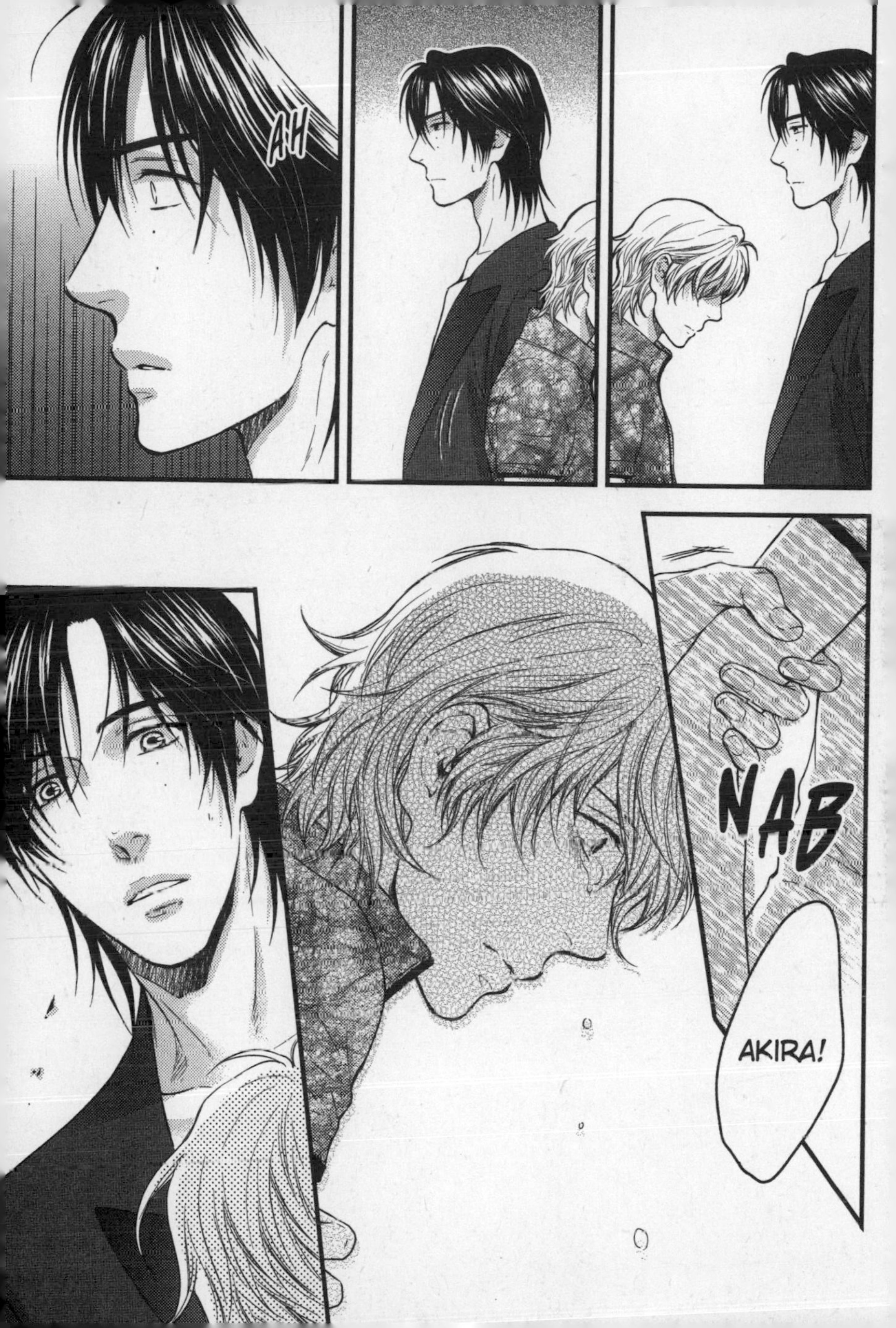
AH
NAB
AKIRA!

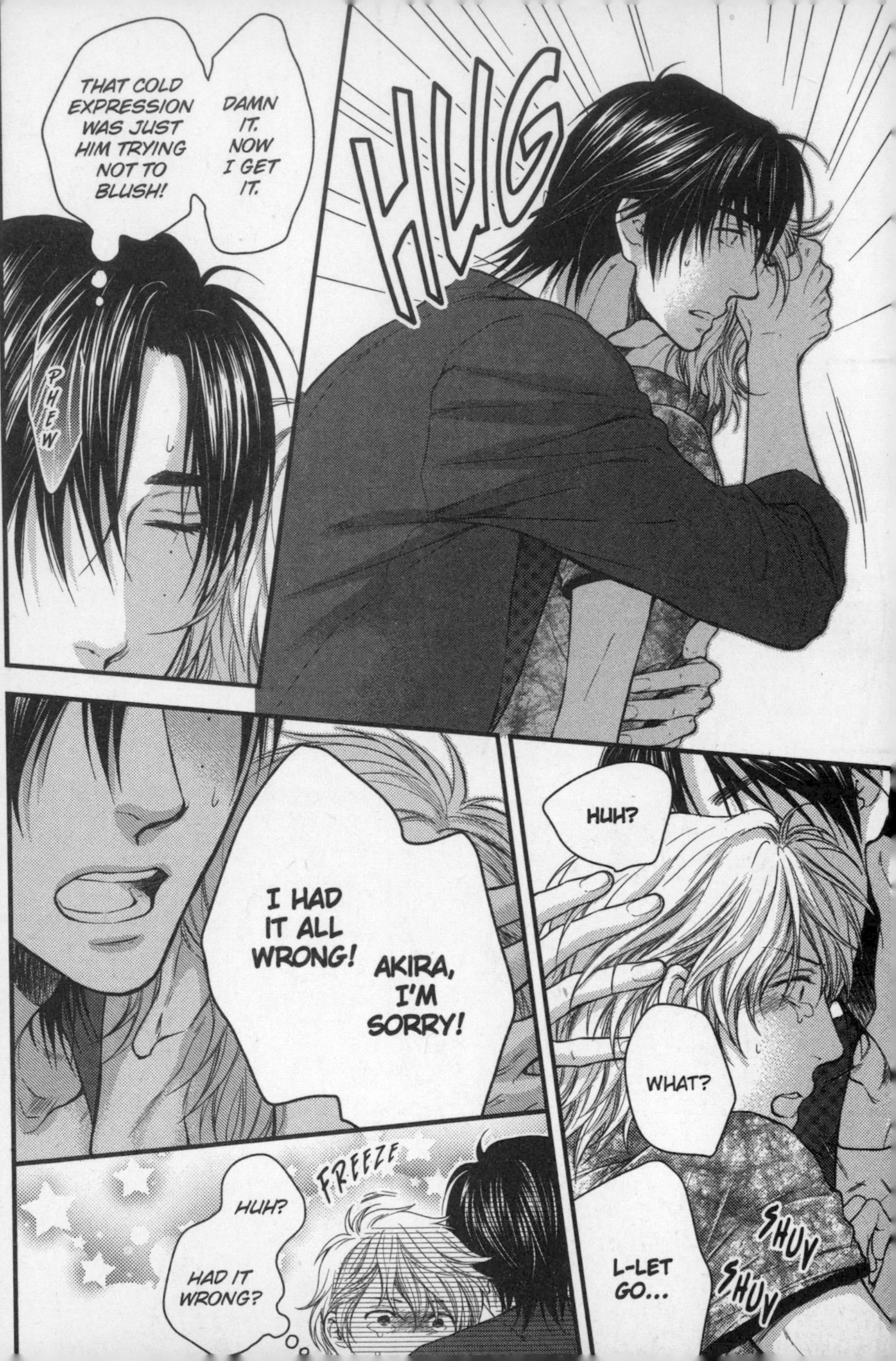
HUG
DAMN IT. NOW I GET IT.
THAT COLD EXPRESSION WAS JUST HIM TRYING NOT TO BLUSH!
PHEW
HUH?
WHAT?
SHUV
SHUV
L-LET GO...
I HAD IT ALL WRONG!
AKIRA, I'M SORRY!
FREEZE
HUH?
HAD IT WRONG?

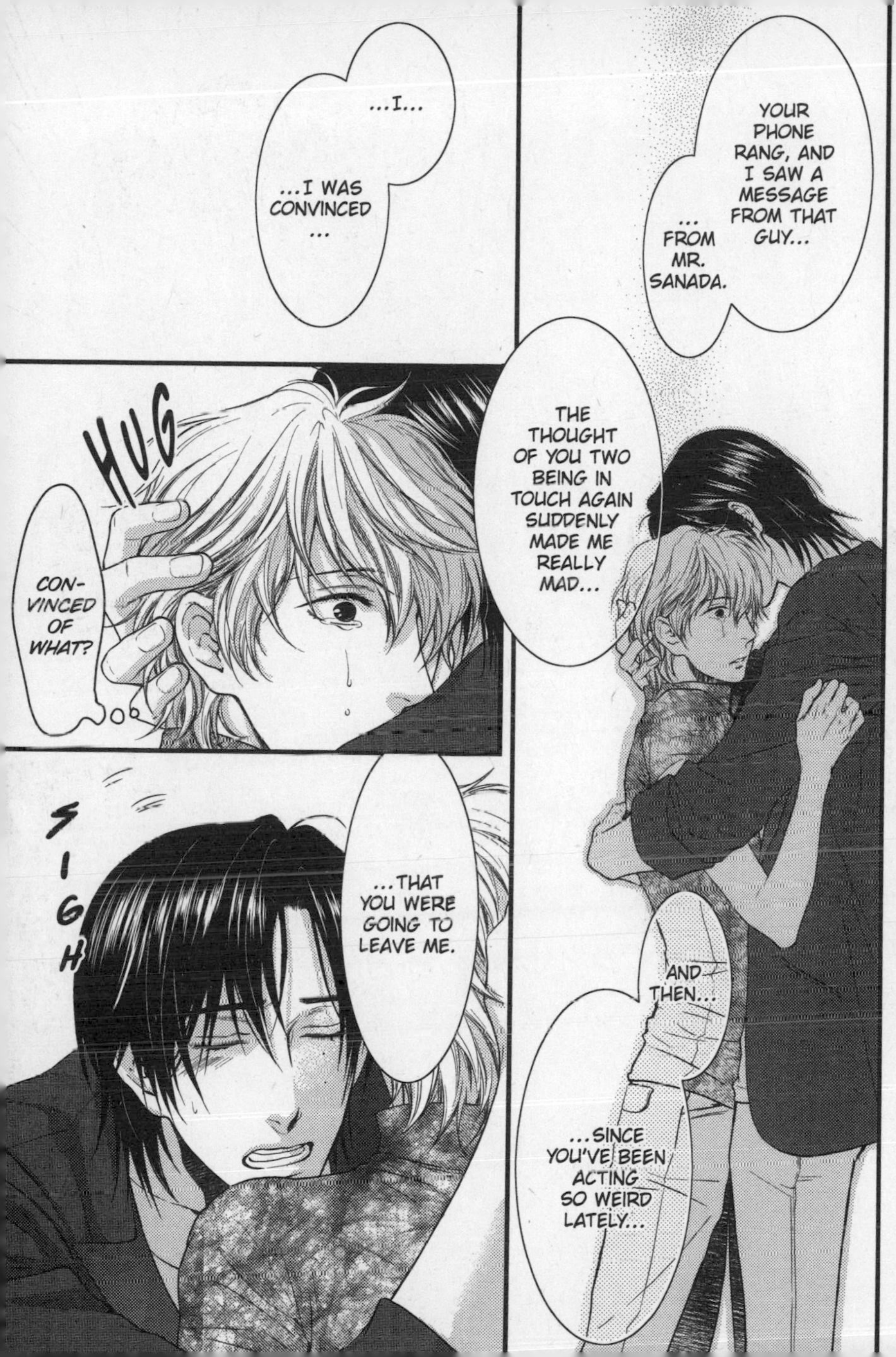
YOUR PHONE RANG, AND I SAW A MESSAGE FROM THAT GUY...
...FROM MR. SANADA.
THE THOUGHT OF YOU TWO BEING IN TOUCH AGAIN SUDDENLY MADE ME REALLY MAD...
AND THEN...
...SINCE YOU'VE BEEN ACTING SO WEIRD LATELY...
...I...
...I WAS CONVINCED ...
HUG
CON-VINCED OF WHAT?
SIGH
...THAT YOU WERE GOING TO LEAVE ME.

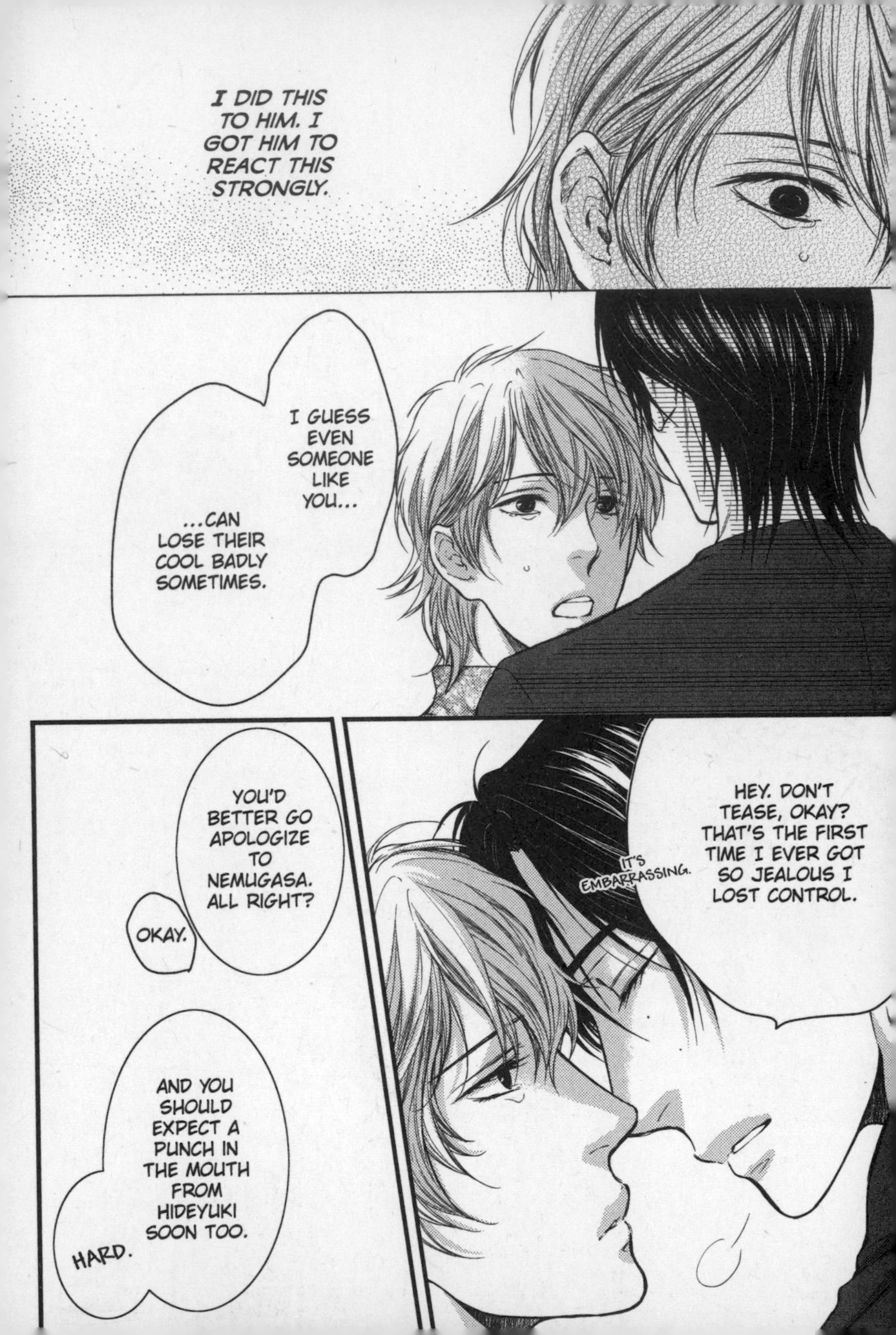
I DID THIS TO HIM. I GOT HIM TO REACT THIS STRONGLY.
I GUESS EVEN SOMEONE LIKE YOU...
...CAN LOSE THEIR COOL BADLY SOMETIMES.
HEY. DON'T TEASE, OKAY? THAT'S THE FIRST TIME I EVER GOT SO JEALOUS I LOST CONTROL.
IT'S EMBARRASSING.
YOU'D BETTER GO APOLOGIZE TO NEMUGASA. ALL RIGHT?
OKAY.
AND YOU SHOULD EXPECT A PUNCH IN THE MOUTH FROM HIDEYUKI SOON TOO.
HARD.

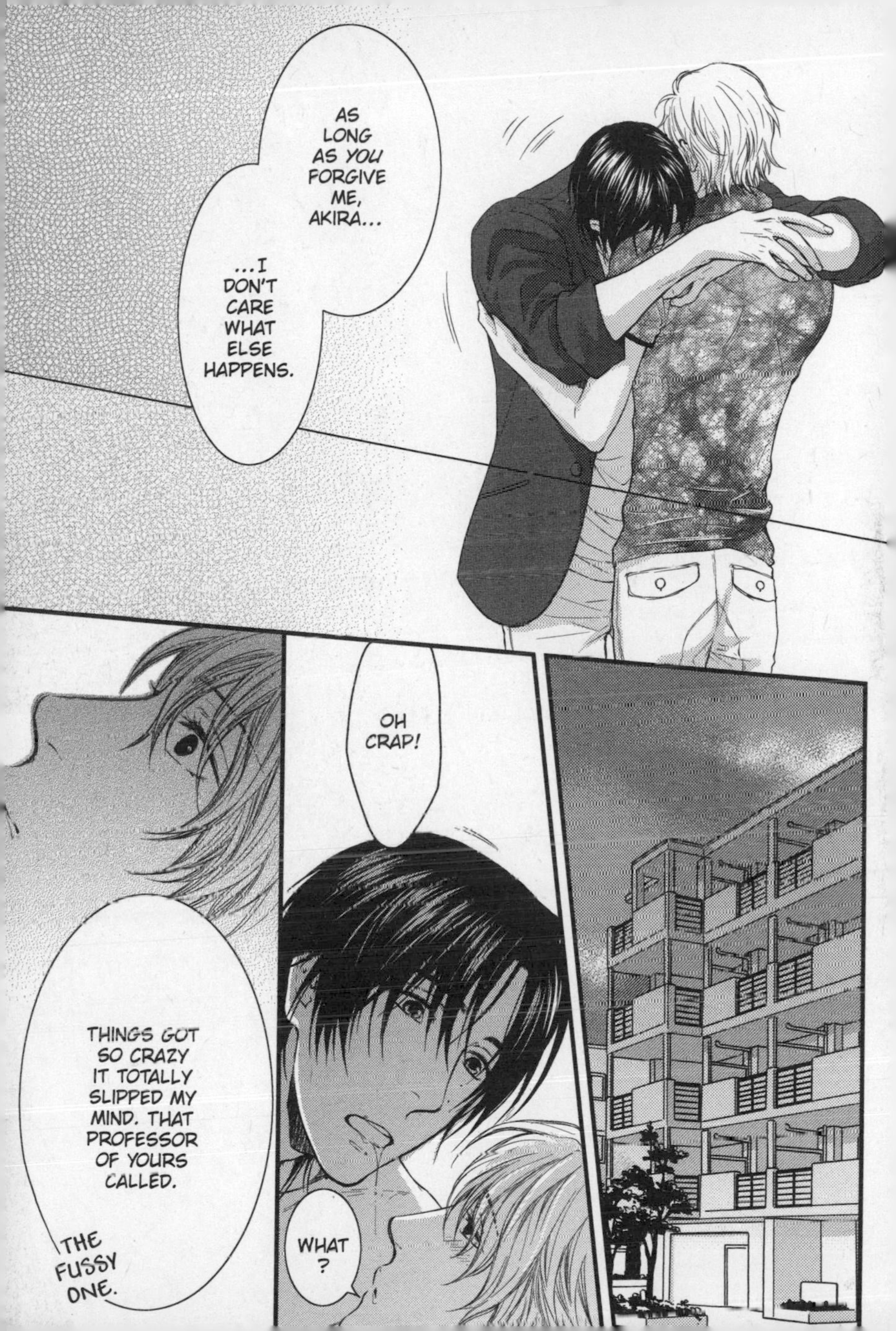
AS LONG AS YOU FORGIVE ME, AKIRA...
...I DON'T CARE WHAT ELSE HAPPENS.
OH CRAP!
WHAT?
THINGS GOT SO CRAZY IT TOTALLY SLIPPED MY MIND. THAT PROFESSOR OF YOURS CALLED.
THE FUSSY ONE.

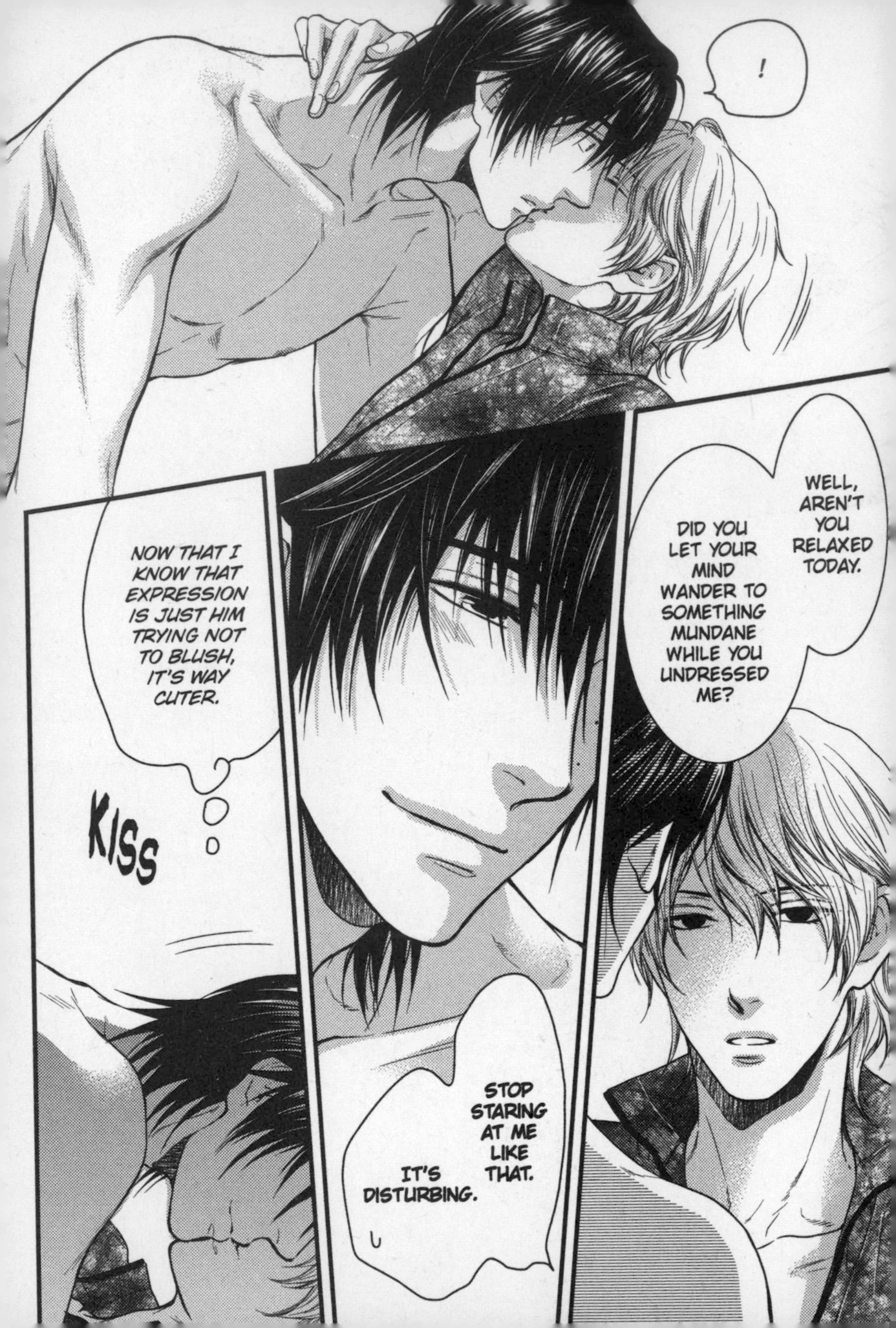
!
WELL, AREN'T YOU RELAXED TODAY.
DID YOU LET YOUR MIND WANDER TO SOMETHING MUNDANE WHILE YOU UNDRESSED ME?
STOP STARING AT ME LIKE THAT.
IT'S DISTURBING.
NOW THAT I KNOW THAT EXPRESSION IS JUST HIM TRYING NOT TO BLUSH, IT'S WAY CUTER.
KISS

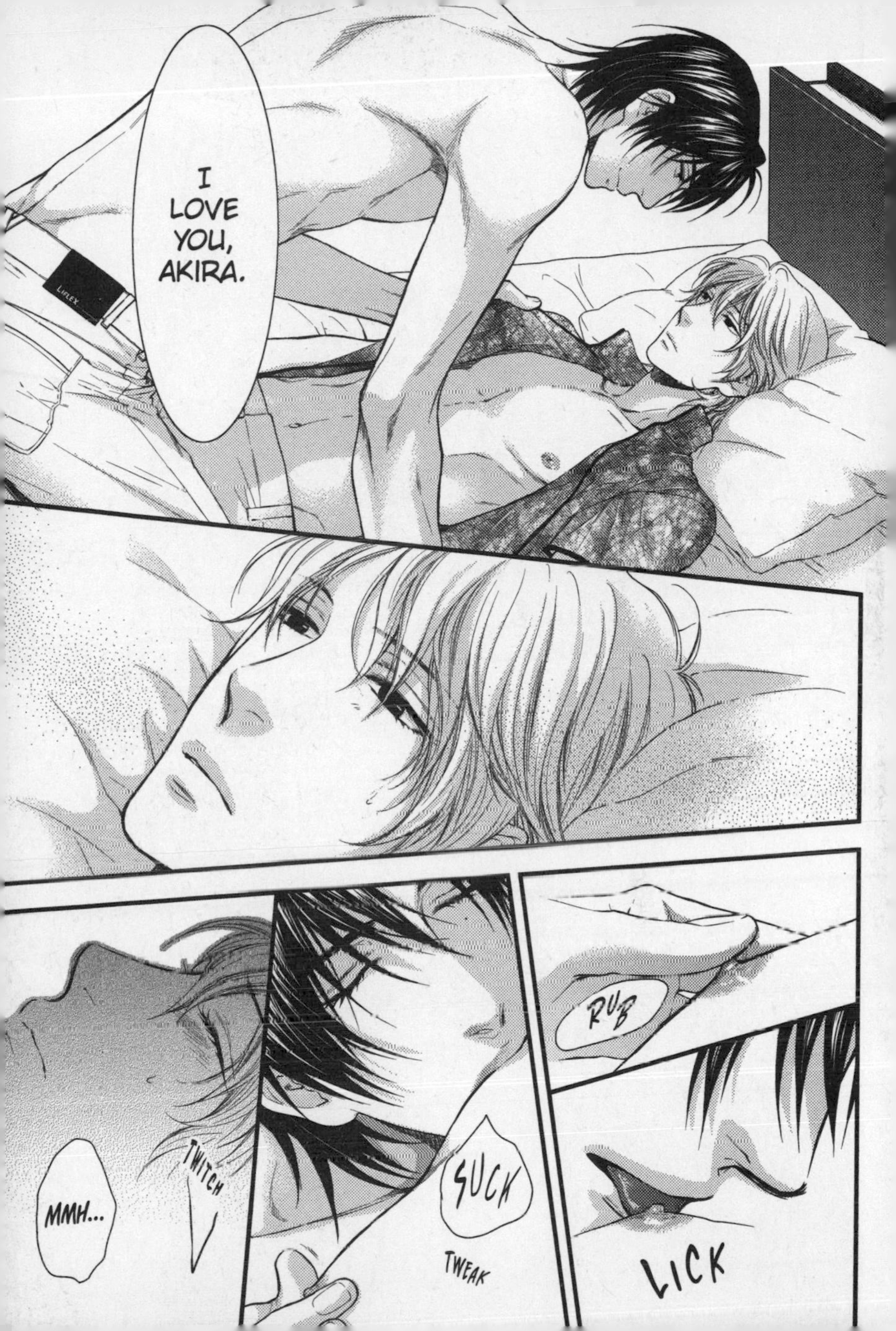
I LOVE YOU, AKIRA.
RUB
LICK
SUCK
TWEAK
TWITCH
MMH...

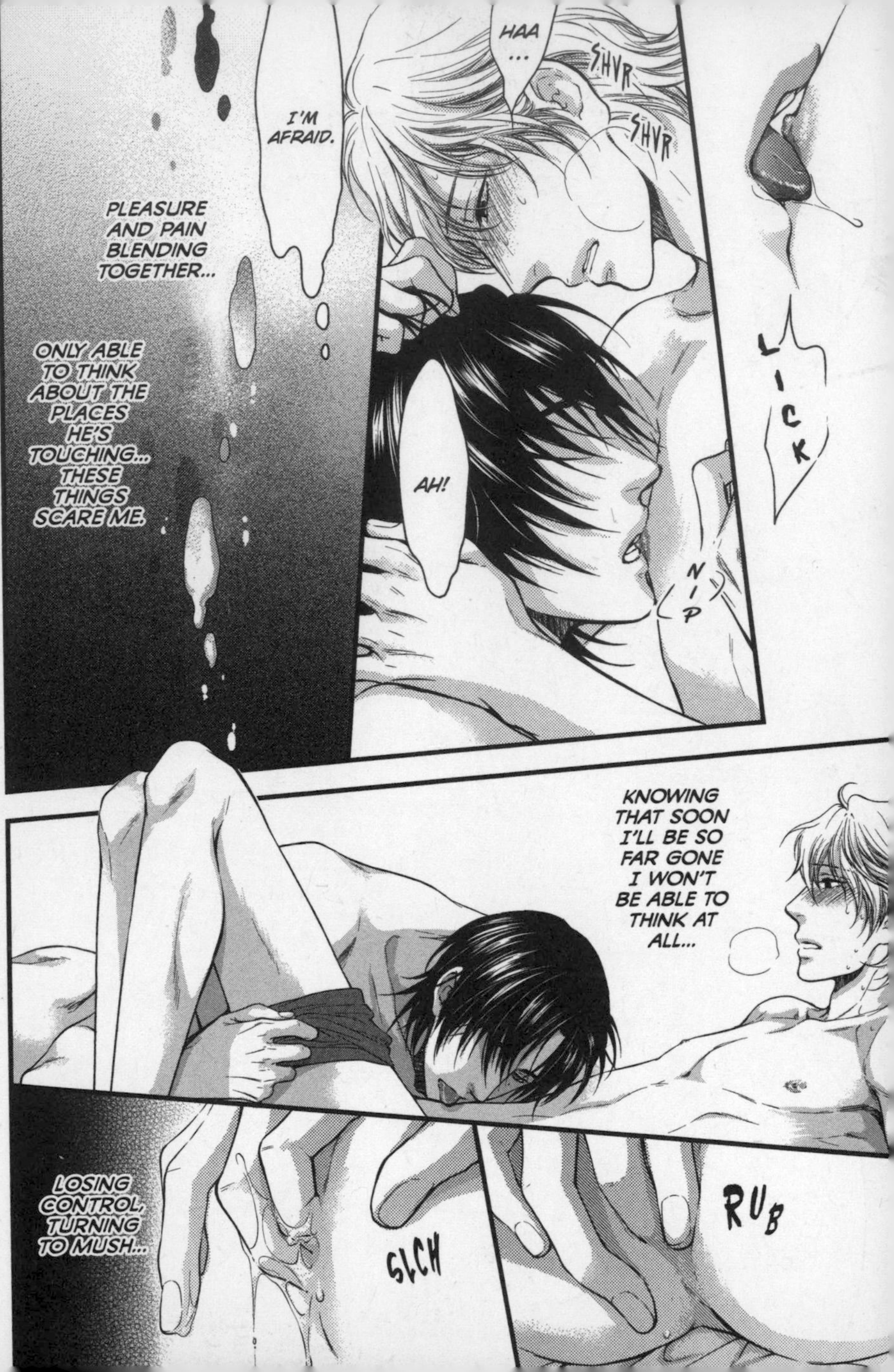
LICK
HAA...
SHVR
SHVR
I'M AFRAID.
AH!
NIP
PLEASURE AND PAIN BLENDING TOGETHER...
ONLY ABLE TO THINK ABOUT THE PLACES HE'S TOUCHING... THESE THINGS SCARE ME.
KNOWING THAT SOON I'LL BE SO FAR GONE I WON'T BE ABLE TO THINK AT ALL...
RUB
SLCH
LOSING CONTROL, TURNING TO MUSH...

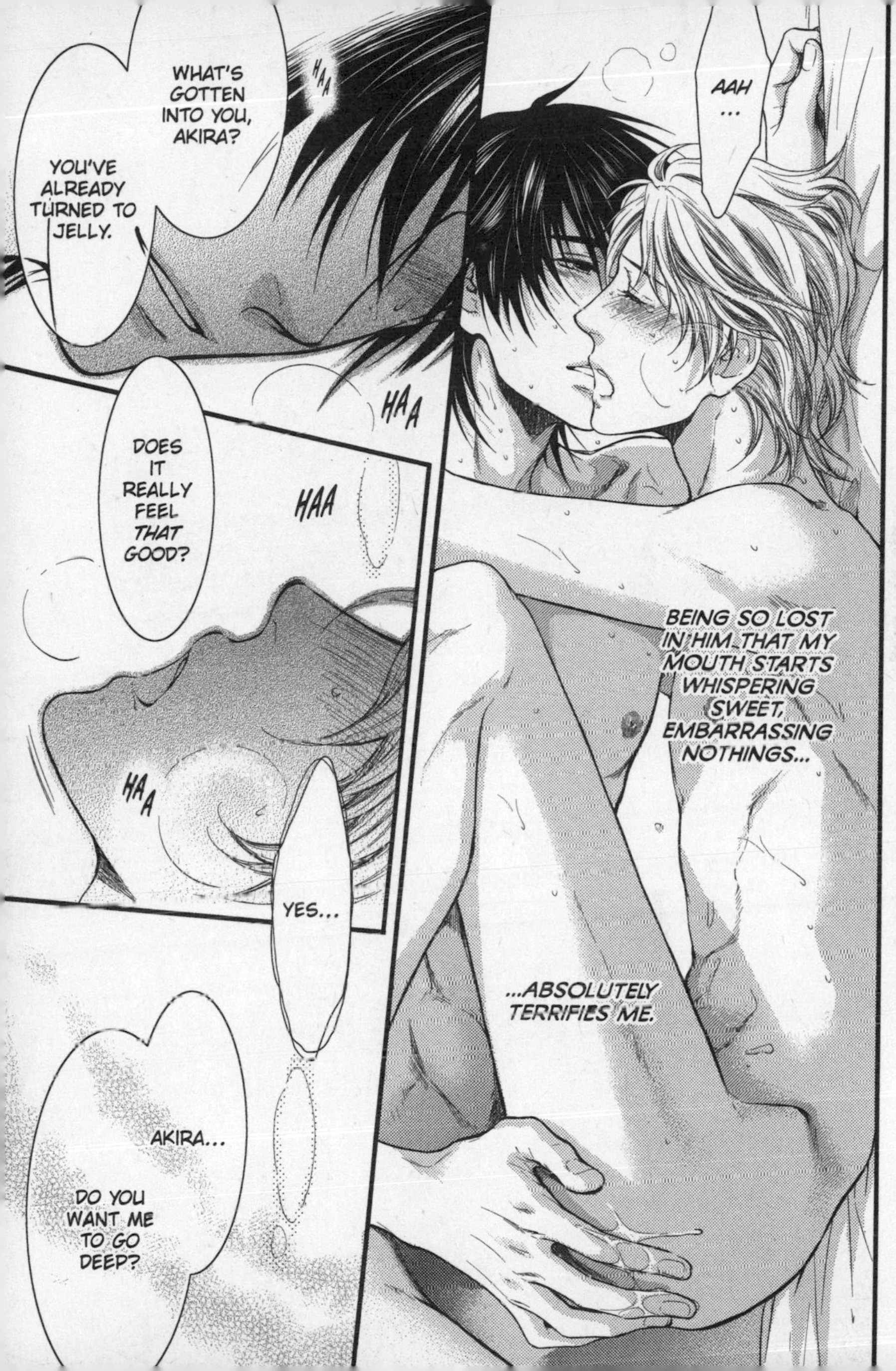
AAH ...
BEING SO LOST IN HIM THAT MY MOUTH STARTS WHISPERING SWEET, EMBARRASSING NOTHINGS...
...ABSOLUTELY TERRIFIES ME.
HAA
WHAT'S GOTTEN INTO YOU, AKIRA?
YOU'VE ALREADY TURNED TO JELLY.
HAA
DOES IT REALLY FEEL THAT GOOD?
HAA
HAA
YES...
AKIRA...
DO YOU WANT ME TO GO DEEP?

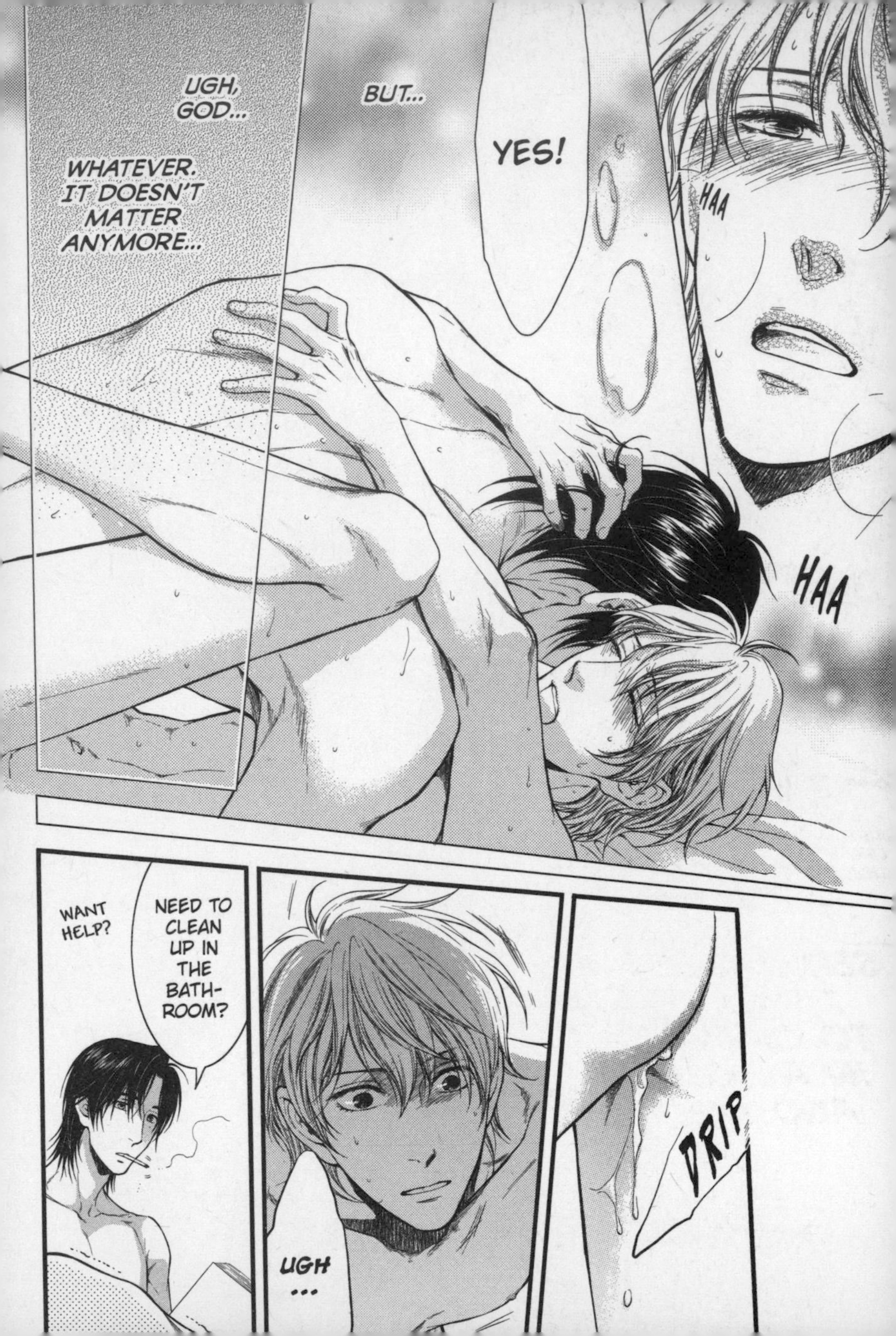
HAA
YES!
HAA
BUT...
UGH, GOD...
WHATEVER. IT DOESN'T MATTER ANYMORE...
DRIP
UGH ...
NEED TO CLEAN UP IN THE BATH-ROOM?
WANT HELP?

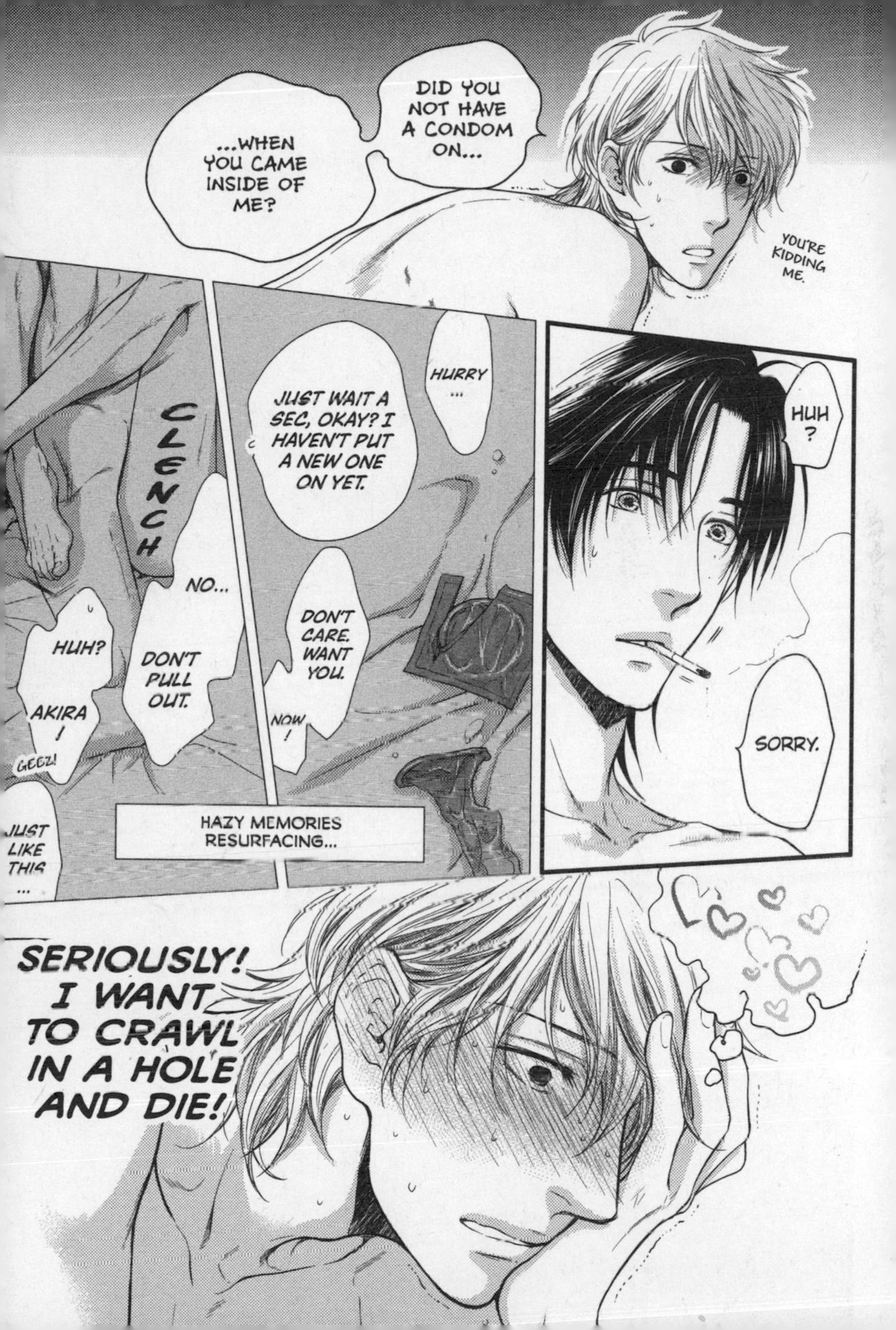
DID YOU NOT HAVE A CONDOM ON...
...WHEN YOU CAME INSIDE OF ME?
YOU'RE KIDDING ME.
HUH?
SORRY.
HURRY...
JUST WAIT A SEC, OKAY? I HAVEN'T PUT A NEW ONE ON YET.
DON'T CARE. WANT YOU.
NOW!
CLENCH
NO...
DON'T PULL OUT.
HUH?
AKIRA!
GEEZ!
JUST LIKE THIS...
HAZY MEMORIES RESURFACING...
SERIOUSLY! I WANT TO CRAWL IN A HOLE AND DIE!

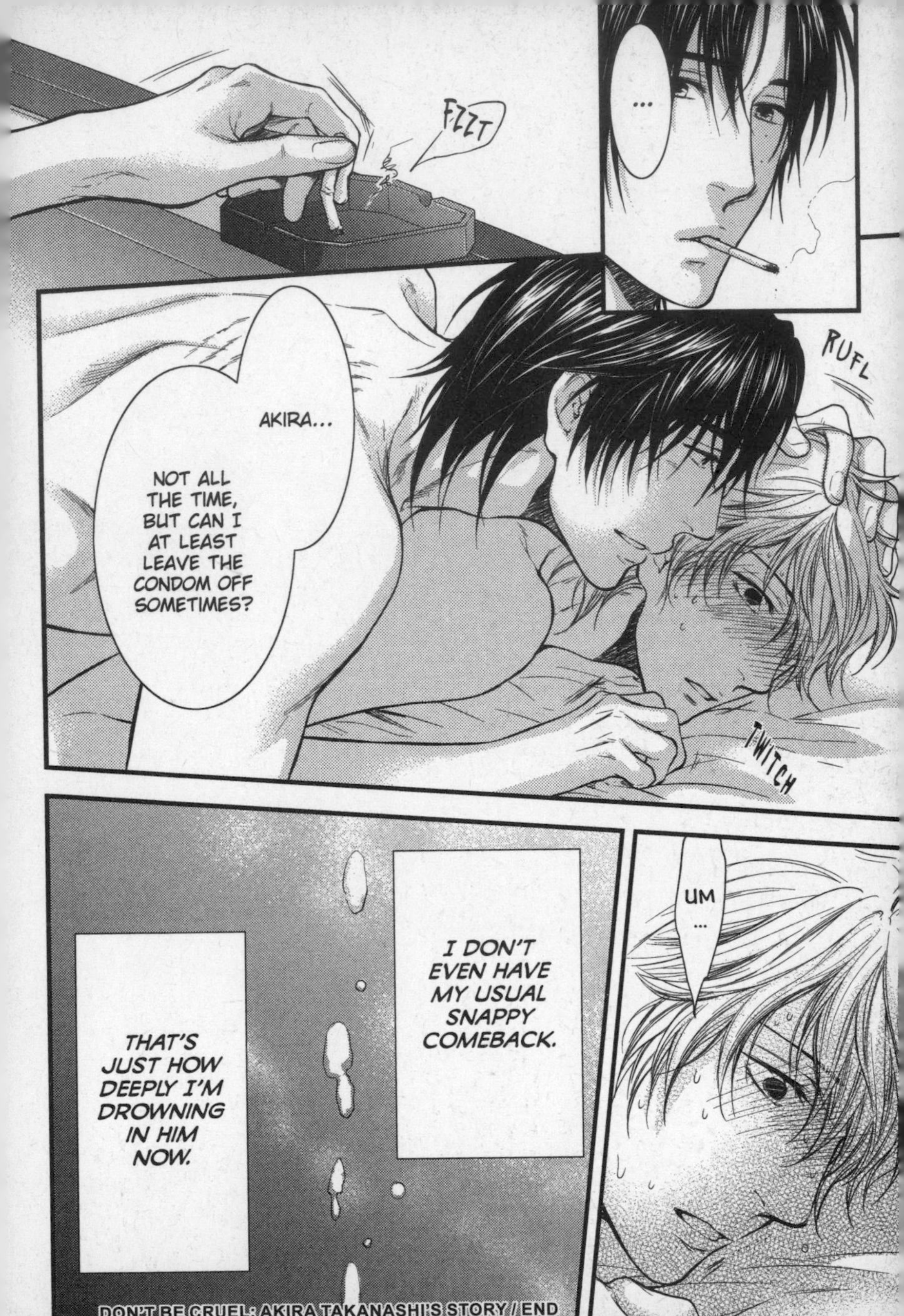
...
FZZT
RUFL
AKIRA...
NOT ALL THE TIME, BUT CAN I AT LEAST LEAVE THE CONDOM OFF SOMETIMES?
TWITCH
UM ...
I DON'T EVEN HAVE MY USUAL SNAPPY COMEBACK.
THAT'S JUST HOW DEEPLY I'M DROWNING IN HIM NOW.

DON'T BE CRUEL: AKIRA TAKANASHI'S STORY / END

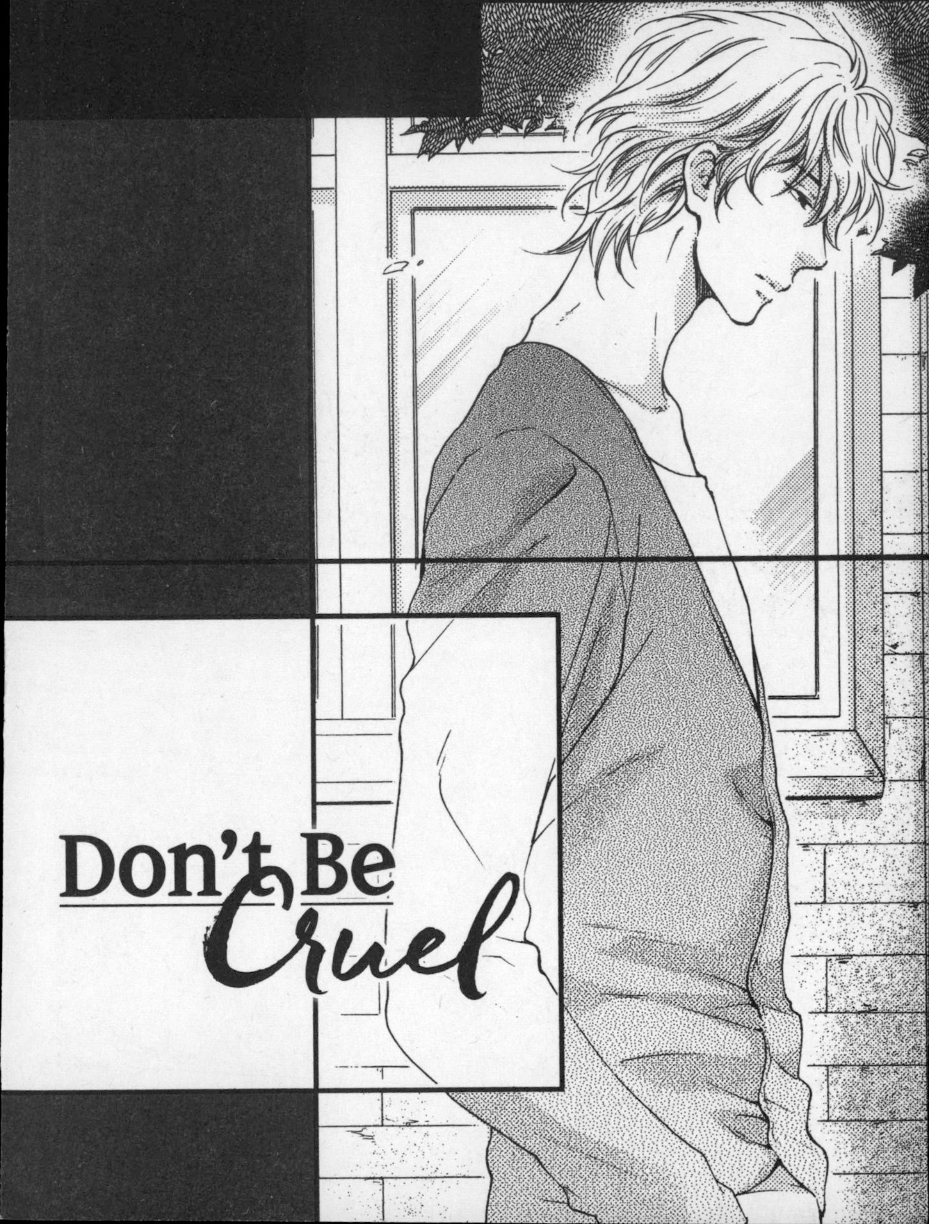
Don't Be
Cruel

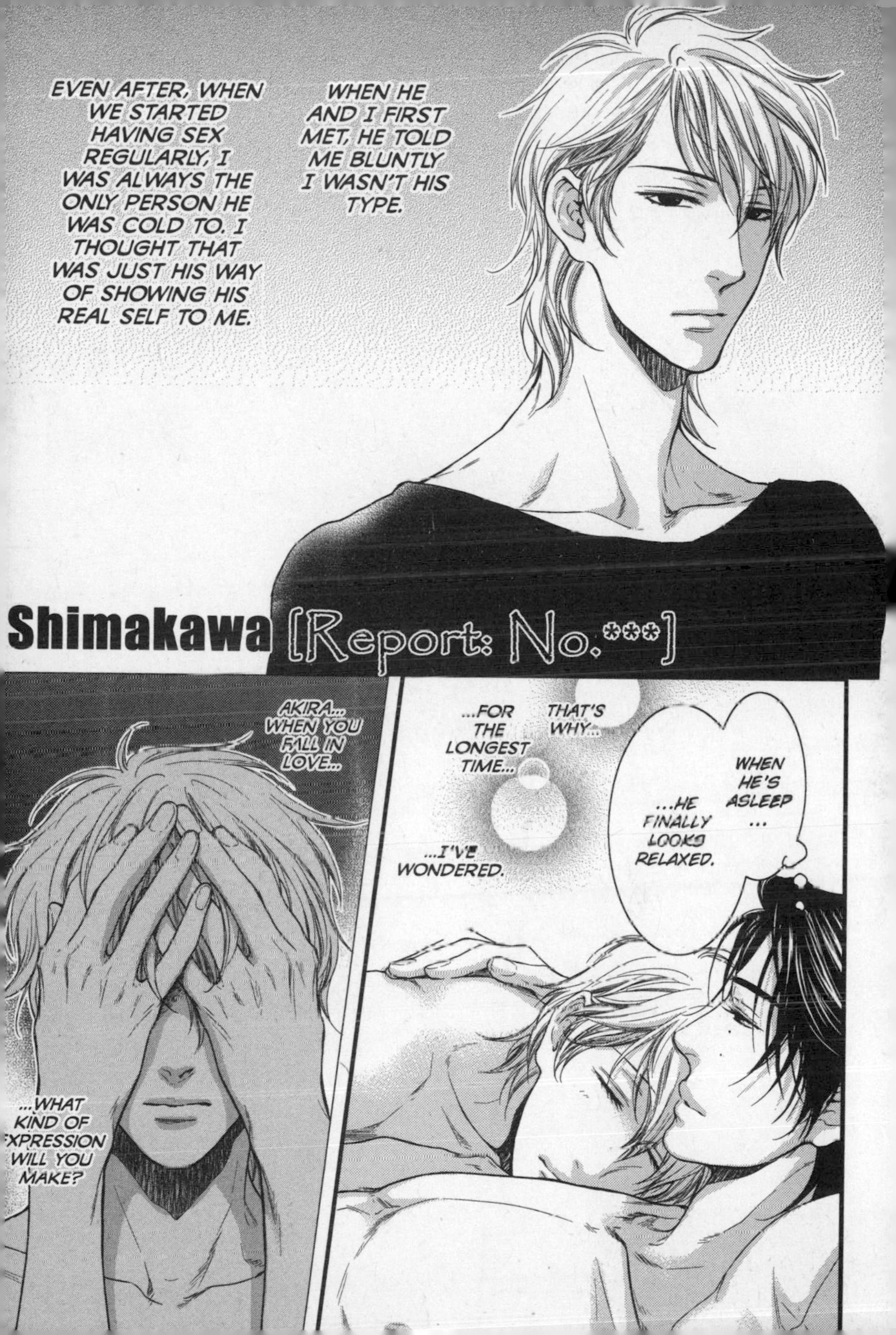
WHEN HE AND I FIRST MET, HE TOLD ME BLUNTLY I WASN'T HIS TYPE.
EVEN AFTER, WHEN WE STARTED HAVING SEX REGULARLY, I WAS ALWAYS THE ONLY PERSON HE WAS COLD TO. I THOUGHT THAT WAS JUST HIS WAY OF SHOWING HIS REAL SELF TO ME.
Shimakawa [Report: No.***]
WHEN HE'S ASLEEP...
...HE FINALLY LOOKS RELAXED.
THAT'S WHY...
...FOR THE LONGEST TIME...
...I'VE WONDERED.
AKIRA... WHEN YOU FALL IN LOVE...
...WHAT KIND OF EXPRESSION WILL YOU MAKE?

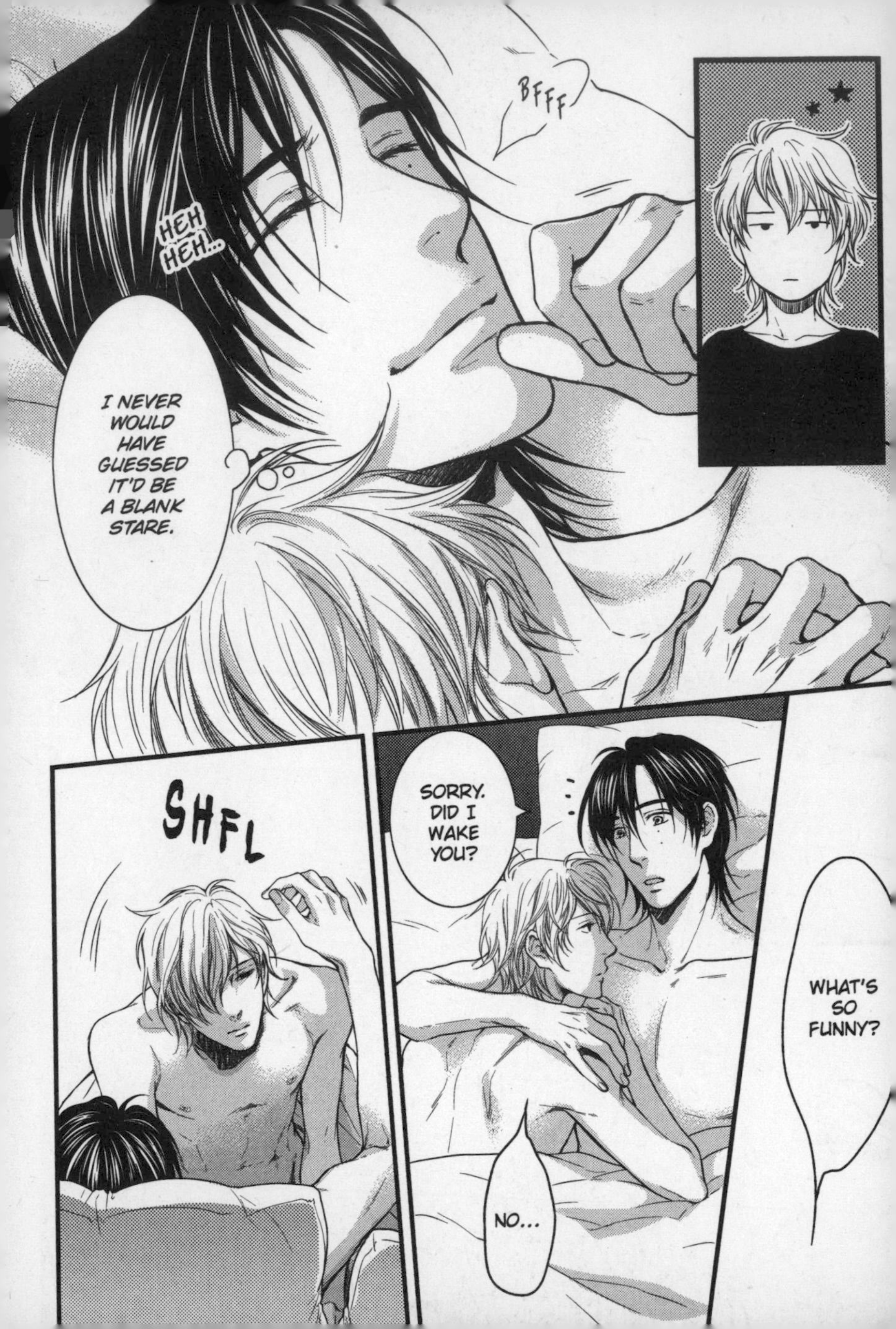
BFFF
HEH HEH...
I NEVER WOULD HAVE GUESSED IT'D BE A BLANK STARE.
WHAT'S SO FUNNY?
SORRY. DID I WAKE YOU?
NO...
SHFL

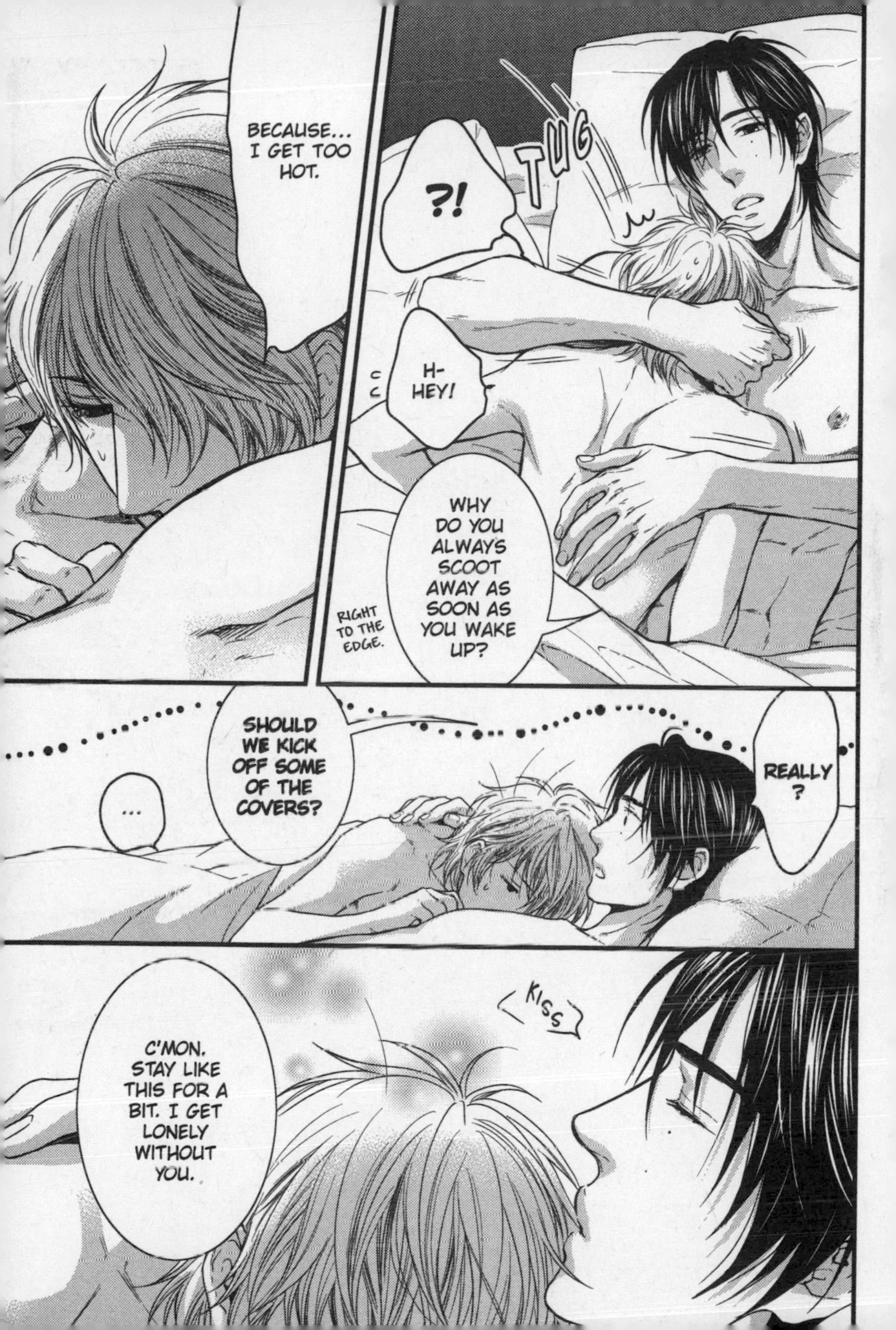
TUG
?!
H-HEY!
WHY DO YOU ALWAYS SCOOT AWAY AS SOON AS YOU WAKE UP?
RIGHT TO THE EDGE.
BECAUSE... I GET TOO HOT.
REALLY?
SHOULD WE KICK OFF SOME OF THE COVERS?
...
KISS
C'MON. STAY LIKE THIS FOR A BIT. I GET LONELY WITHOUT YOU.

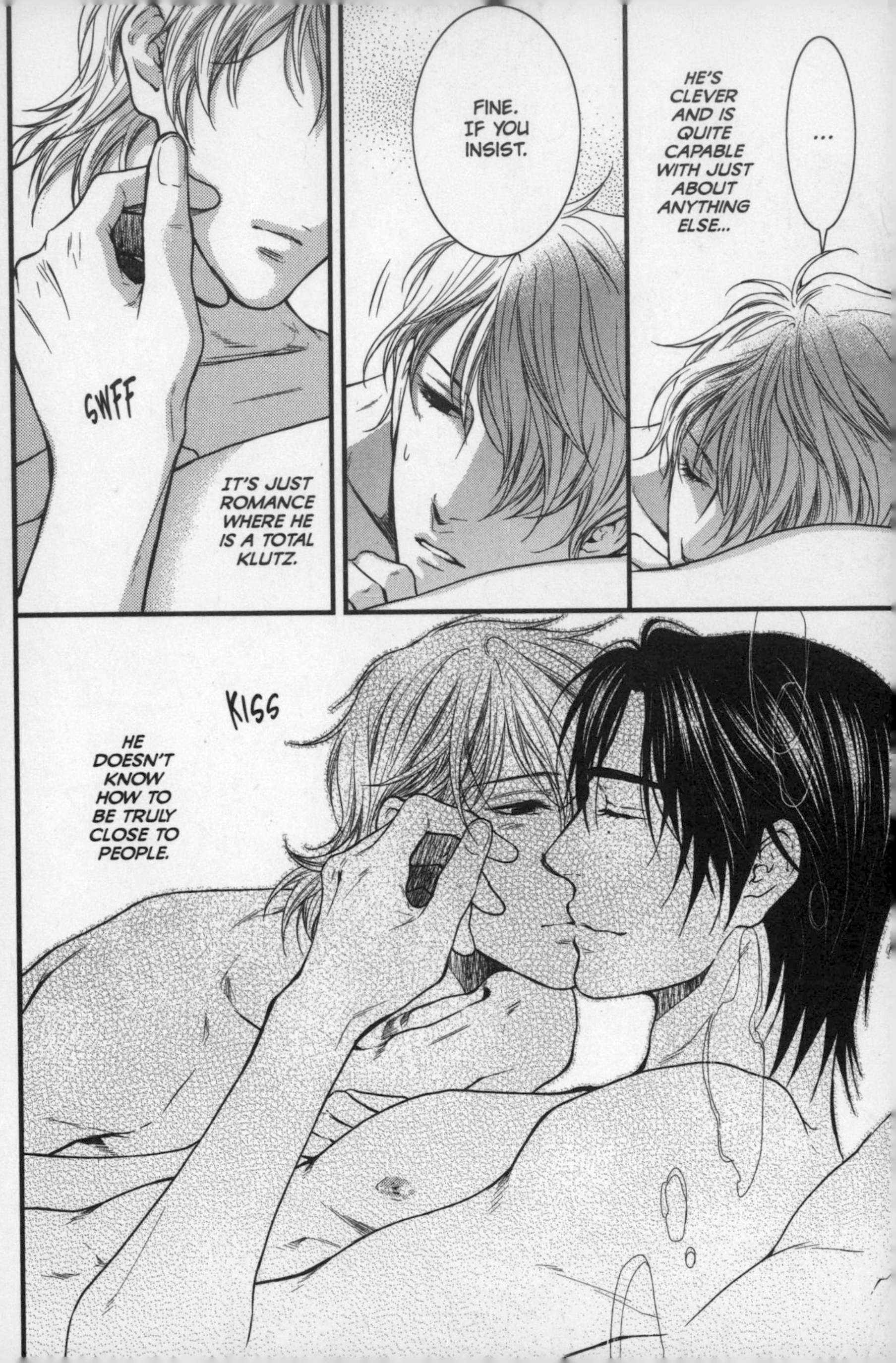
...
HE'S CLEVER AND IS QUITE CAPABLE WITH JUST ABOUT ANYTHING ELSE...
FINE. IF YOU INSIST.
SWFF
IT'S JUST ROMANCE WHERE HE IS A TOTAL KLUTZ.
KISS
HE DOESN'T KNOW HOW TO BE TRULY CLOSE TO PEOPLE.

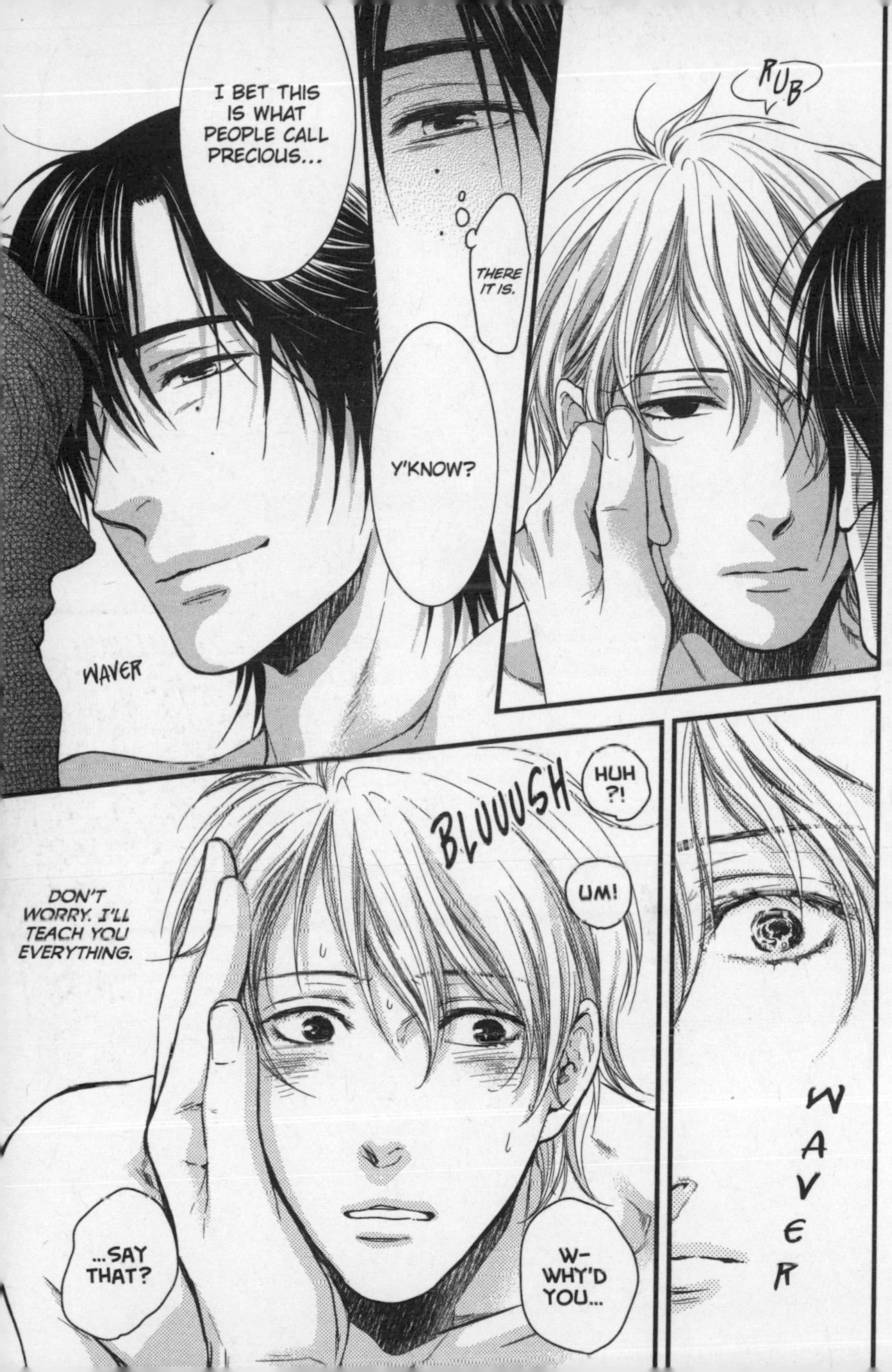
RUB
THERE IT IS.
I BET THIS IS WHAT PEOPLE CALL PRECIOUS...
Y'KNOW?
WAVER
WAVER
HUH ?!
BLUUUSH
UM!
W-WHY'D YOU...
...SAY THAT?
DON'T WORRY. I'LL TEACH YOU EVERYTHING.

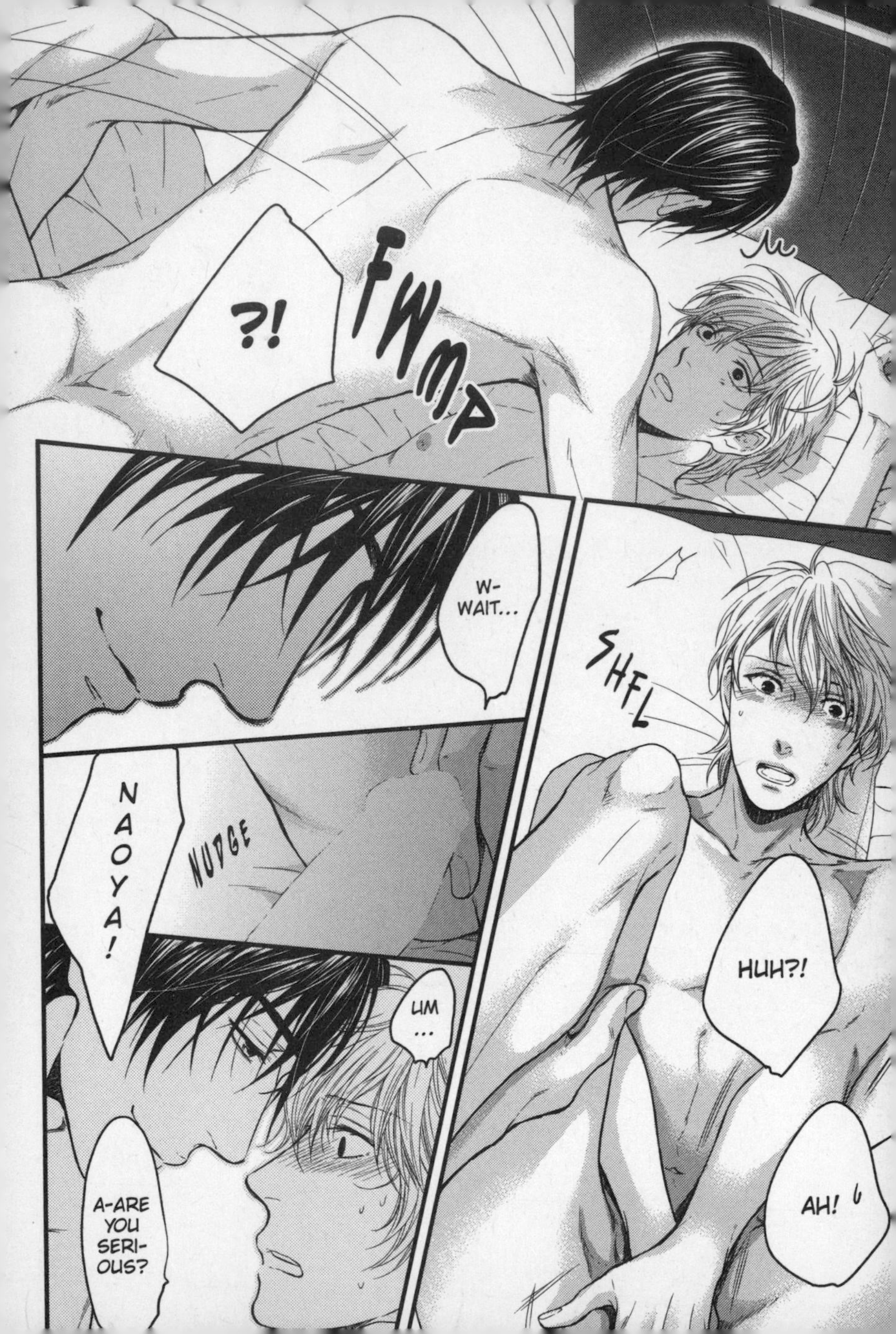
?!
FWMP
SHFL
HUH?!
AH!
W-WAIT...
NAOYA!
NUDGE
UM...
A-ARE YOU SERIOUS?

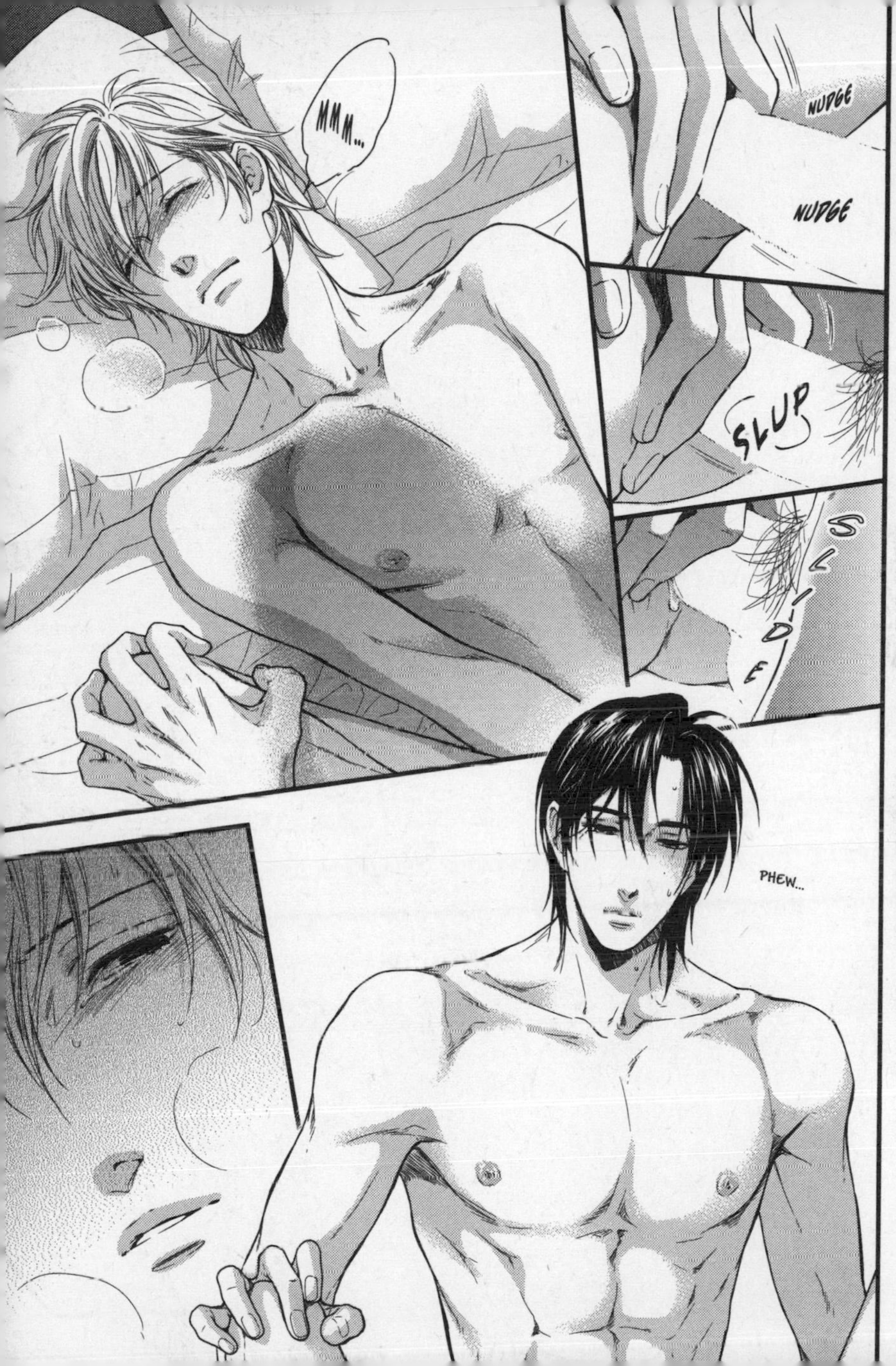
NUDGE
NUDGE
SLUP
SLIDE
MMM...
PHEW...

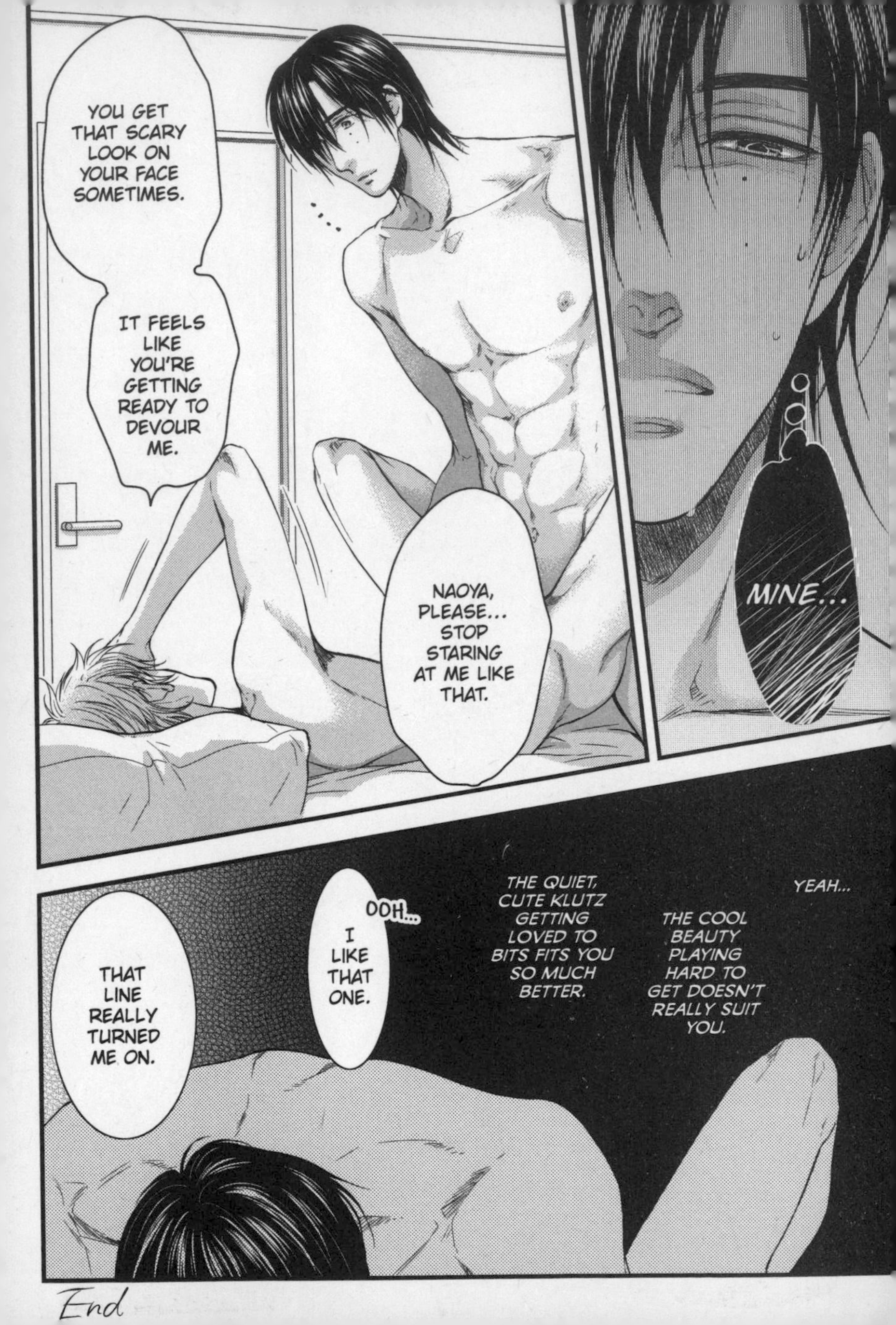
MINE...
YOU GET THAT SCARY LOOK ON YOUR FACE SOMETIMES.
...
IT FEELS LIKE YOU'RE GETTING READY TO DEVOUR ME.
NAOYA, PLEASE... STOP STARING AT ME LIKE THAT.
YEAH...
THE COOL BEAUTY PLAYING HARD TO GET DOESN'T REALLY SUIT YOU.
THE QUIET, CUTE KLUTZ GETTING LOVED TO BITS FITS YOU SO MUCH BETTER.
OOH...
I LIKE THAT ONE.
THAT LINE REALLY TURNED ME ON.
End

AFTERWORD

HUMAN ANAT

HUMAN ANAT

Did everyone enjoy Akira's side story? There are many Akira fans out there, and I can't wait to hear what they think about this volume in light of what they thought about him before. I added a little of his history with Mr. Sanada too. With those two, I wanted to write a story that shows that even in BL, sometimes young love doesn't work out. Of course, I'll sometimes pull stunts in stories like these, so apparently there are more than a few of you out there who were on pins and needles reading this one. (laughs) In the end, it was going through those events in his life that made Akira the beautiful and popular, yet passive and suspicious, young man he is. At least, that's what I was aiming to write. (grimace) Anyway! I'm glad Akira's habit of going blank when he feels loved went over well with my editors.

For someone as passive and beta male as Akira, he gets aggressive alpha male Shimakawa for his lover. I had Shimakawa make a quick cameo appearance in volume 4, and apparently a lot of you suspected he was yandere. But see? Isn't he actually a decent guy? Believe it or not, there is a real-life model for him—a bear, like the animal. Bears are supposed to be really possessive and determined. When they decide something is their prey, they will stubbornly chase it until they catch it. They'll be clever about it too. And if something else comes along trying to snatch their prey away, they'll chase the thief down until they get their prey back...stubbornly...relentlessly... (No, this isn't a horror story. Honest.) Anyway, that's the image I had in mind when I wrote Shimakawa. (Did I overdo it with the horror?) Oh well. I guess in that way, deep down he might really be yandere. I went for a gentle and neutral seme image with him. Someone who may be extremely possessive but doesn't do anything nasty, like tie his uke up. Personally. I really enjoyed writing him with such a gap between his outer speech and inner monologue. I hope at least some of you out there enjoyed reading it.

Come to think of it...did you all notice the silver I used in the cover illustration? It's something I've done for a while with my doujinshi, but I never thought the day would come when I could use it in a formal comic! I can hardly wait to see how it turns out! ♡ Not only that, the color pages from the first chapter were left as color for the volume release! ♡ ♡ ♡ Volume 4 had such a good reception we got to do it again for this volume. I hear some who picked up volume 4 felt they had to put a cover over it, but I should hope this volume turned out okay. It did, right? Right?!

Oh! Oh! Soon after this volume hits the shelves, the volume 2 drama CD will go on sale too! It's only been six years since volume 1. (laughs) If possible, someday I'd like to hear Akira's volume fully voiced too. Will we ever reach this volume at that pace? It is the fifth one...and if there're six years in between...then there's at least 18 years to go... Ouch... (laughs)

Anyway... The Don't Be Cruel series has reached five full volumes. Thanks to all the great people out there who enjoy watching the main couple, Maya and Nemu, I've been able to keep telling their story. I hope Akira and Shimakawa will get at least as much love as those two.

Thank you very much for following along this far!

Nekota Yonezou 10.2014

COME HERE, LITTLE RABBIT. I'M A NICE BEAR. I WON'T EAT YOU.

... o

Special Thanx!

Editor: Miyoshi-san

Graphic Novel Editor: Sato-san

Super Assistants: Mucchi, M-ko, Ito, Watabe

And you!

So with nothing to say about myself this time, I instead show off a sketch I had available at Comiket... Anyway, Maya and Nemugasa are on a break this volume, but I hope you'll enjoy this story anyway.

About the Author

This may be **Yonezou Nekota**'s first English-language manga, but she is already well-known for the Japanese release of her title *Mousou Elektel* (Elektel Delusion). A prolific *doujinshi* (independent comics) creator, she was born in Tokyo in August and is a Leo with an A blood type. You can find out more about Yonezou Nekota at her website, **kmy.blog.jp**, or her Twitter page, **@yonekozoh**.

Don't Be Cruel
Akira Takanashi's Story
SuBLime Manga Edition

Story and Art by **Yonezou Nekota**

Translation—**Adrienne Beck**
Touch-Up Art and Lettering—**NRP Studios**
Cover and Graphic Design—**Fawn Lau**
Editor—**Jennifer LeBlanc**

Hidokushinaide Takanashi Akira-hen © 2014 Yonezou Nekota
Originally published in Japan in 2014 by Libre Publishing Co., Ltd.
English translation rights arranged with Libre Inc.

libre

Printed in the U.S.A.

Published by SuBLime Manga
P.O. Box 77010
San Francisco, CA 94107

10 9 8 7 6 5 4 3 2 1
First printing, December 2016

www.SuBLimeManga.com

For more information

on all our products, along with the most up-to-date news on releases, series announcements, and contests, please visit us at:

 SuBLimeManga.com

 twitter.com/**SuBLimeManga**

 facebook.com/**SuBLimeManga**

 SuBLimeManga.tumblr.com

Downloading is as easy as:

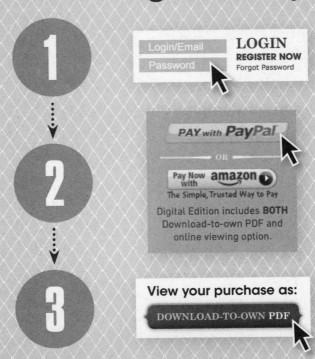

1 Login/Email · Password — LOGIN · REGISTER NOW · Forgot Password

2 PAY with PayPal · OR · Pay Now with amazon — The Simple, Trusted Way to Pay · Digital Edition includes **BOTH** Download-to-own PDF and online viewing option.

3 View your purchase as: DOWNLOAD-TO-OWN PDF